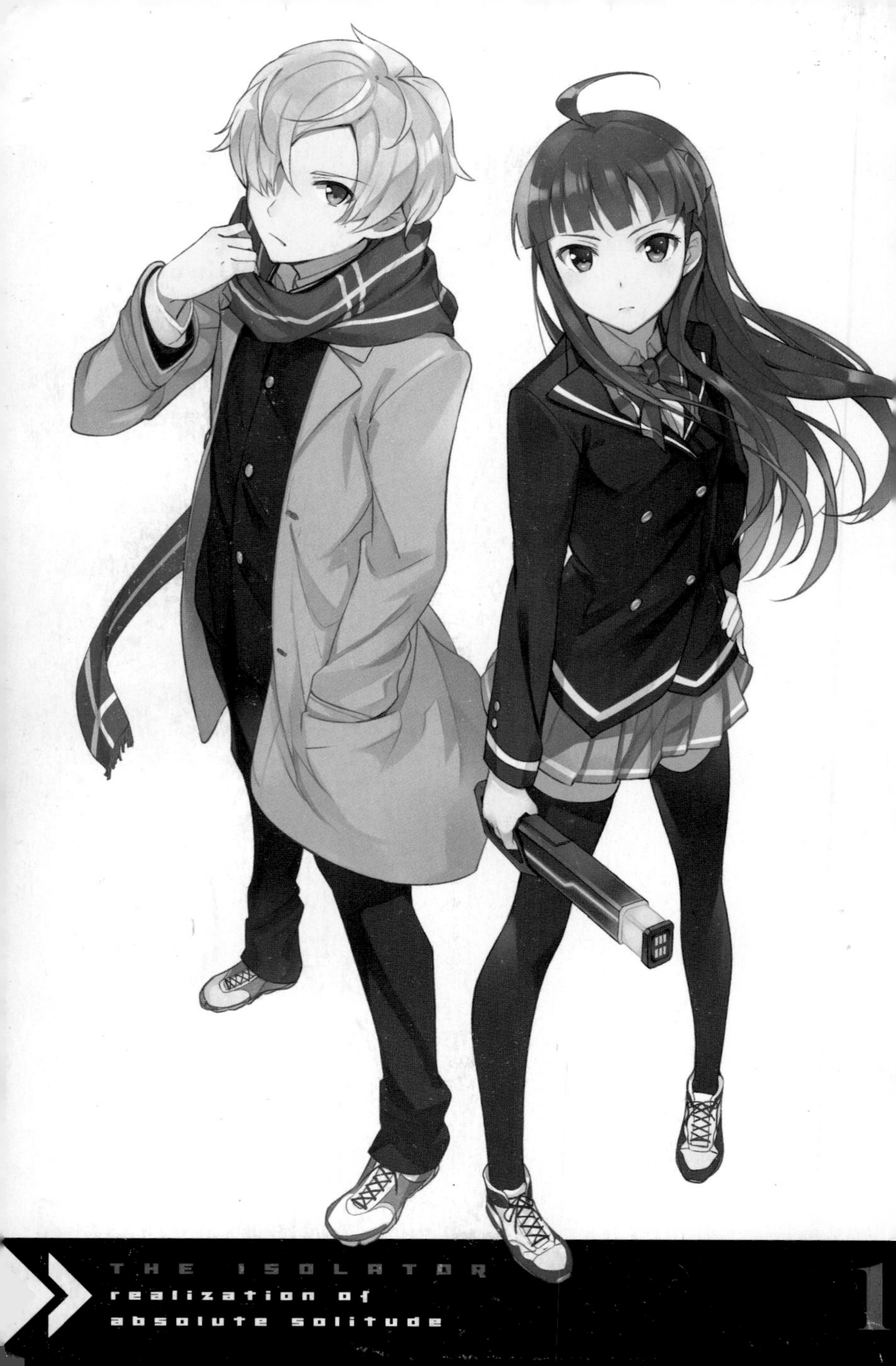
THE ISOLATOR
realization of
absolute solitude
1

CONTENTS

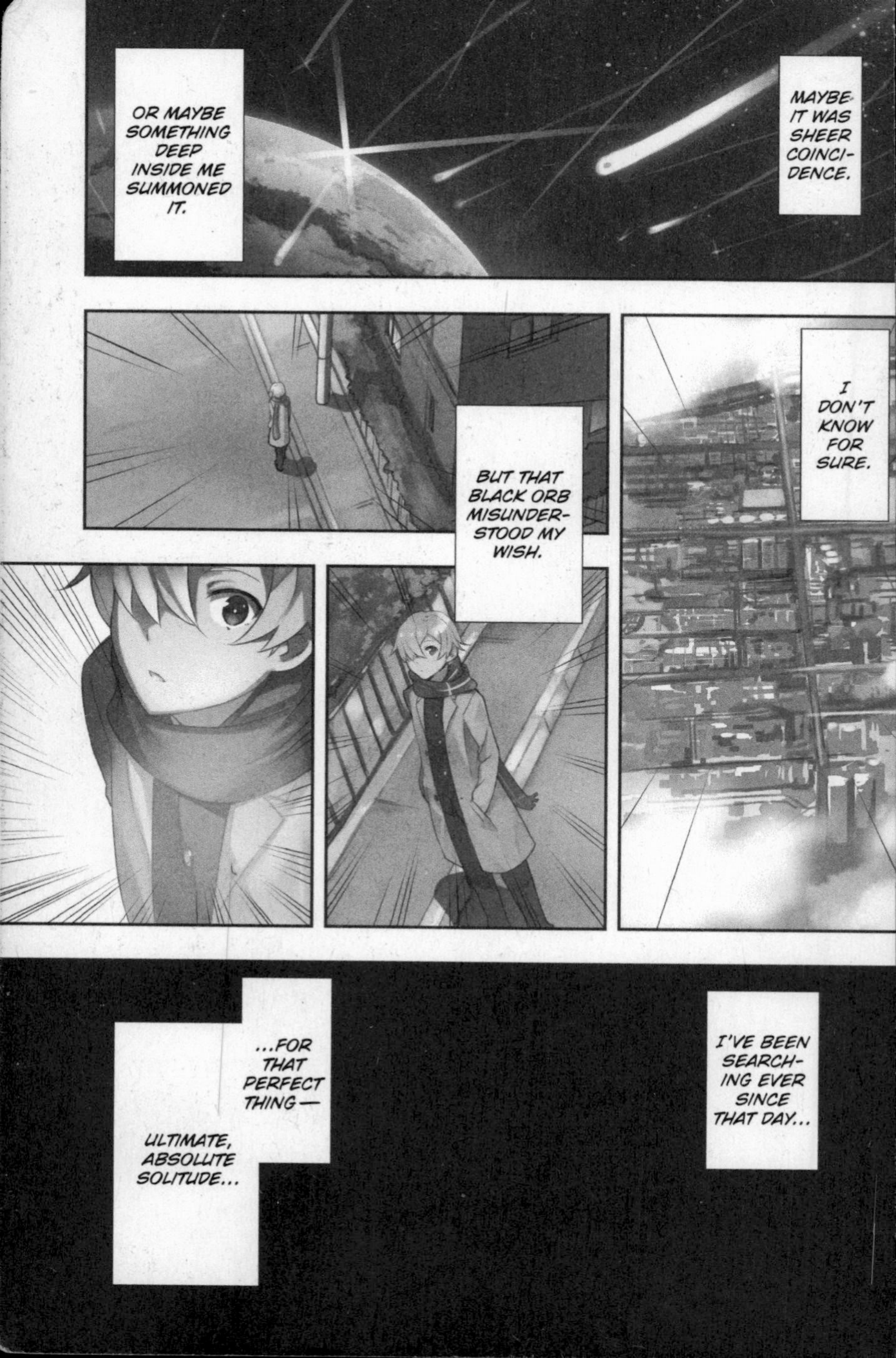
MAYBE IT WAS SHEER COINCI-DENCE.
OR MAYBE SOMETHING DEEP INSIDE ME SUMMONED IT.
I DON'T KNOW FOR SURE.
BUT THAT BLACK ORB MISUNDER-STOOD MY WISH.
I'VE BEEN SEARCH-ING EVER SINCE THAT DAY...
...FOR THAT PERFECT THING—
ULTIMATE, ABSOLUTE SOLITUDE...

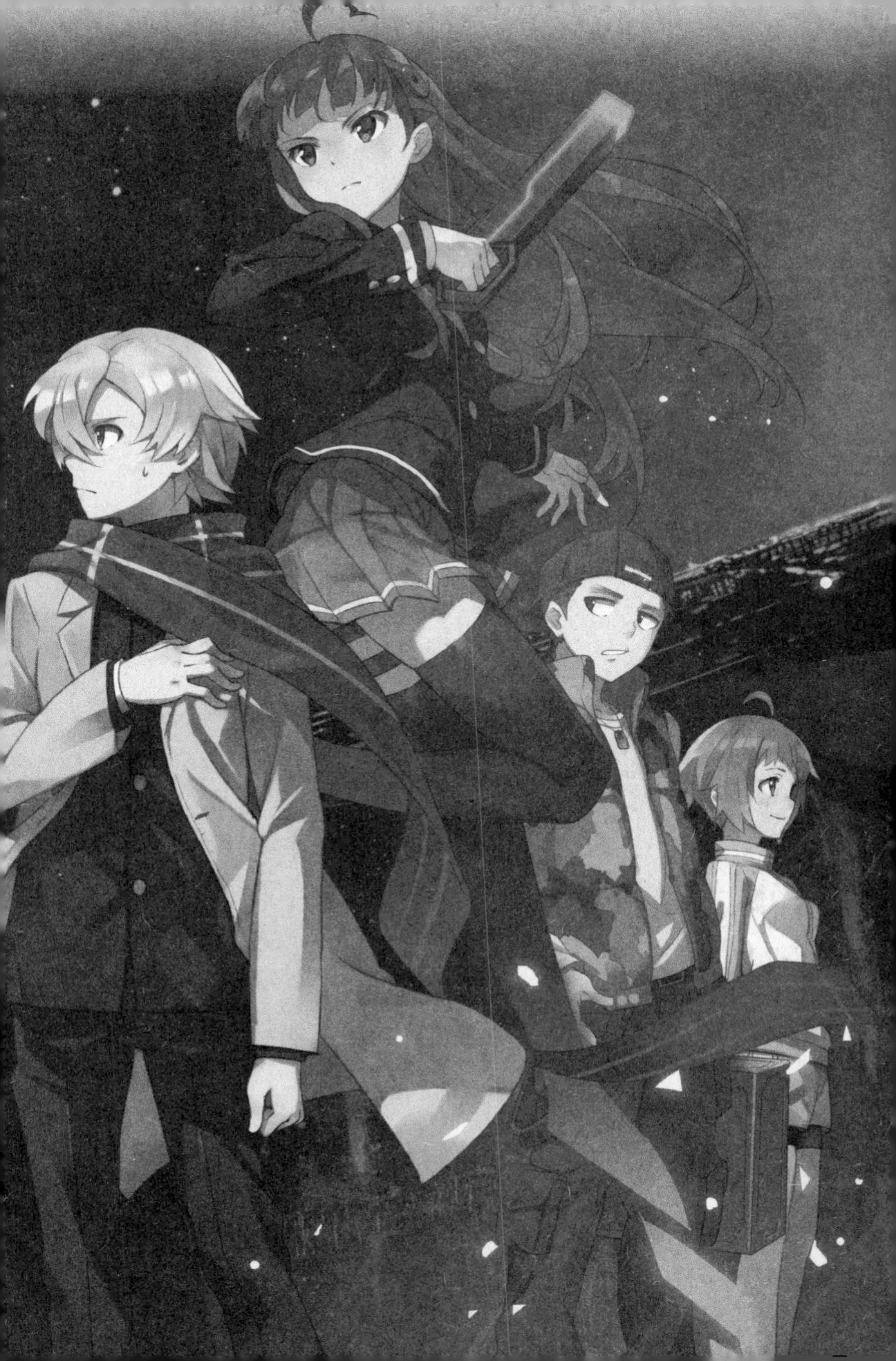

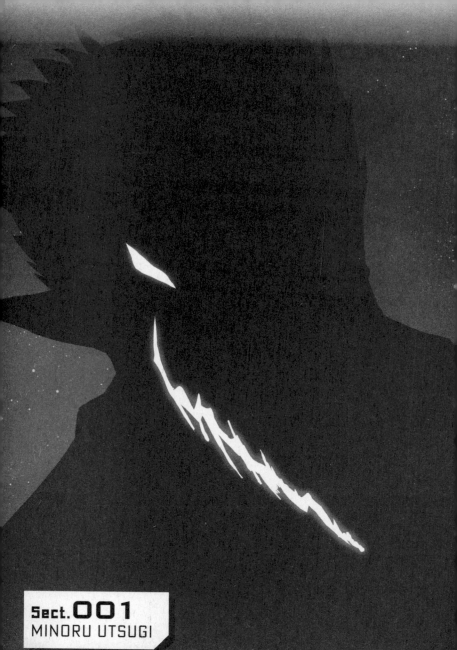

Sect.**001**
MINORU UTSUGI

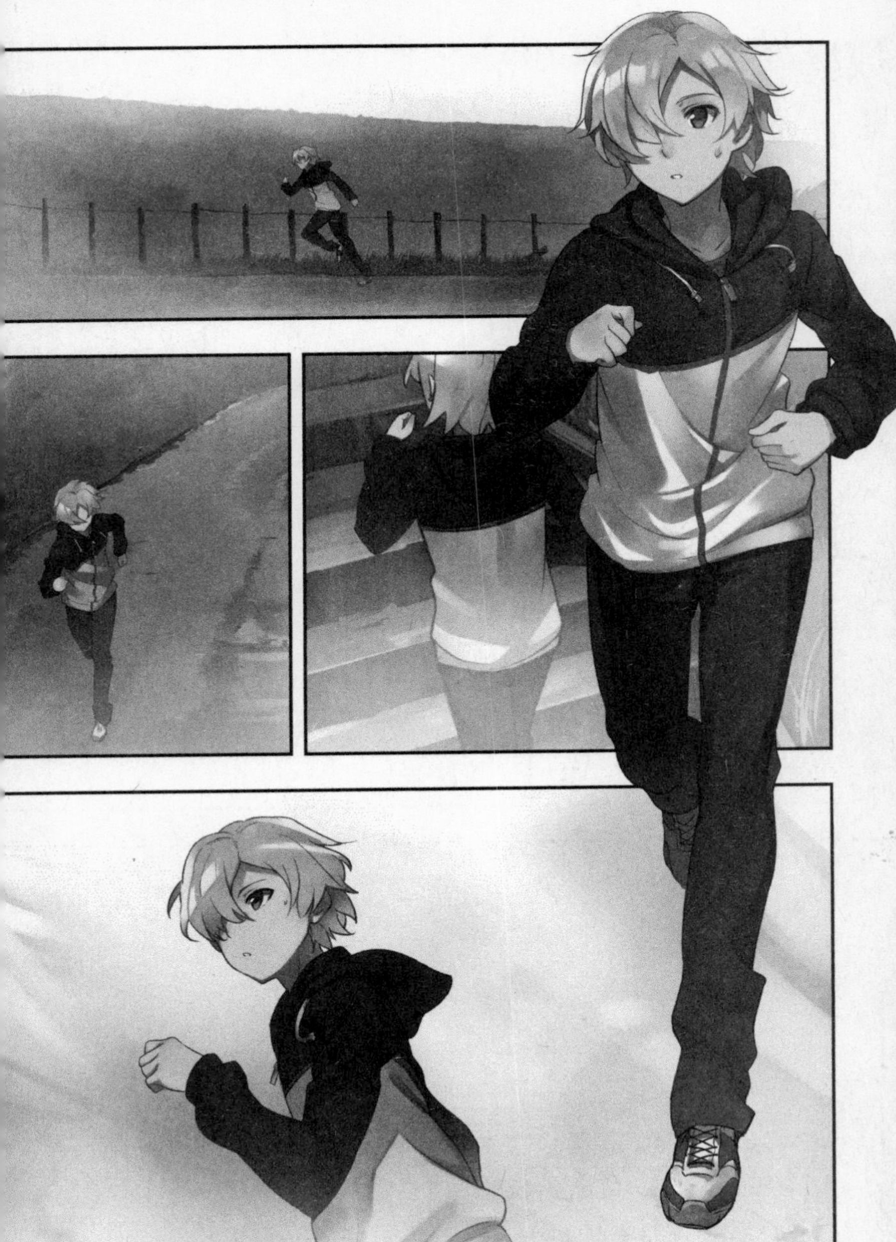

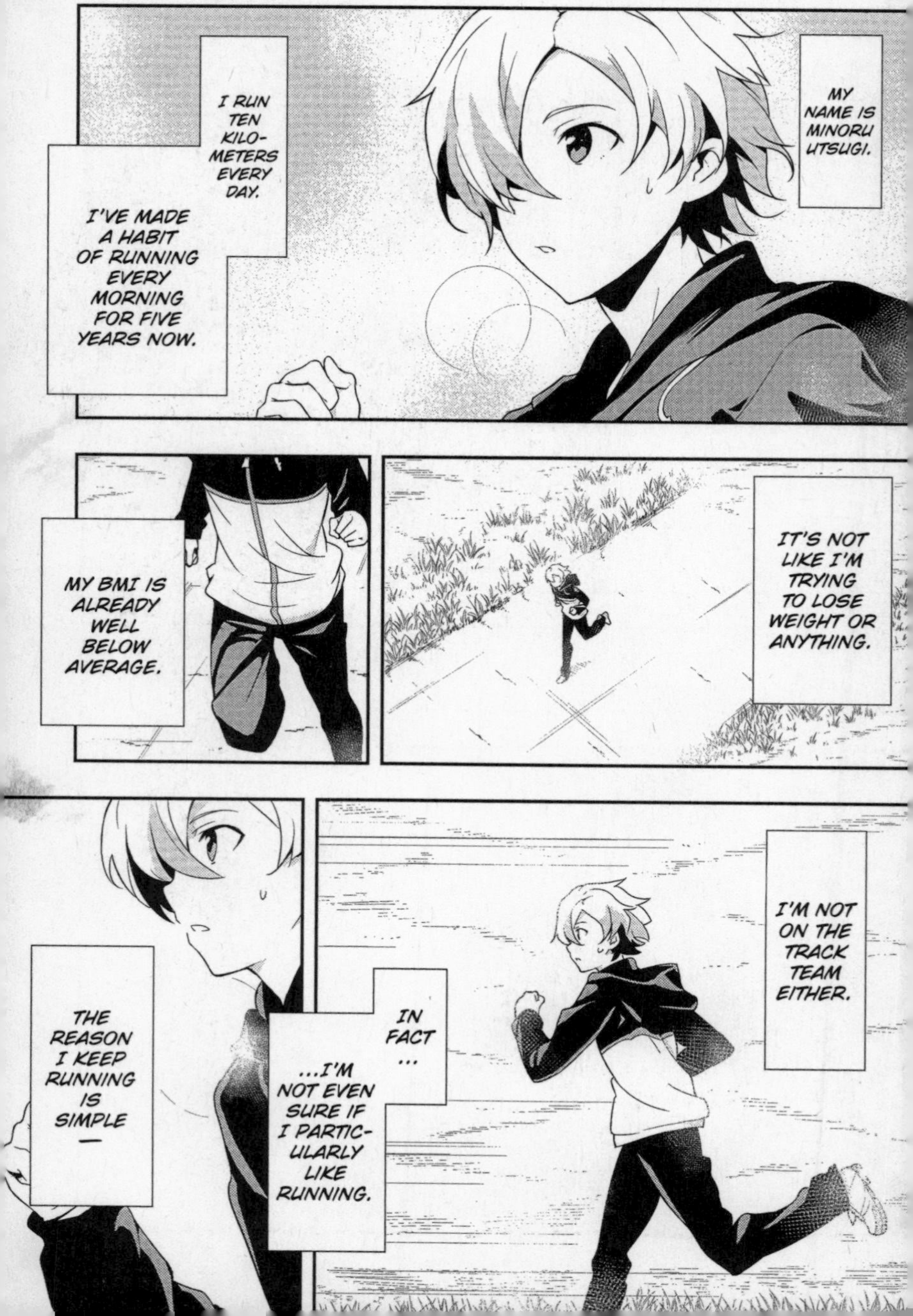
MY NAME IS MINORU UTSUGI.
I RUN TEN KILO-METERS EVERY DAY.
I'VE MADE A HABIT OF RUNNING EVERY MORNING FOR FIVE YEARS NOW.
IT'S NOT LIKE I'M TRYING TO LOSE WEIGHT OR ANYTHING.
MY BMI IS ALREADY WELL BELOW AVERAGE.
I'M NOT ON THE TRACK TEAM EITHER.
IN FACT...
...I'M NOT EVEN SURE IF I PARTIC-ULARLY LIKE RUNNING.
THE REASON I KEEP RUNNING IS SIMPLE—

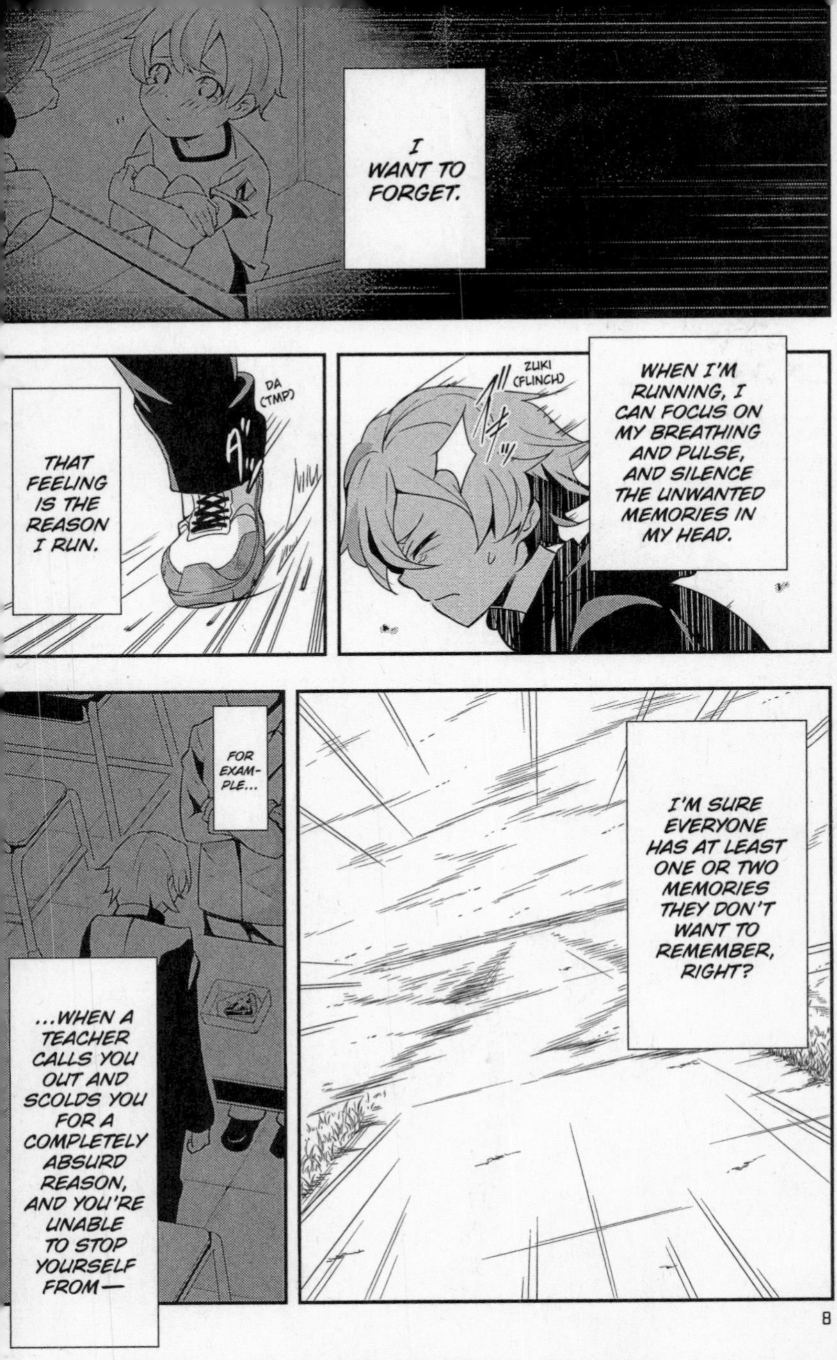
I WANT TO FORGET.
ZUKI (FLINCH)
WHEN I'M RUNNING, I CAN FOCUS ON MY BREATHING AND PULSE, AND SILENCE THE UNWANTED MEMORIES IN MY HEAD.
DA (TMP)
THAT FEELING IS THE REASON I RUN.
I'M SURE EVERYONE HAS AT LEAST ONE OR TWO MEMORIES THEY DON'T WANT TO REMEMBER, RIGHT?
FOR EXAMPLE...
...WHEN A TEACHER CALLS YOU OUT AND SCOLDS YOU FOR A COMPLETELY ABSURD REASON, AND YOU'RE UNABLE TO STOP YOURSELF FROM—

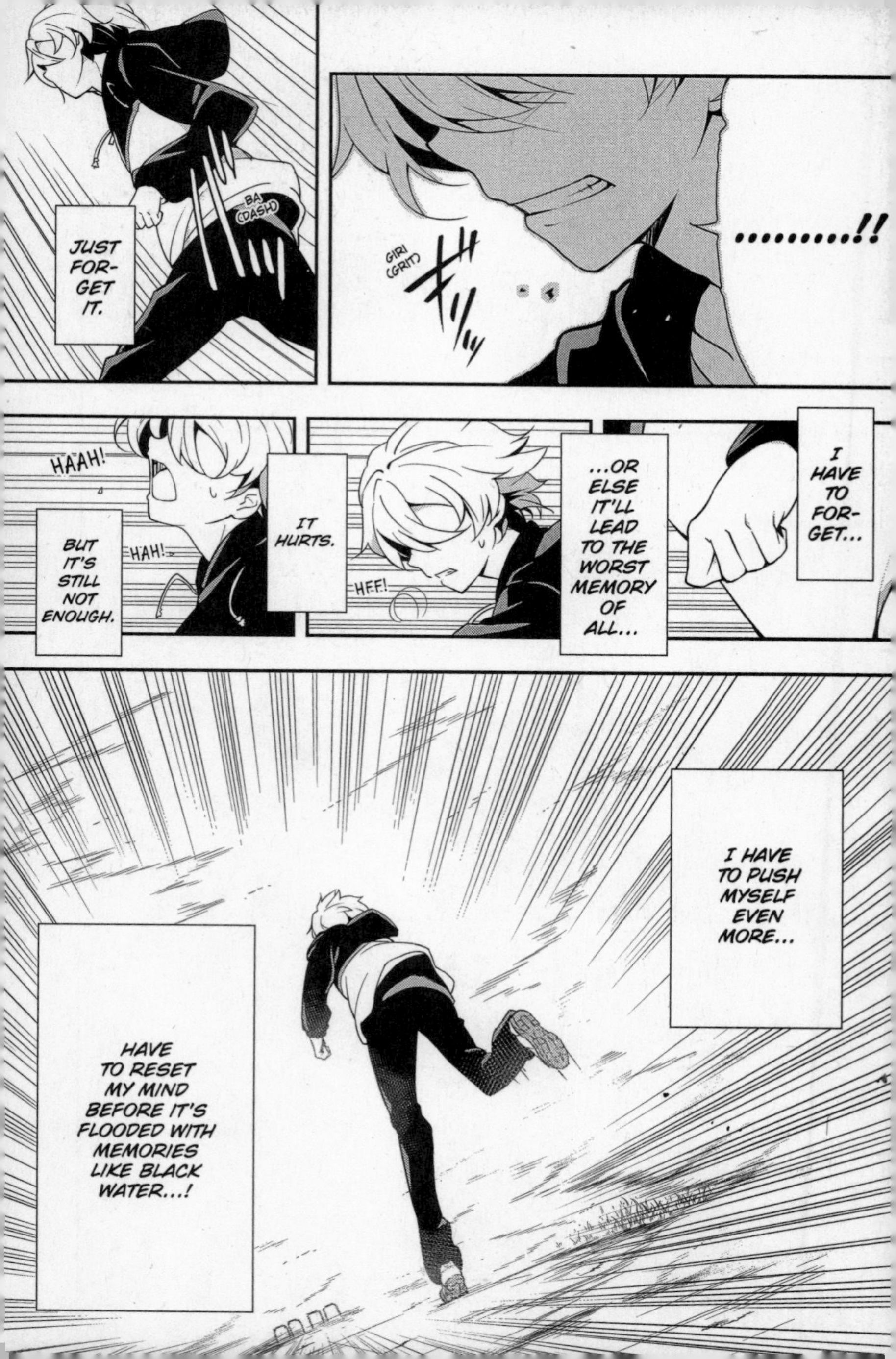
........!!
GIRI (GRIT)
BA (DASH)
JUST FOR-GET IT.
I HAVE TO FOR-GET...
...OR ELSE IT'LL LEAD TO THE WORST MEMORY OF ALL...
HFF!
IT HURTS.
HAAH!
HAH!
BUT IT'S STILL NOT ENOUGH.
I HAVE TO PUSH MYSELF EVEN MORE...
HAVE TO RESET MY MIND BEFORE IT'S FLOODED WITH MEMORIES LIKE BLACK WATER...!

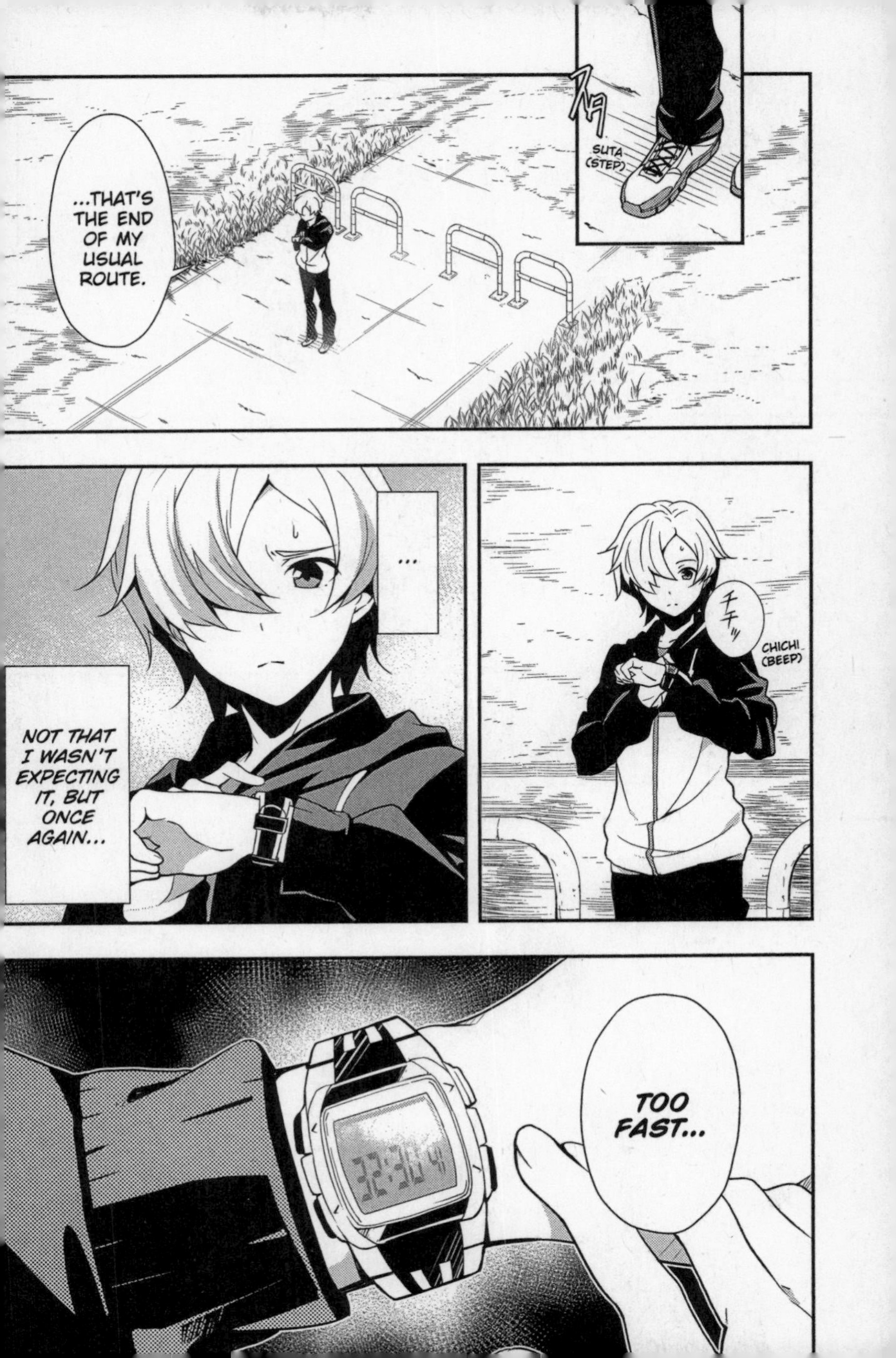
スタ
SUTA (STEP)
...THAT'S THE END OF MY USUAL ROUTE.
チチッ
CHICHI (BEEP)
...
NOT THAT I WASN'T EXPECTING IT, BUT ONCE AGAIN...
TOO FAST...

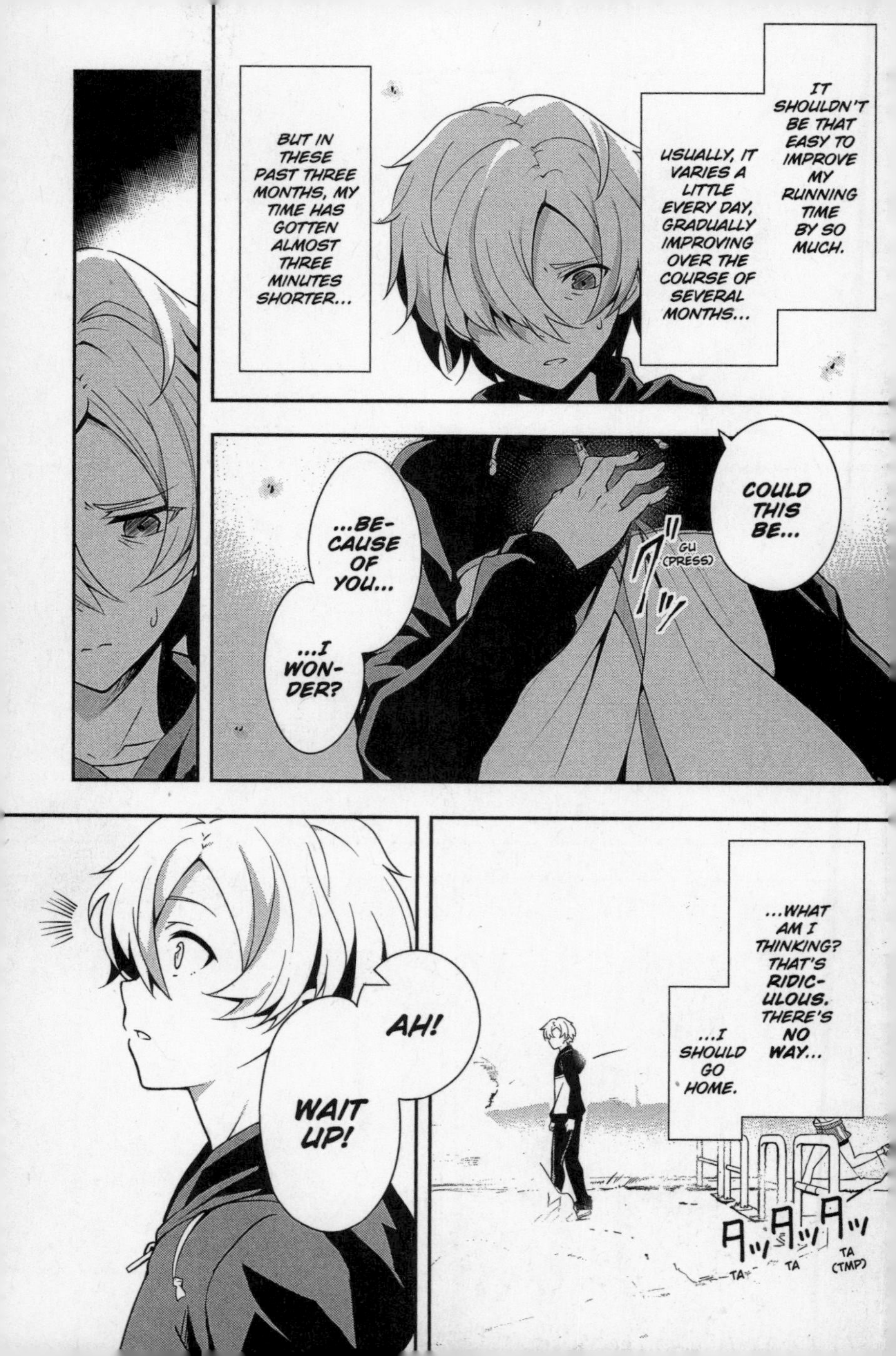
IT SHOULDN'T BE THAT EASY TO IMPROVE MY RUNNING TIME BY SO MUCH.
USUALLY, IT VARIES A LITTLE EVERY DAY, GRADUALLY IMPROVING OVER THE COURSE OF SEVERAL MONTHS...
BUT IN THESE PAST THREE MONTHS, MY TIME HAS GOTTEN ALMOST THREE MINUTES SHORTER...
COULD THIS BE...
GU (PRESS)
...BE-CAUSE OF YOU...
...I WON-DER?
...WHAT AM I THINKING? THAT'S RIDIC-ULOUS. THERE'S NO WAY...
...I SHOULD GO HOME.
TA TA TA (TMP)
AH!
WAIT UP!

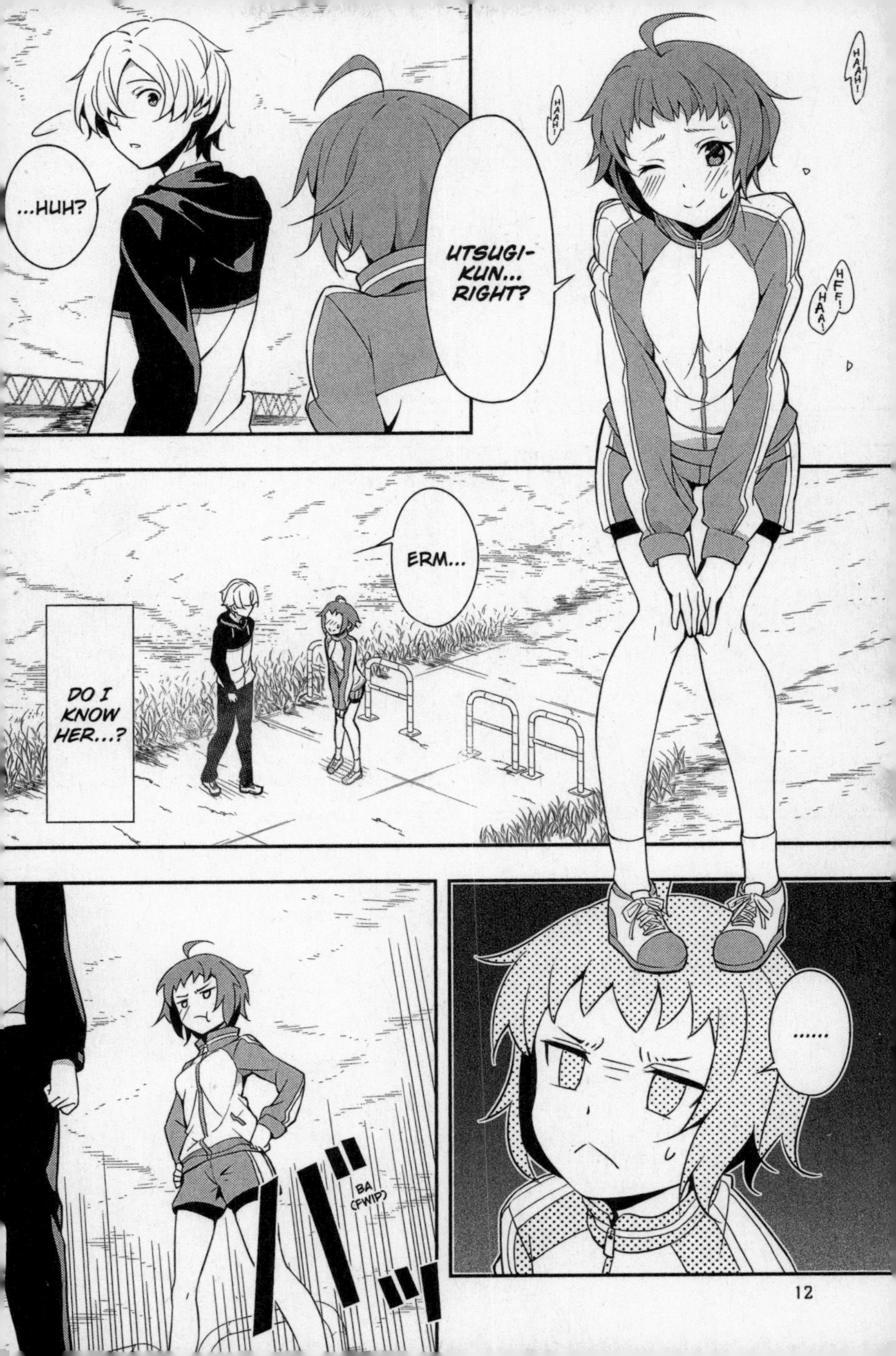
HAAH!
HAAH!
HFF!
HAA!
UTSUGI-KUN... RIGHT?
...HUH?
ERM...
DO I KNOW HER...?
......
BA (FWIP)

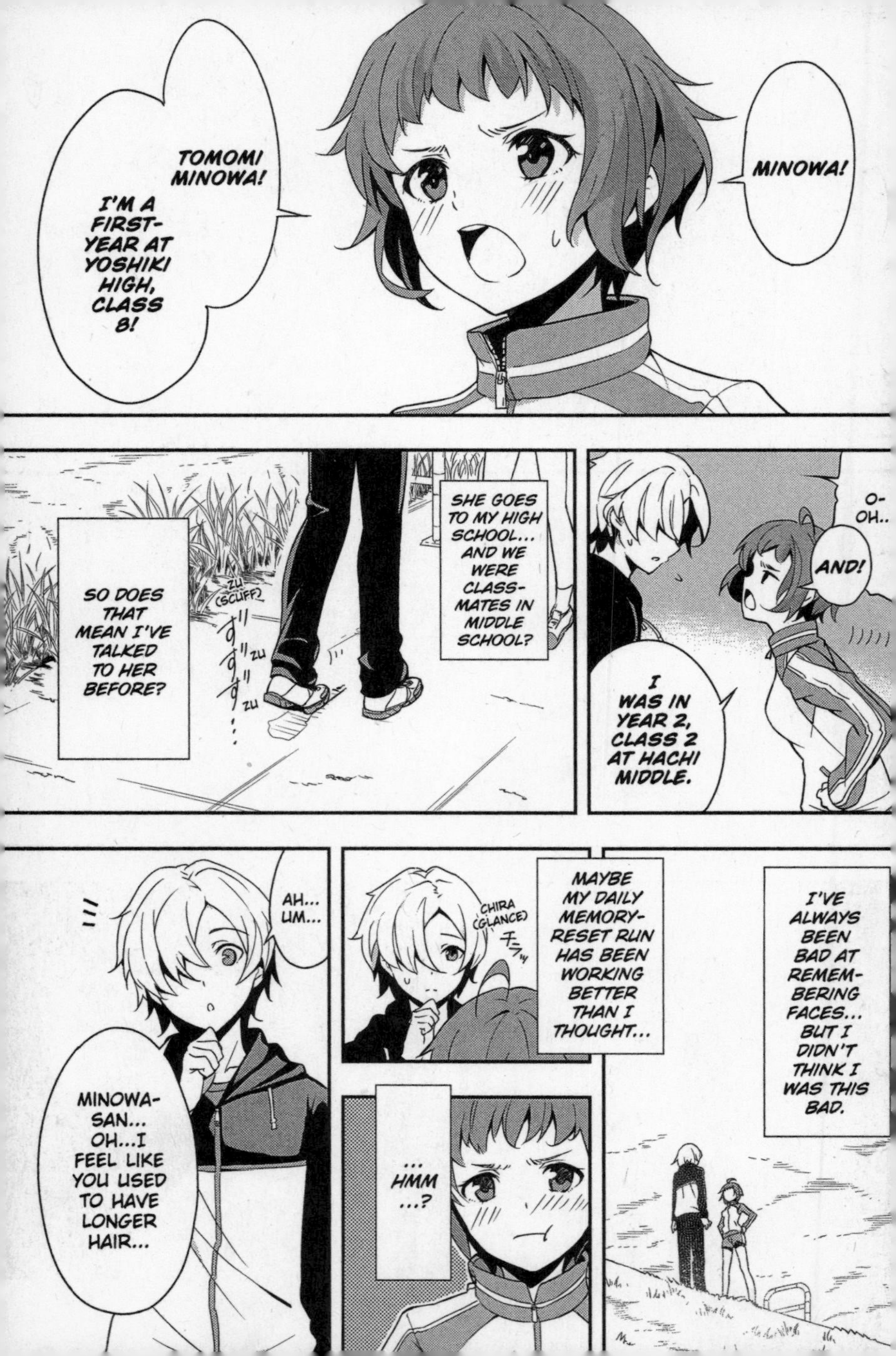
MINOWA!
TOMOMI MINOWA!
I'M A FIRST-YEAR AT YOSHIKI HIGH, CLASS 8!
O-OH..
AND!
I WAS IN YEAR 2, CLASS 2 AT HACHI MIDDLE.
SHE GOES TO MY HIGH SCHOOL... AND WE WERE CLASSMATES IN MIDDLE SCHOOL?
ZU (SCUFF)
SO DOES THAT MEAN I'VE TALKED TO HER BEFORE?
I'VE ALWAYS BEEN BAD AT REMEMBERING FACES... BUT I DIDN'T THINK I WAS THIS BAD.
MAYBE MY DAILY MEMORY-RESET RUN HAS BEEN WORKING BETTER THAN I THOUGHT...
CHIRA (GLANCE)
... HMM ...?
AH... UM...
MINOWA-SAN... OH...I FEEL LIKE YOU USED TO HAVE LONGER HAIR...

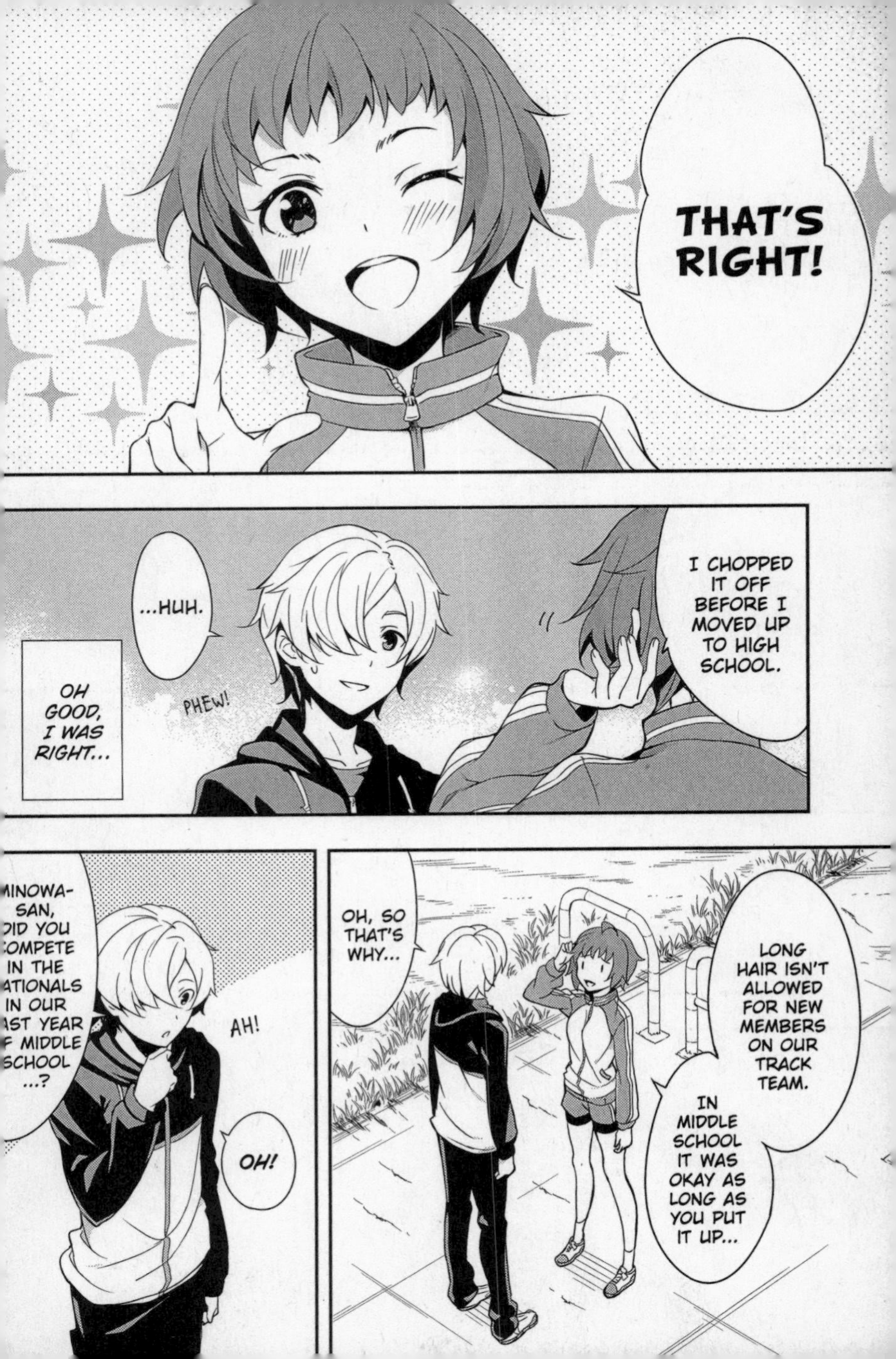
THAT'S RIGHT!
I CHOPPED IT OFF BEFORE I MOVED UP TO HIGH SCHOOL.
...HUH.
PHEW!
OH GOOD, I WAS RIGHT...
LONG HAIR ISN'T ALLOWED FOR NEW MEMBERS ON OUR TRACK TEAM.
IN MIDDLE SCHOOL IT WAS OKAY AS LONG AS YOU PUT IT UP...
OH, SO THAT'S WHY...
AH!
OH!
MINOWA-SAN, DID YOU COMPETE IN THE ATIONALS IN OUR AST YEAR F MIDDLE SCHOOL ...?

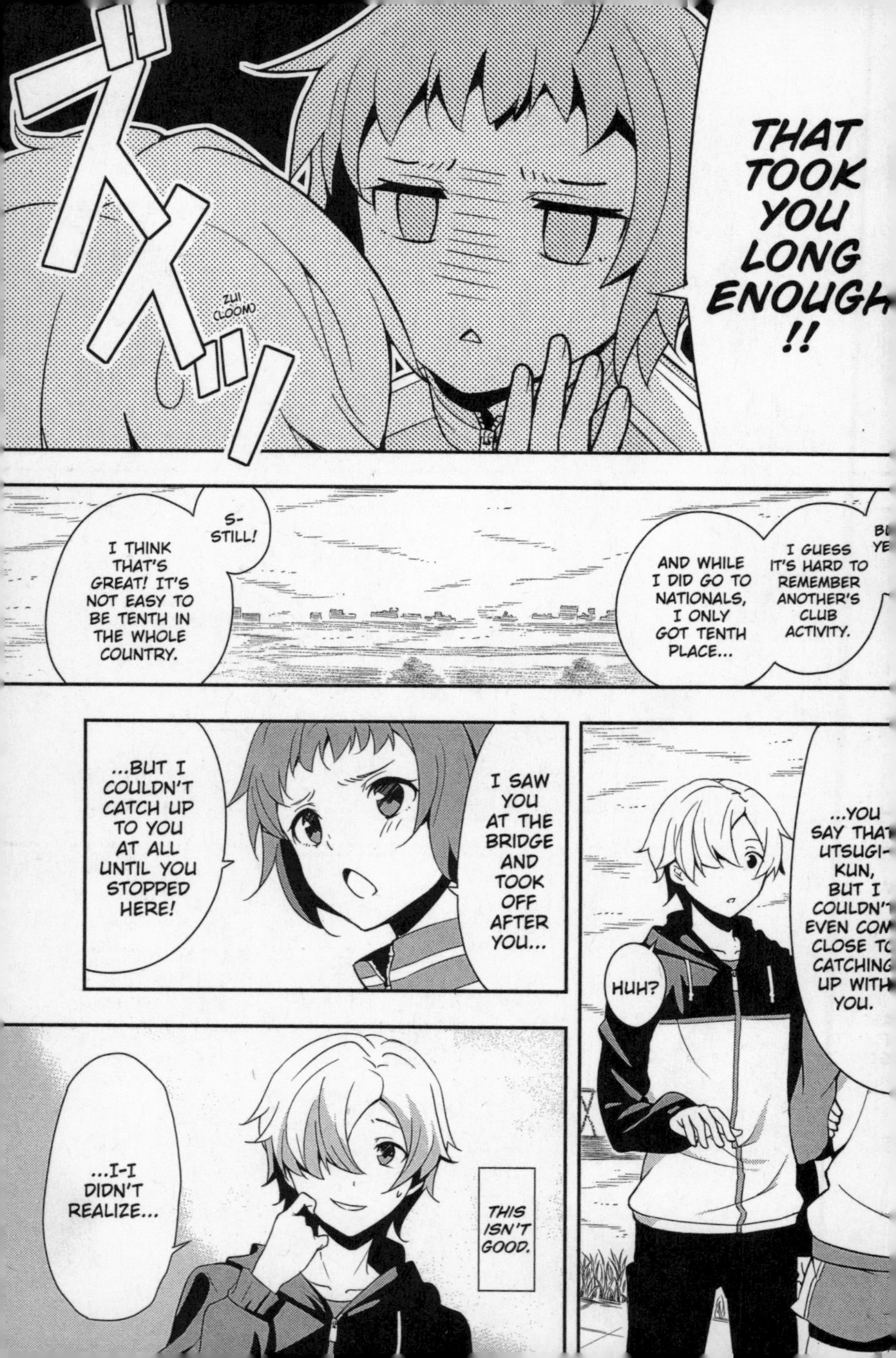
THAT TOOK YOU LONG ENOUGH!!
ZUI (LOOM)
I GUESS IT'S HARD TO REMEMBER ANOTHER'S CLUB ACTIVITY.
AND WHILE I DID GO TO NATIONALS, I ONLY GOT TENTH PLACE...
S-STILL!
I THINK THAT'S GREAT! IT'S NOT EASY TO BE TENTH IN THE WHOLE COUNTRY.
...YOU SAY THAT UTSUGI-KUN, BUT I COULDN'T EVEN COME CLOSE TO CATCHING UP WITH YOU.
HUH?
I SAW YOU AT THE BRIDGE AND TOOK OFF AFTER YOU...
...BUT I COULDN'T CATCH UP TO YOU AT ALL UNTIL YOU STOPPED HERE!
THIS ISN'T GOOD.
...I-I DIDN'T REALIZE...

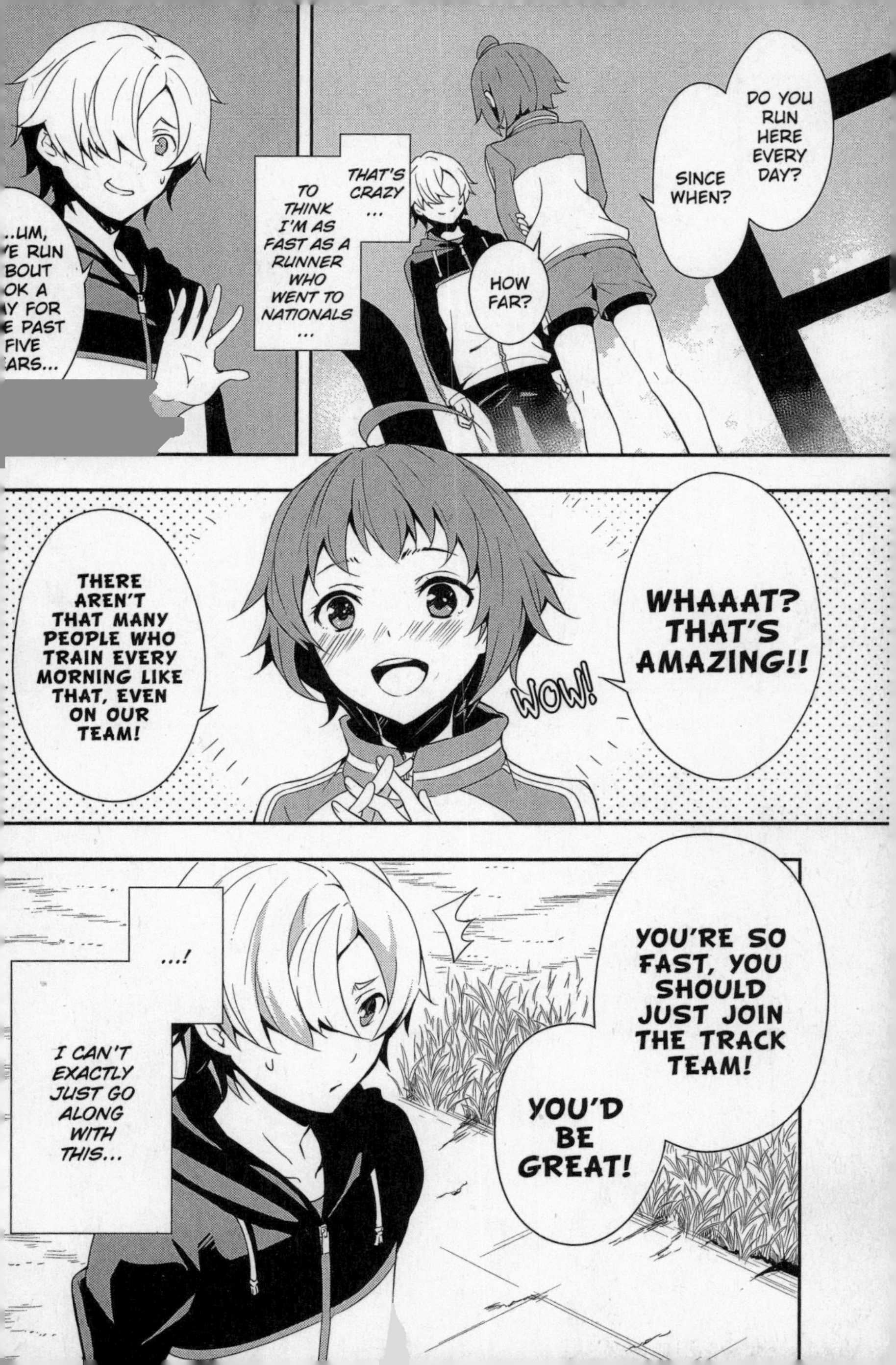
DO YOU RUN HERE EVERY DAY?
SINCE WHEN?
HOW FAR?
THAT'S CRAZY... TO THINK I'M AS FAST AS A RUNNER WHO WENT TO NATIONALS...
..UM, 'E RUN BOUT OK A Y FOR E PAST FIVE ARS...
WHAAAT? THAT'S AMAZING!!
WOW!
THERE AREN'T THAT MANY PEOPLE WHO TRAIN EVERY MORNING LIKE THAT, EVEN ON OUR TEAM!
YOU'RE SO FAST, YOU SHOULD JUST JOIN THE TRACK TEAM!
YOU'D BE GREAT!
...!
I CAN'T EXACTLY JUST GO ALONG WITH THIS...

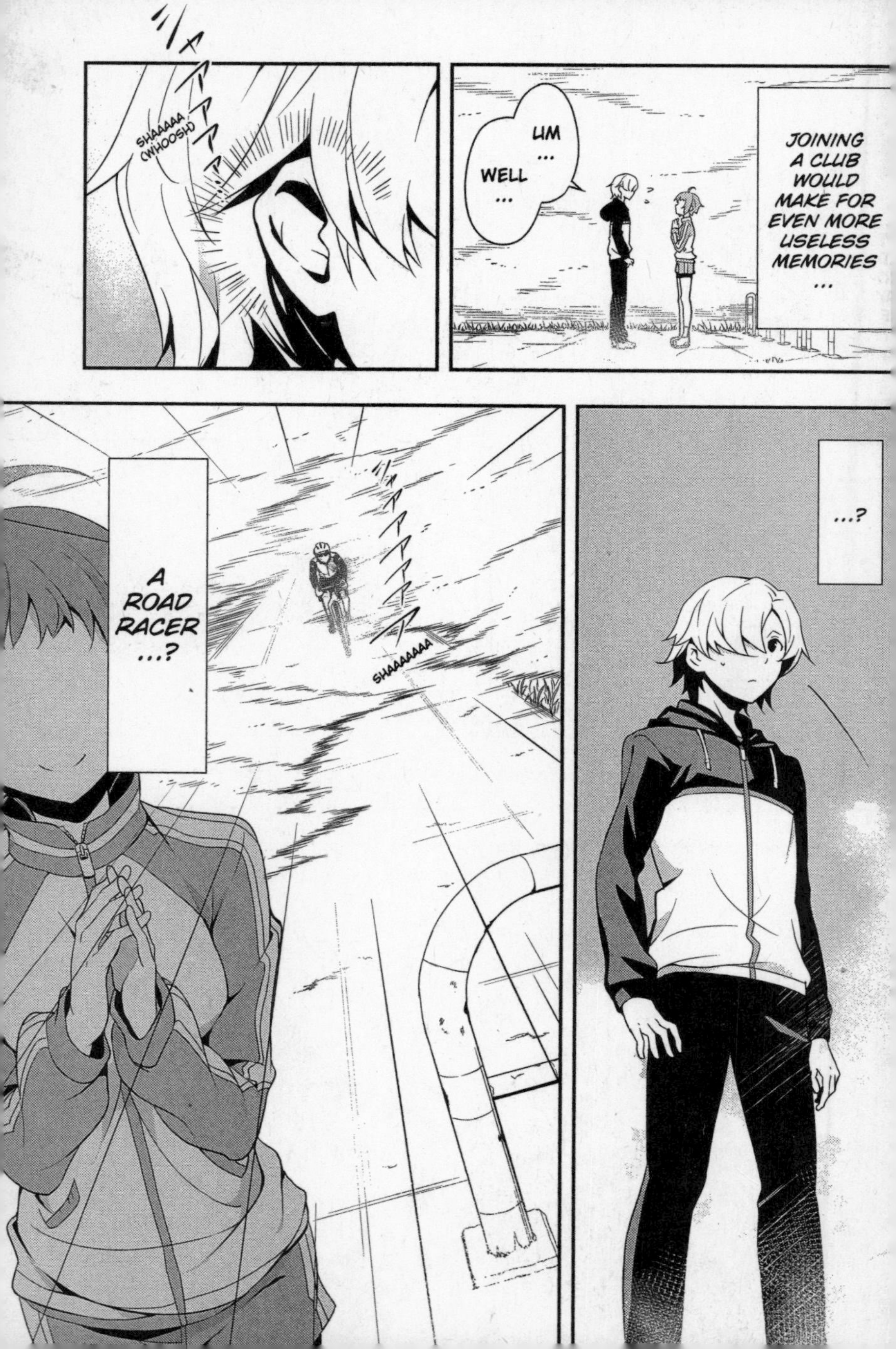

JOINING A CLUB WOULD MAKE FOR EVEN MORE USELESS MEMORIES ...
UM ... WELL ...
?
SHAAAAAA (WHOOSH)
...?
A ROAD RACER ...?
SHAAAAAAA

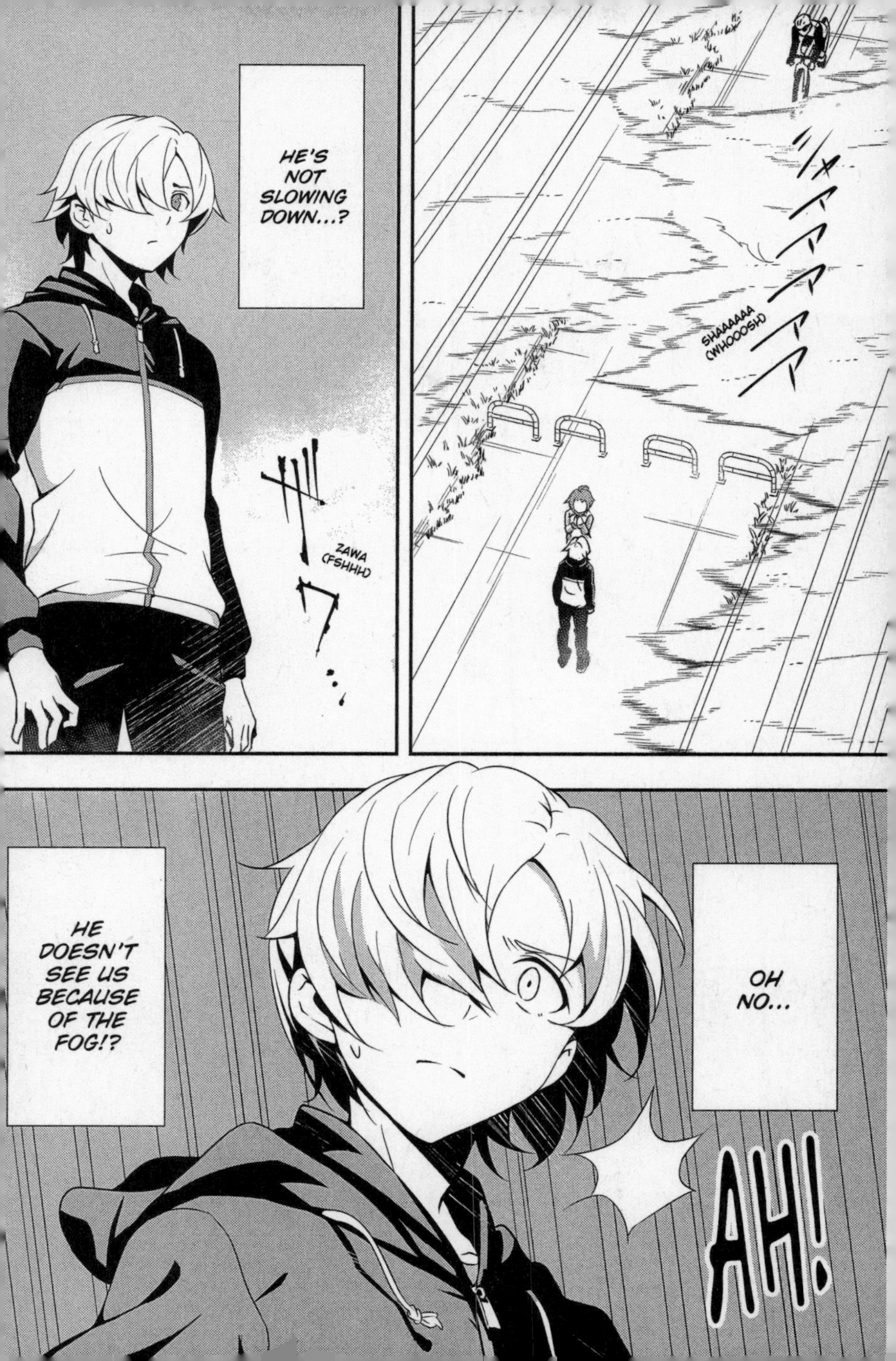
SHAAAAAA (WHOOOSH)
HE'S NOT SLOWING DOWN...?
ZAWA (FSHHH)
OH NO...
HE DOESN'T SEE US BECAUSE OF THE FOG!?
AH!

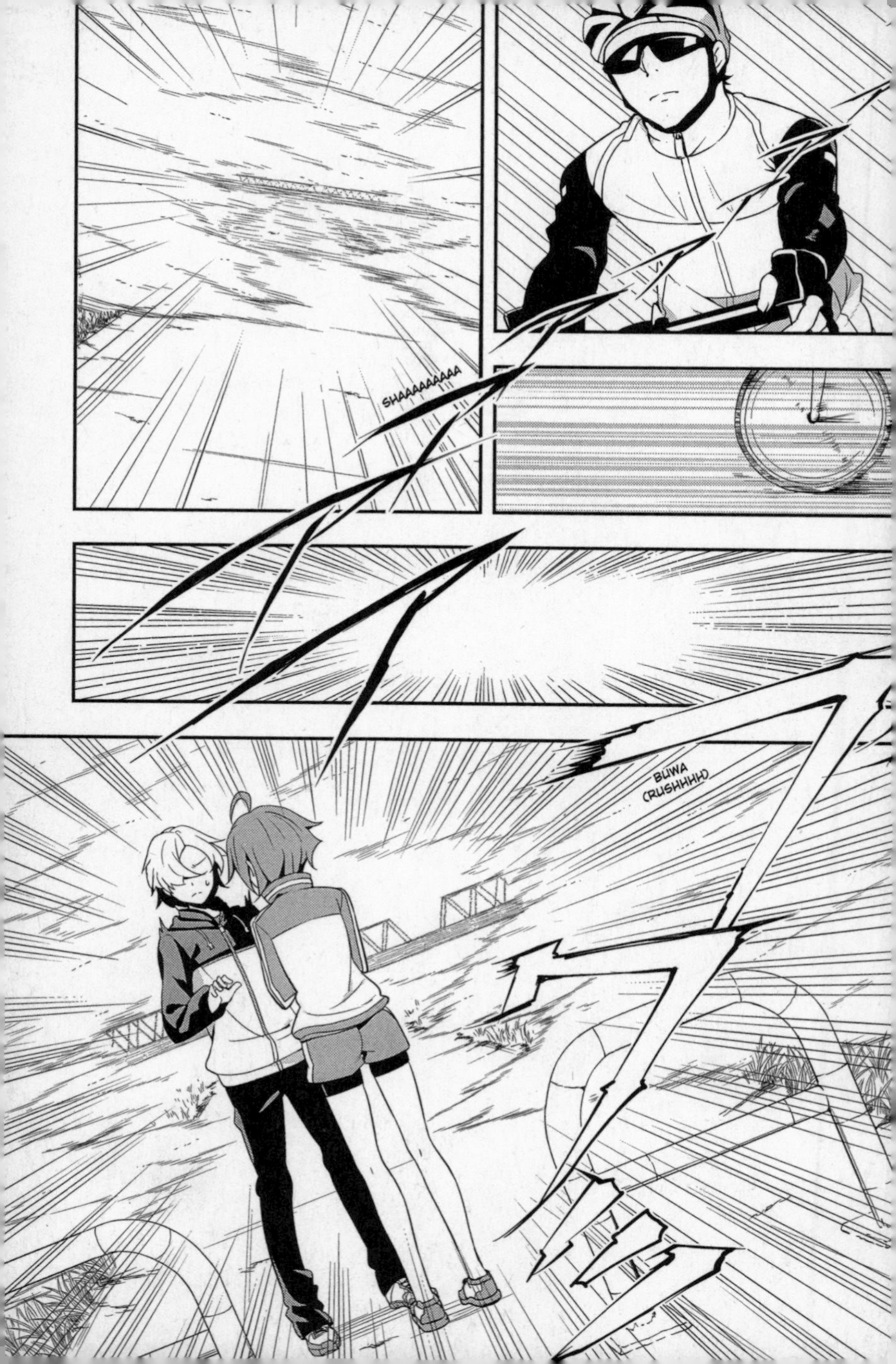
SHAAAAAAAAA
BUWA
(RUSHHHH)

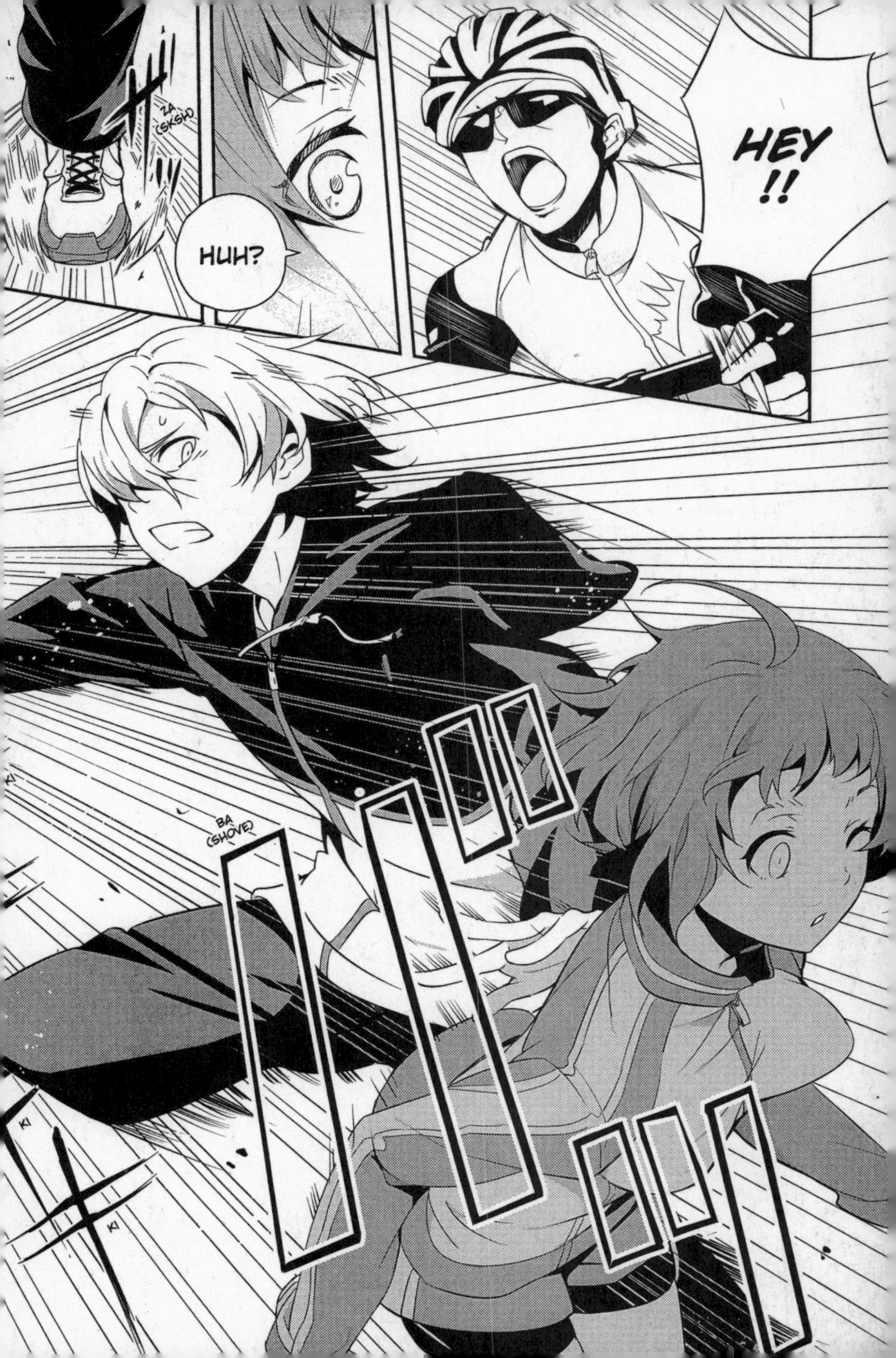

HEY!!
HUH?
ZA (SKSH)
BA (SHOVE)
KI
KI
KI

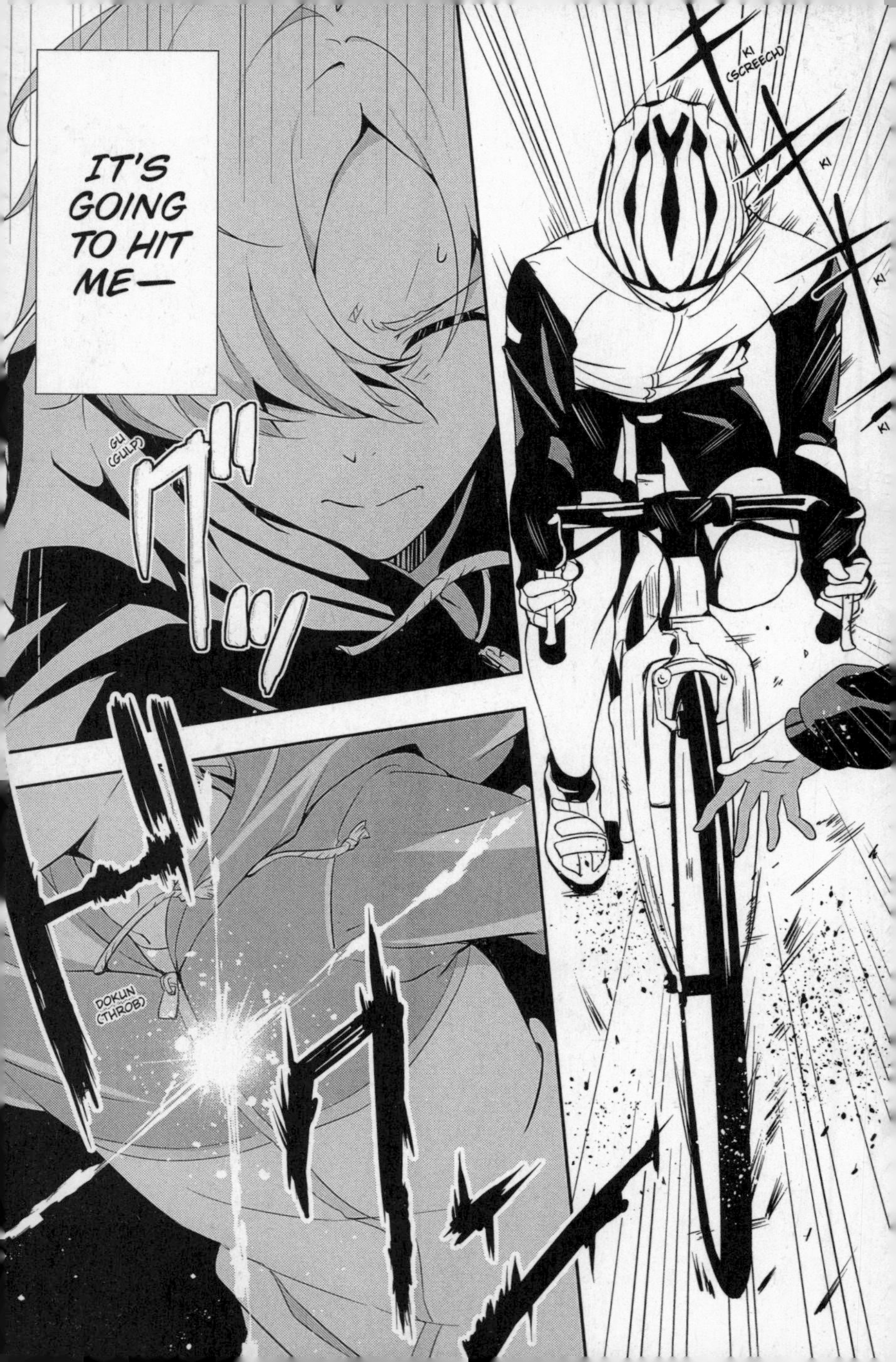
KI (SCREECH)
KI
KI
KI
IT'S GOING TO HIT ME—
GU (GULP)
DOKUN (THROB)

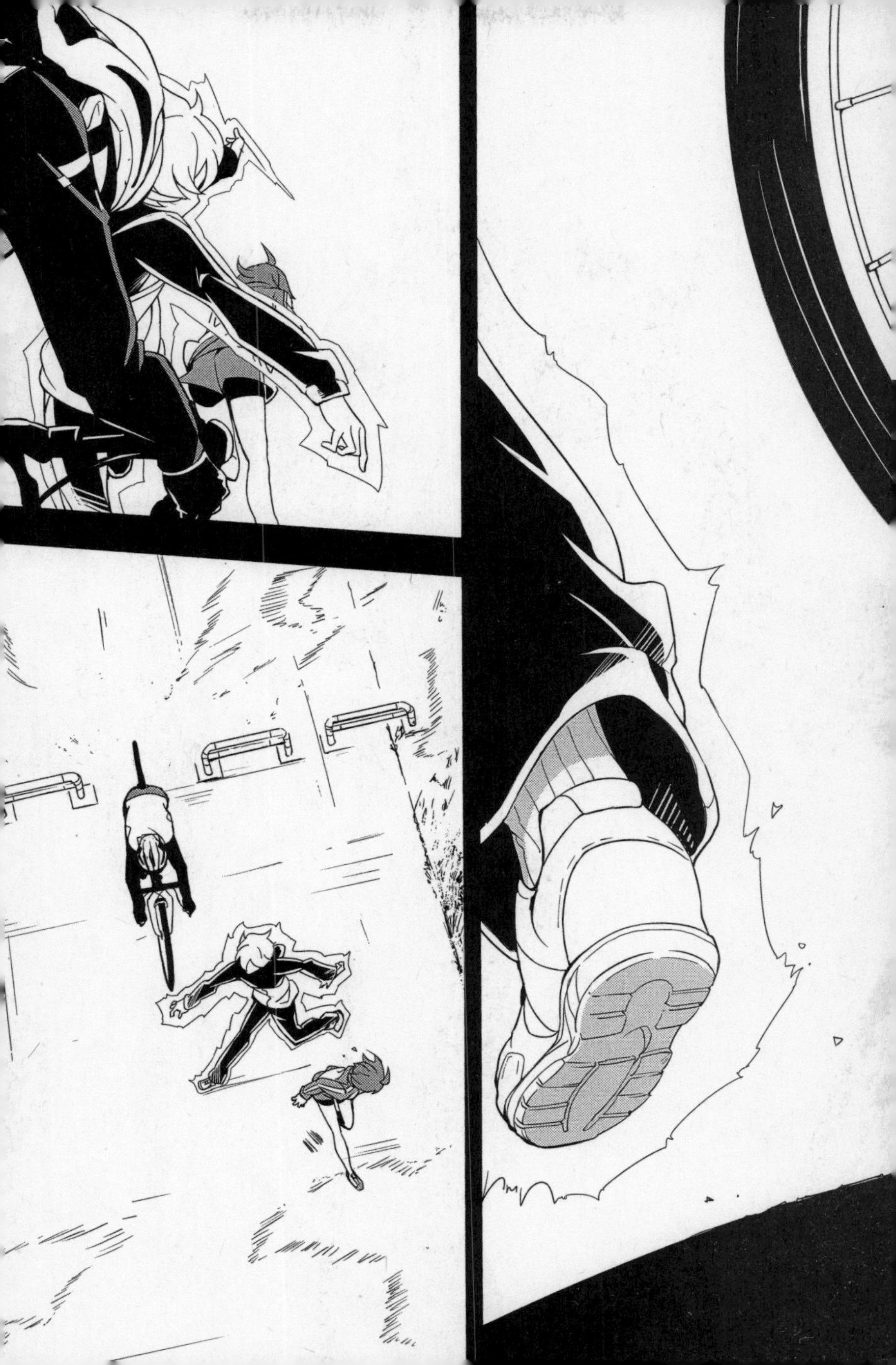

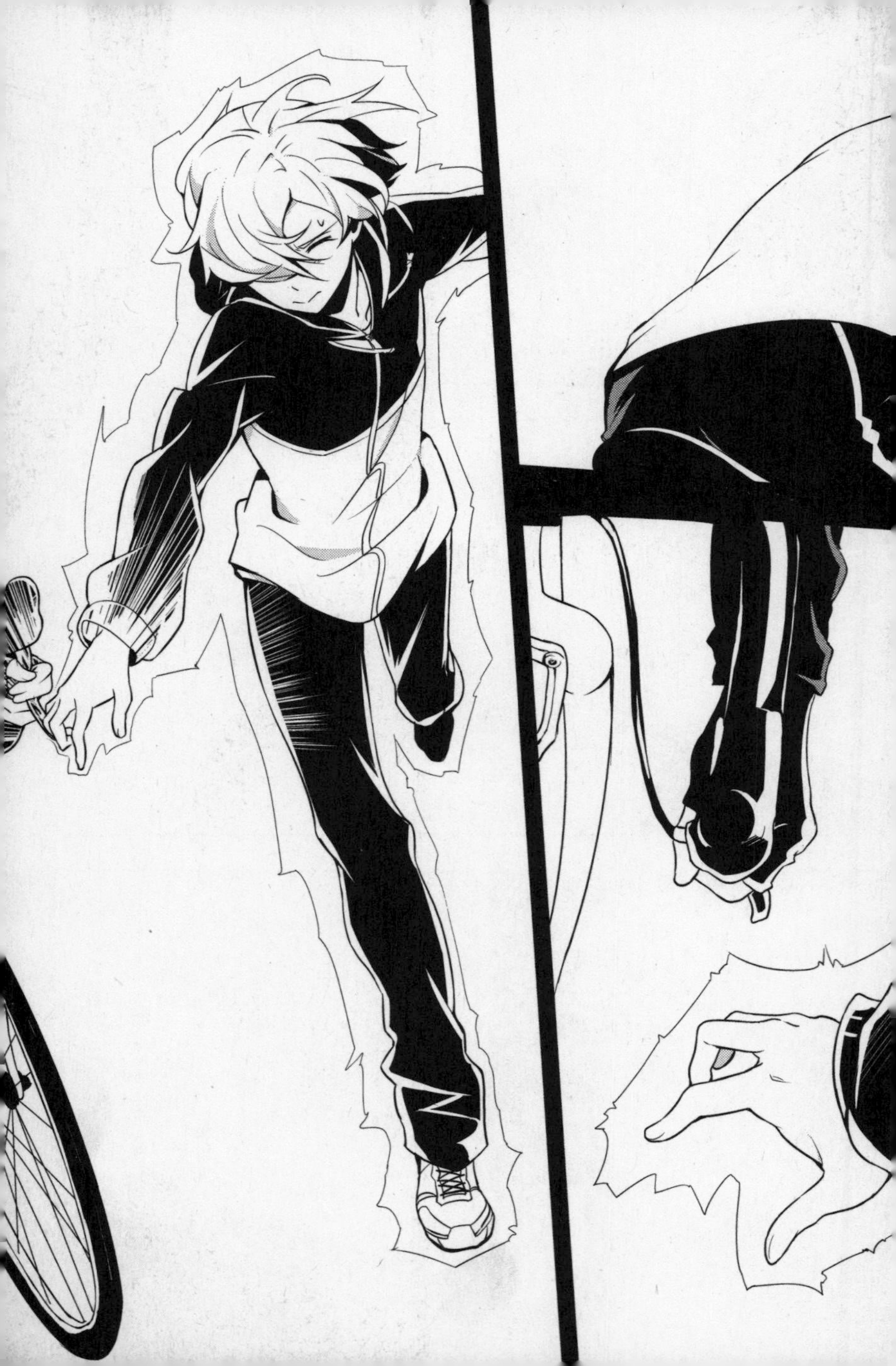

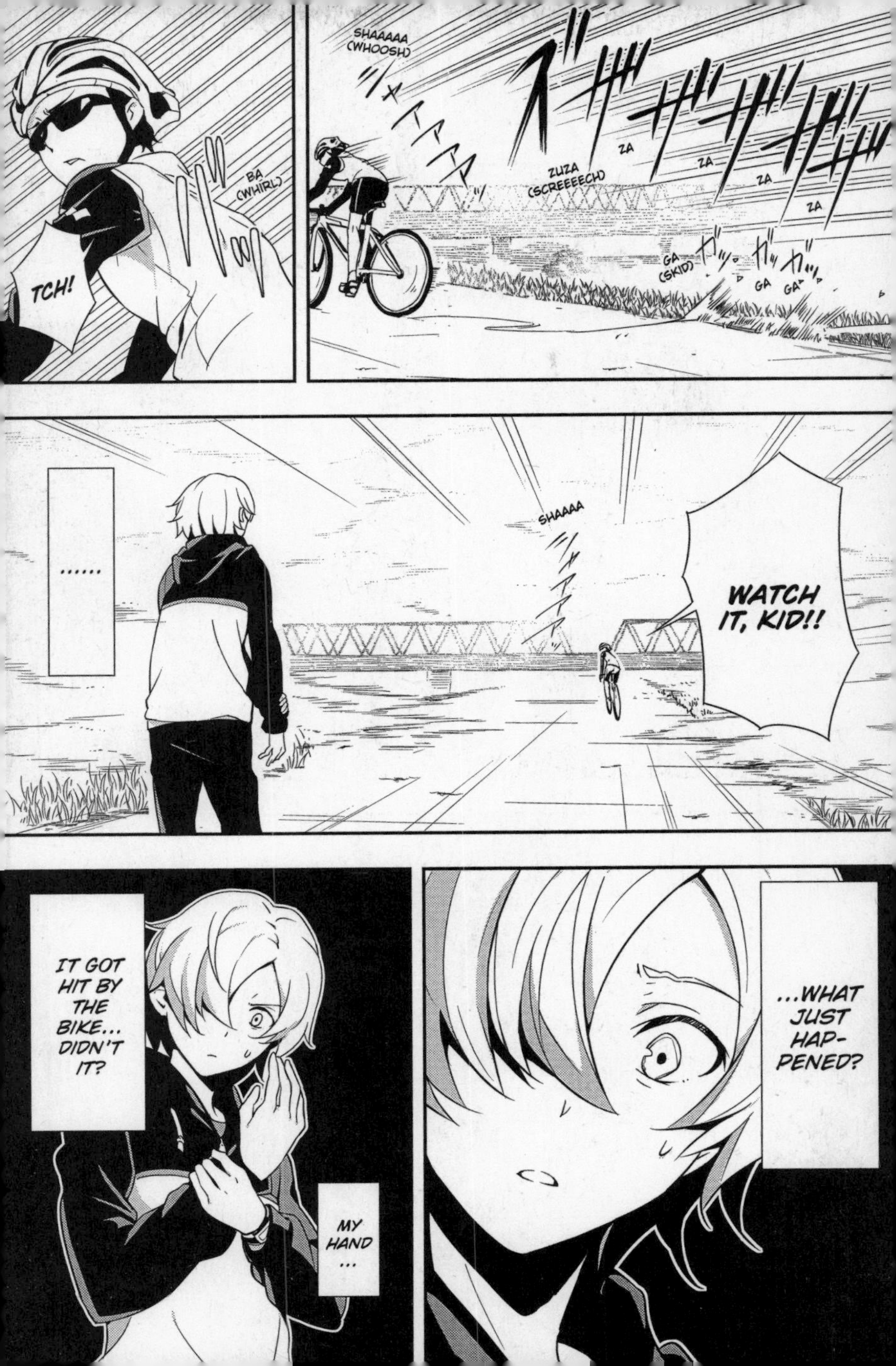
SHAAAAA (WHOOSH)
ZUZA (SCREEEECH)
ZA ZA ZA ZA
GA (SKID)
GA GA
BA (WHIRL)
TCH!
WATCH IT, KID!!
SHAAAA
......
...WHAT JUST HAP-PENED?
IT GOT HIT BY THE BIKE... DIDN'T IT?
MY HAND ...

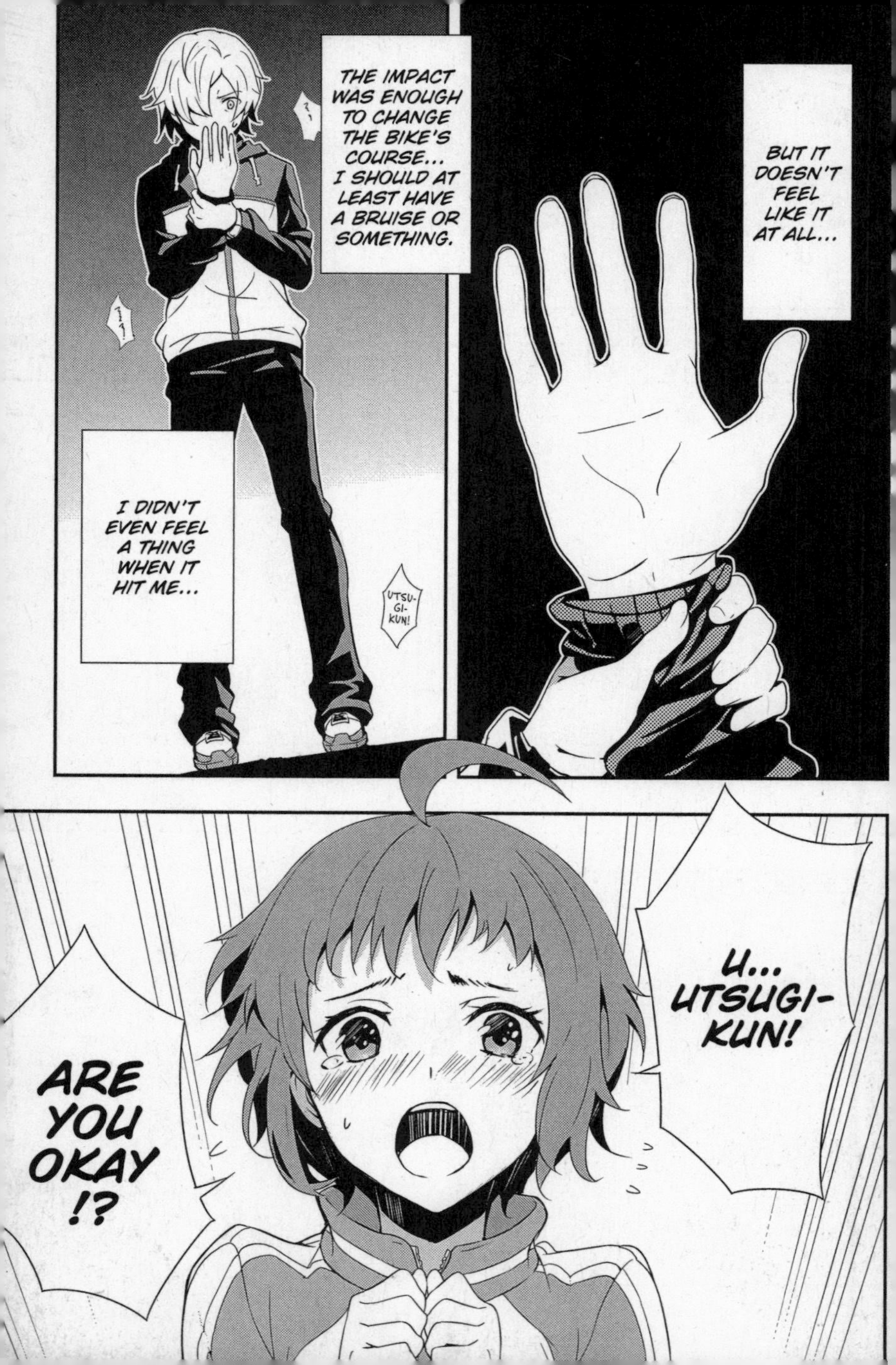
BUT IT DOESN'T FEEL LIKE IT AT ALL...
THE IMPACT WAS ENOUGH TO CHANGE THE BIKE'S COURSE... I SHOULD AT LEAST HAVE A BRUISE OR SOMETHING.
I DIDN'T EVEN FEEL A THING WHEN IT HIT ME...
UTSUGI-KUN!
U... UTSUGI-KUN!
ARE YOU OKAY!?

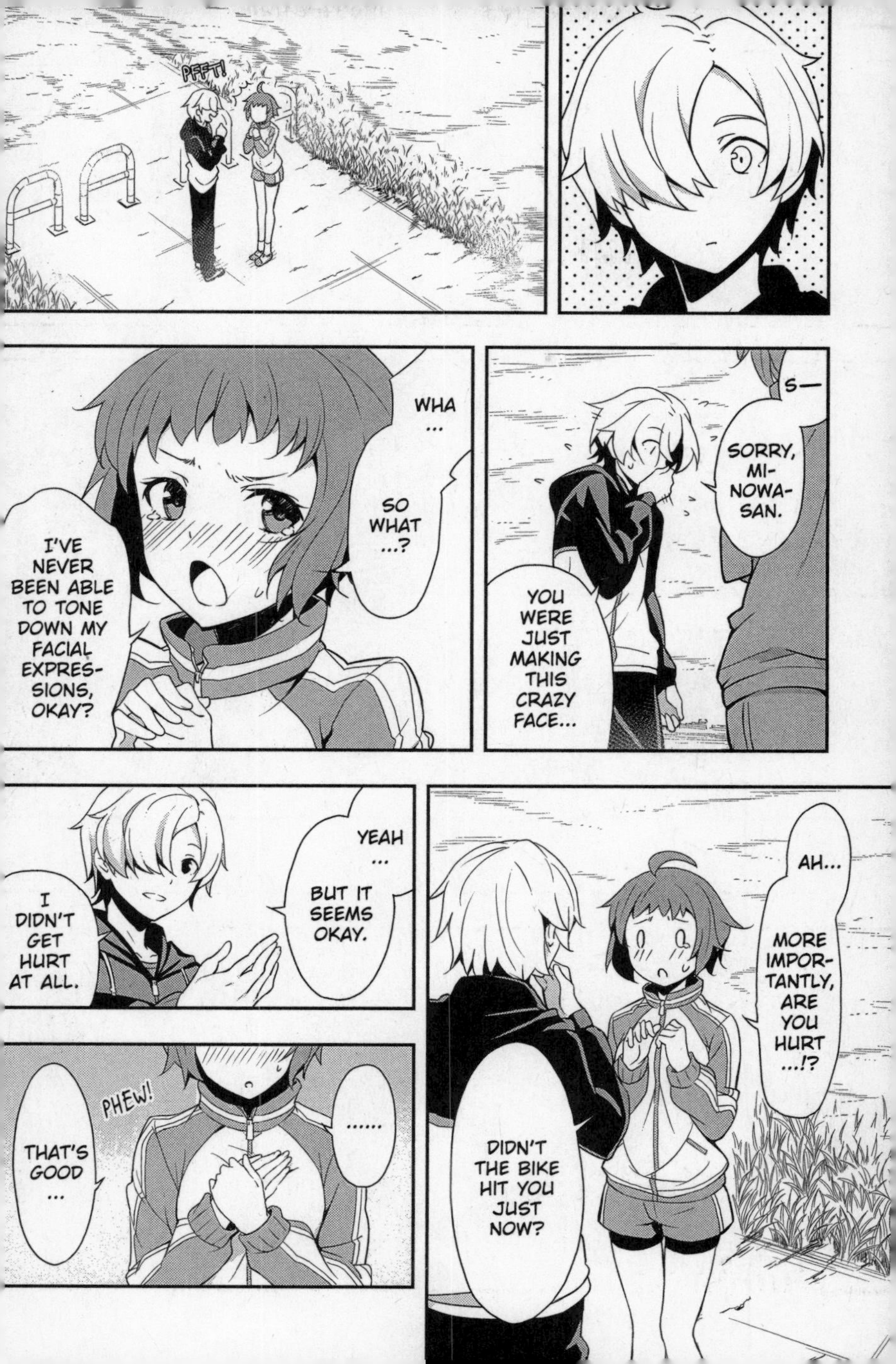
PFFT!
S—
SORRY, MI-NOWA-SAN.
YOU WERE JUST MAKING THIS CRAZY FACE...
WHA...
SO WHAT...?
I'VE NEVER BEEN ABLE TO TONE DOWN MY FACIAL EXPRES-SIONS, OKAY?
AH...
MORE IMPOR-TANTLY, ARE YOU HURT...!?
DIDN'T THE BIKE HIT YOU JUST NOW?
YEAH...
BUT IT SEEMS OKAY.
I DIDN'T GET HURT AT ALL.
......
PHEW!
THAT'S GOOD...

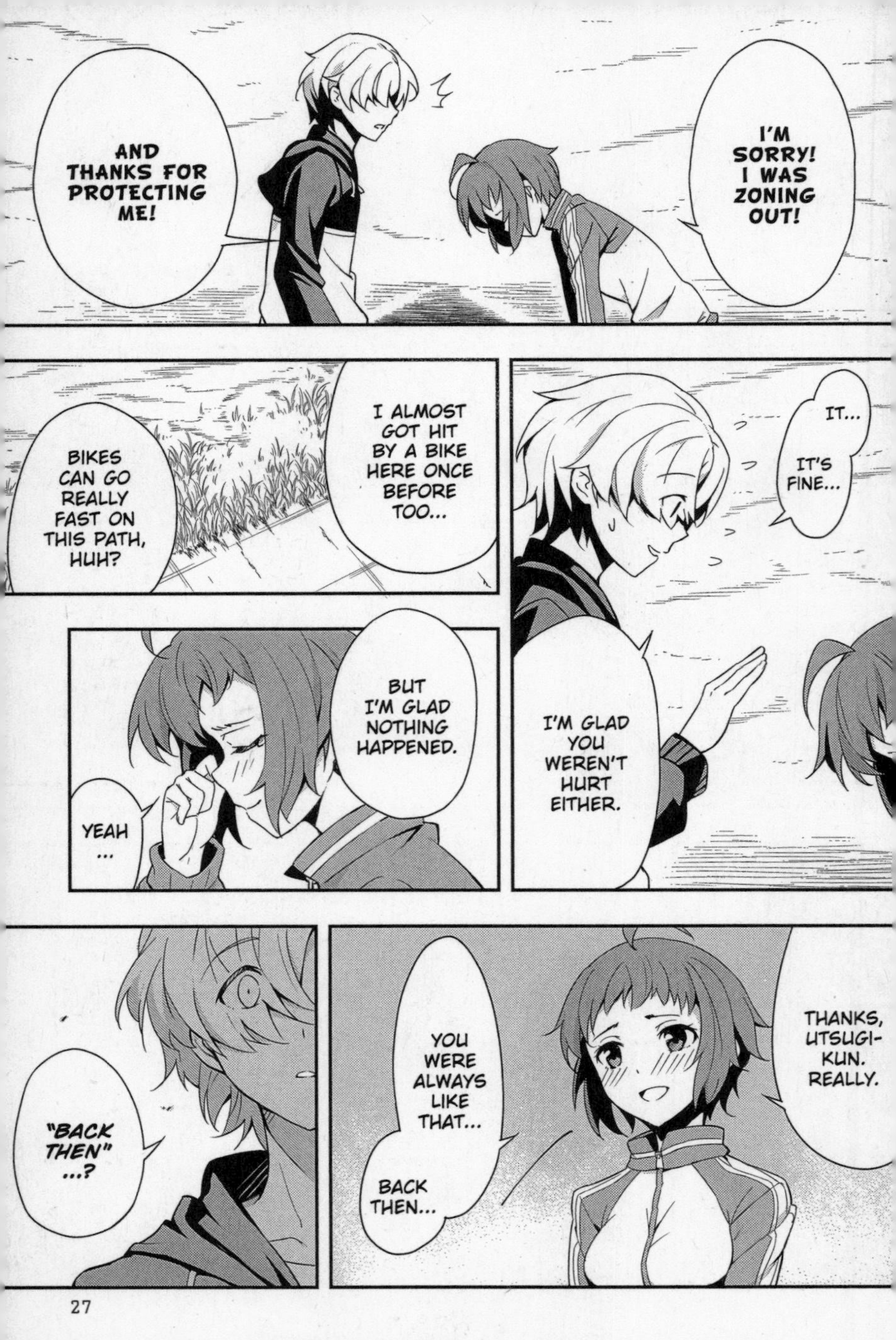
I'M SORRY! I WAS ZONING OUT!
AND THANKS FOR PROTECTING ME!
IT...
IT'S FINE...
I'M GLAD YOU WEREN'T HURT EITHER.
I ALMOST GOT HIT BY A BIKE HERE ONCE BEFORE TOO...
BIKES CAN GO REALLY FAST ON THIS PATH, HUH?
BUT I'M GLAD NOTHING HAPPENED.
YEAH ...
THANKS, UTSUGI-KUN. REALLY.
YOU WERE ALWAYS LIKE THAT...
BACK THEN...
"BACK THEN" ...?

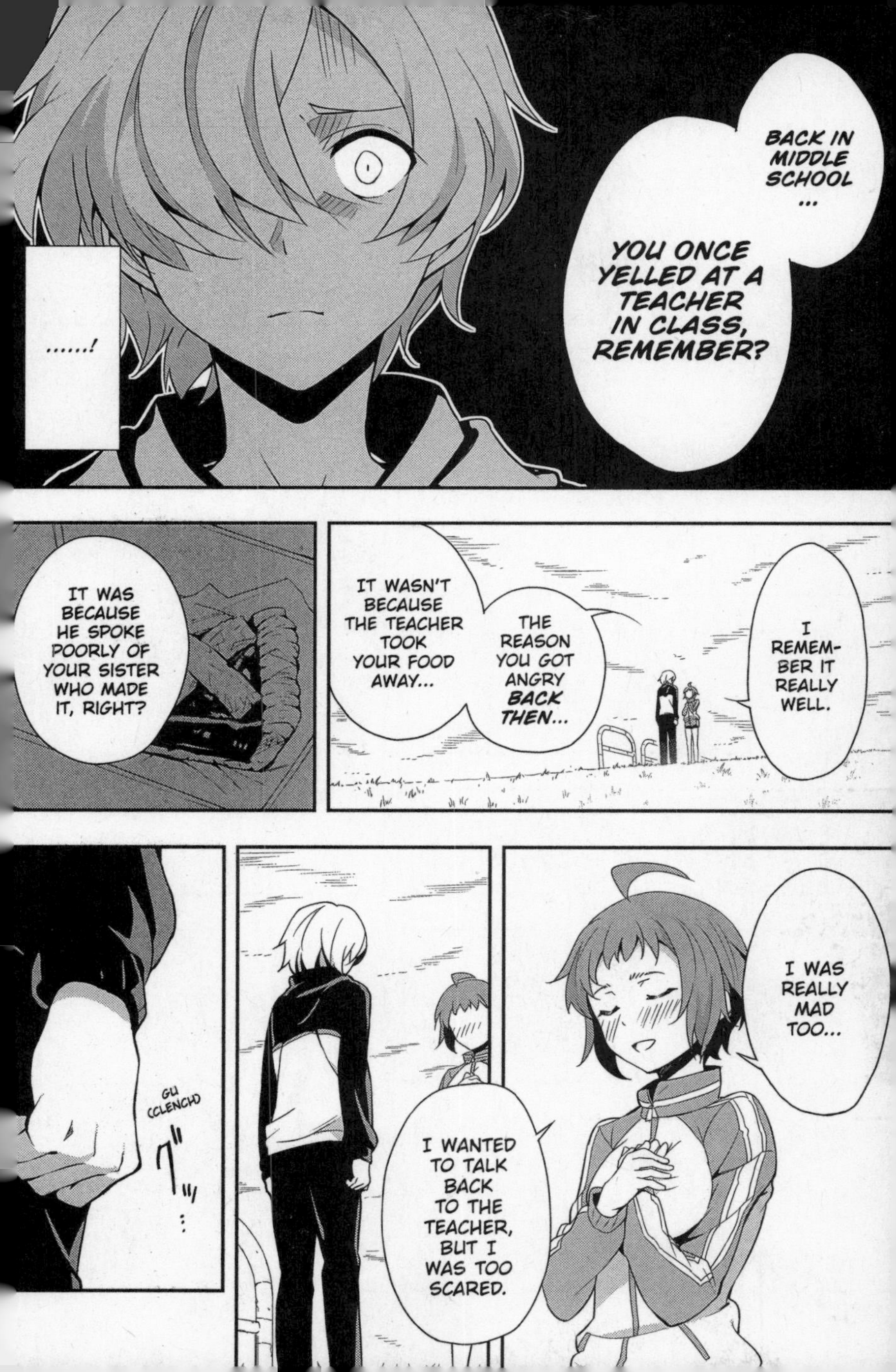
BACK IN MIDDLE SCHOOL ...
YOU ONCE YELLED AT A TEACHER IN CLASS, REMEMBER?
......!
I REMEMBER IT REALLY WELL.
THE REASON YOU GOT ANGRY BACK THEN...
IT WASN'T BECAUSE THE TEACHER TOOK YOUR FOOD AWAY...
IT WAS BECAUSE HE SPOKE POORLY OF YOUR SISTER WHO MADE IT, RIGHT?
I WAS REALLY MAD TOO...
I WANTED TO TALK BACK TO THE TEACHER, BUT I WAS TOO SCARED.
GU (CLENCH)

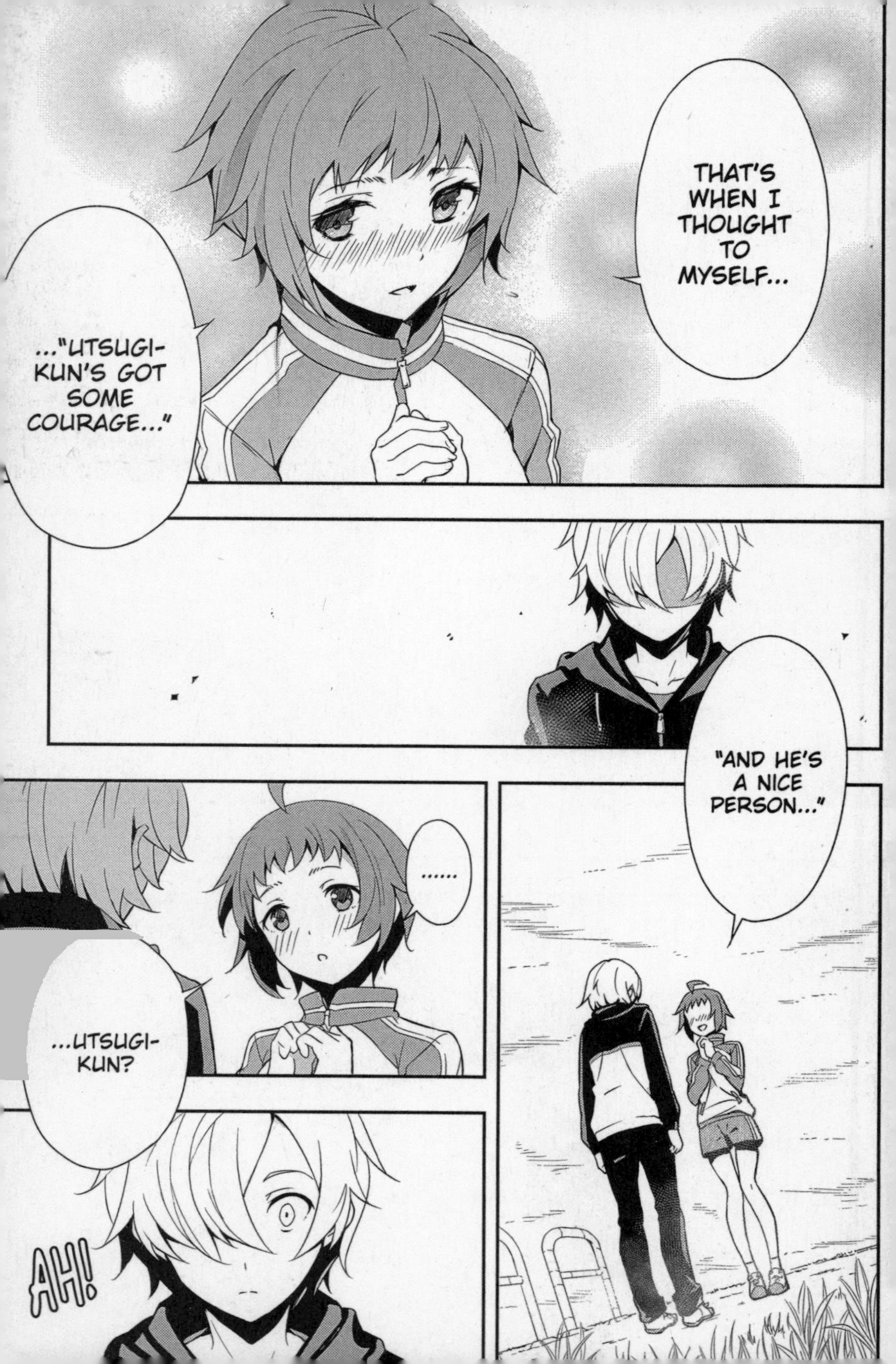
THAT'S WHEN I THOUGHT TO MYSELF...
..."UTSUGI-KUN'S GOT SOME COURAGE..."
"AND HE'S A NICE PERSON..."
......
...UTSUGI-KUN?
AH!

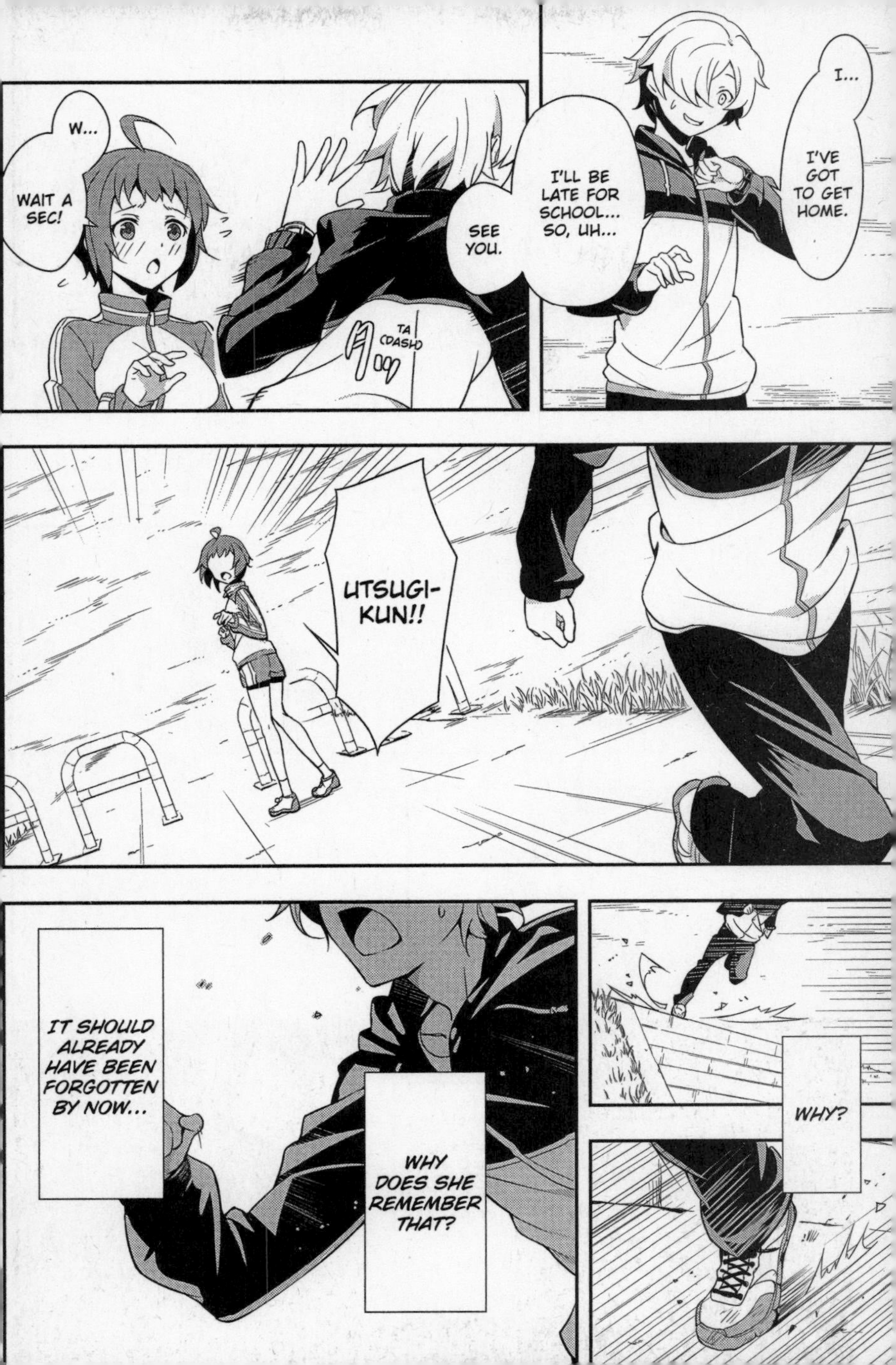
I...
I'VE GOT TO GET HOME.
I'LL BE LATE FOR SCHOOL... SO, UH...
SEE YOU.
TA (DASH)
W...
WAIT A SEC!
UTSUGI-KUN!!
WHY?
WHY DOES SHE REMEMBER THAT?
IT SHOULD ALREADY HAVE BEEN FORGOTTEN BY NOW...

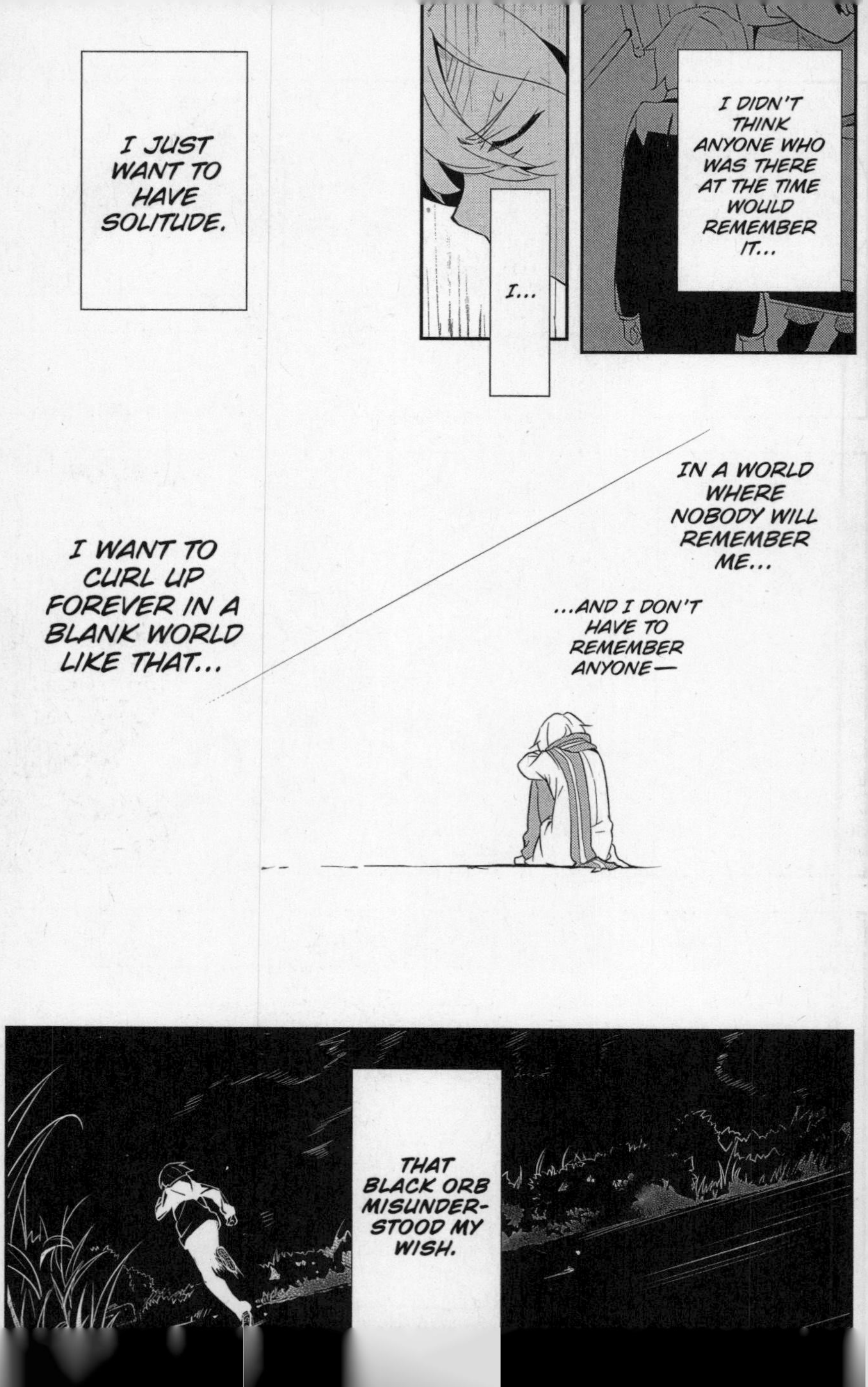
I DIDN'T THINK ANYONE WHO WAS THERE AT THE TIME WOULD REMEMBER IT...
I...
I JUST WANT TO HAVE SOLITUDE.
IN A WORLD WHERE NOBODY WILL REMEMBER ME...
...AND I DON'T HAVE TO REMEMBER ANYONE—
I WANT TO CURL UP FOREVER IN A BLANK WORLD LIKE THAT...
THAT BLACK ORB MISUNDERSTOOD MY WISH.

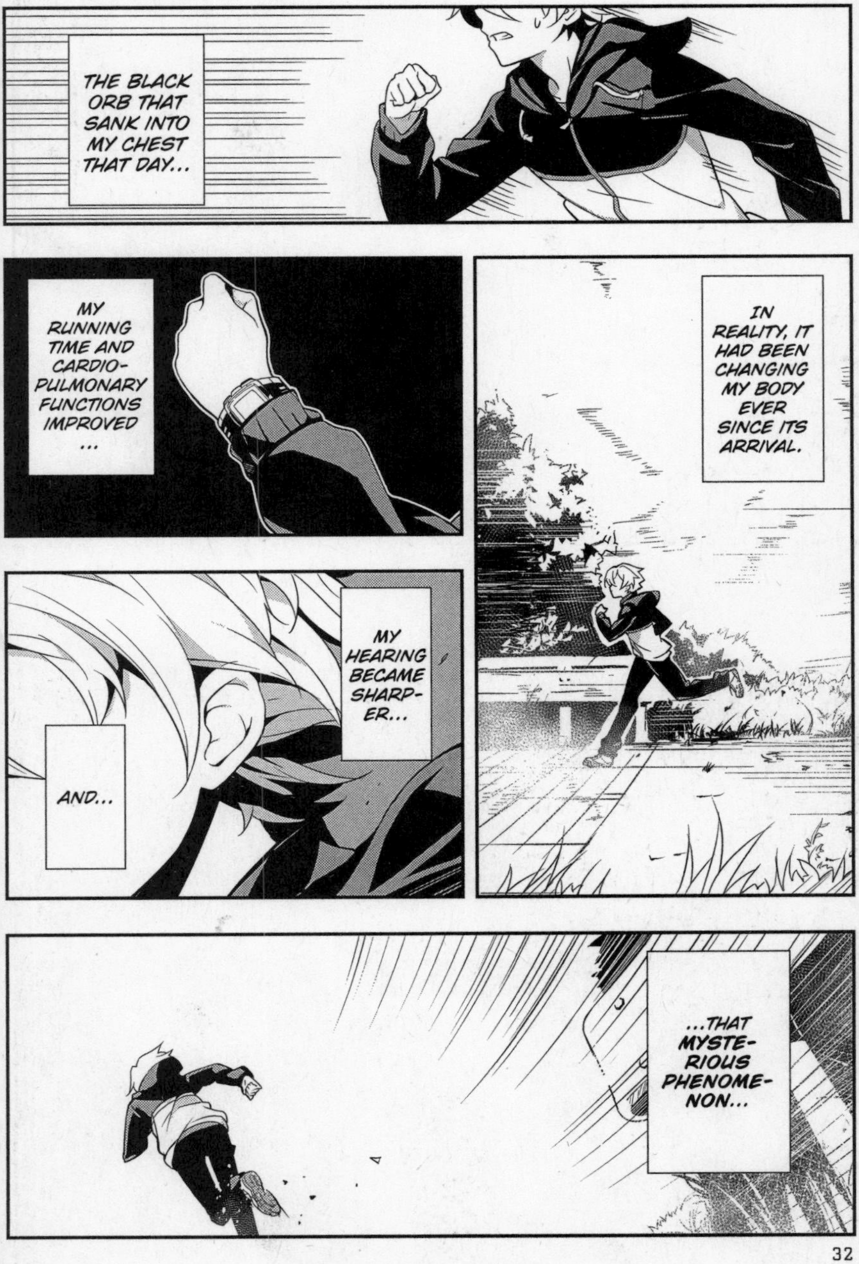
THE BLACK ORB THAT SANK INTO MY CHEST THAT DAY...
IN REALITY, IT HAD BEEN CHANGING MY BODY EVER SINCE ITS ARRIVAL.
MY RUNNING TIME AND CARDIO-PULMONARY FUNCTIONS IMPROVED ...
MY HEARING BECAME SHARP-ER...
AND...
...THAT MYSTE-RIOUS PHENOME-NON...

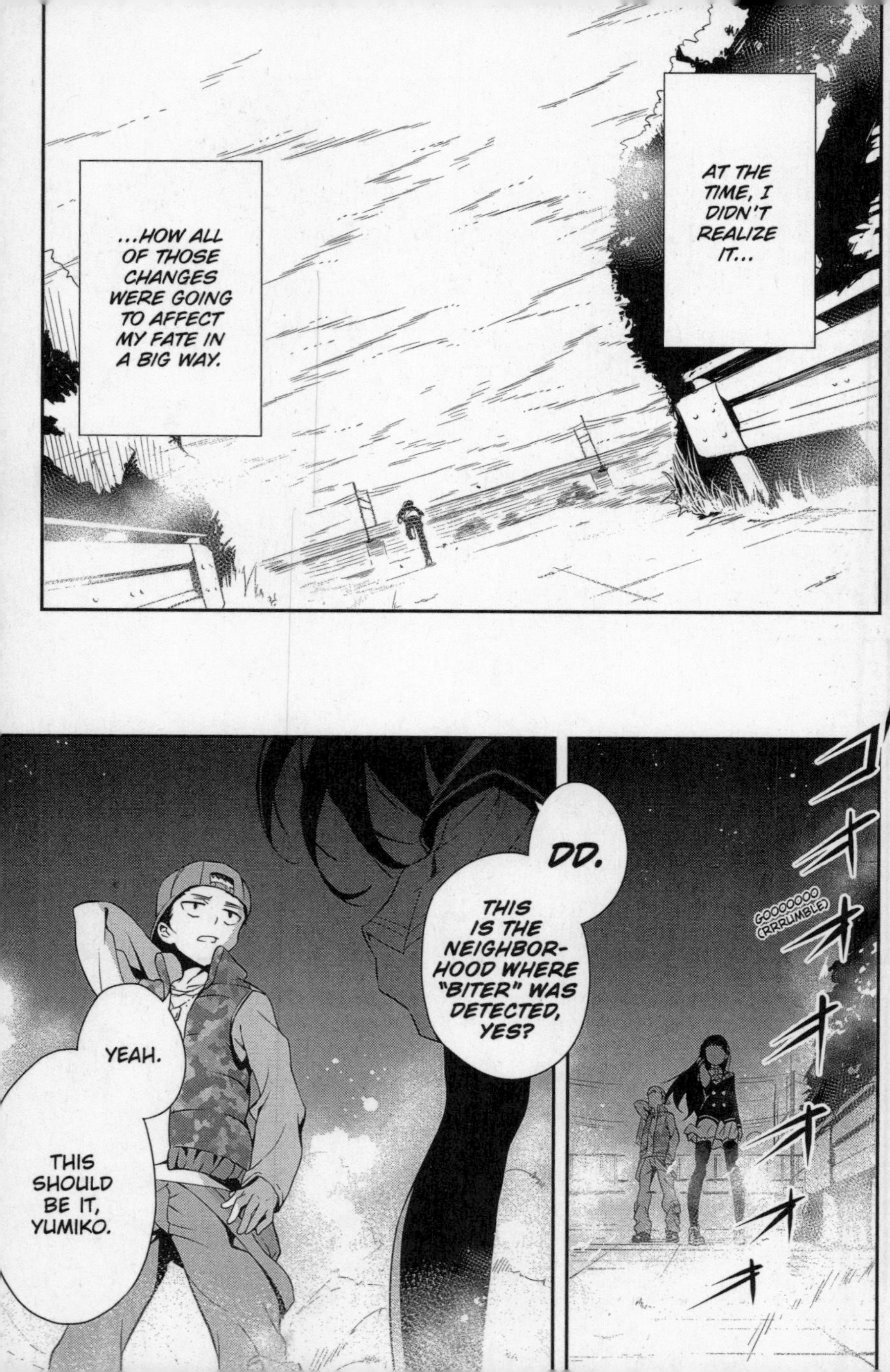
AT THE TIME, I DIDN'T REALIZE IT...
...HOW ALL OF THOSE CHANGES WERE GOING TO AFFECT MY FATE IN A BIG WAY.
GOOOOOOO (RRRUMBLE)
DD.
THIS IS THE NEIGHBORHOOD WHERE "BITER" WAS DETECTED, YES?
YEAH.
THIS SHOULD BE IT, YUMIKO.

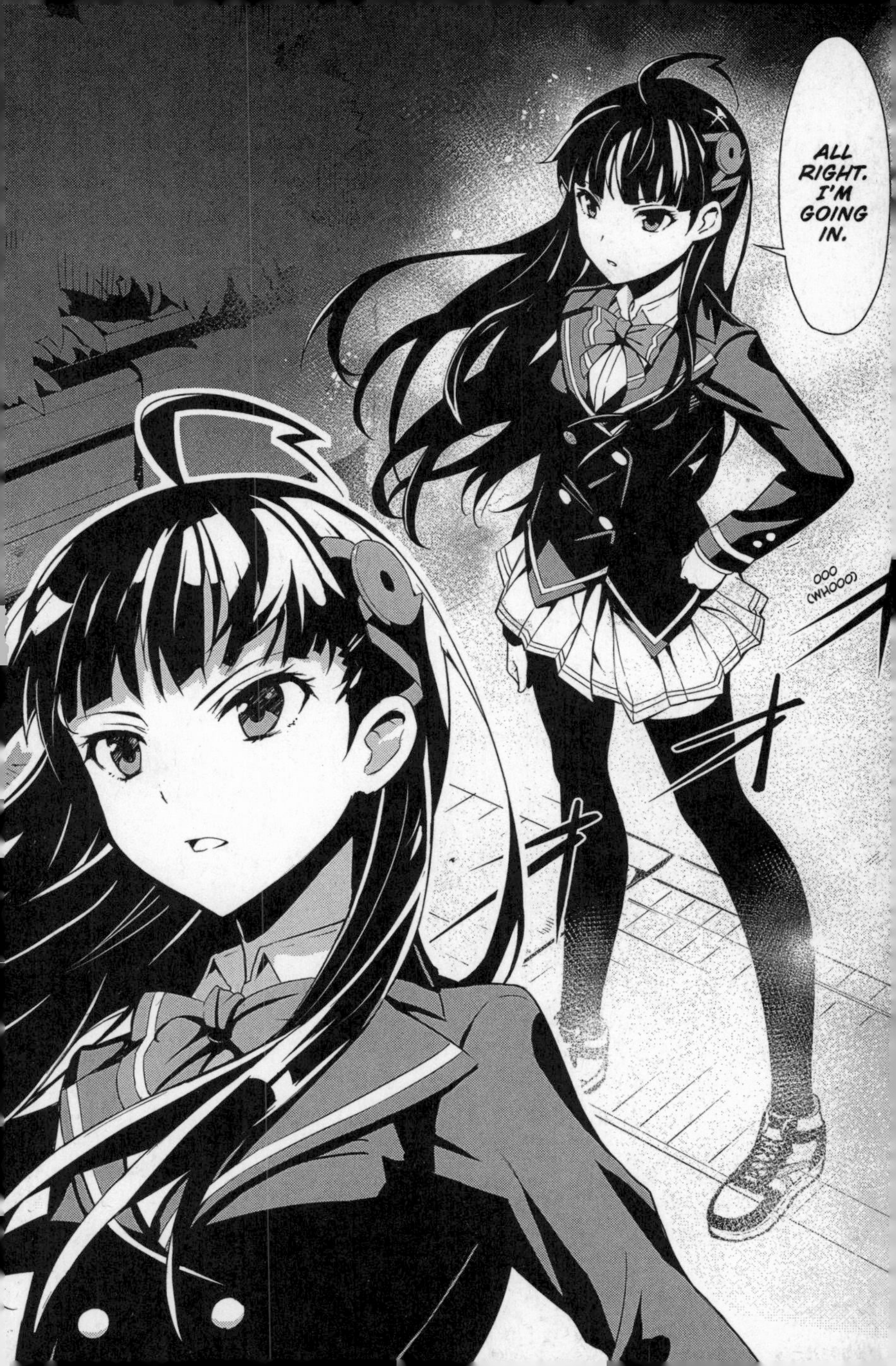
ALL RIGHT. I'M GOING IN.
OOO (WHOOO)

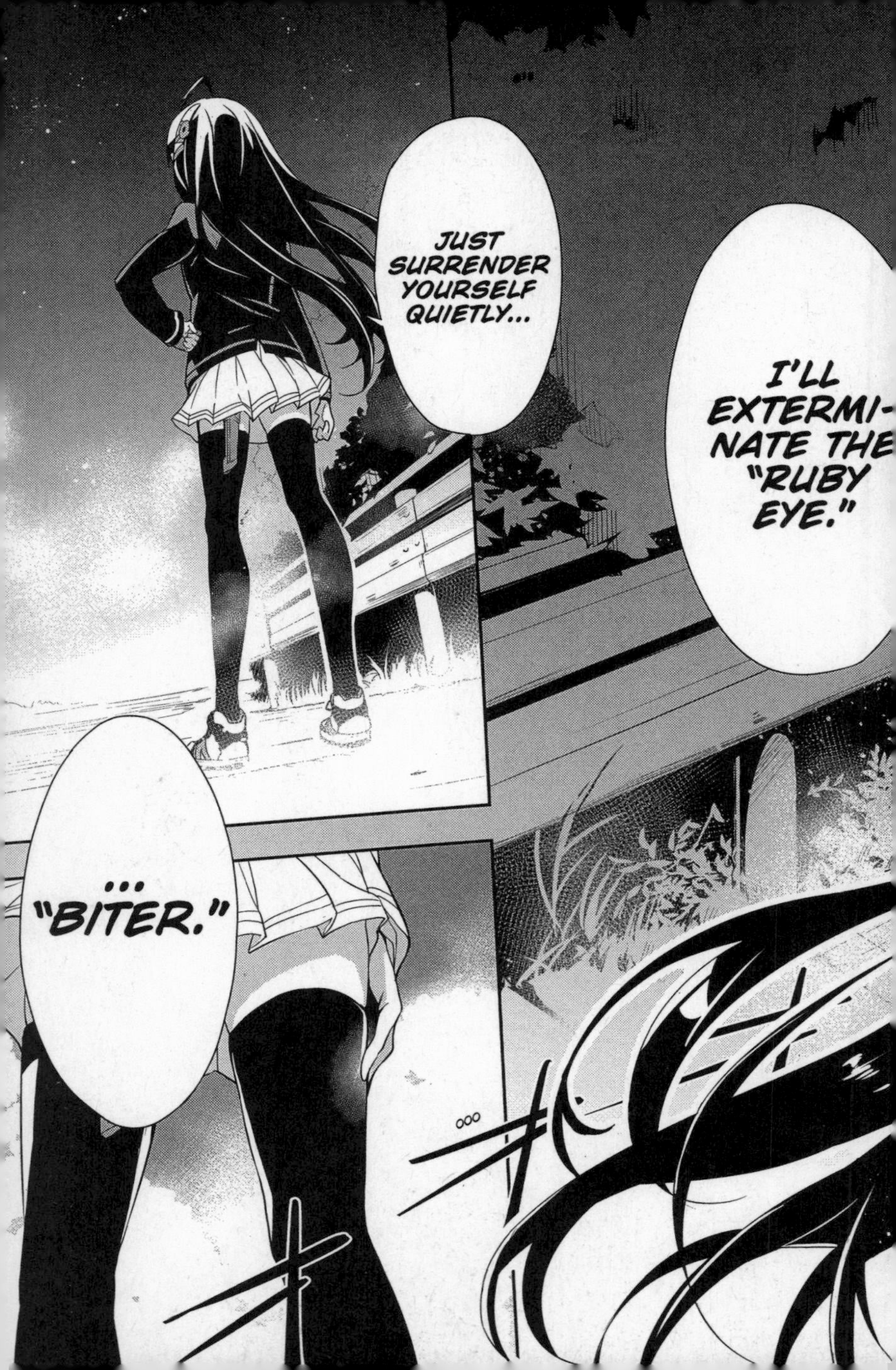
JUST SURRENDER YOURSELF QUIETLY...
I'LL EXTERMINATE THE "RUBY EYE."
... "BITER."

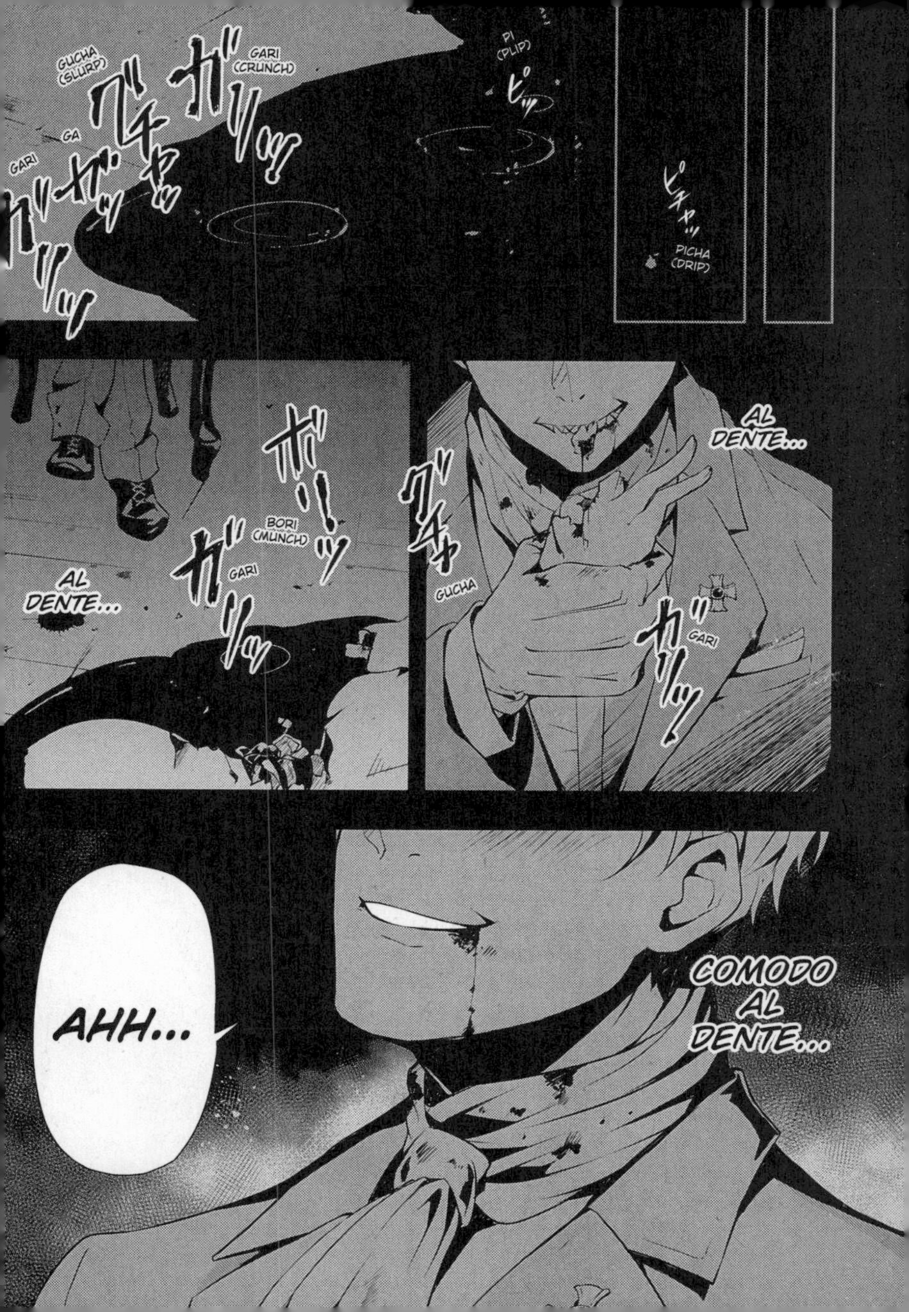
PICHA (DRIP)
PI (PLIP)
GARI (CRUNCH)
GUCHA (SLURP)
GA
GARI
AL DENTE...
GUCHA
GARI
BORI (MUNCH)
GARI
AL DENTE...
COMODO AL DENTE...
AHH...

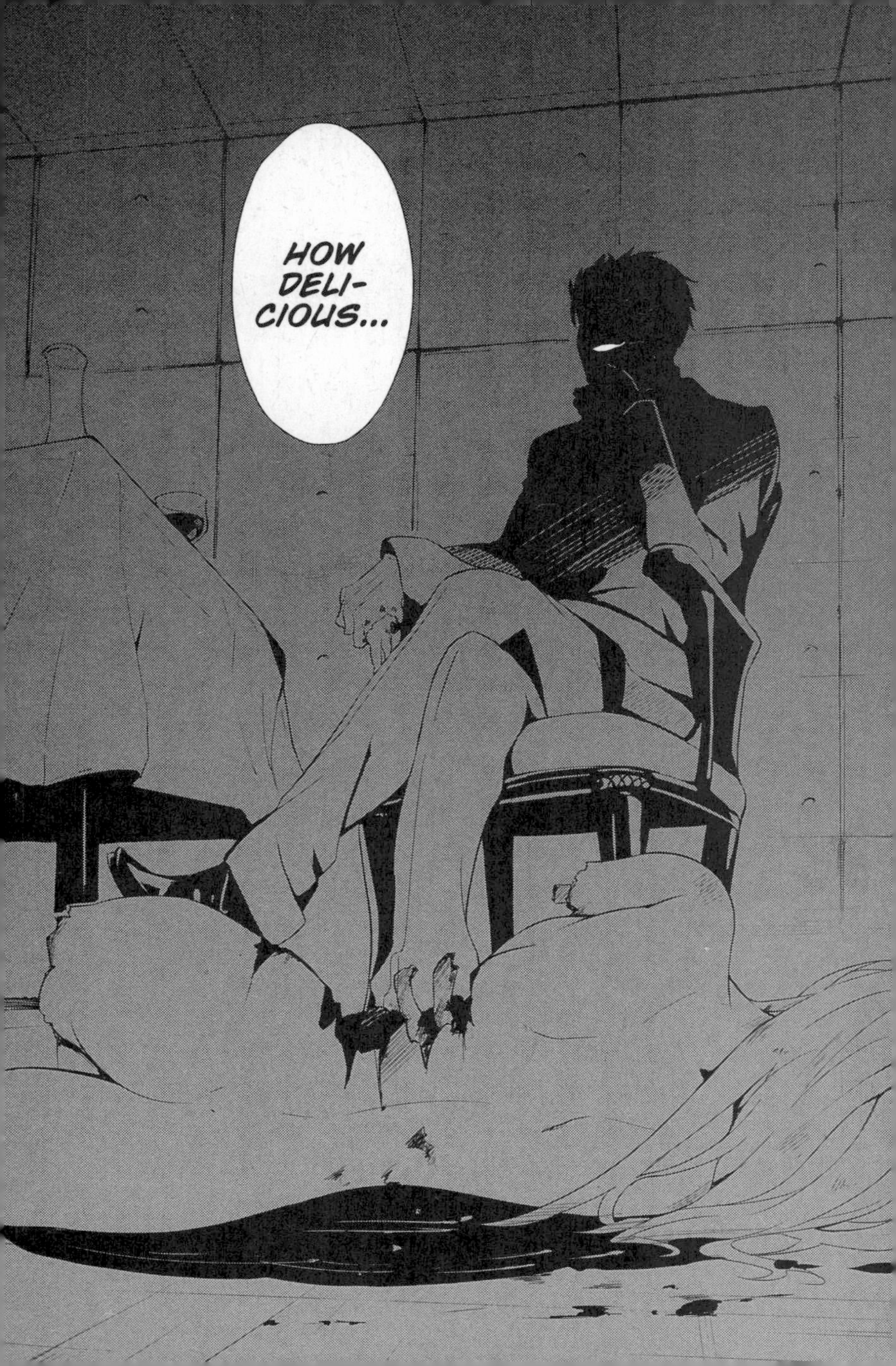
HOW DELI- CIOUS...

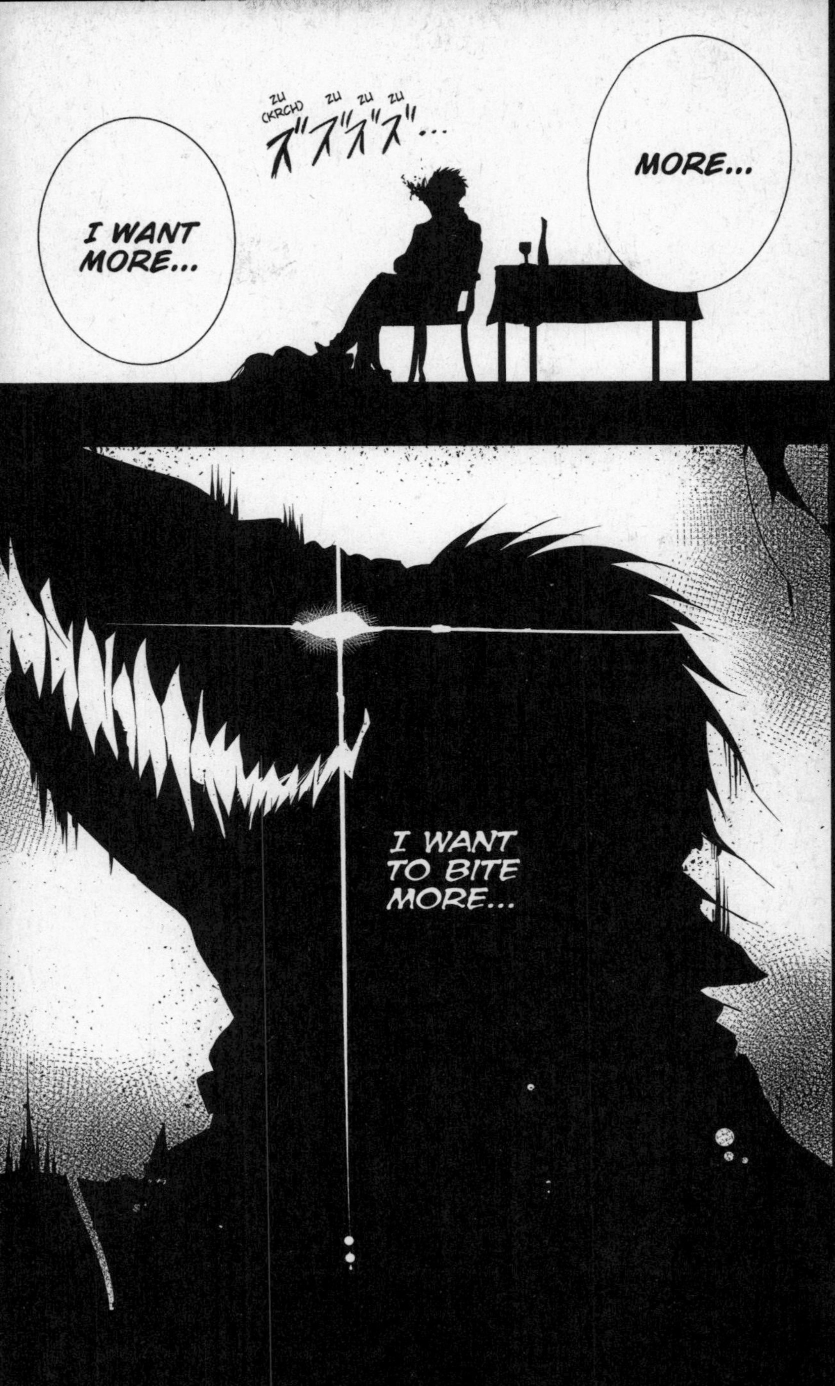
MORE...
ZU (KRCH) ZU ZU ZU
ズズズズ...
I WANT MORE...
I WANT TO BITE MORE...

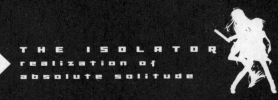

THE ISOLATOR
realization of
absolute solitude

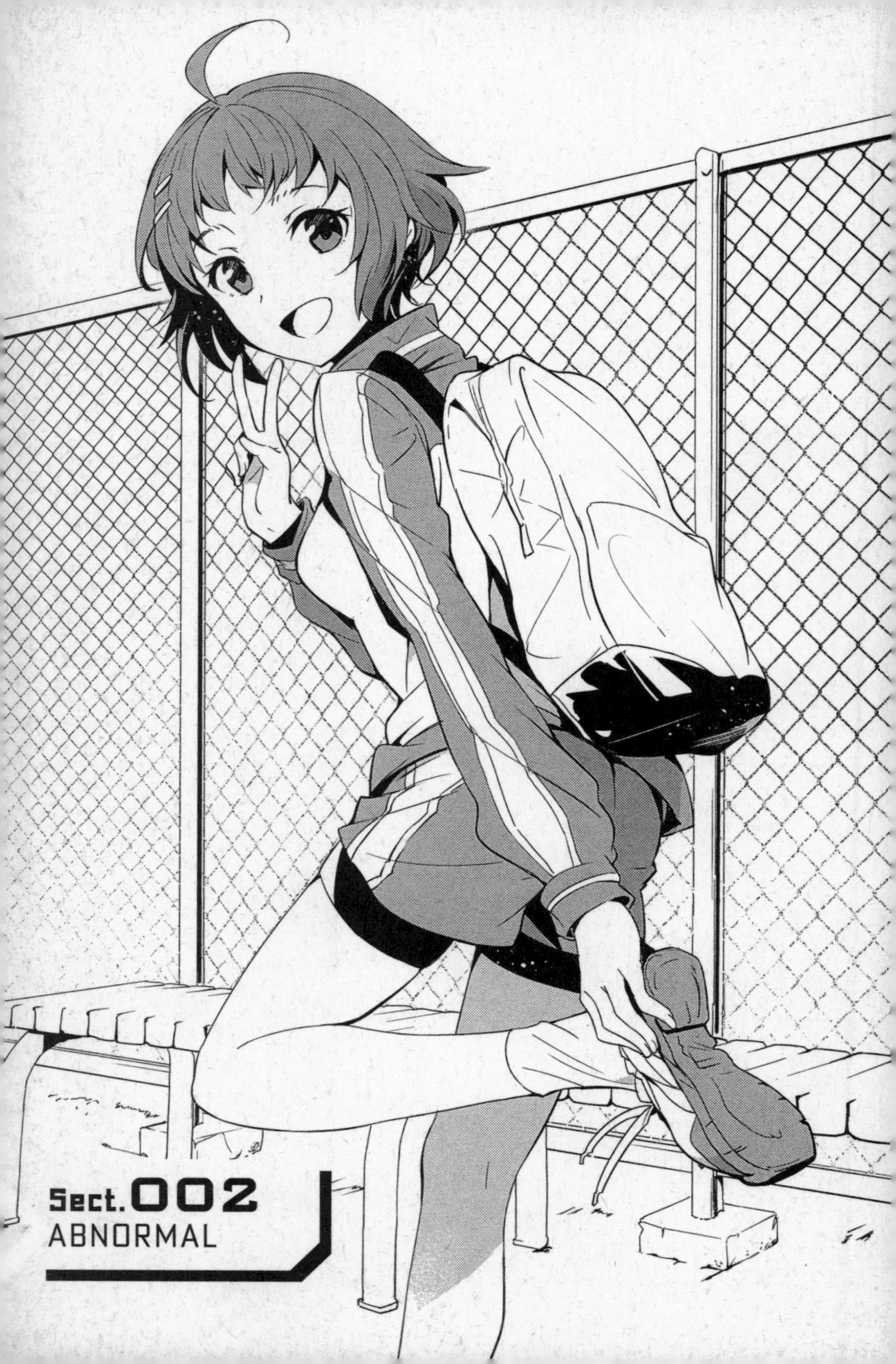

Sect.002
ABNORMAL

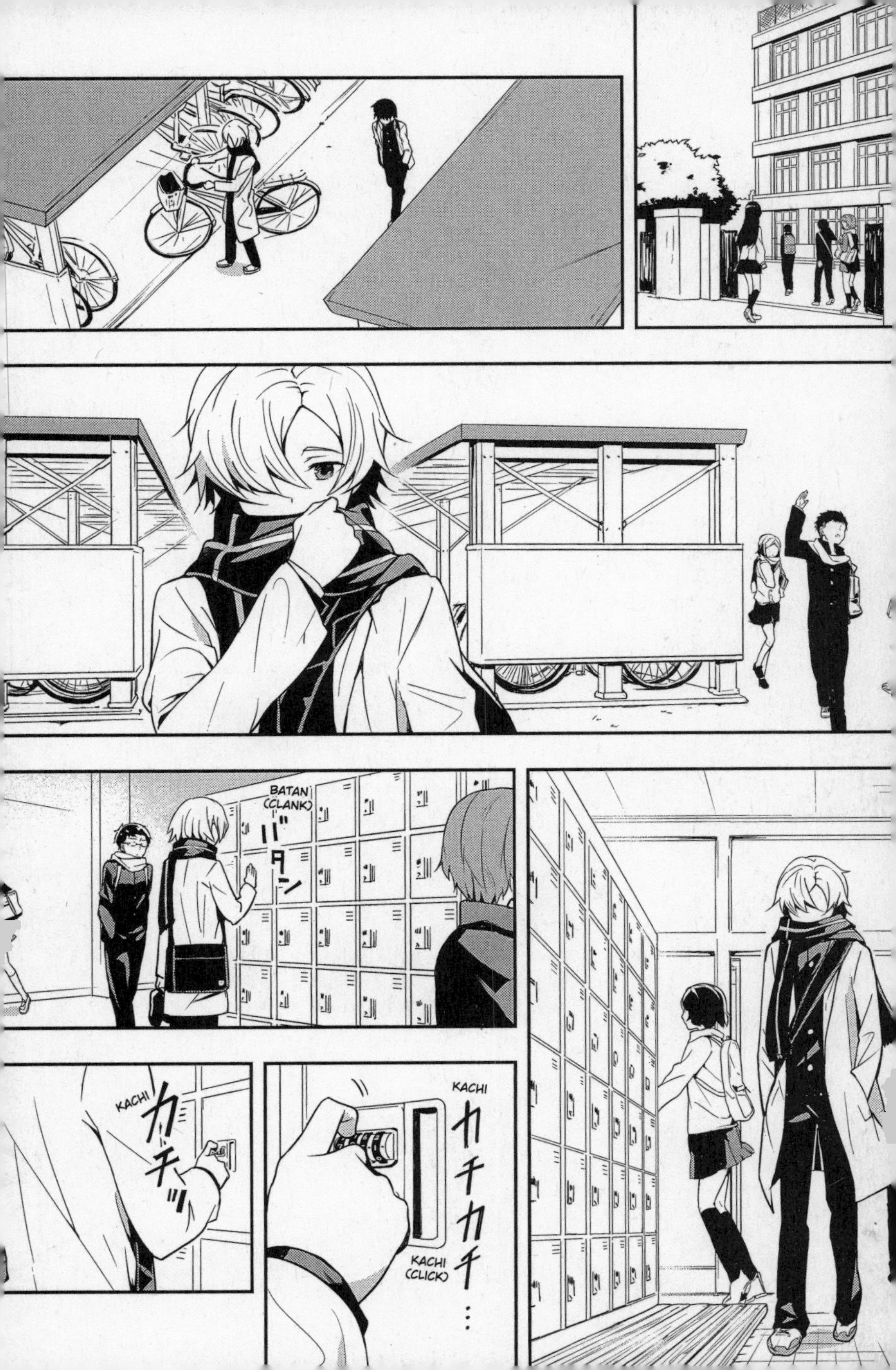
BATAN (CLANK)
バタン
KACHI
カチカチ
KACHI (CLICK)
…
KACHI
カチッ

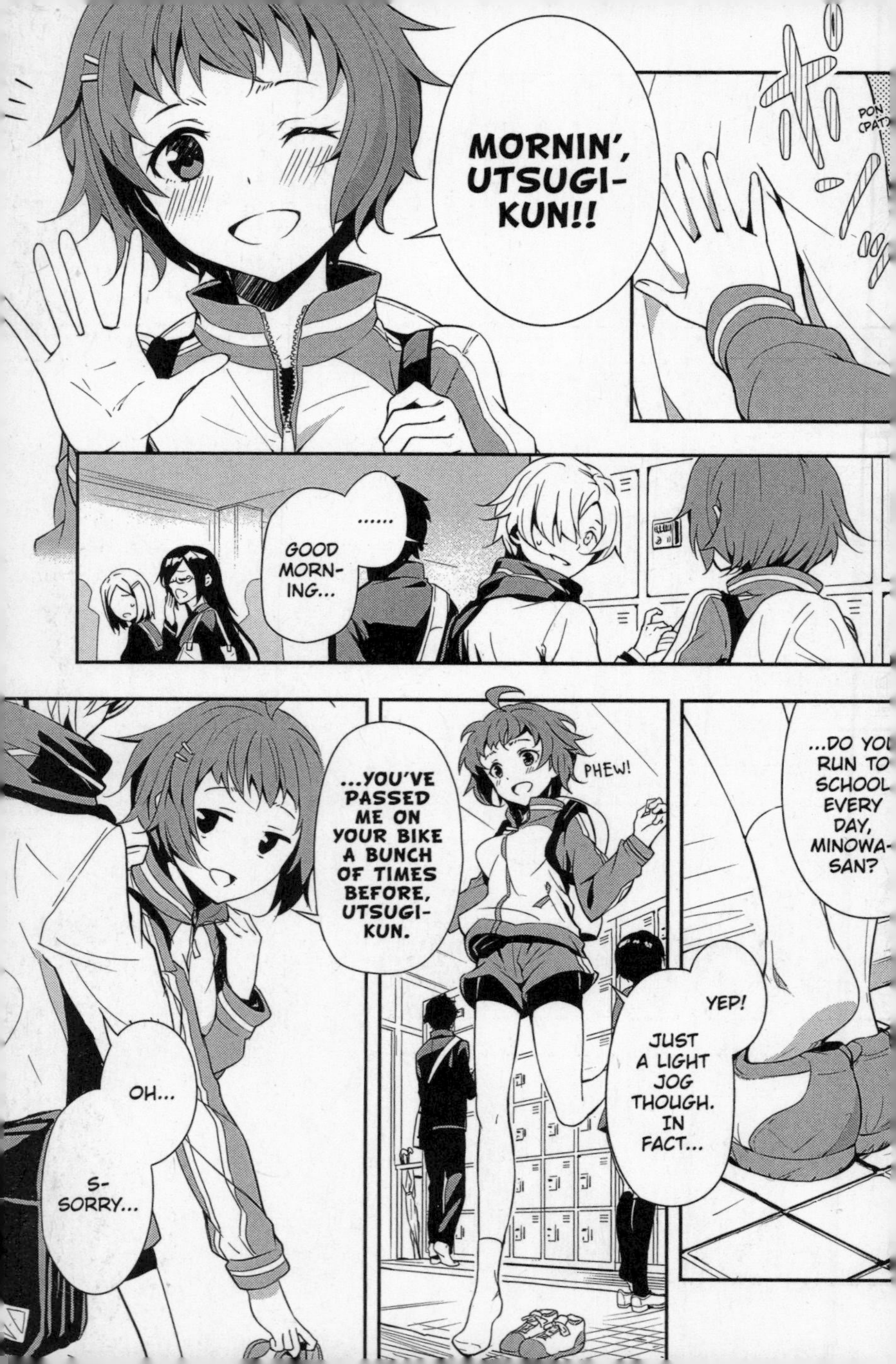
PON (PAT)
MORNIN', UTSUGI-KUN!!
......
GOOD MORNING...
...DO YOU RUN TO SCHOOL EVERY DAY, MINOWA-SAN?
PHEW!
YEP!
JUST A LIGHT JOG THOUGH. IN FACT...
...YOU'VE PASSED ME ON YOUR BIKE A BUNCH OF TIMES BEFORE, UTSUGI-KUN.
OH...
S-SORRY...

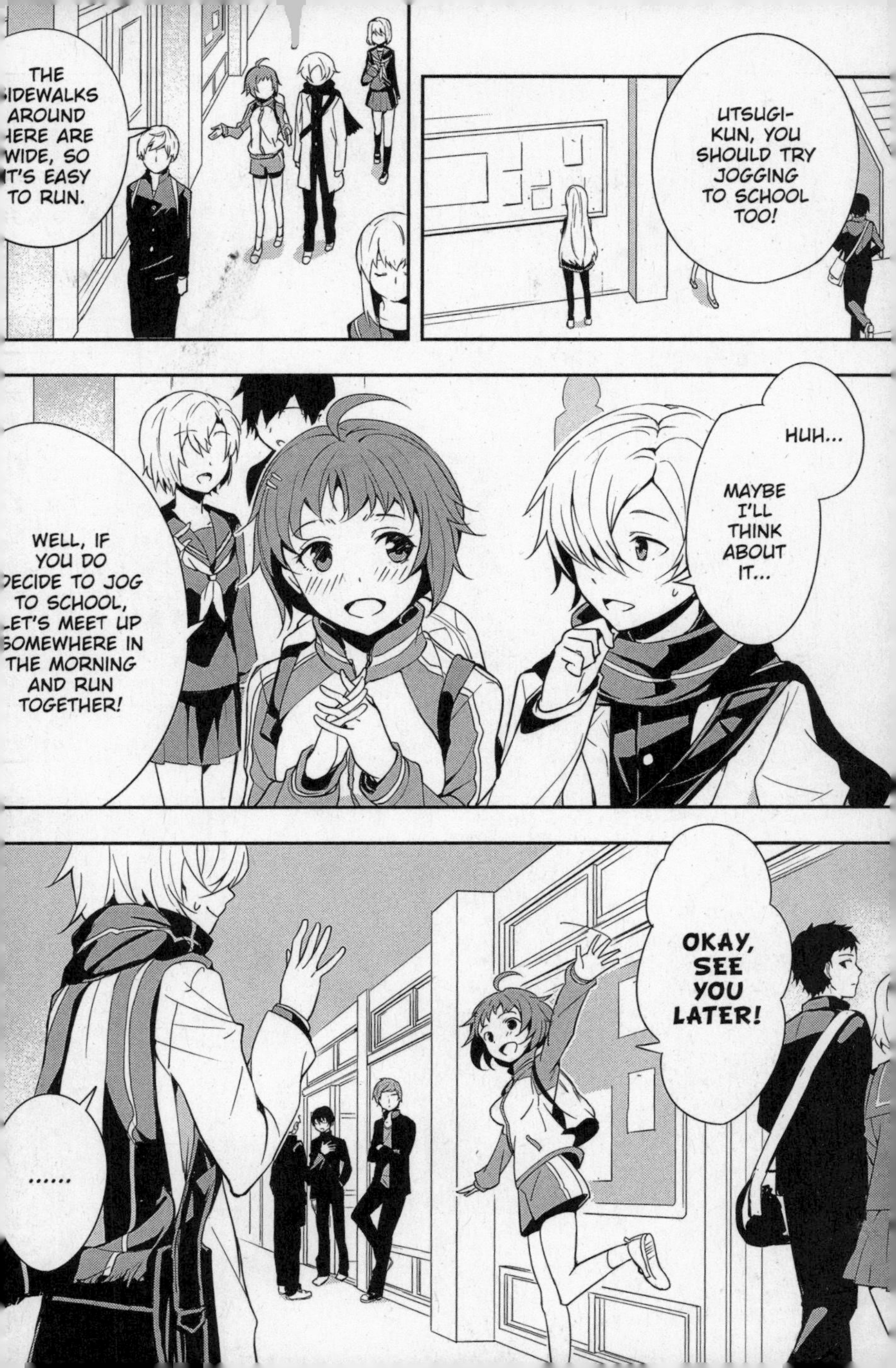
UTSUGI-KUN, YOU SHOULD TRY JOGGING TO SCHOOL TOO!
THE SIDEWALKS AROUND HERE ARE WIDE, SO IT'S EASY TO RUN.
HUH...
MAYBE I'LL THINK ABOUT IT...
WELL, IF YOU DO DECIDE TO JOG TO SCHOOL, LET'S MEET UP SOMEWHERE IN THE MORNING AND RUN TOGETHER!
OKAY, SEE YOU LATER!
......

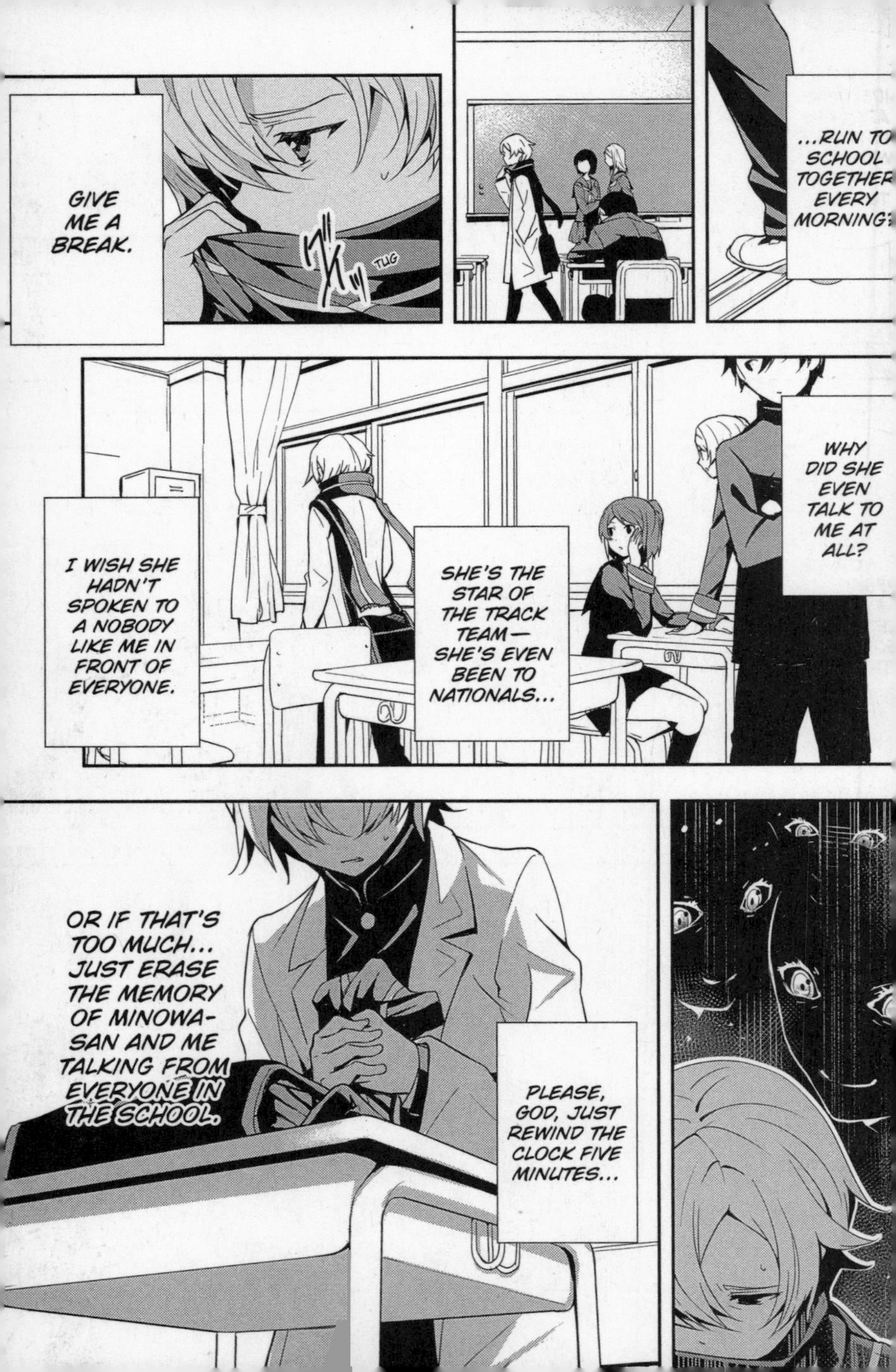
...RUN TO SCHOOL TOGETHER EVERY MORNING?
GIVE ME A BREAK.
TUG
WHY DID SHE EVEN TALK TO ME AT ALL?
SHE'S THE STAR OF THE TRACK TEAM—SHE'S EVEN BEEN TO NATIONALS...
I WISH SHE HADN'T SPOKEN TO A NOBODY LIKE ME IN FRONT OF EVERYONE.
PLEASE, GOD, JUST REWIND THE CLOCK FIVE MINUTES...
OR IF THAT'S TOO MUCH... JUST ERASE THE MEMORY OF MINOWA-SAN AND ME TALKING FROM EVERYONE IN THE SCHOOL.

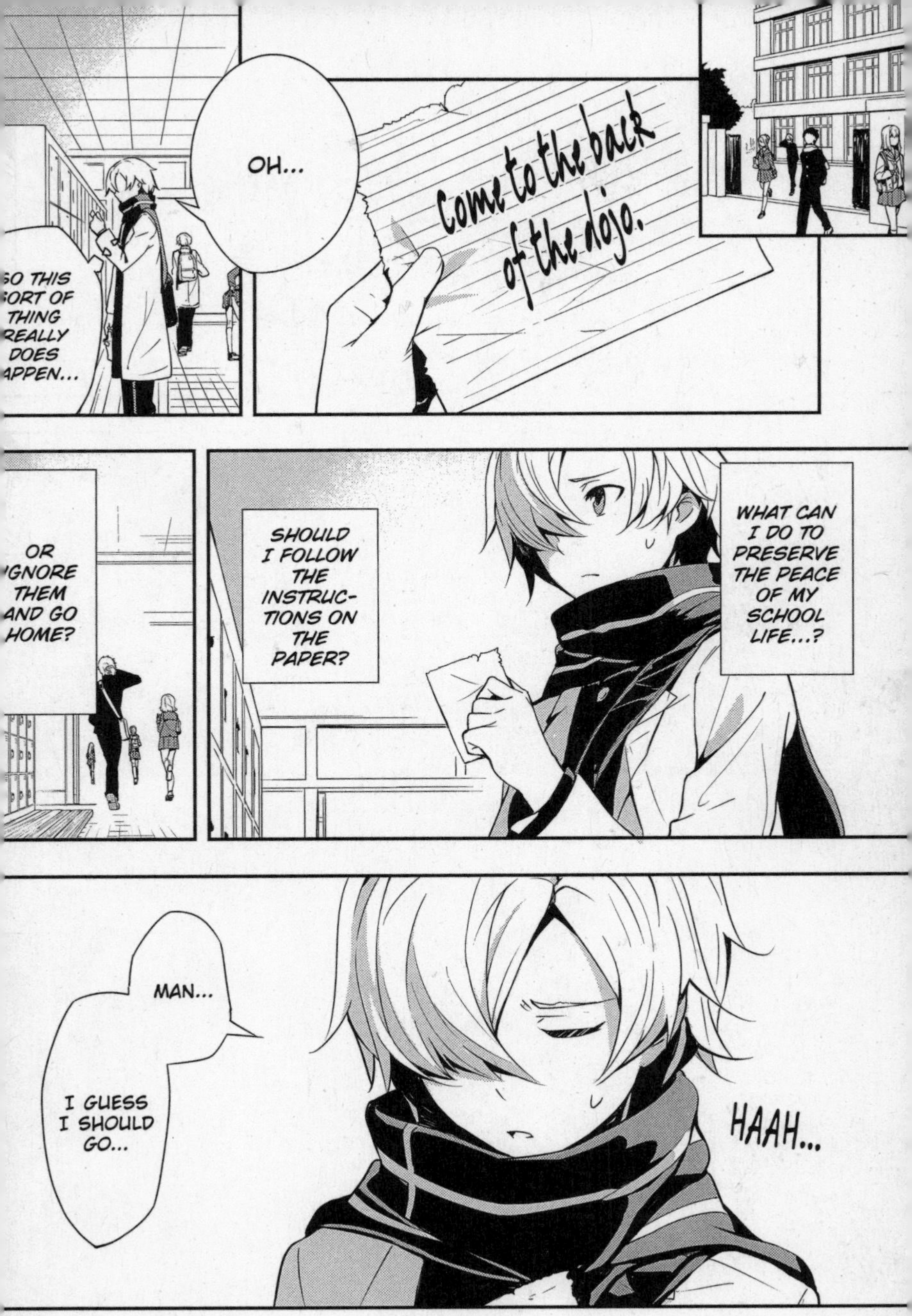
Come to the back of the dojo.
OH...
SO THIS SORT OF THING REALLY DOES APPEN...
WHAT CAN I DO TO PRESERVE THE PEACE OF MY SCHOOL LIFE...?
SHOULD I FOLLOW THE INSTRUC-TIONS ON THE PAPER?
OR GNORE THEM AND GO HOME?
HAAH...
MAN...
I GUESS I SHOULD GO...

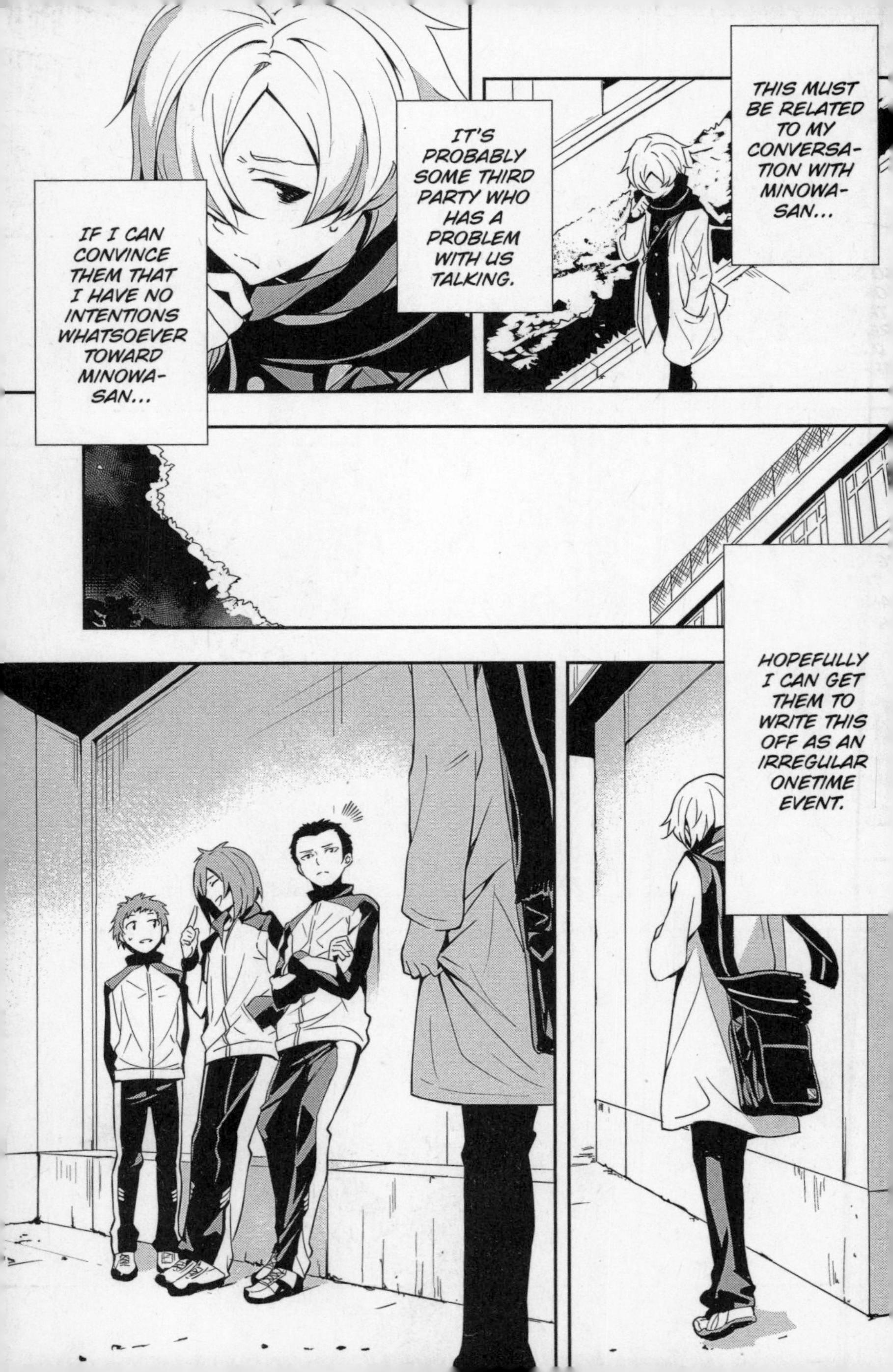
THIS MUST BE RELATED TO MY CONVERSATION WITH MINOWA-SAN...
IT'S PROBABLY SOME THIRD PARTY WHO HAS A PROBLEM WITH US TALKING.
IF I CAN CONVINCE THEM THAT I HAVE NO INTENTIONS WHATSOEVER TOWARD MINOWA-SAN...
HOPEFULLY I CAN GET THEM TO WRITE THIS OFF AS AN IRREGULAR ONETIME EVENT.

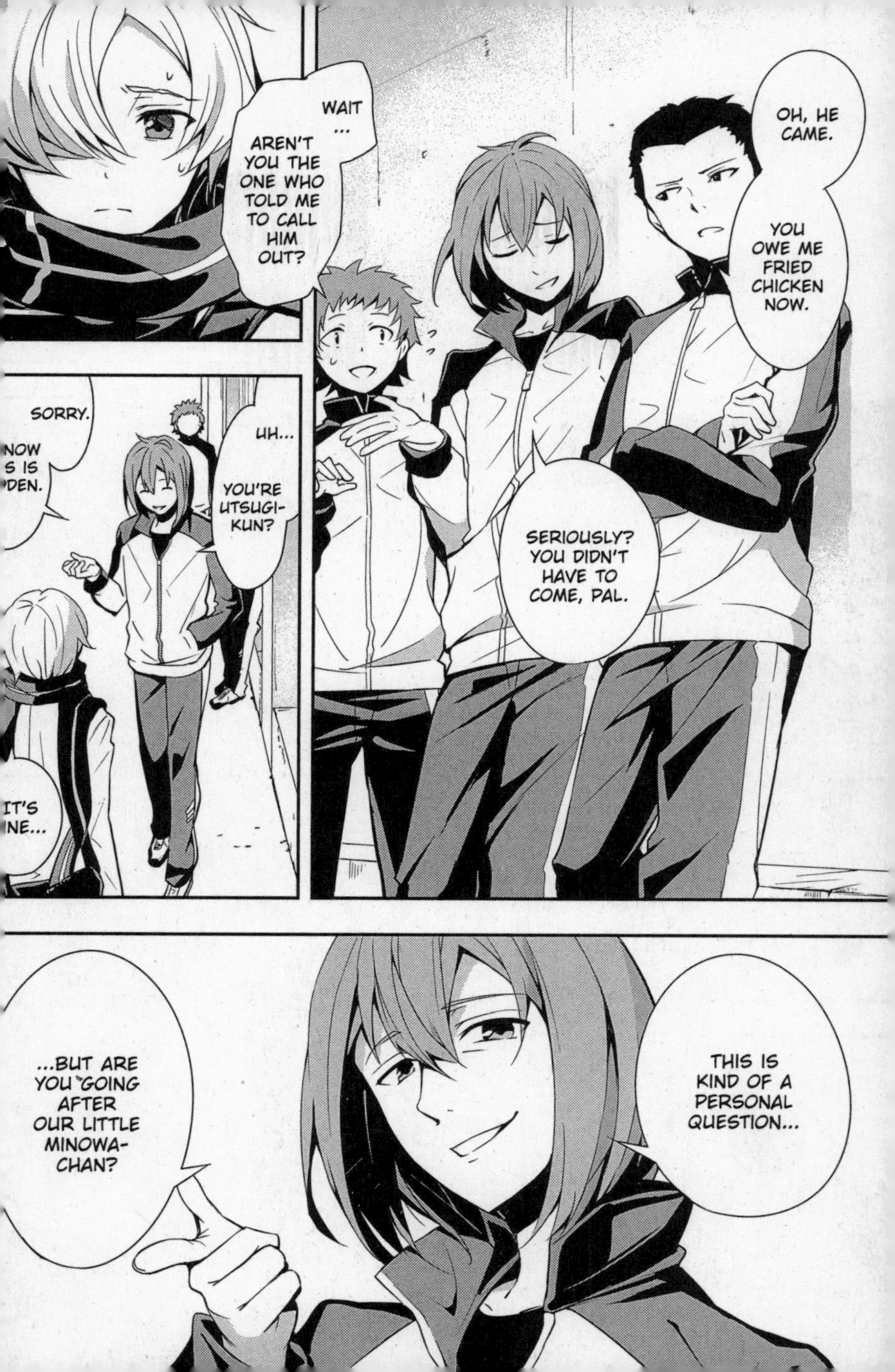
OH, HE CAME.
YOU OWE ME FRIED CHICKEN NOW.
SERIOUSLY? YOU DIDN'T HAVE TO COME, PAL.
WAIT...
AREN'T YOU THE ONE WHO TOLD ME TO CALL HIM OUT?
UH...
YOU'RE UTSUGI-KUN?
SORRY.
NOW
S IS
DEN.
IT'S
NE...
THIS IS KIND OF A PERSONAL QUESTION...
...BUT ARE YOU GOING AFTER OUR LITTLE MINOWA-CHAN?

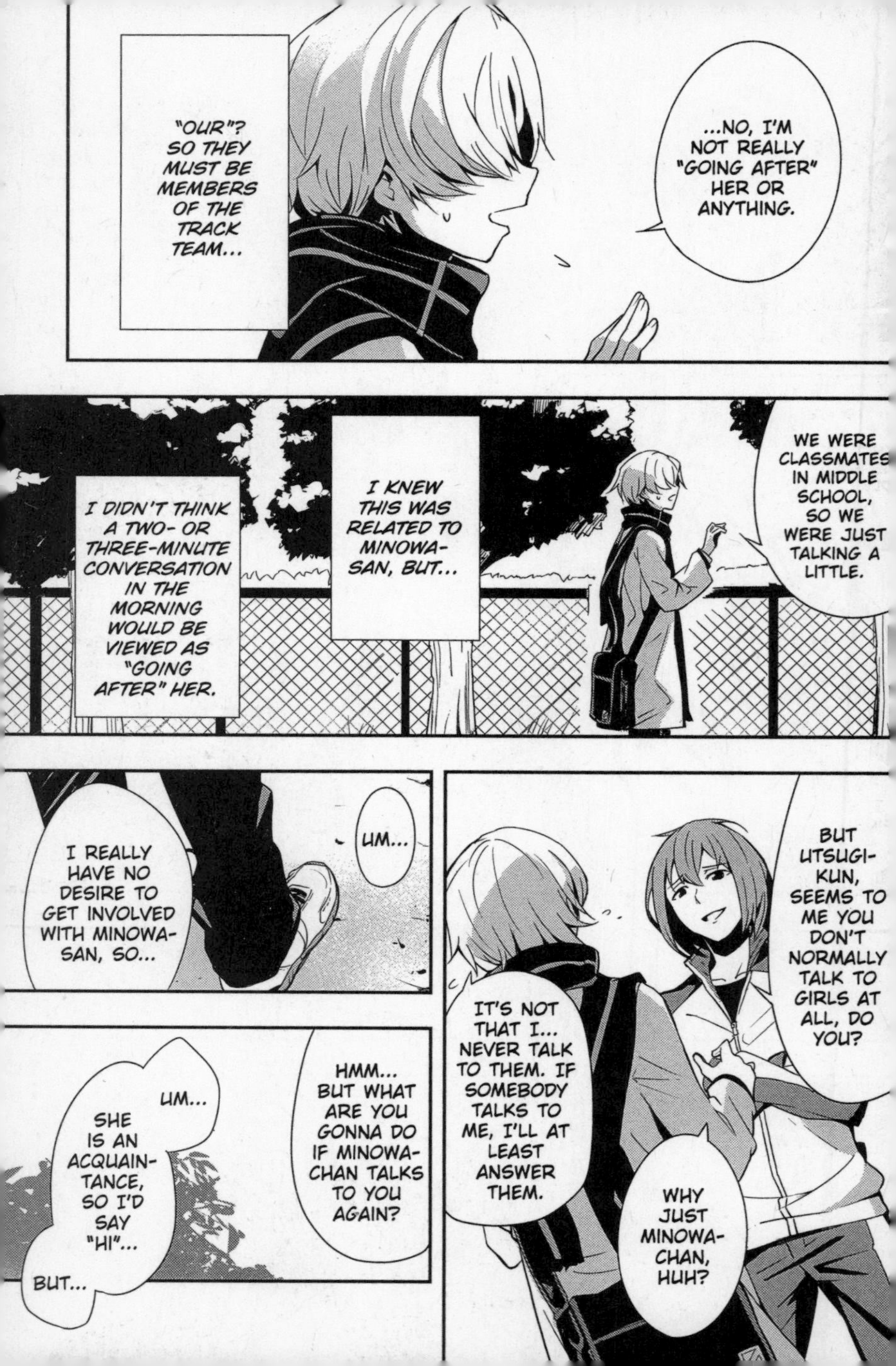
...NO, I'M NOT REALLY "GOING AFTER" HER OR ANYTHING.
"OUR"? SO THEY MUST BE MEMBERS OF THE TRACK TEAM...
WE WERE CLASSMATES IN MIDDLE SCHOOL, SO WE WERE JUST TALKING A LITTLE.
I KNEW THIS WAS RELATED TO MINOWA-SAN, BUT...
I DIDN'T THINK A TWO- OR THREE-MINUTE CONVERSATION IN THE MORNING WOULD BE VIEWED AS "GOING AFTER" HER.
BUT UTSUGI-KUN, SEEMS TO ME YOU DON'T NORMALLY TALK TO GIRLS AT ALL, DO YOU?
IT'S NOT THAT I... NEVER TALK TO THEM. IF SOMEBODY TALKS TO ME, I'LL AT LEAST ANSWER THEM.
WHY JUST MINOWA-CHAN, HUH?
UM...
I REALLY HAVE NO DESIRE TO GET INVOLVED WITH MINOWA-SAN, SO...
HMM... BUT WHAT ARE YOU GONNA DO IF MINOWA-CHAN TALKS TO YOU AGAIN?
UM...
SHE IS AN ACQUAINTANCE, SO I'D SAY "HI"...
BUT...

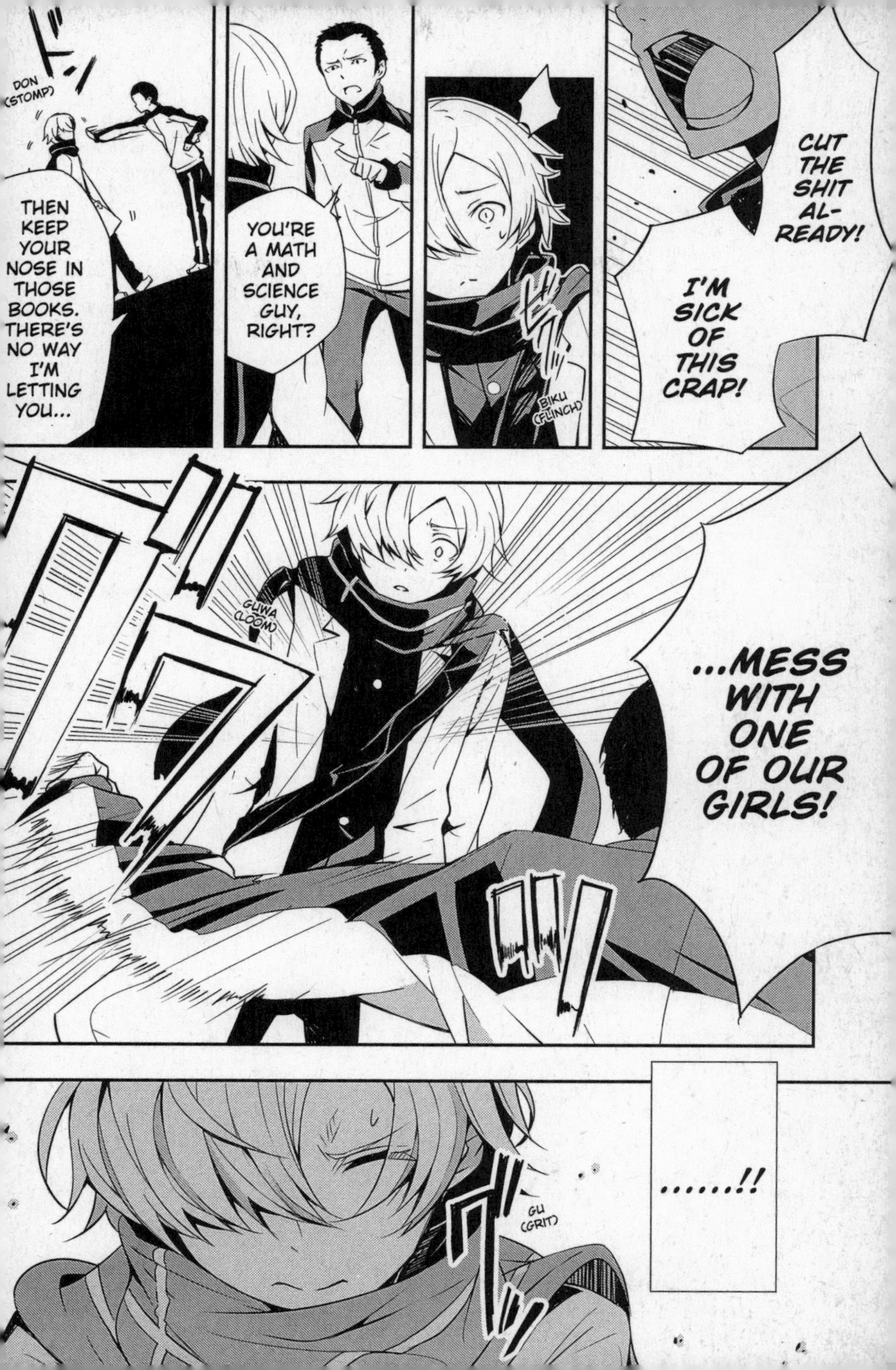
CUT THE SHIT AL-READY!
I'M SICK OF THIS CRAP!
BIKU (FLINCH)
YOU'RE A MATH AND SCIENCE GUY, RIGHT?
DON (STOMP)
THEN KEEP YOUR NOSE IN THOSE BOOKS. THERE'S NO WAY I'M LETTING YOU...
...MESS WITH ONE OF OUR GIRLS!
GUWA (LOOM)
......!!
GU (GRIT)

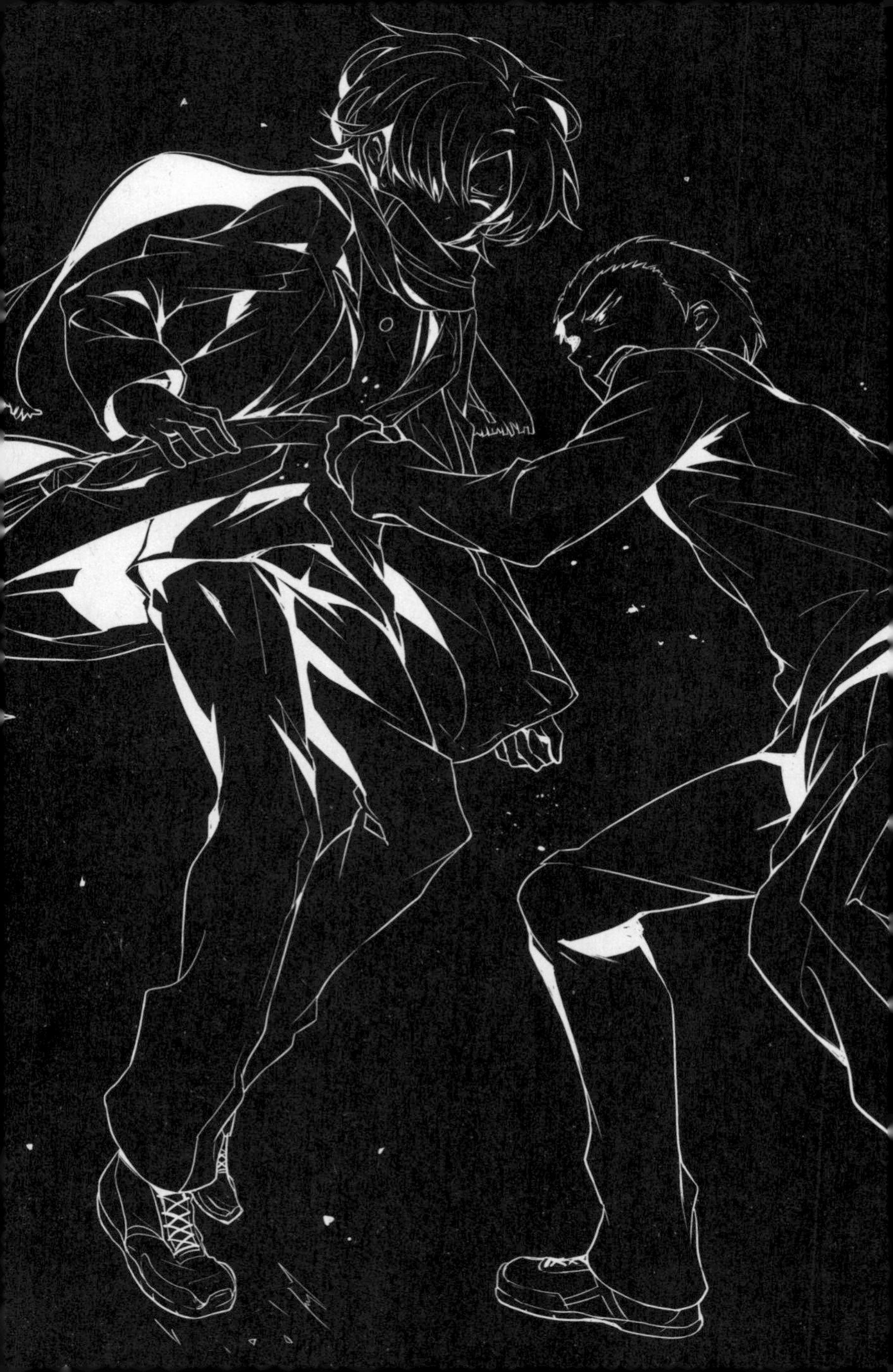

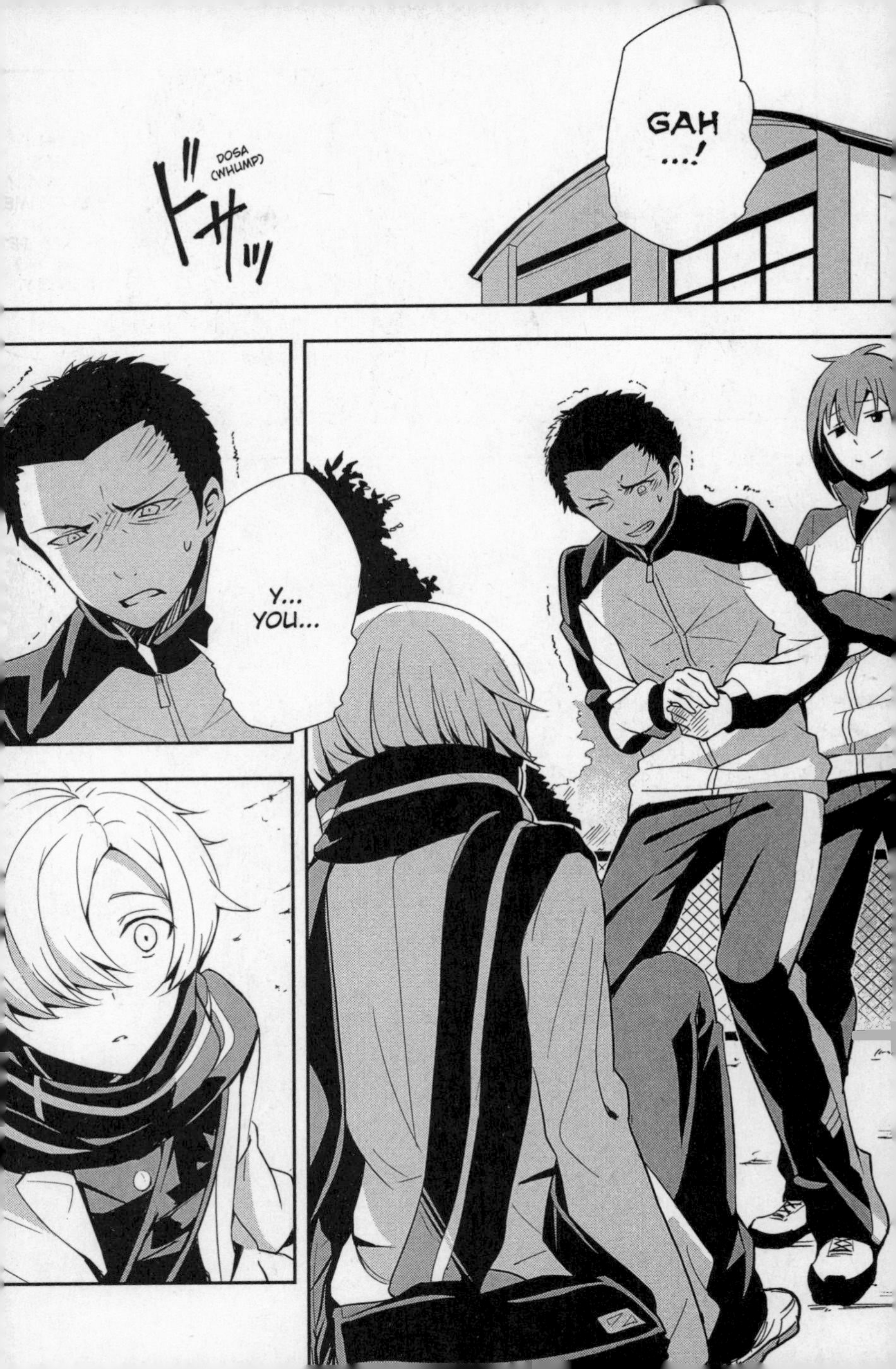
GAH ...!
ドサッ
DOSA (WHUMP)
Y... YOU...

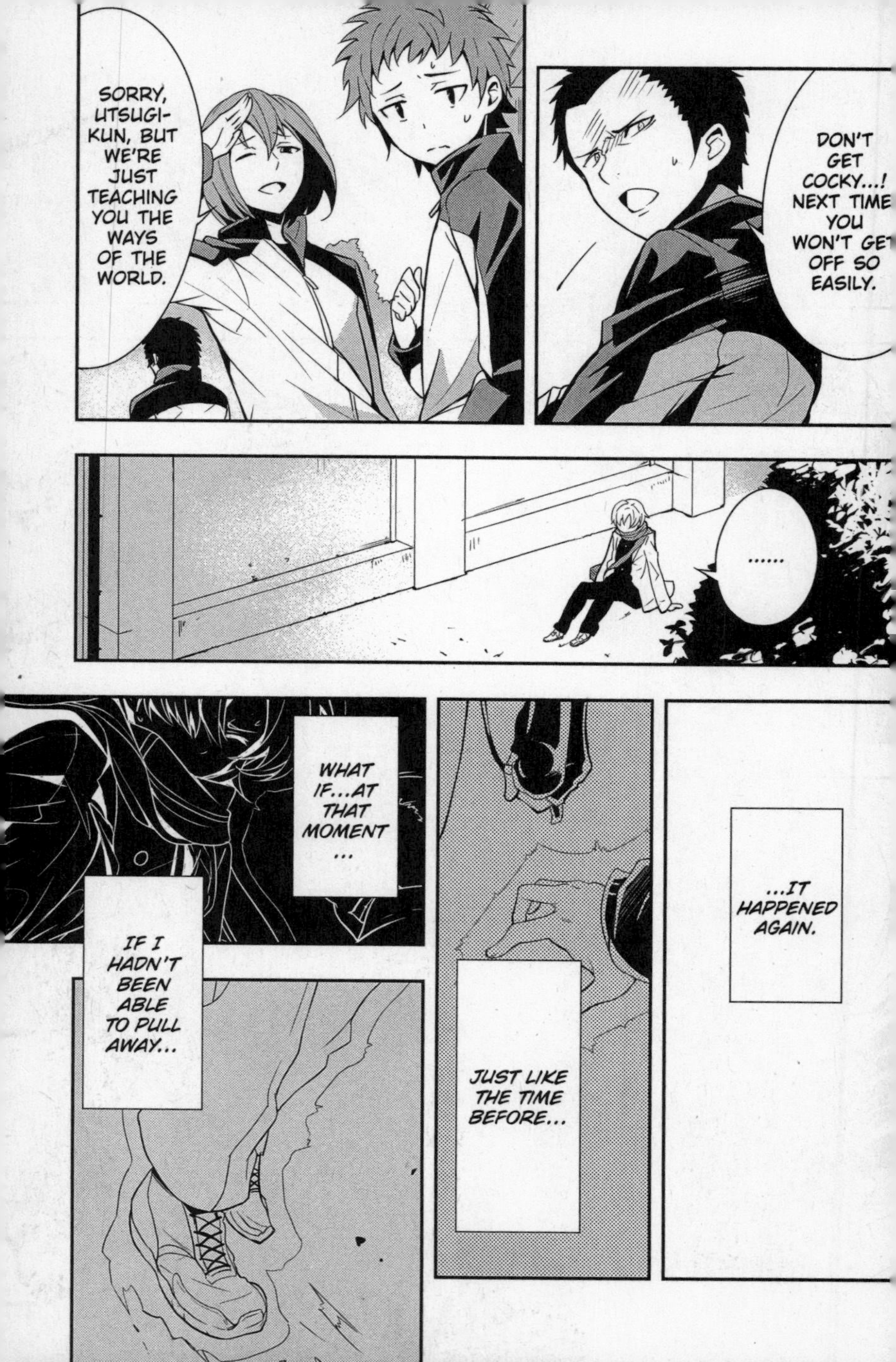
DON'T GET COCKY...! NEXT TIME YOU WON'T GET OFF SO EASILY.
SORRY, UTSUGI-KUN, BUT WE'RE JUST TEACHING YOU THE WAYS OF THE WORLD.
......
...IT HAPPENED AGAIN.
JUST LIKE THE TIME BEFORE...
WHAT IF...AT THAT MOMENT...
IF I HADN'T BEEN ABLE TO PULL AWAY...

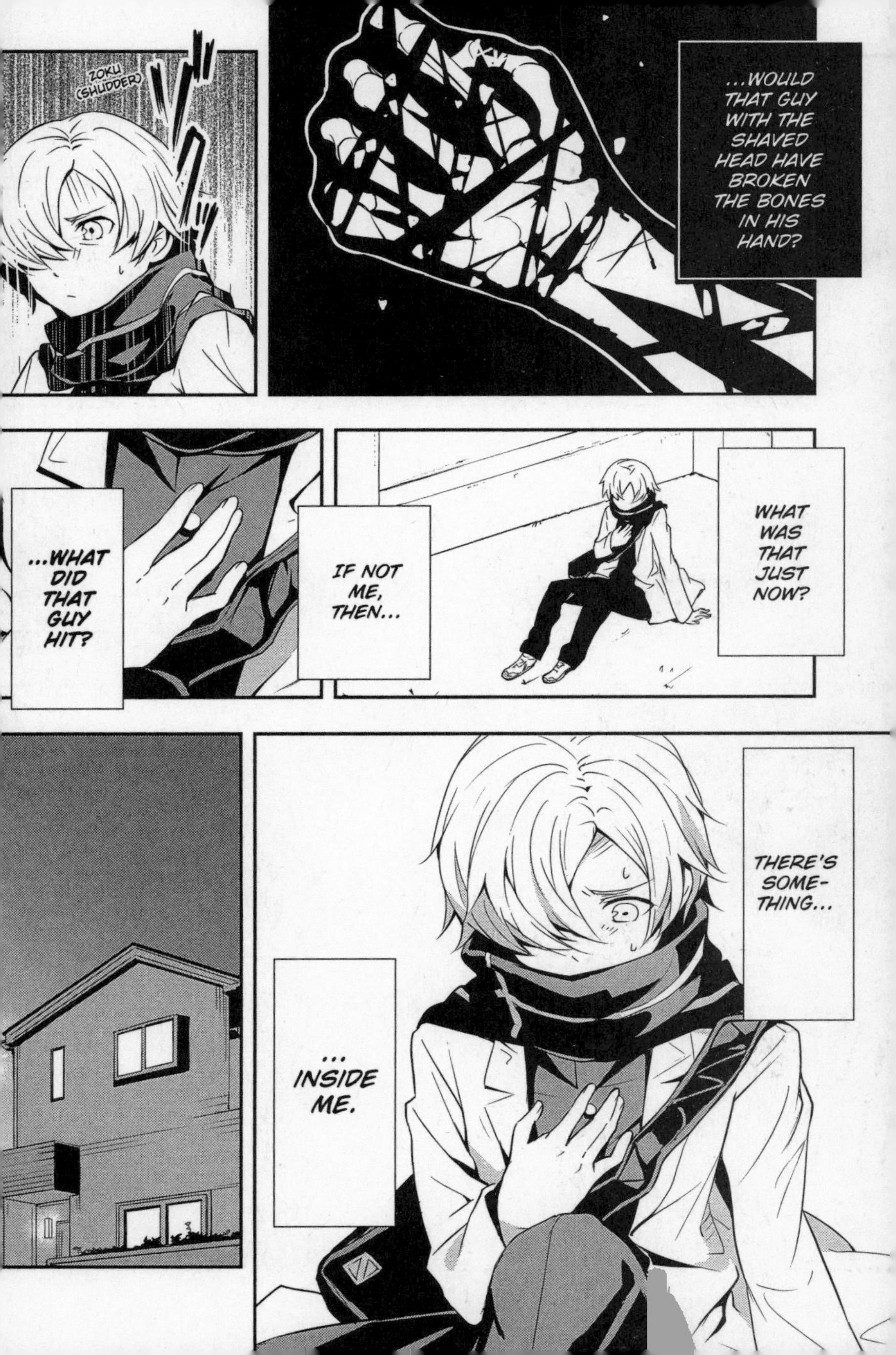
...WOULD THAT GUY WITH THE SHAVED HEAD HAVE BROKEN THE BONES IN HIS HAND?
ZOKU (SHUDDER)
WHAT WAS THAT JUST NOW?
IF NOT ME, THEN...
...WHAT DID THAT GUY HIT?
THERE'S SOME-THING...
... INSIDE ME.

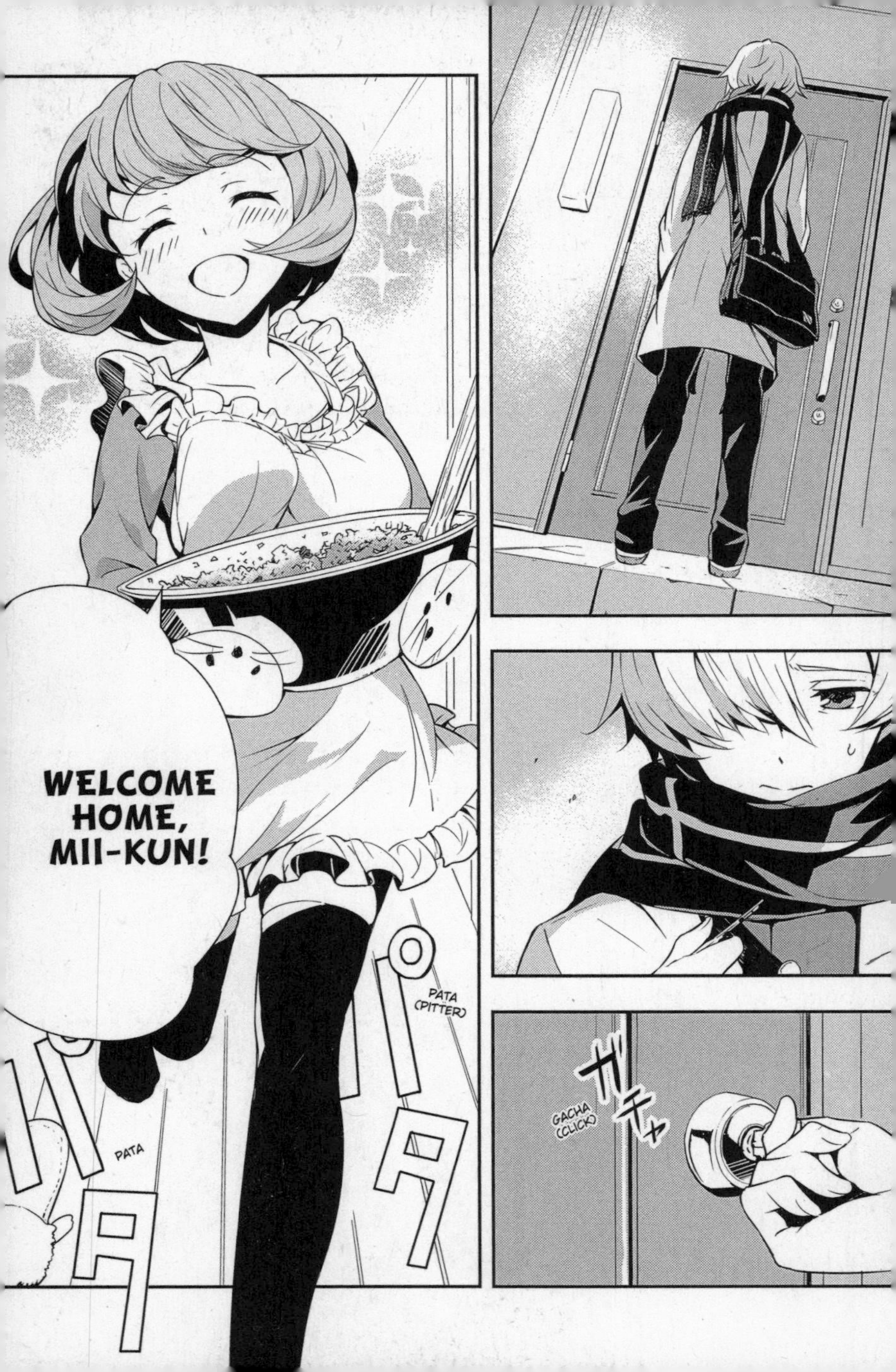
ガチャ
GACHA (CLICK)
WELCOME HOME, MII-KUN!
PATA (PITTER)
PATA

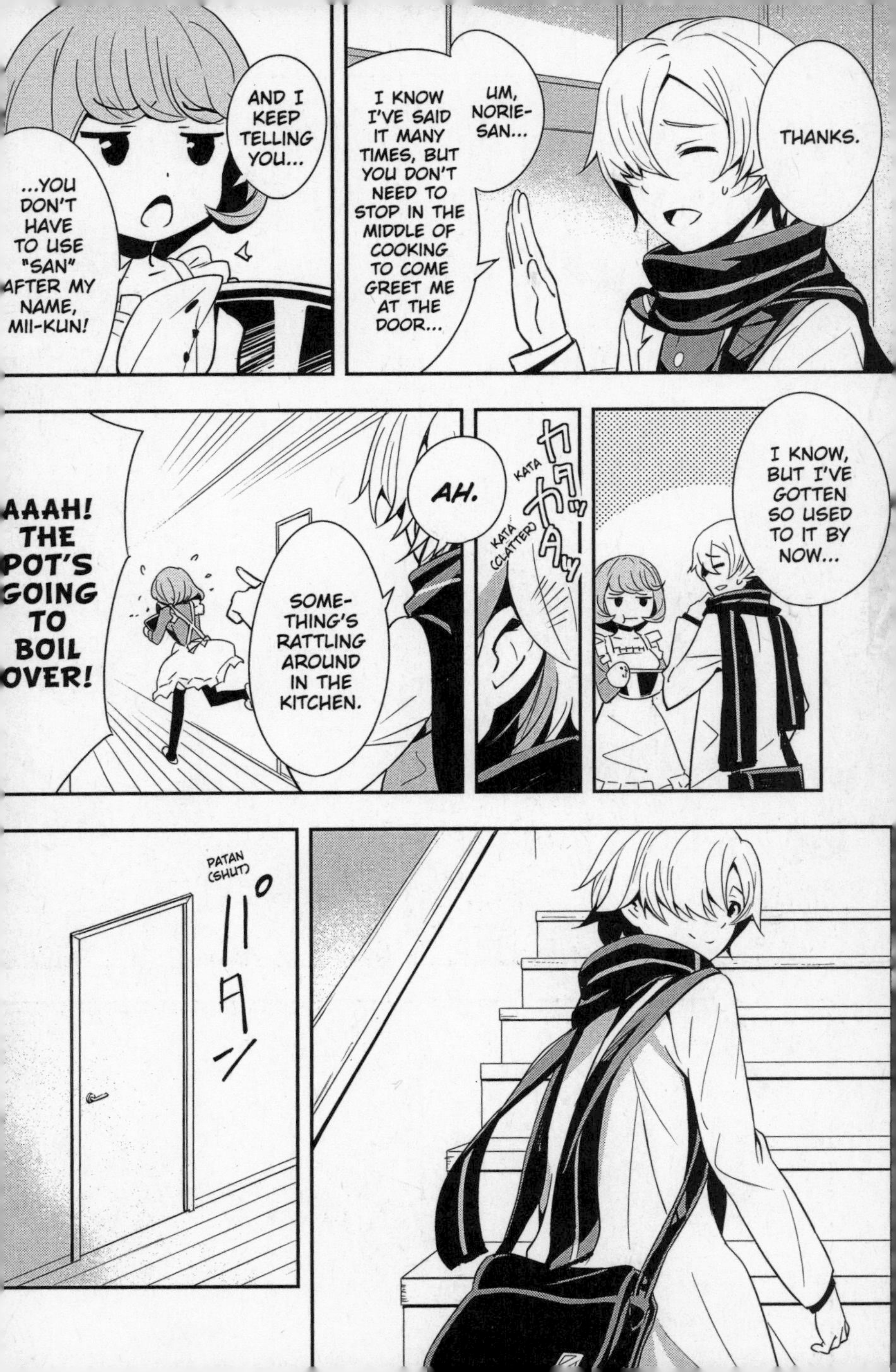
THANKS.
UM, NORIE-SAN...
I KNOW I'VE SAID IT MANY TIMES, BUT YOU DON'T NEED TO STOP IN THE MIDDLE OF COOKING TO COME GREET ME AT THE DOOR...
AND I KEEP TELLING YOU...
...YOU DON'T HAVE TO USE "SAN" AFTER MY NAME, MII-KUN!
I KNOW, BUT I'VE GOTTEN SO USED TO IT BY NOW...
KATA
KATA (CLATTER)
AH.
SOME-THING'S RATTLING AROUND IN THE KITCHEN.
AAAH! THE POT'S GOING TO BOIL OVER!
PATAN (SHUT)

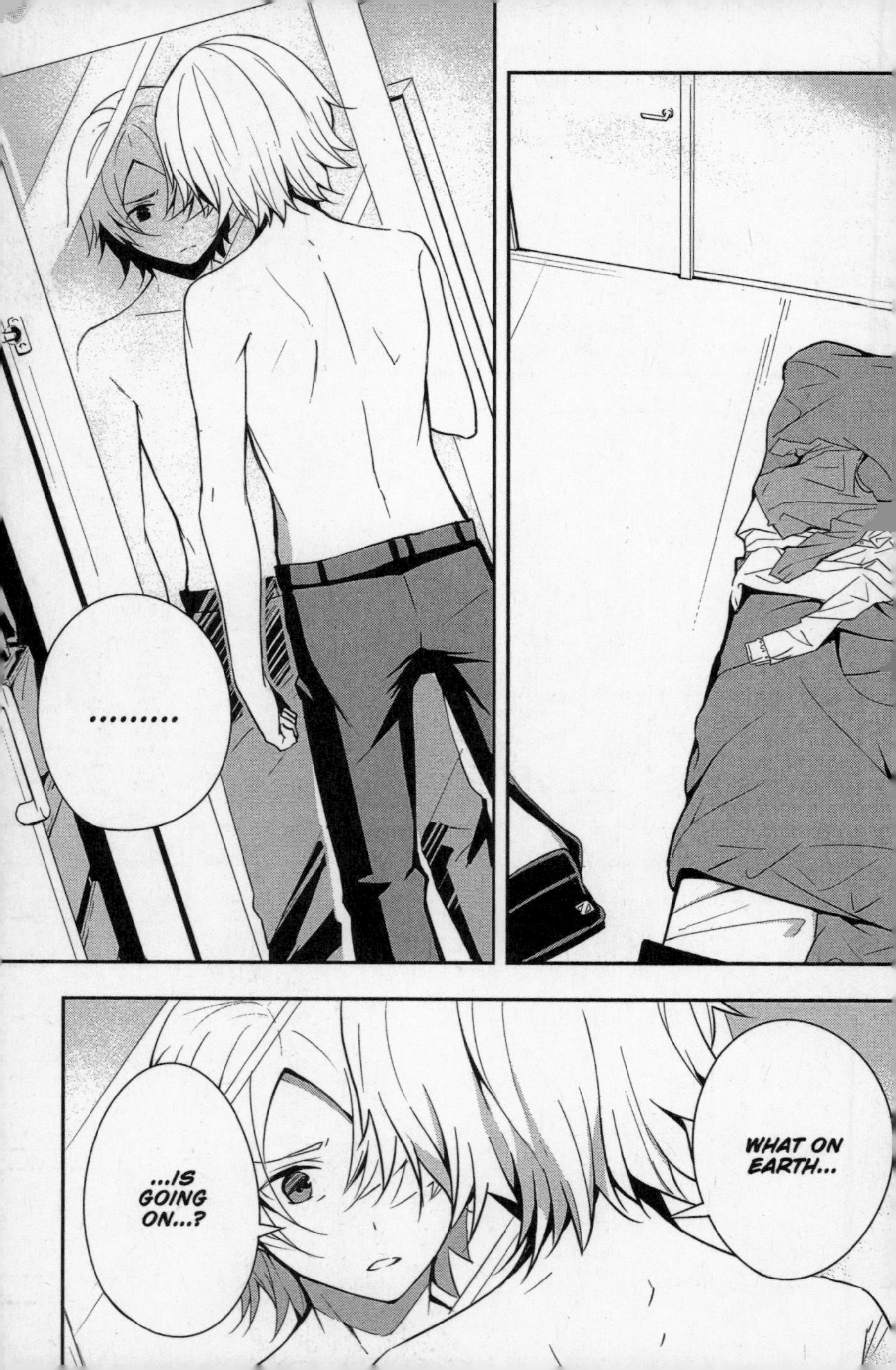
....
WHAT ON EARTH...
...IS GOING ON...?

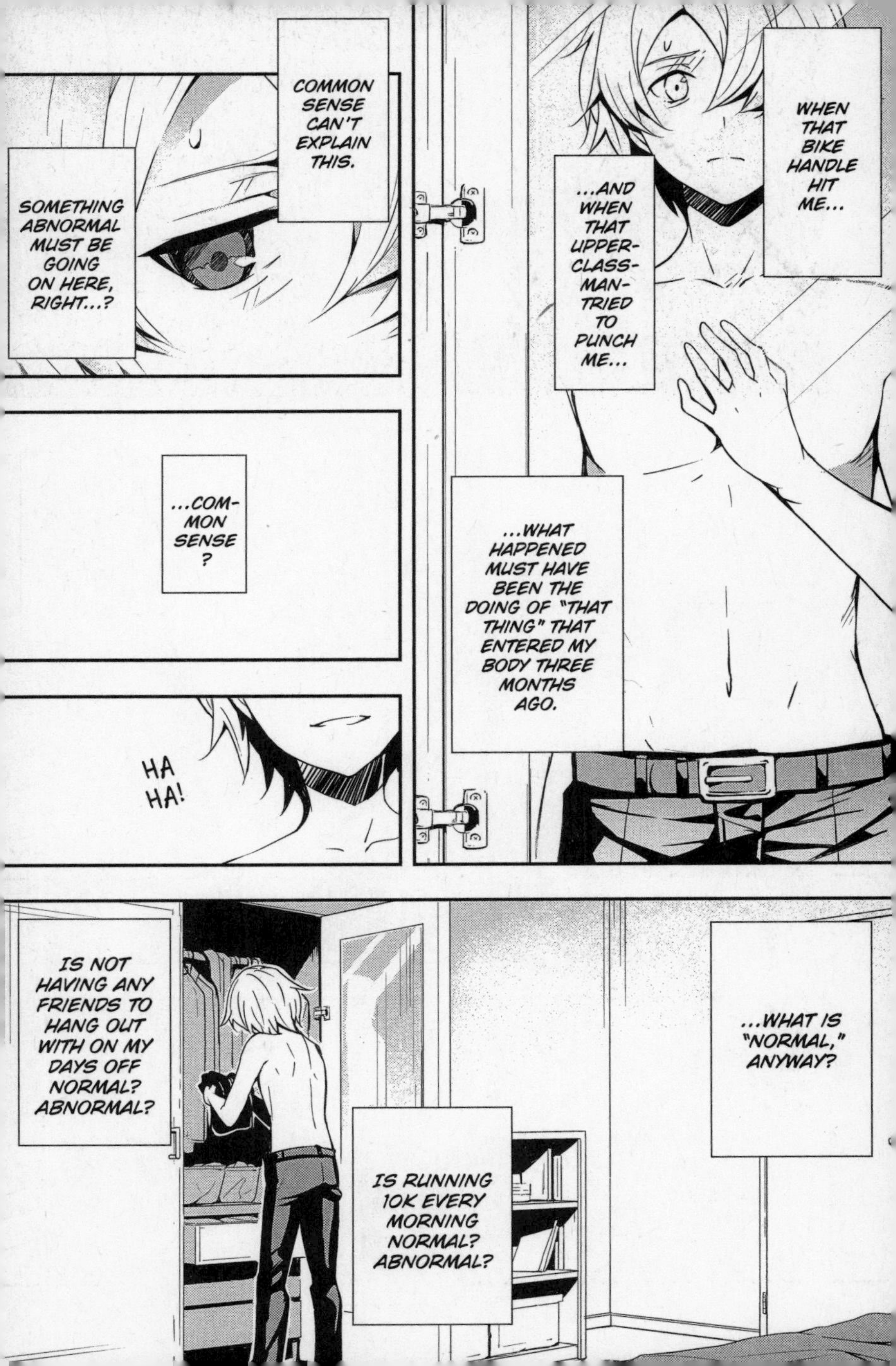

WHEN THAT BIKE HANDLE HIT ME...
...AND WHEN THAT UPPER-CLASS-MAN TRIED TO PUNCH ME...
...WHAT HAPPENED MUST HAVE BEEN THE DOING OF "THAT THING" THAT ENTERED MY BODY THREE MONTHS AGO.
COMMON SENSE CAN'T EXPLAIN THIS.
SOMETHING ABNORMAL MUST BE GOING ON HERE, RIGHT...?
...COM-MON SENSE?
HA HA!
...WHAT IS "NORMAL," ANYWAY?
IS RUNNING 10K EVERY MORNING NORMAL? ABNORMAL?
IS NOT HAVING ANY FRIENDS TO HANG OUT WITH ON MY DAYS OFF NORMAL? ABNORMAL?

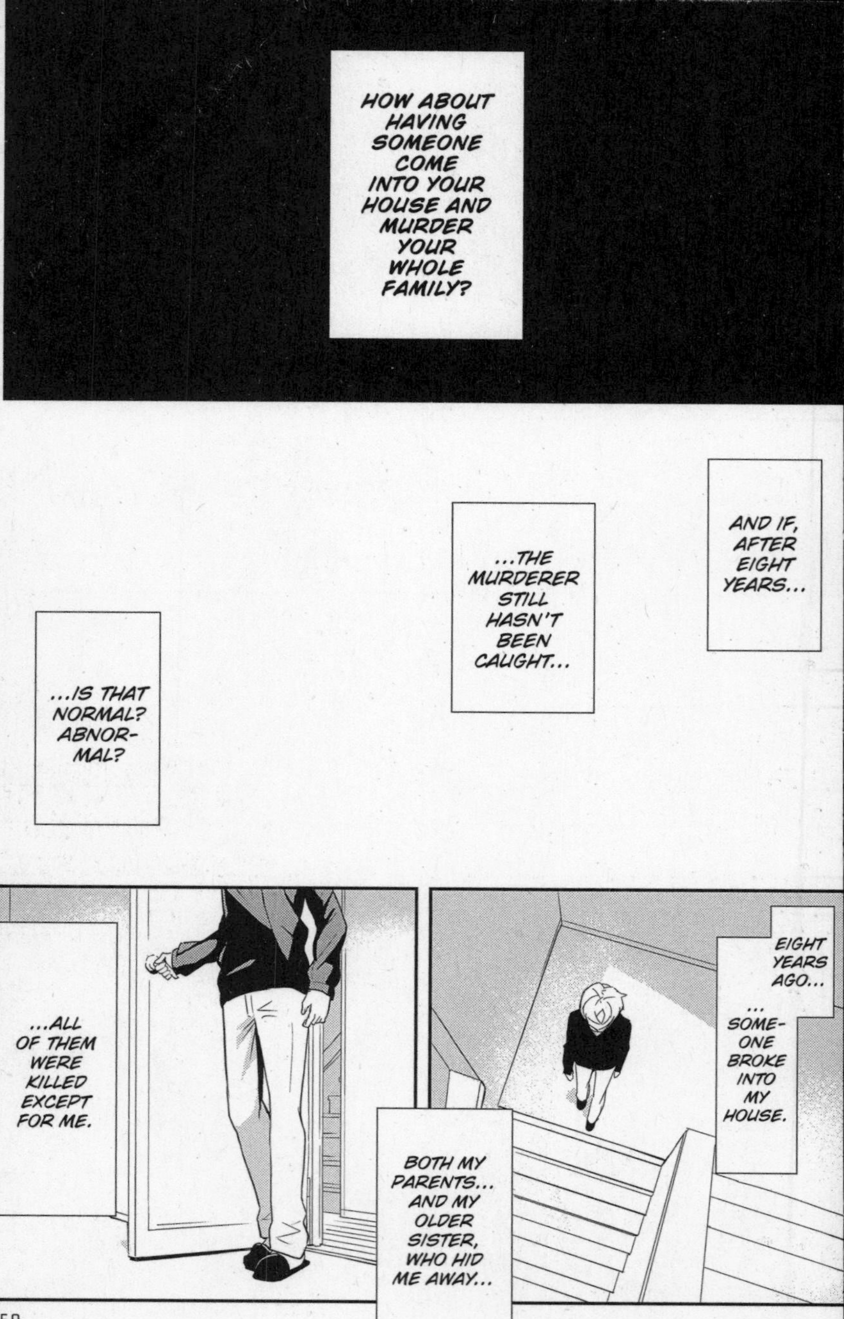

HOW ABOUT HAVING SOMEONE COME INTO YOUR HOUSE AND MURDER YOUR WHOLE FAMILY?
AND IF, AFTER EIGHT YEARS...
...THE MURDERER STILL HASN'T BEEN CAUGHT...
...IS THAT NORMAL? ABNOR-MAL?
EIGHT YEARS AGO...
...SOME-ONE BROKE INTO MY HOUSE.
BOTH MY PARENTS... AND MY OLDER SISTER, WHO HID ME AWAY...
...ALL OF THEM WERE KILLED EXCEPT FOR ME.

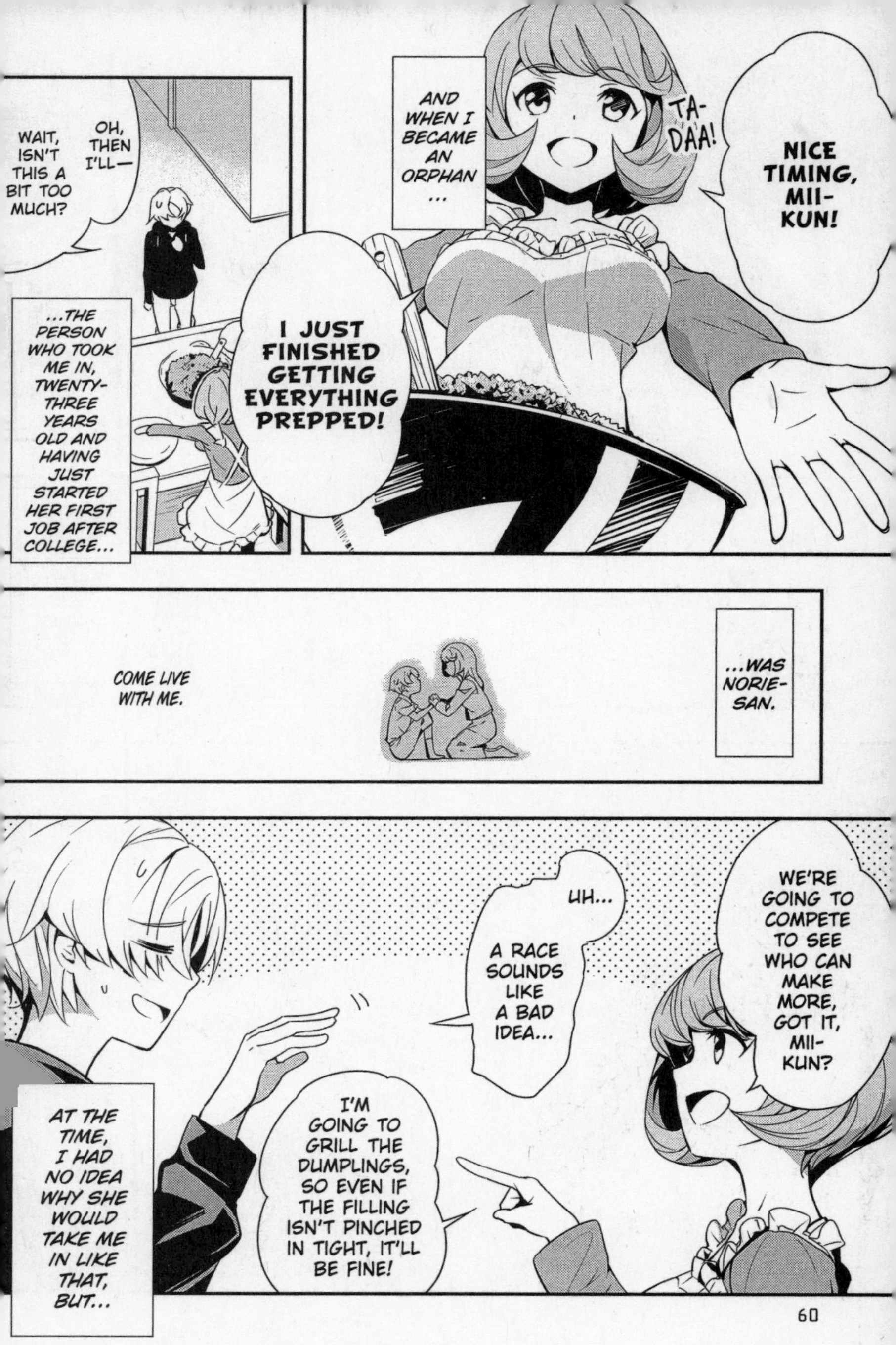
AND WHEN I BECAME AN ORPHAN...
TA-DAA!
NICE TIMING, MII-KUN!
I JUST FINISHED GETTING EVERYTHING PREPPED!
OH, THEN I'LL—
WAIT, ISN'T THIS A BIT TOO MUCH?
...THE PERSON WHO TOOK ME IN, TWENTY-THREE YEARS OLD AND HAVING JUST STARTED HER FIRST JOB AFTER COLLEGE...
...WAS NORIE-SAN.
COME LIVE WITH ME.
WE'RE GOING TO COMPETE TO SEE WHO CAN MAKE MORE, GOT IT, MII-KUN?
I'M GOING TO GRILL THE DUMPLINGS, SO EVEN IF THE FILLING ISN'T PINCHED IN TIGHT, IT'LL BE FINE!
UH...
A RACE SOUNDS LIKE A BAD IDEA...
AT THE TIME, I HAD NO IDEA WHY SHE WOULD TAKE ME IN LIKE THAT, BUT...

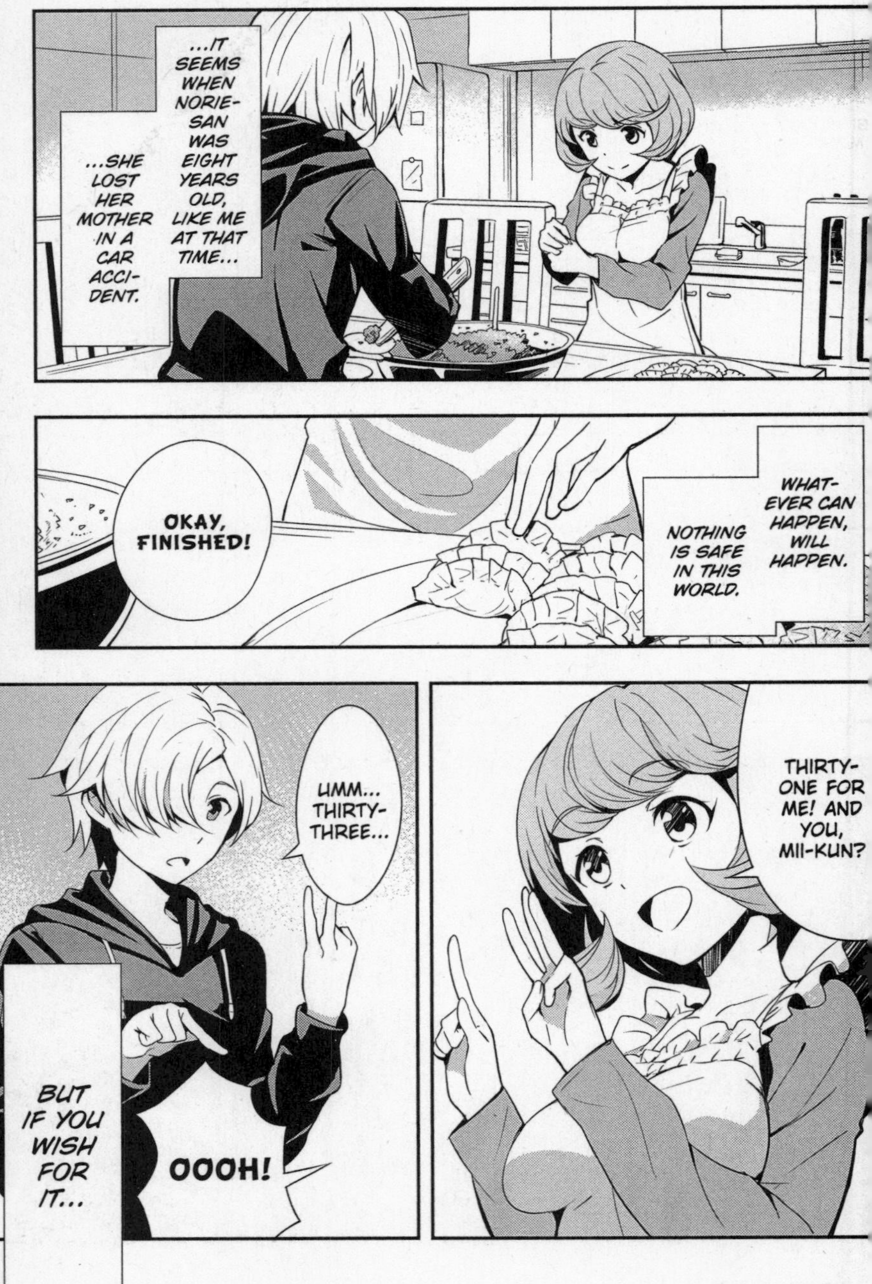

...IT SEEMS WHEN NORIE-SAN WAS EIGHT YEARS OLD, LIKE ME AT THAT TIME...
...SHE LOST HER MOTHER IN A CAR ACCIDENT.
WHATEVER CAN HAPPEN, WILL HAPPEN.
NOTHING IS SAFE IN THIS WORLD.
OKAY, FINISHED!
THIRTY-ONE FOR ME! AND YOU, MII-KUN?
UMM... THIRTY-THREE...
OOOH!
BUT IF YOU WISH FOR IT...

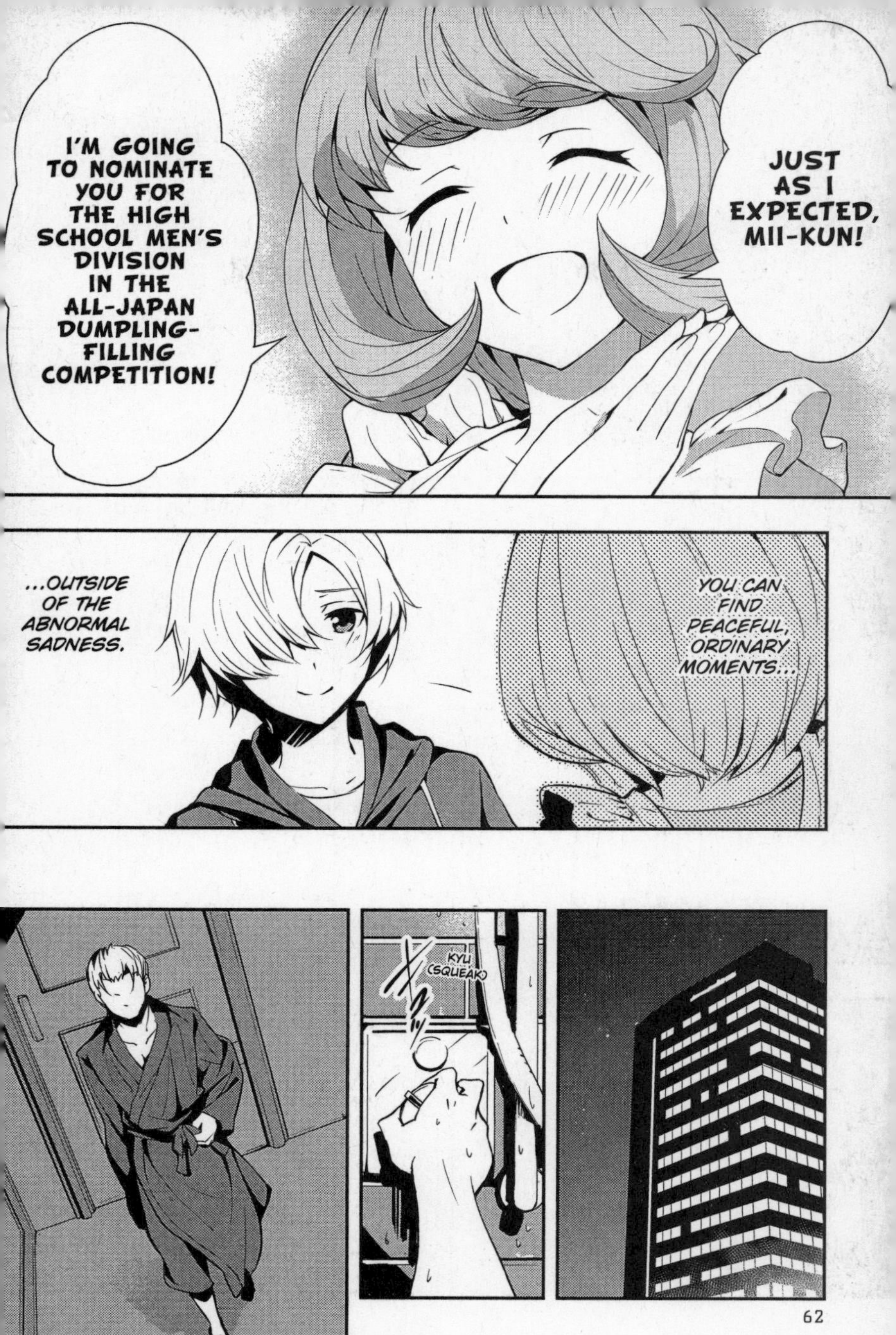
JUST AS I EXPECTED, MII-KUN!
I'M GOING TO NOMINATE YOU FOR THE HIGH SCHOOL MEN'S DIVISION IN THE ALL-JAPAN DUMPLING-FILLING COMPETITION!
YOU CAN FIND PEACEFUL, ORDINARY MOMENTS...
...OUTSIDE OF THE ABNORMAL SADNESS.
KYU (SQUEAK)

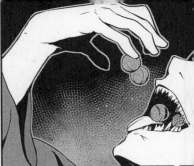

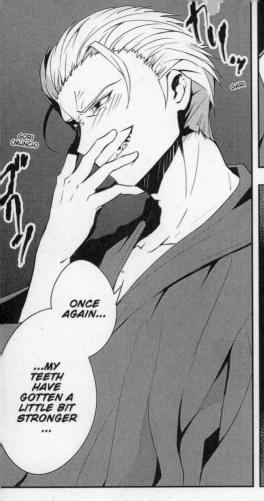

GORI
(MUNCH)

ONCE AGAIN...

...MY TEETH HAVE GOTTEN A LITTLE BIT STRONGER...

GARI

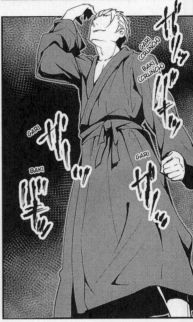

GARI
(CRUNCH)

BAKI
(CRUNCH)

GARI

BAKI

GARI

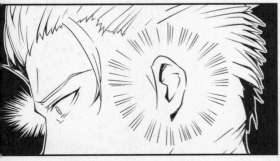

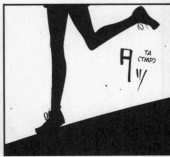

TA
(TMP)

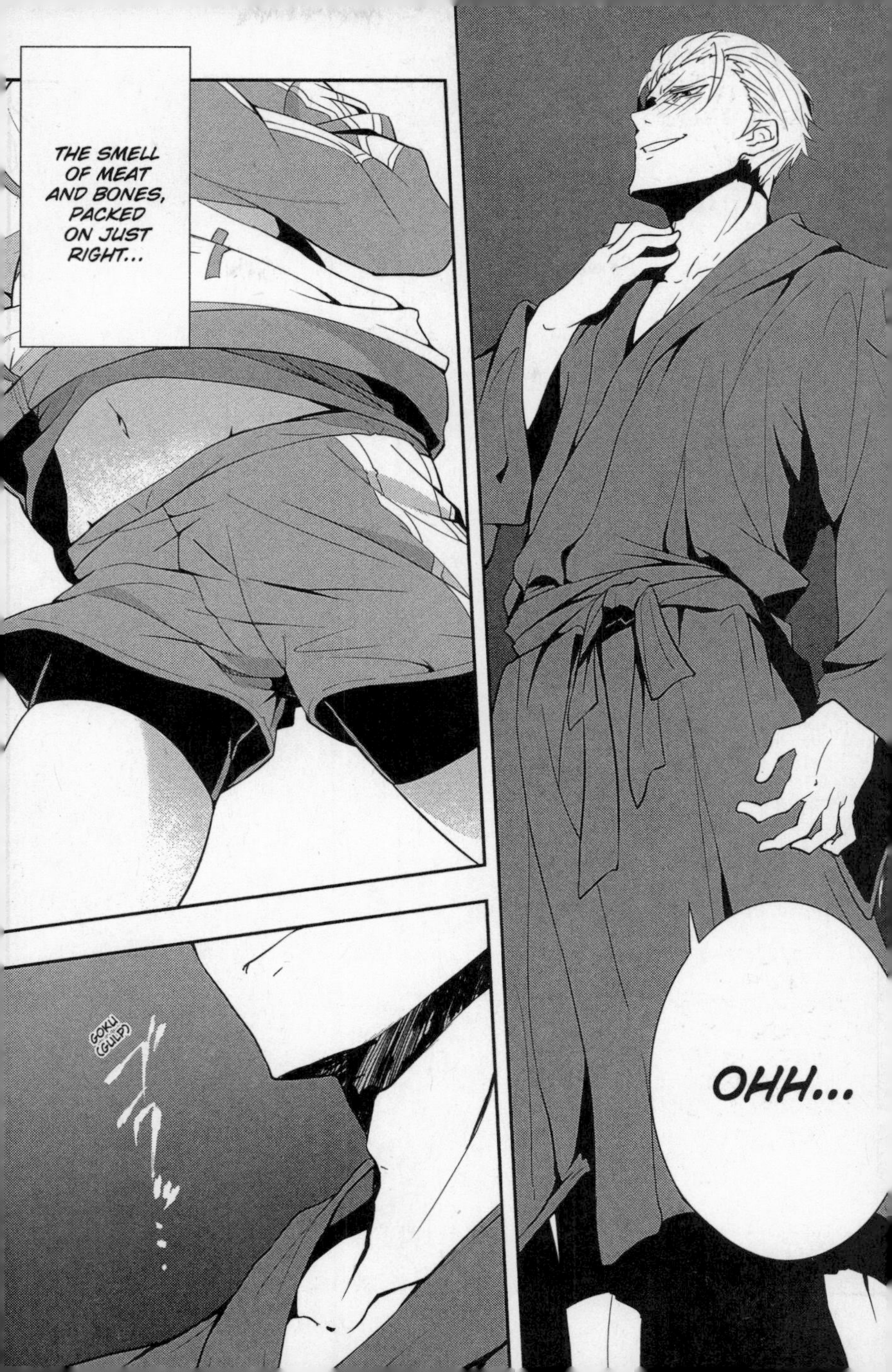
OHH...
THE SMELL OF MEAT AND BONES, PACKED ON JUST RIGHT...
GOKU (GULP)

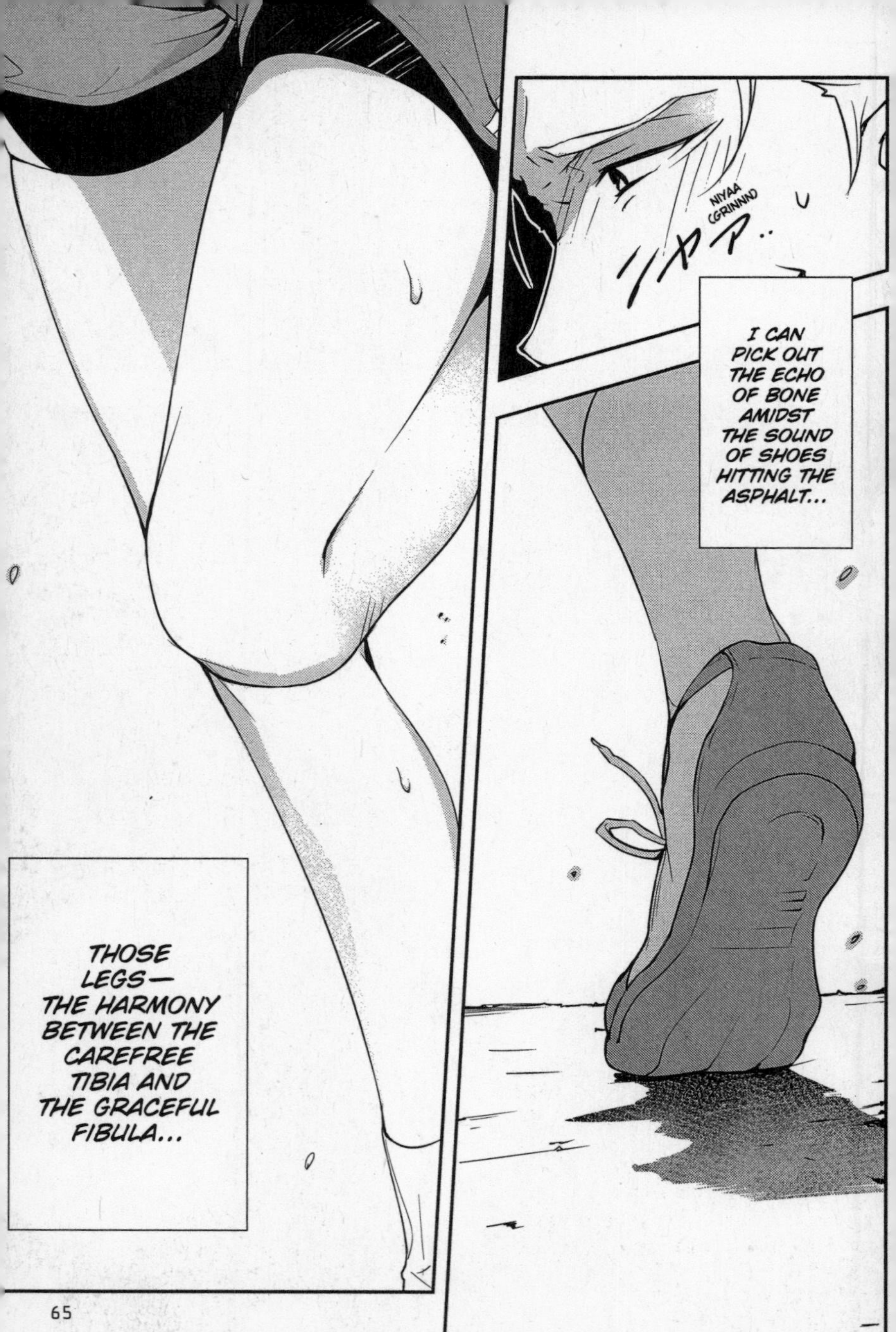
ニヤア‥
NIYAA (GRINNN)
I CAN PICK OUT THE ECHO OF BONE AMIDST THE SOUND OF SHOES HITTING THE ASPHALT...
THOSE LEGS— THE HARMONY BETWEEN THE CAREFREE TIBIA AND THE GRACEFUL FIBULA...

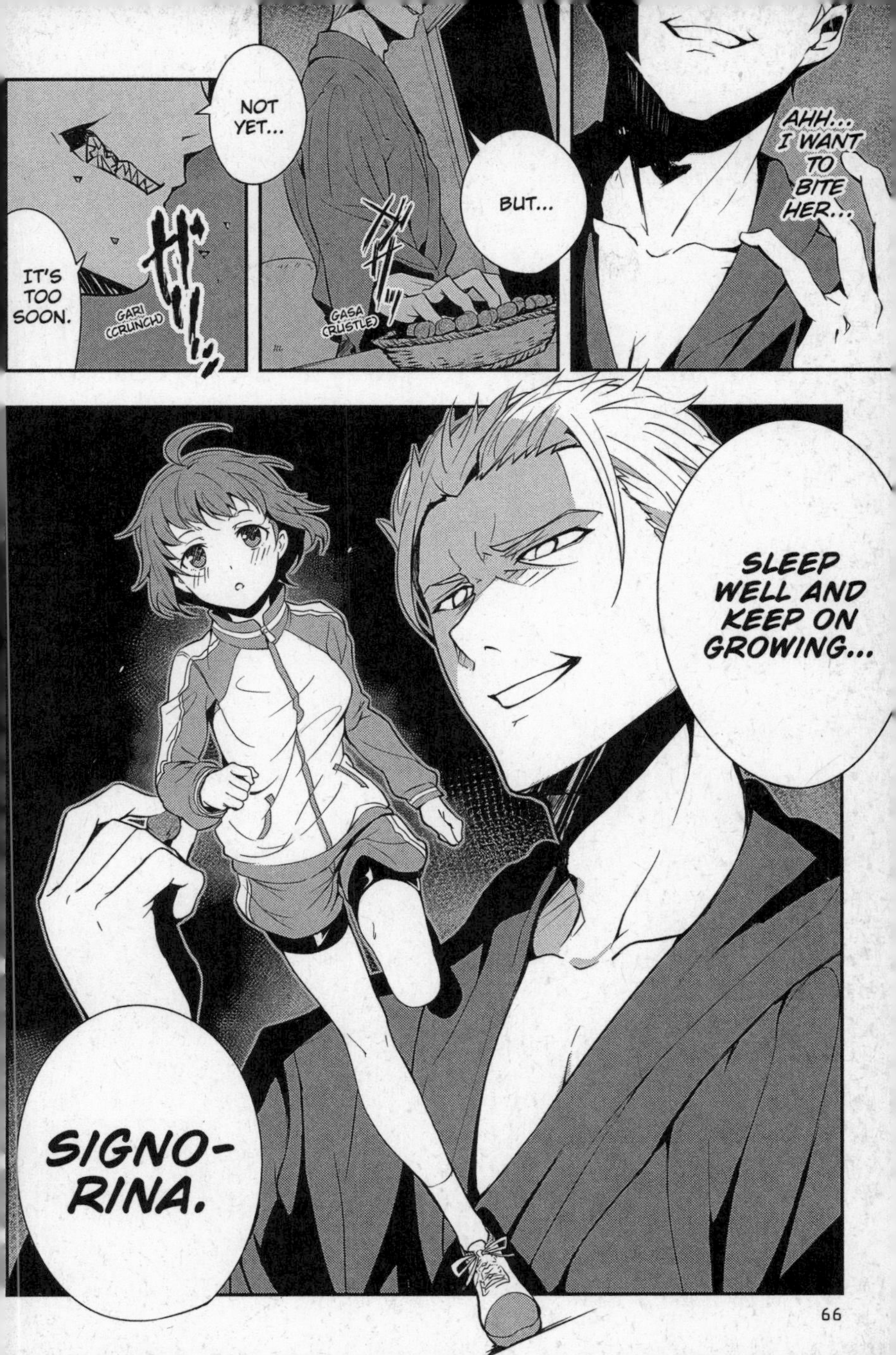
AHH... I WANT TO BITE HER...
BUT...
GASA (RUSTLE)
NOT YET...
IT'S TOO SOON.
GARI (CRUNCH)
SLEEP WELL AND KEEP ON GROWING...
SIGNO-RINA.

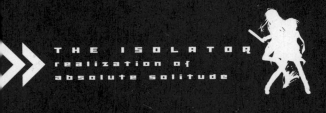

THE ISOLATOR
realization of
absolute solitude

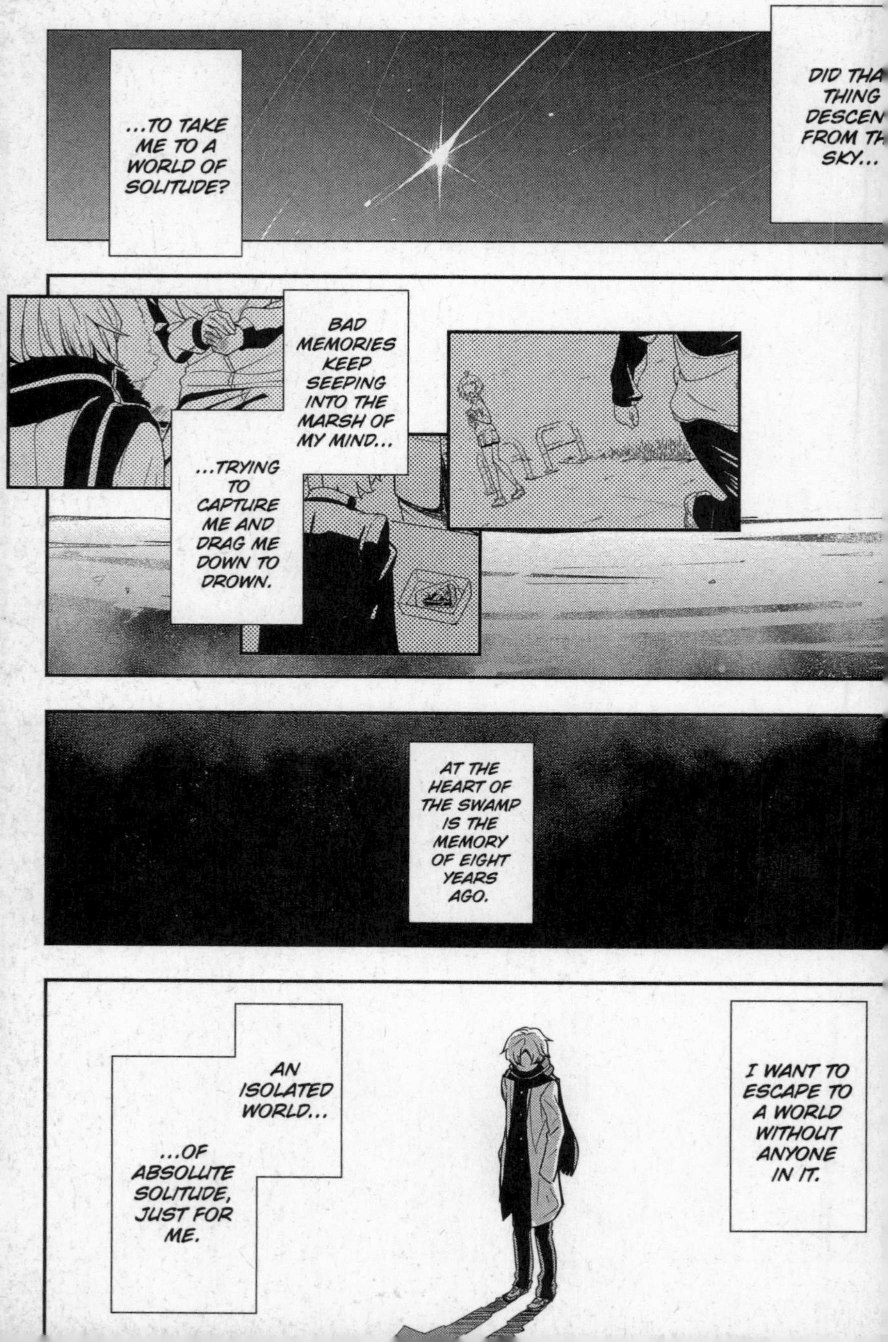
DID THA THING DESCEN FROM TH SKY...
...TO TAKE ME TO A WORLD OF SOLITUDE?
BAD MEMORIES KEEP SEEPING INTO THE MARSH OF MY MIND...
...TRYING TO CAPTURE ME AND DRAG ME DOWN TO DROWN.
AT THE HEART OF THE SWAMP IS THE MEMORY OF EIGHT YEARS AGO.
I WANT TO ESCAPE TO A WORLD WITHOUT ANYONE IN IT.
AN ISOLATED WORLD...
...OF ABSOLUTE SOLITUDE, JUST FOR ME.

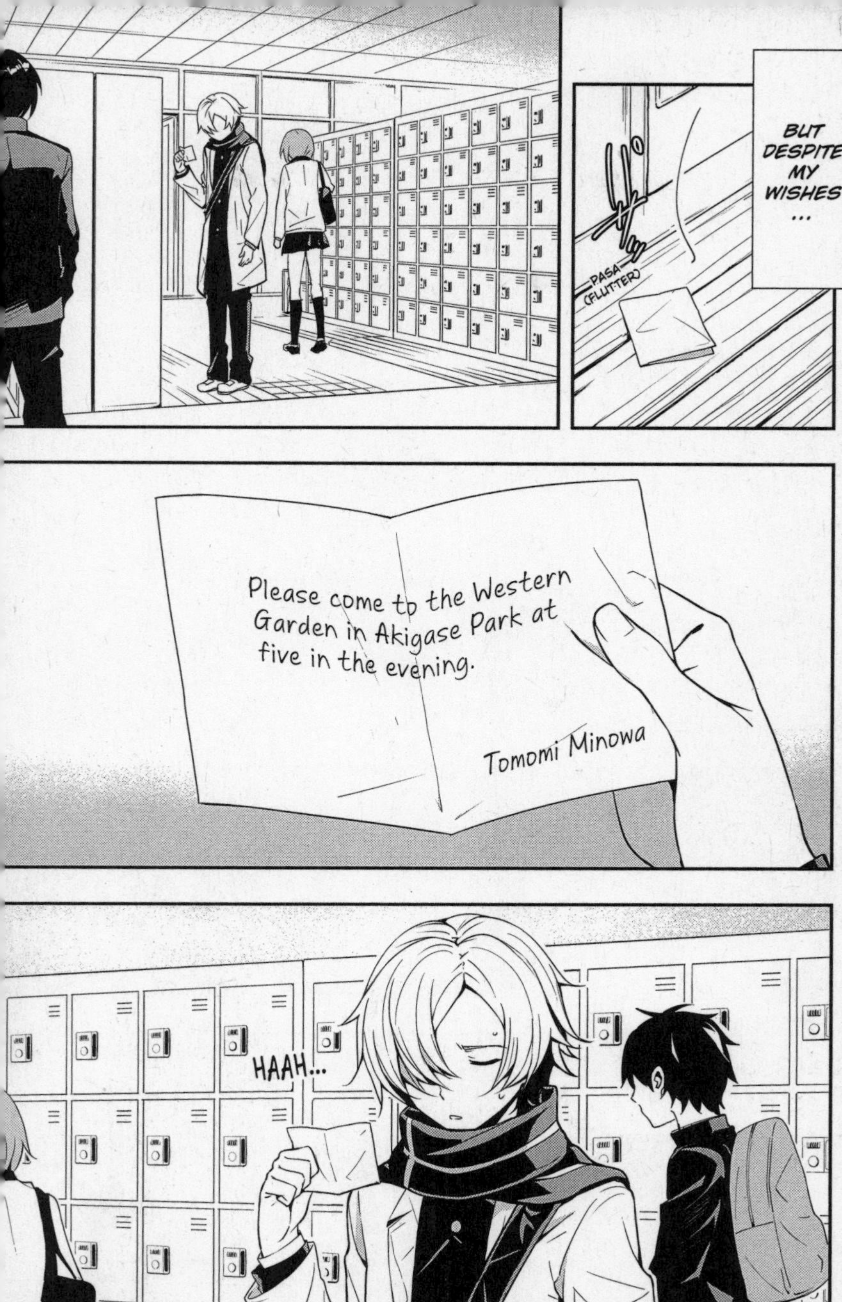
BUT DESPITE MY WISHES ...
PASA (FLUTTER)
Please come to the Western Garden in Akigase Park at five in the evening.
Tomomi Minowa
HAAH...

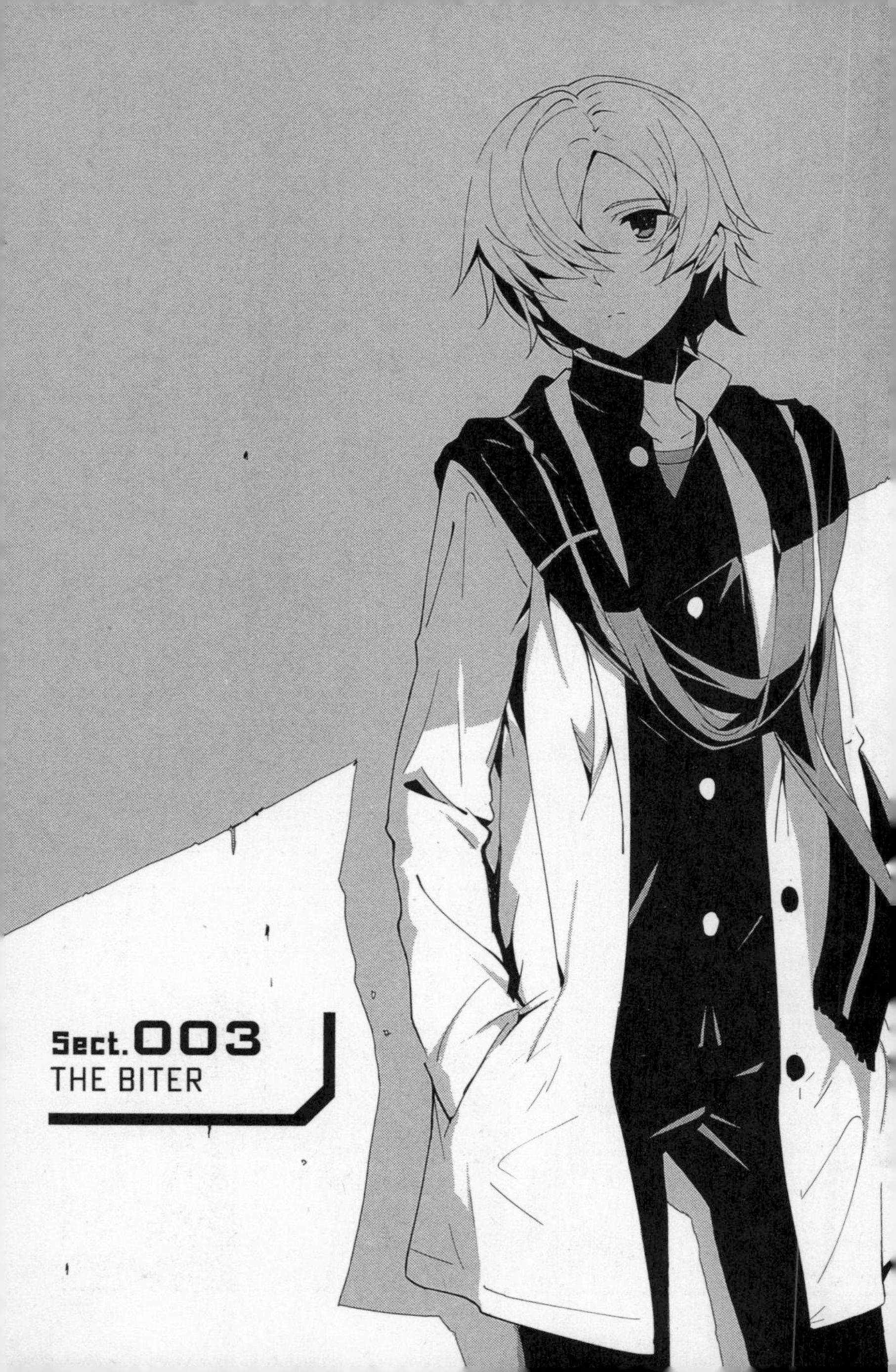

Sect.003
THE BITER

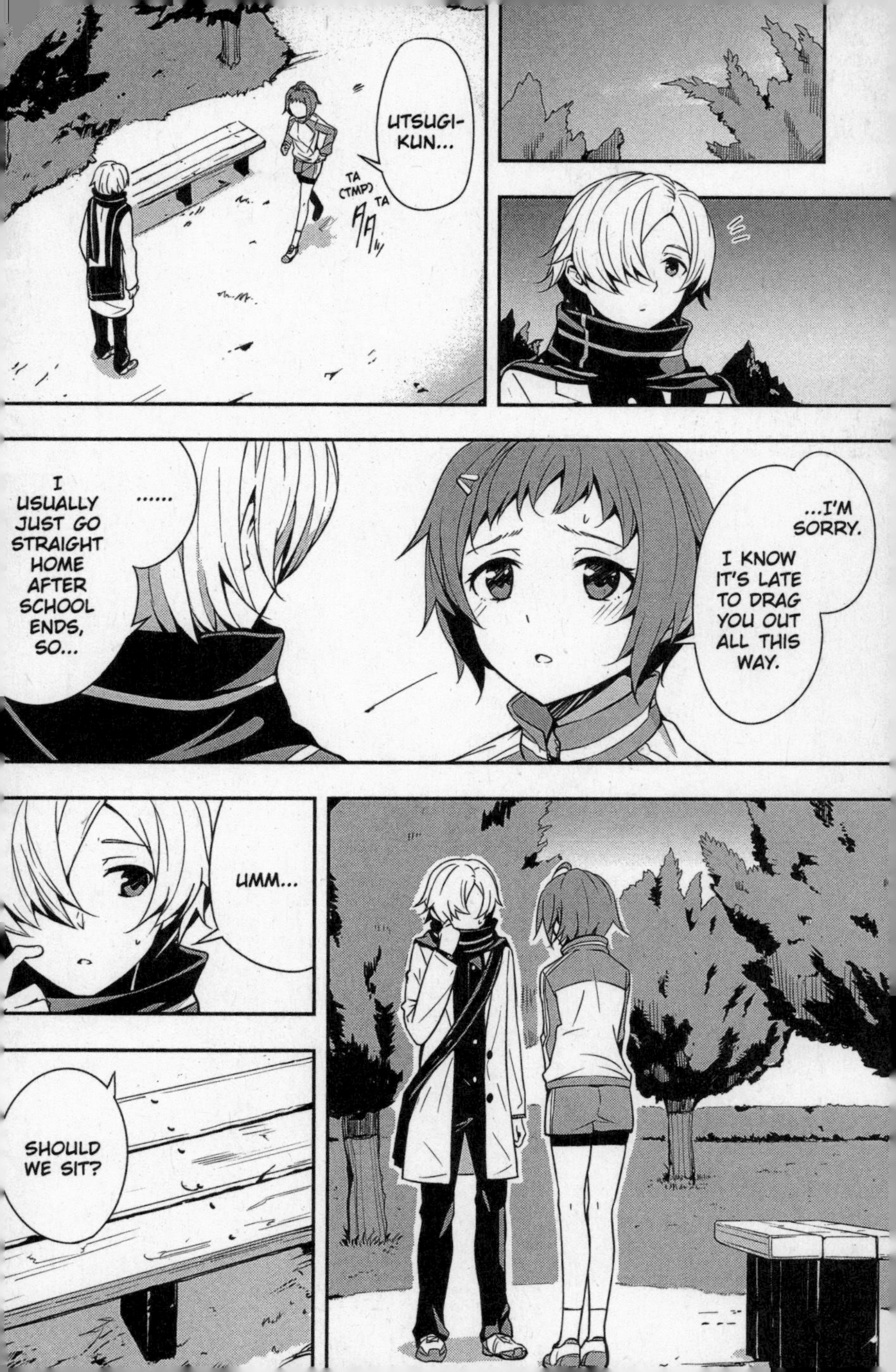
UTSUGI-KUN...
TA (TMP) TA
...I'M SORRY.
I KNOW IT'S LATE TO DRAG YOU OUT ALL THIS WAY.
......
I USUALLY JUST GO STRAIGHT HOME AFTER SCHOOL ENDS, SO...
UMM...
SHOULD WE SIT?

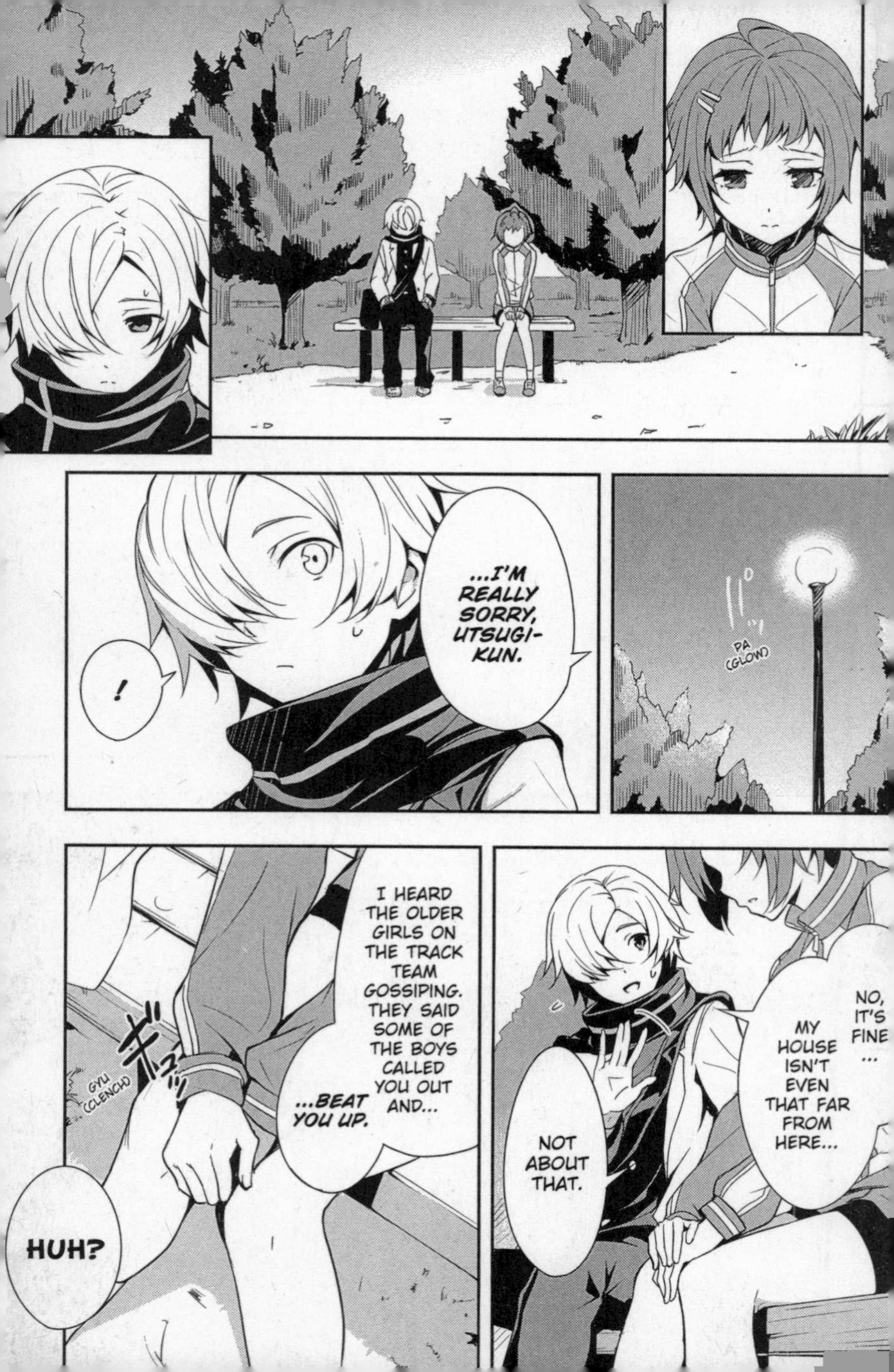
PA (GLOW)
...I'M REALLY SORRY, UTSUGI-KUN.
!
NO, IT'S FINE...
MY HOUSE ISN'T EVEN THAT FAR FROM HERE...
NOT ABOUT THAT.
I HEARD THE OLDER GIRLS ON THE TRACK TEAM GOSSIPING. THEY SAID SOME OF THE BOYS CALLED YOU OUT AND...
...BEAT YOU UP.
GYU (CLENCH)
HUH?

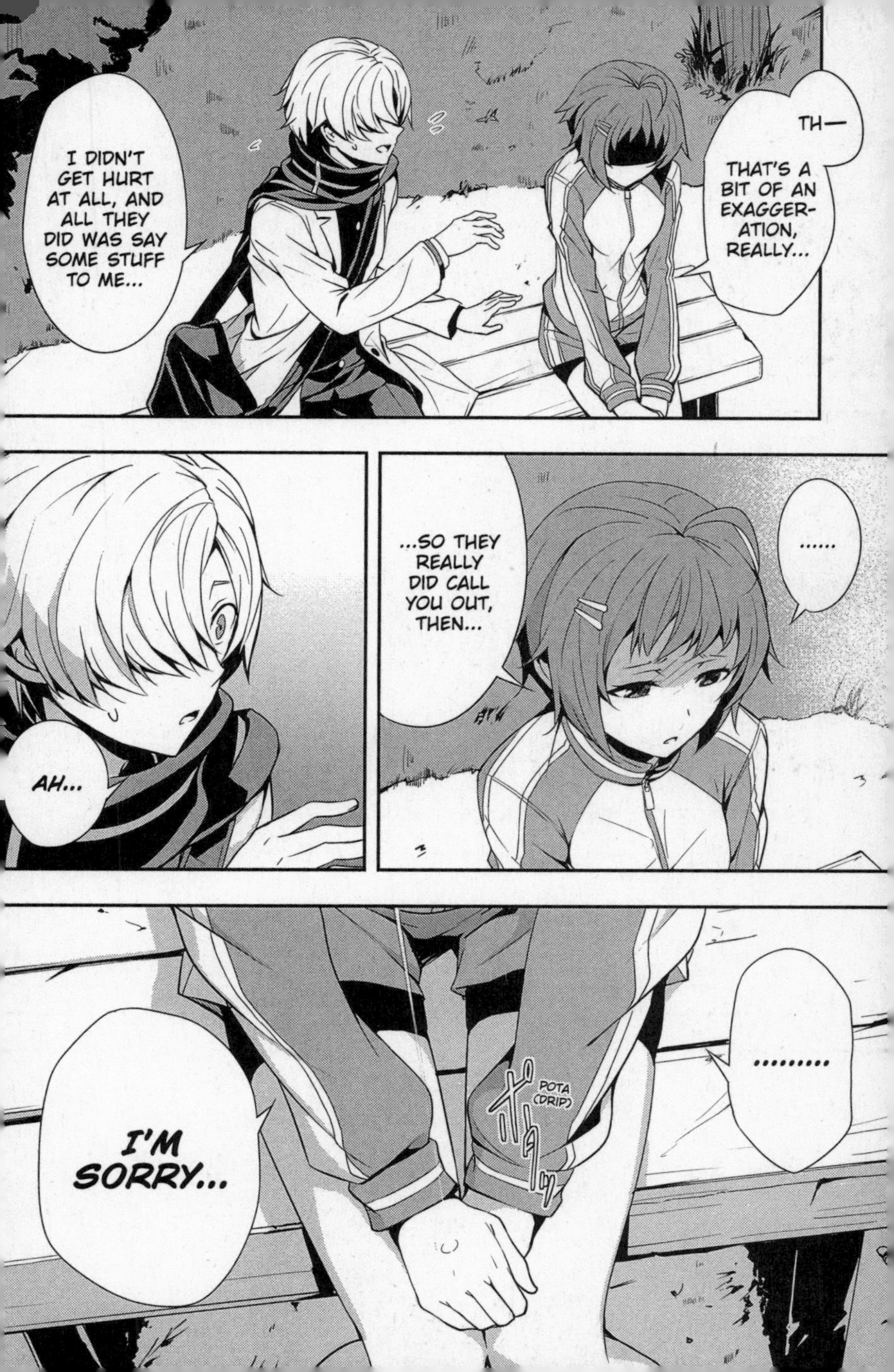
TH— THAT'S A BIT OF AN EXAGGERATION, REALLY...
I DIDN'T GET HURT AT ALL, AND ALL THEY DID WAS SAY SOME STUFF TO ME...
......
...SO THEY REALLY DID CALL YOU OUT, THEN...
AH...
....
POTA (DRIP)
I'M SORRY...

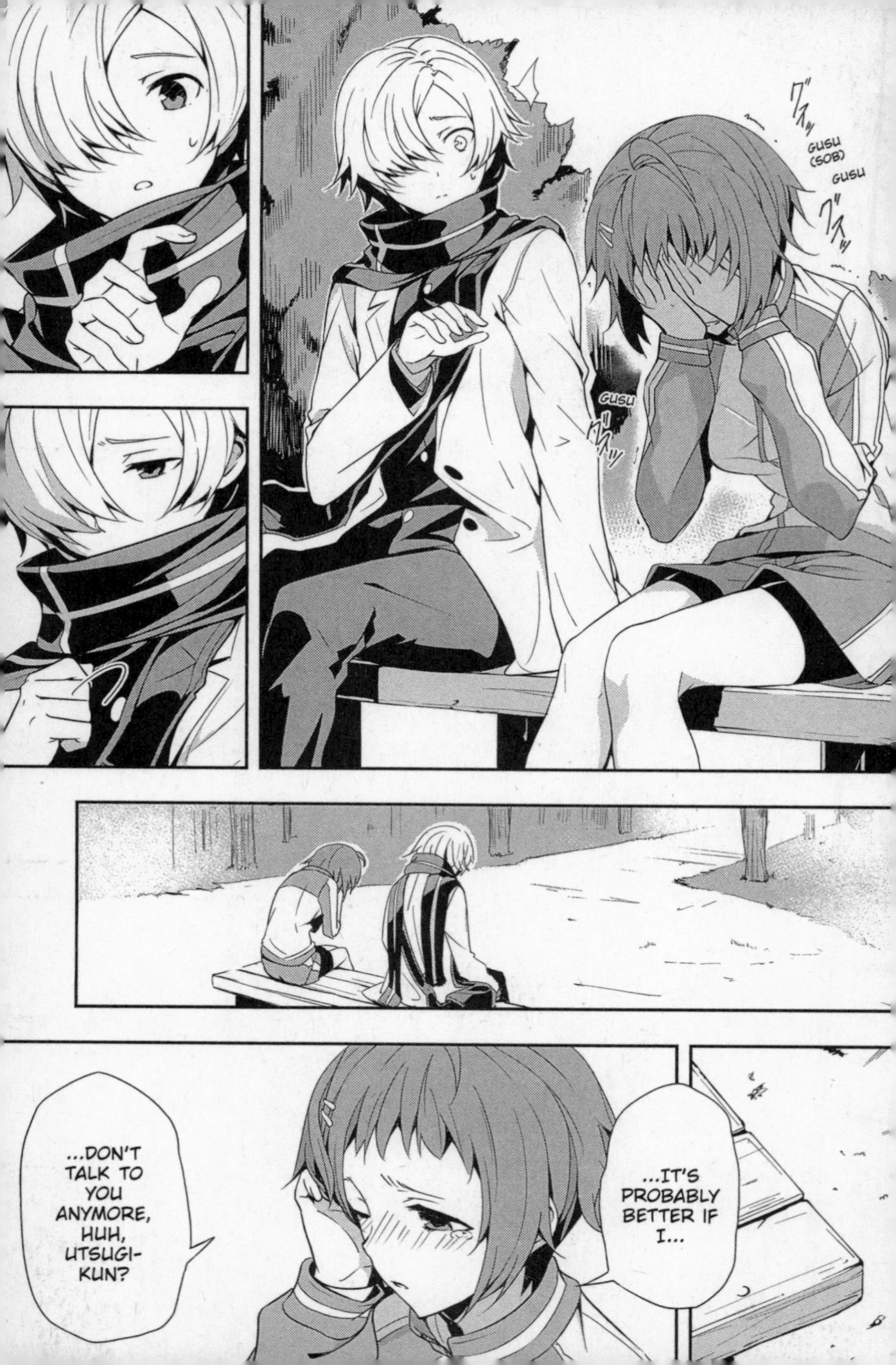
GUSU (SOB)
GUSU
GUSU
...IT'S PROBABLY BETTER IF I...
...DON'T TALK TO YOU ANYMORE, HUH, UTSUGI-KUN?

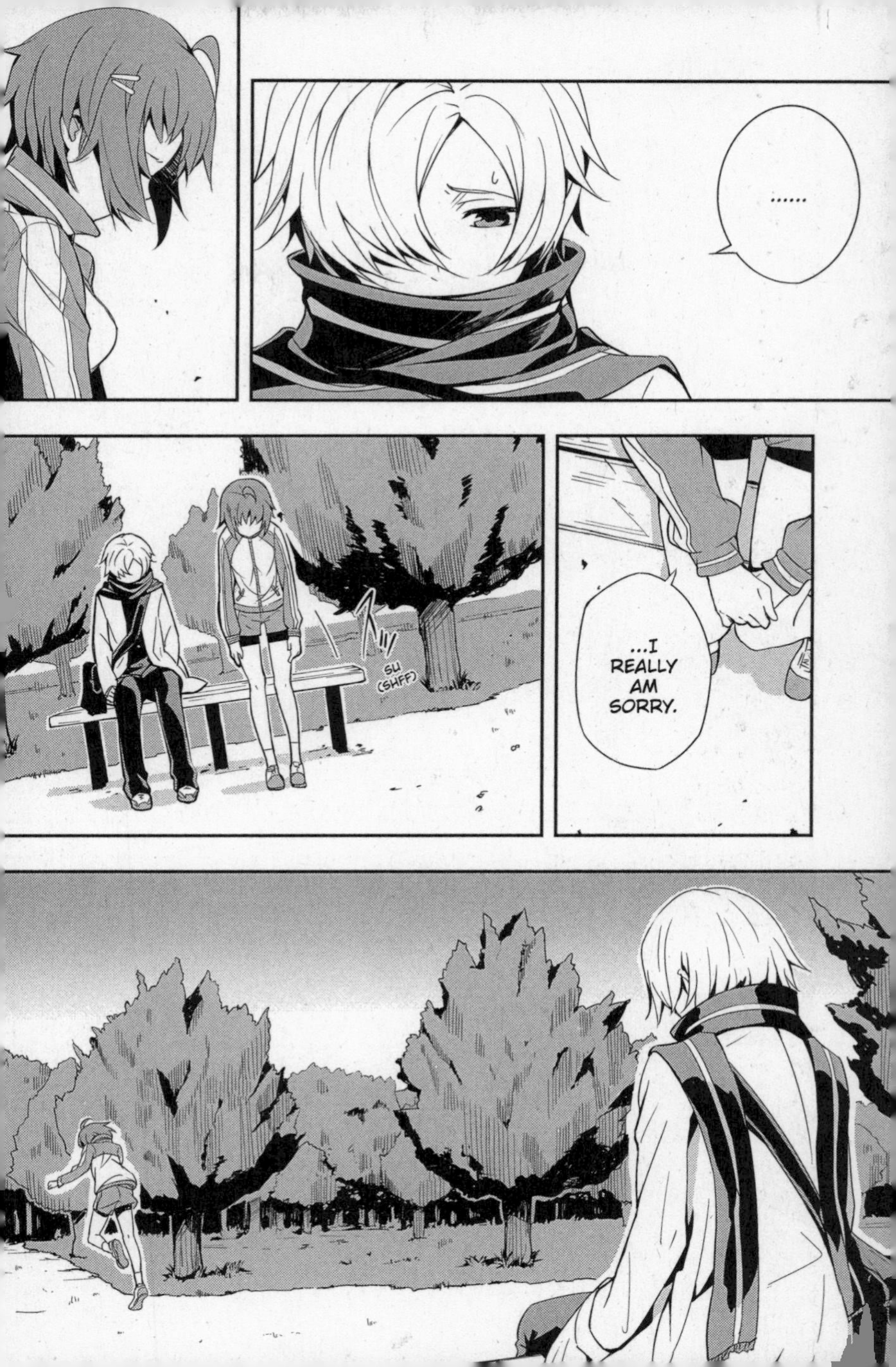
......
...I REALLY AM SORRY.
SU (SHFF)

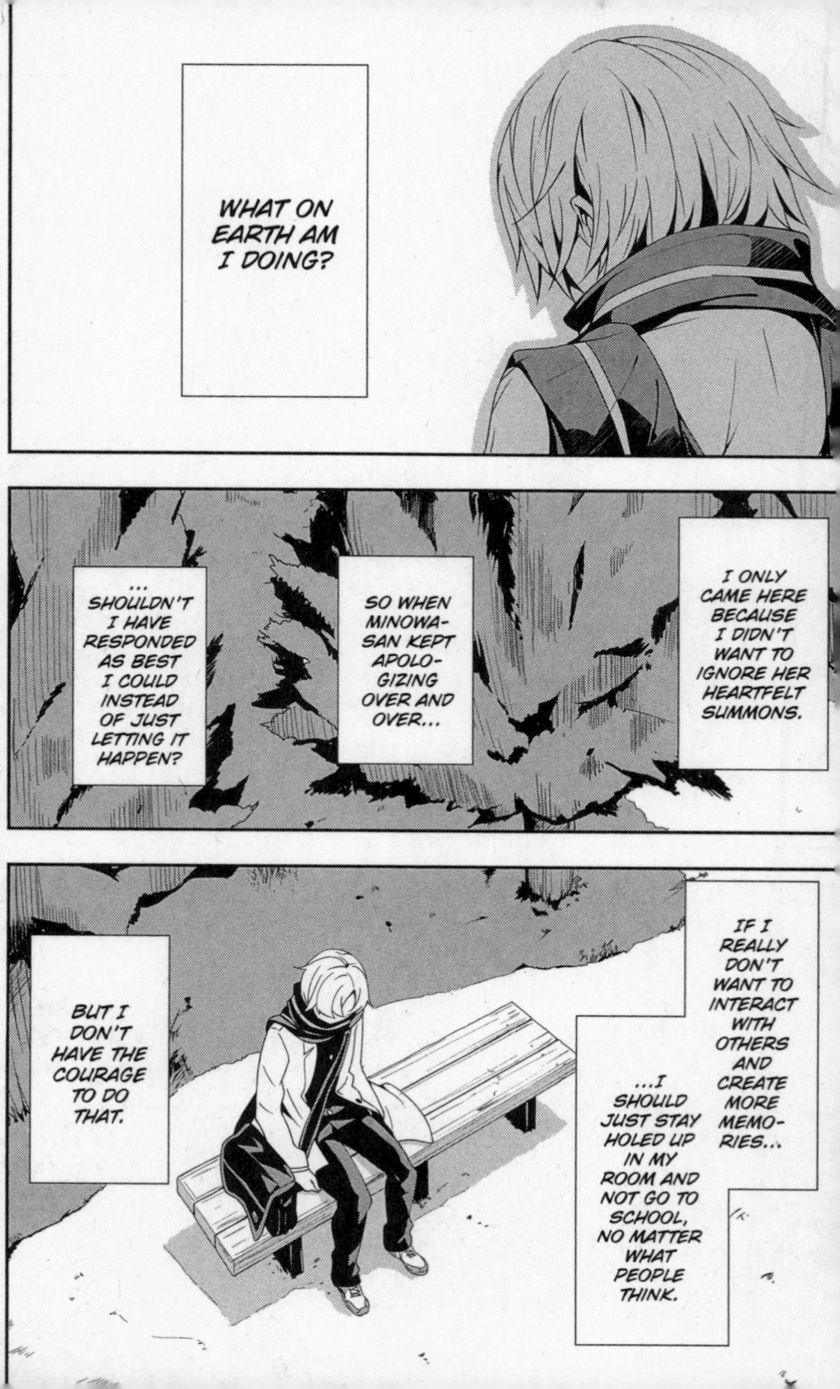
WHAT ON EARTH AM I DOING?
I ONLY CAME HERE BECAUSE I DIDN'T WANT TO IGNORE HER HEARTFELT SUMMONS.
SO WHEN MINOWA-SAN KEPT APOLO-GIZING OVER AND OVER...
...SHOULDN'T I HAVE RESPONDED AS BEST I COULD INSTEAD OF JUST LETTING IT HAPPEN?
IF I REALLY DON'T WANT TO INTERACT WITH OTHERS AND CREATE MORE MEMO-RIES...
...I SHOULD JUST STAY HOLED UP IN MY ROOM AND NOT GO TO SCHOOL, NO MATTER WHAT PEOPLE THINK.
BUT I DON'T HAVE THE COURAGE TO DO THAT.

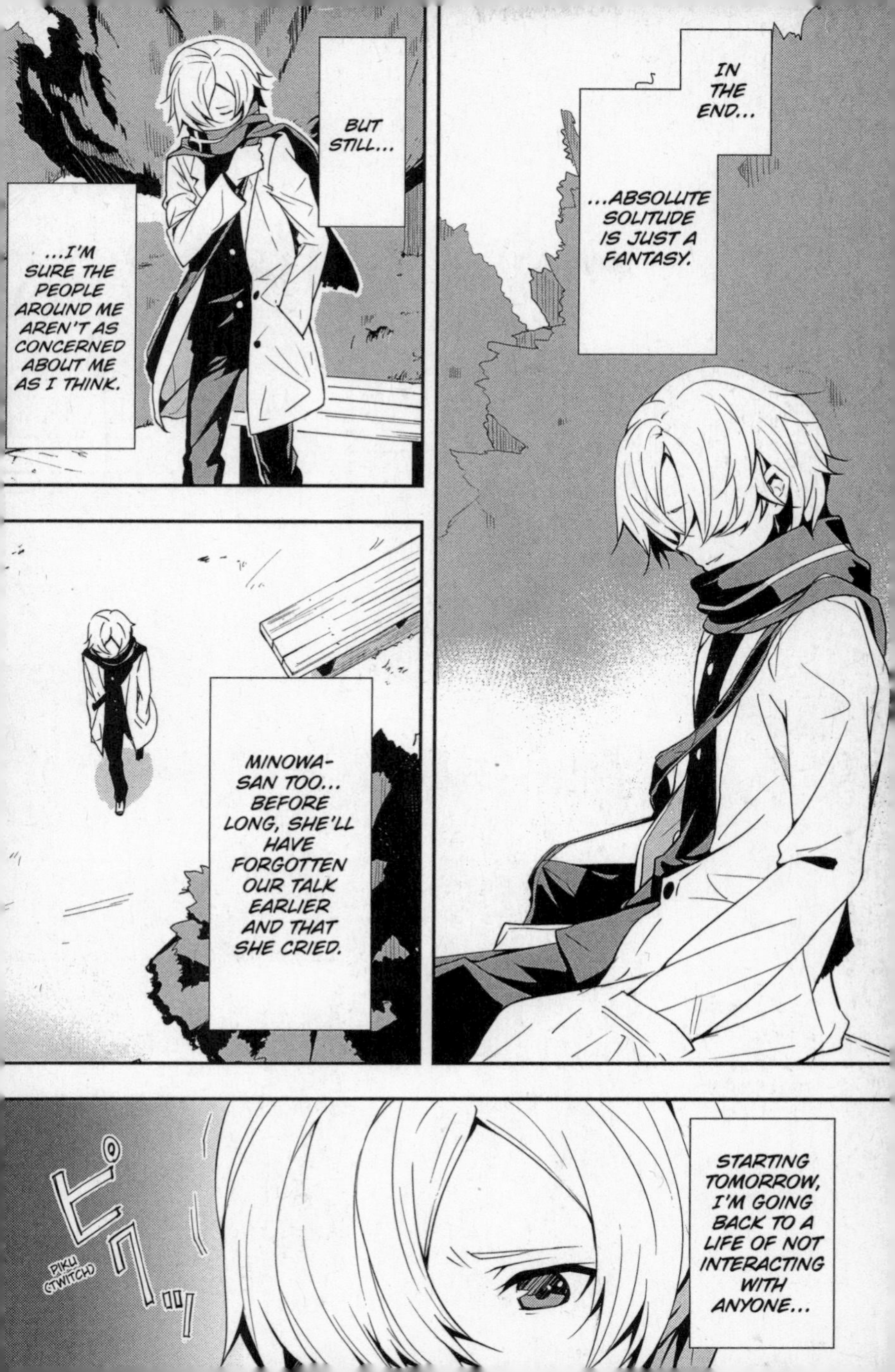
IN THE END...
...ABSOLUTE SOLITUDE IS JUST A FANTASY.
BUT STILL...
...I'M SURE THE PEOPLE AROUND ME AREN'T AS CONCERNED ABOUT ME AS I THINK.
MINOWA-SAN TOO... BEFORE LONG, SHE'LL HAVE FORGOTTEN OUR TALK EARLIER AND THAT SHE CRIED.
STARTING TOMORROW, I'M GOING BACK TO A LIFE OF NOT INTERACTING WITH ANYONE...
PIKU (TWITCH)

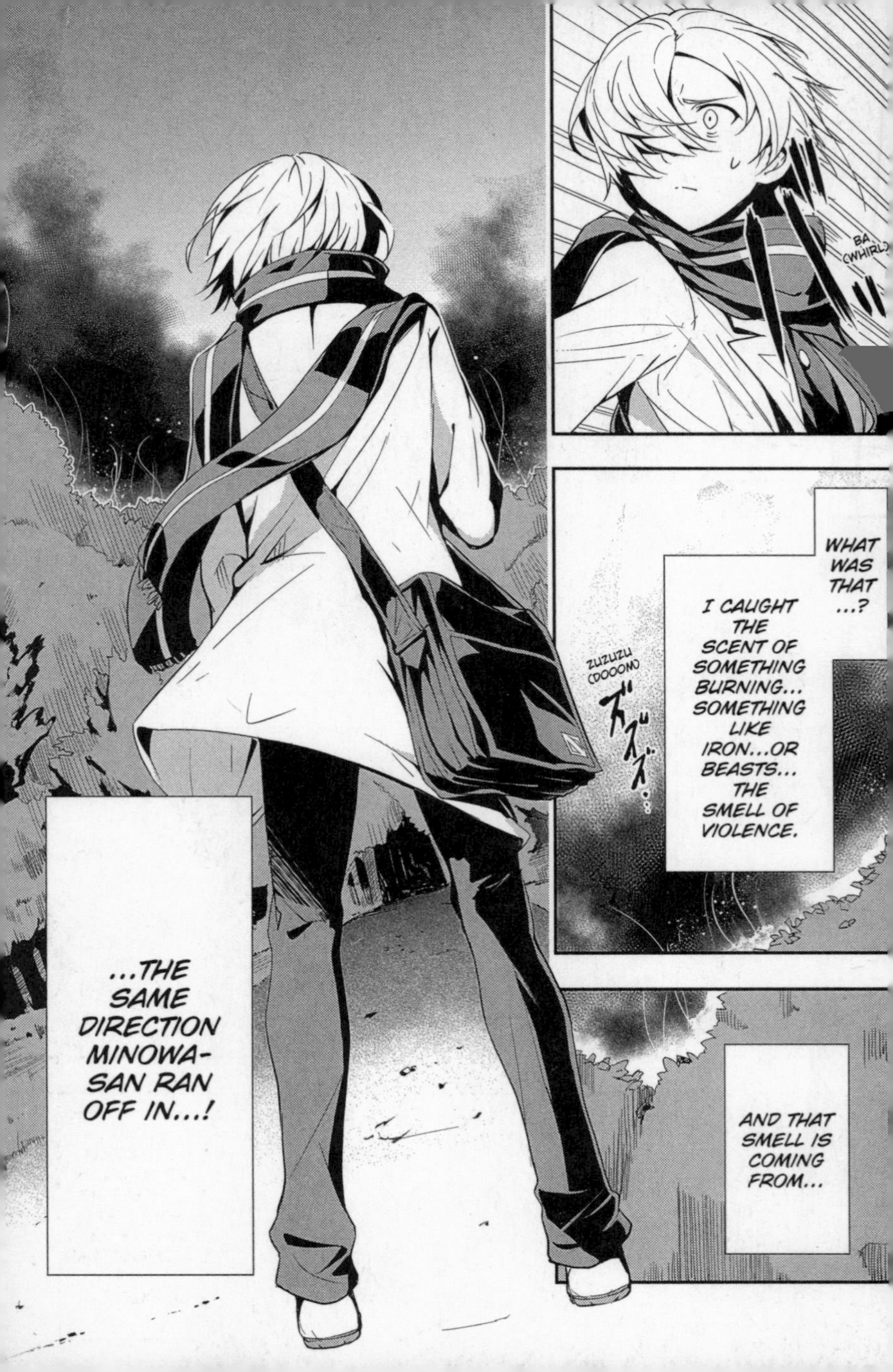
BA (WHIRL)
WHAT WAS THAT ...?
I CAUGHT THE SCENT OF SOMETHING BURNING... SOMETHING LIKE IRON...OR BEASTS... THE SMELL OF VIOLENCE.
ZUZUZU (DOOOM)
ズズズ...
AND THAT SMELL IS COMING FROM...
...THE SAME DIRECTION MINOWA-SAN RAN OFF IN...!

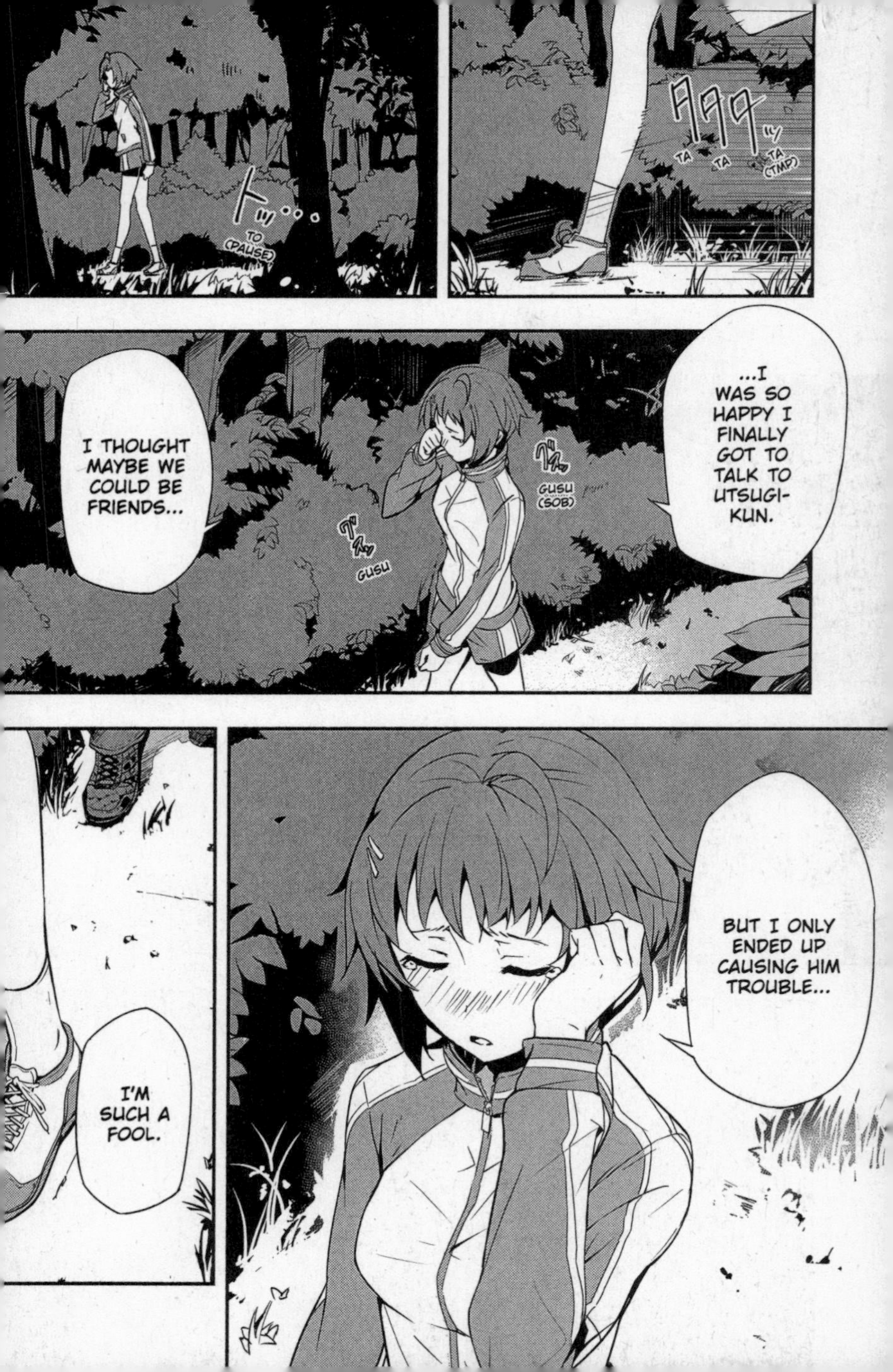

タタタッ
TA TA TA (TMP)
トッ…
TO (PAUSE)
...I WAS SO HAPPY I FINALLY GOT TO TALK TO UTSUGI-KUN.
グスッ
GUSU (SOB)
グスッ
GUSU
I THOUGHT MAYBE WE COULD BE FRIENDS...
BUT I ONLY ENDED UP CAUSING HIM TROUBLE...
I'M SUCH A FOOL.

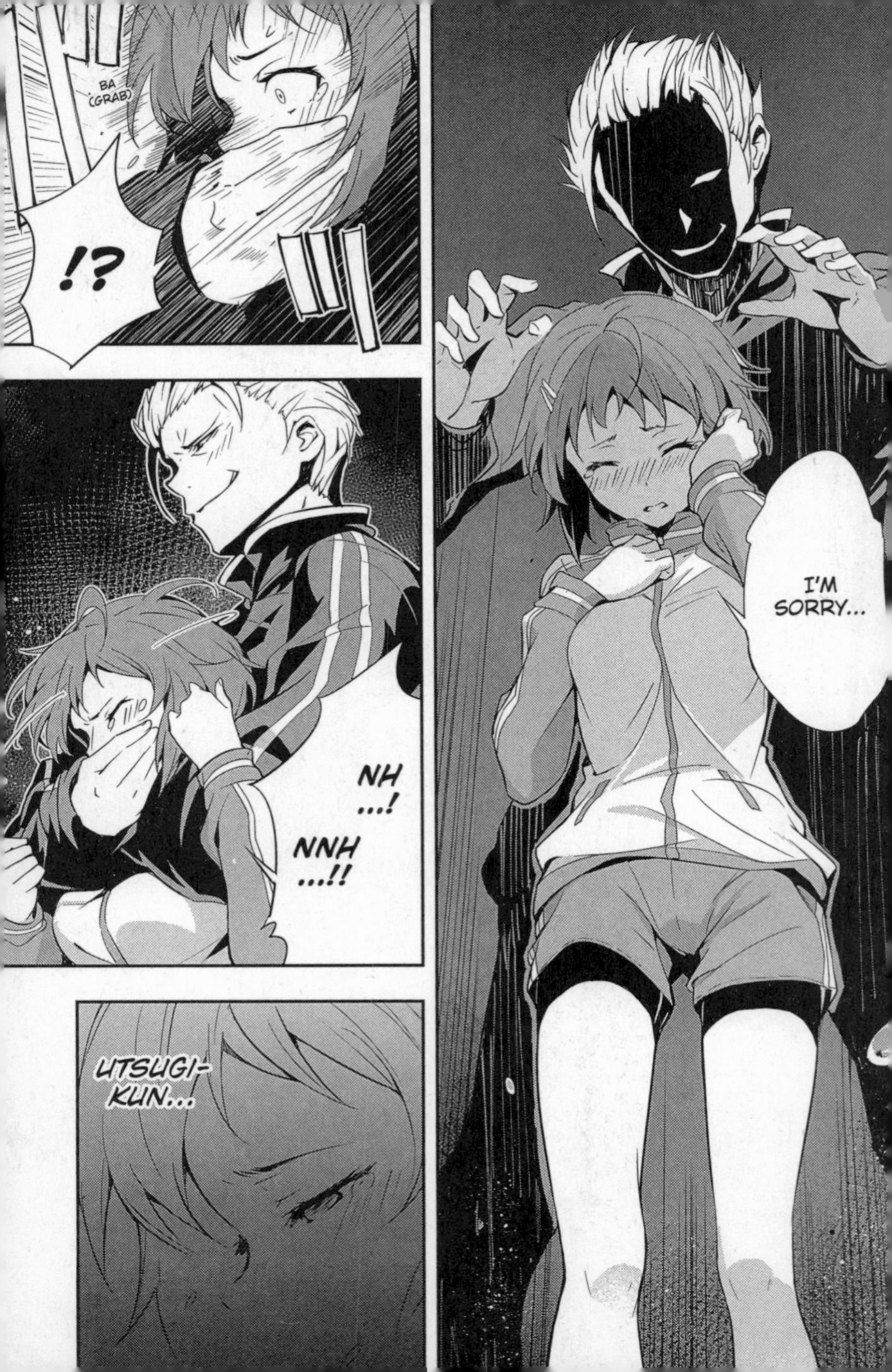
I'M SORRY...
BA (GRAB)
!?
NH ...!
NNH ...!!
UTSUGI-KUN...

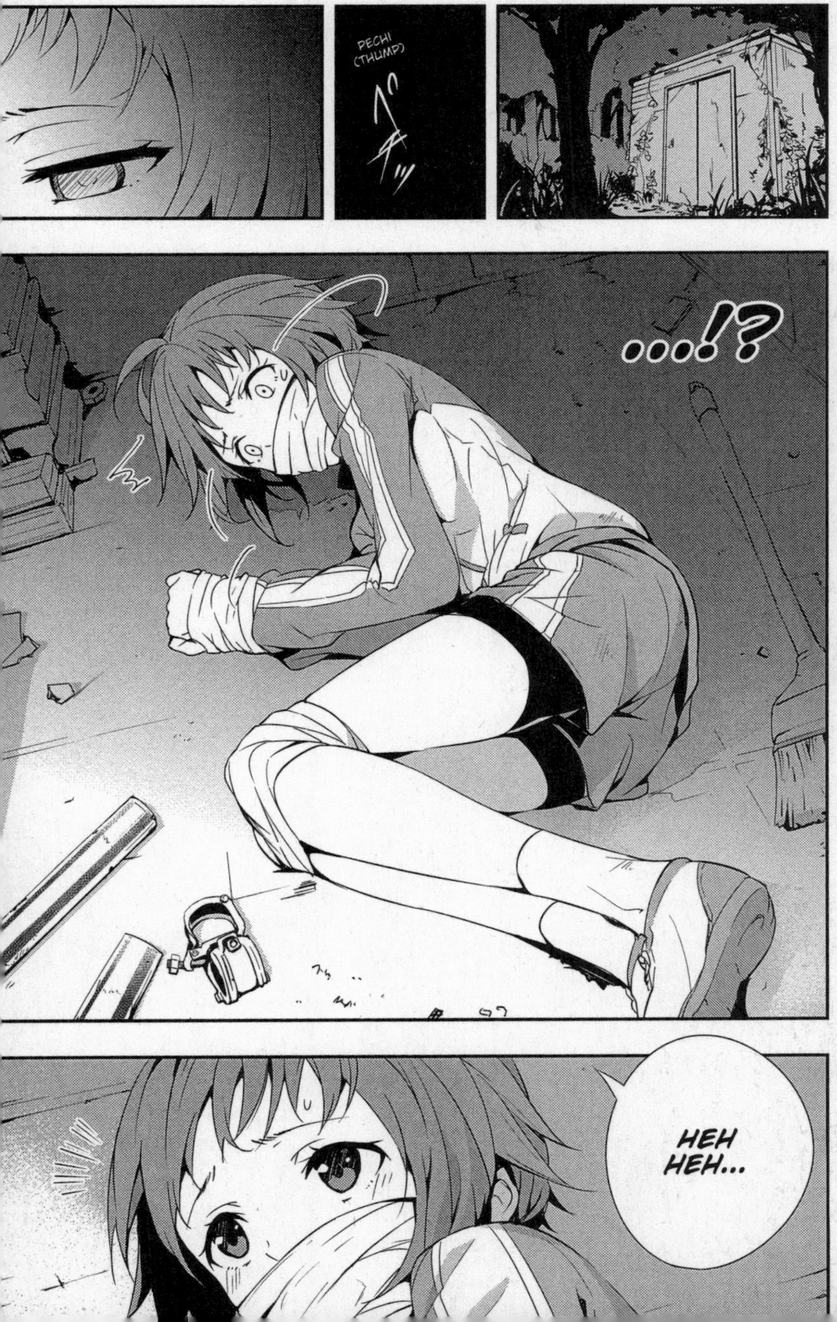
PECHI (THUMP)
...!?
HEH HEH...

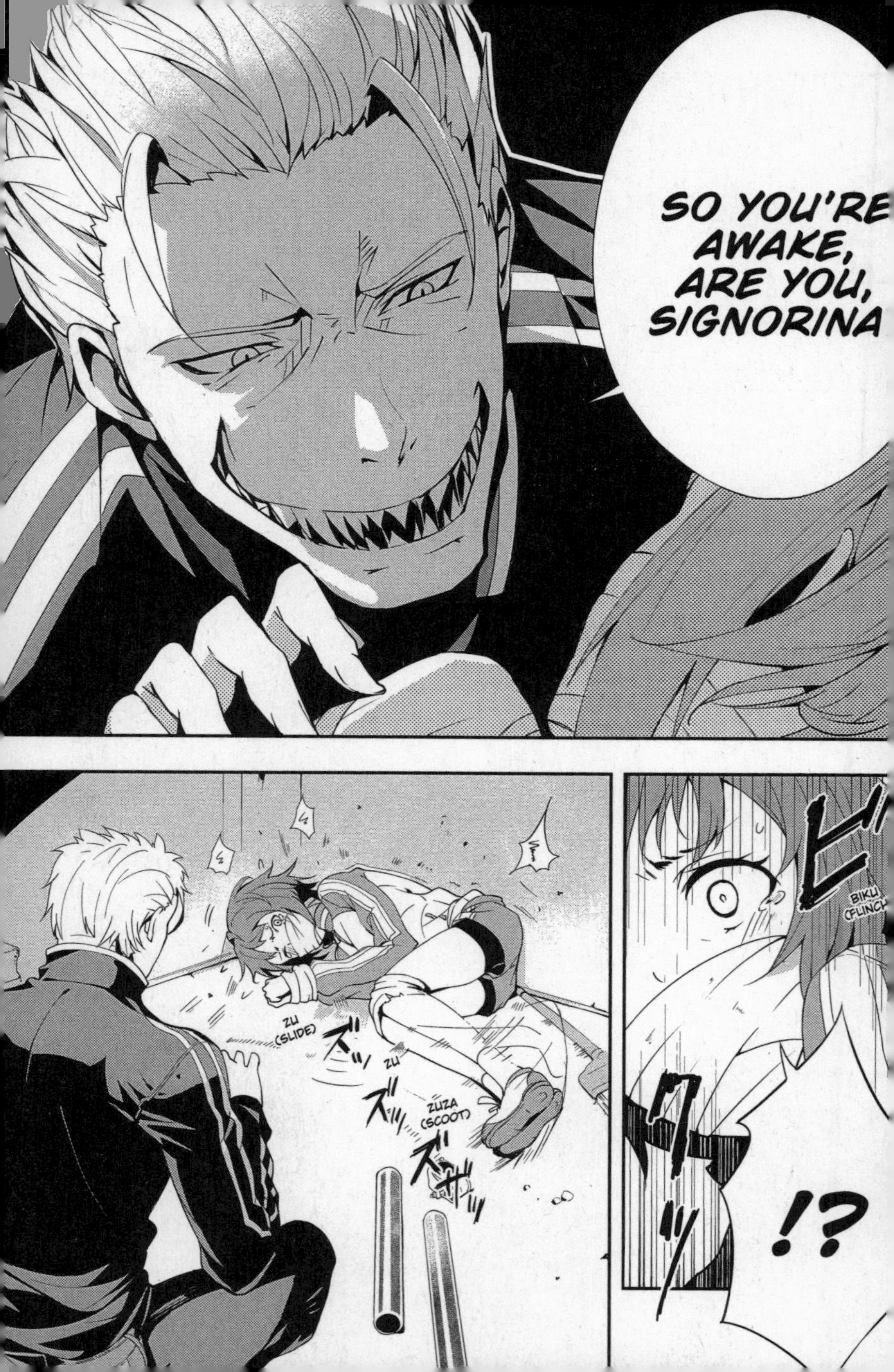
SO YOU'RE AWAKE, ARE YOU, SIGNORINA
BIKU (FLINCH
!?
ZU (SLIDE)
ZU
ZUZA (SCOOT)

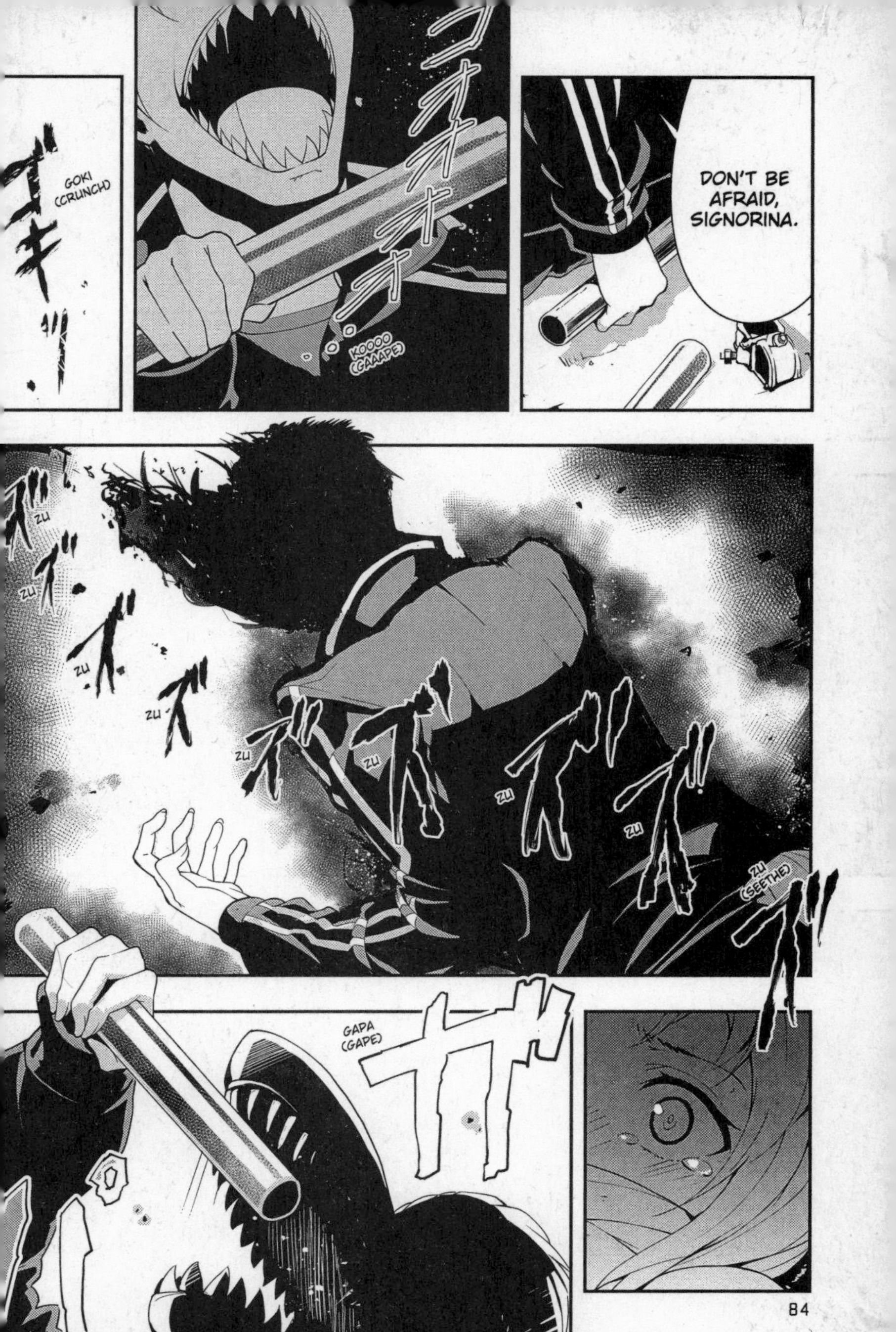
DON'T BE AFRAID, SIGNORINA.
KOOOO (GAAAPE)
GOKI (CRUNCH)
ZU
ZU
ZU
ZU
ZU
ZU
ZU
ZU
ZU (SEETHE)
GAPA (GAPE)

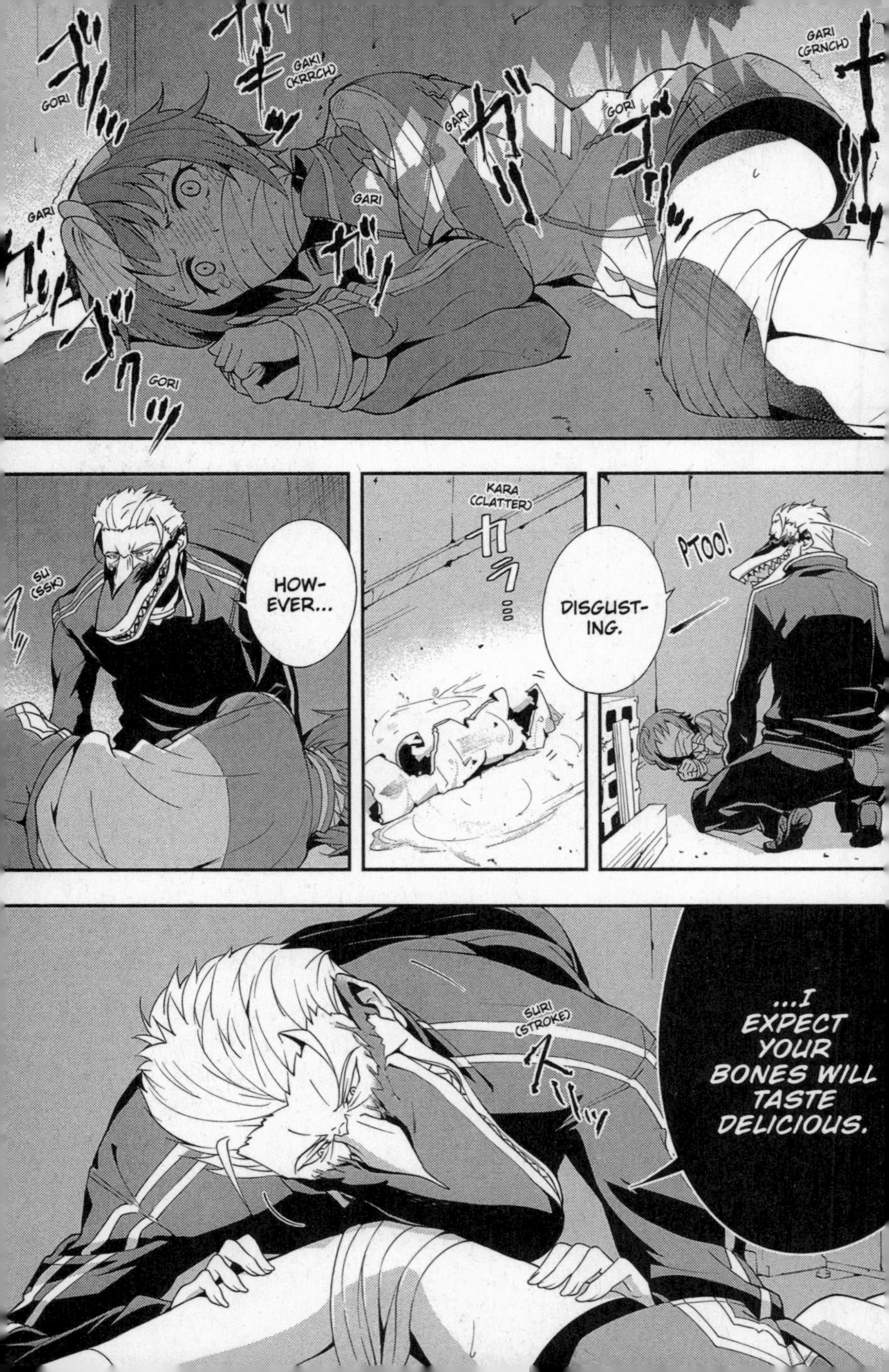
GARI (GRNCH)
GORI
GARI
GAKI (KRRCH)
GORI
GARI
GARI
GORI
PTOO!
DISGUST-ING.
KARA (CLATTER)
HOW-EVER...
SU (SSK)
...I EXPECT YOUR BONES WILL TASTE DELICIOUS.
SURI (STROKE)

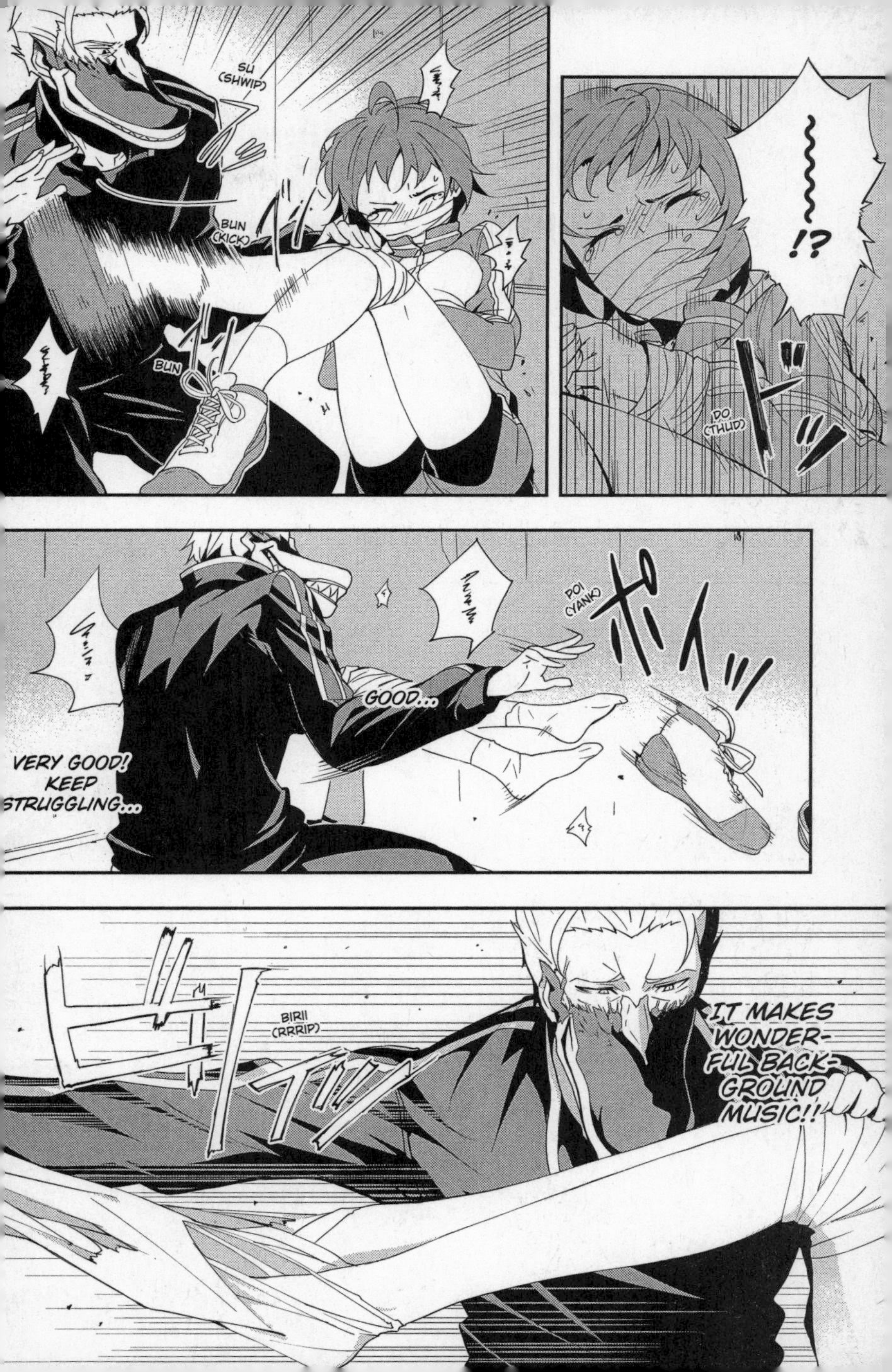

DO (THUD)
SU (SHWIP)
BUN (KICK)
BUN
POI (YANK)
GOOD...
VERY GOOD! KEEP STRUGGLING...
IT MAKES WONDER-FUL BACK-GROUND MUSIC!!
BIRII (RRRIP)

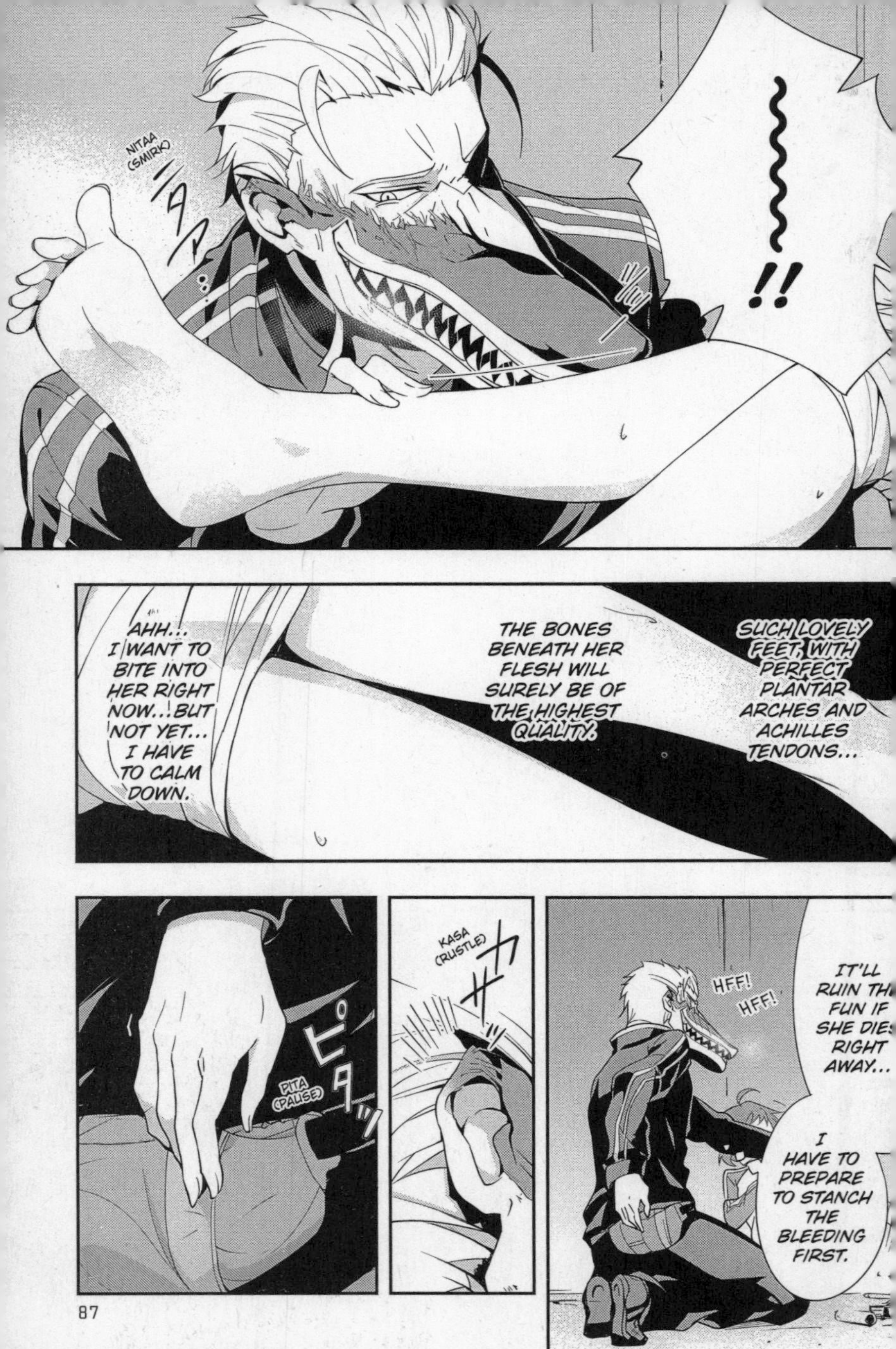

NITAA (SMIRK)
SUCH LOVELY FEET, WITH PERFECT PLANTAR ARCHES AND ACHILLES TENDONS...
THE BONES BENEATH HER FLESH WILL SURELY BE OF THE HIGHEST QUALITY.
AHH... I WANT TO BITE INTO HER RIGHT NOW...BUT NOT YET... I HAVE TO CALM DOWN.
IT'LL RUIN THE FUN IF SHE DIES RIGHT AWAY...
HFF! HFF!
I HAVE TO PREPARE TO STANCH THE BLEEDING FIRST.
KASA (RUSTLE)
PITA (PAUSE)

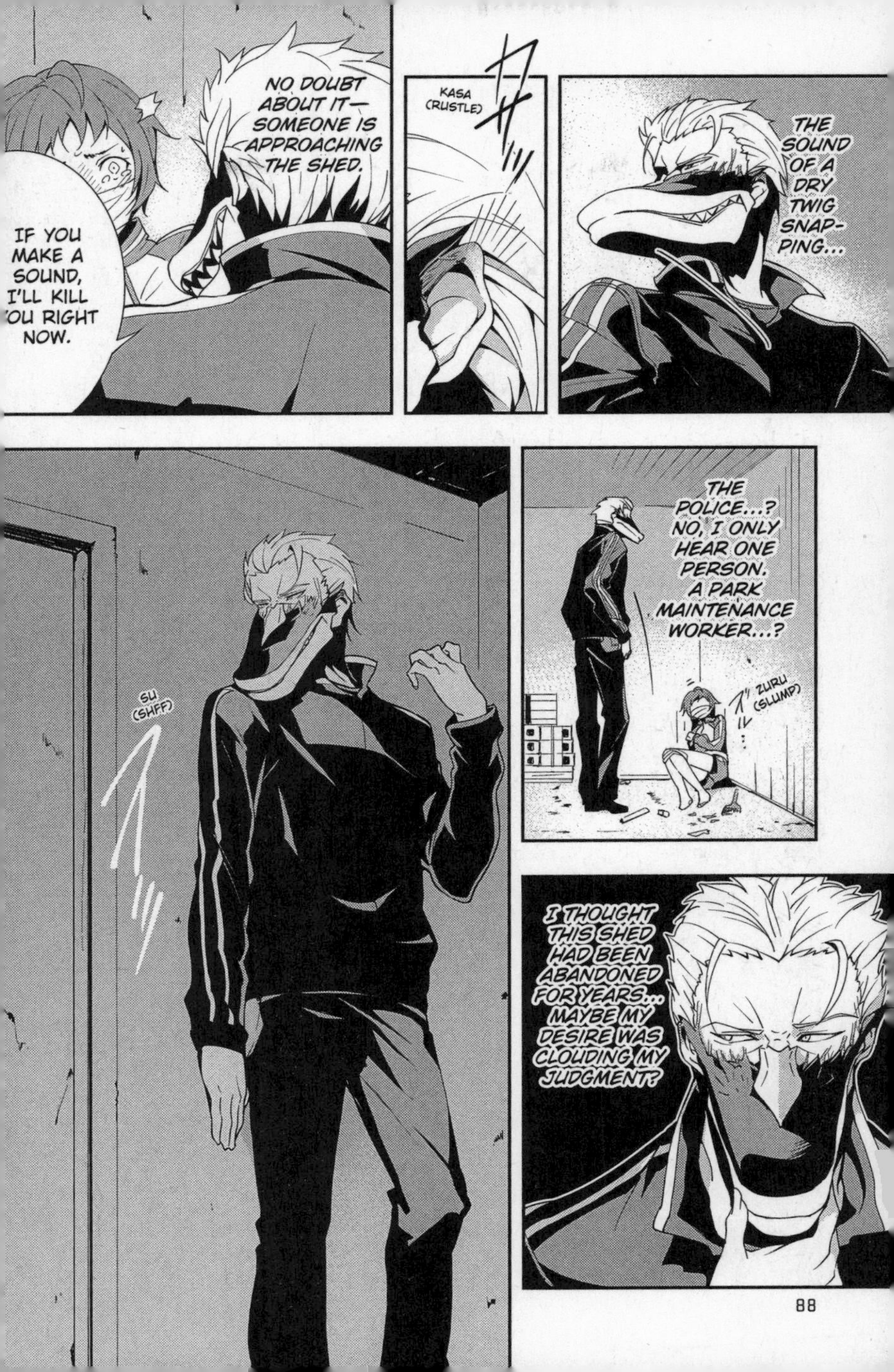
THE SOUND OF A DRY TWIG SNAPPING...
KASA (RUSTLE)
NO DOUBT ABOUT IT— SOMEONE IS APPROACHING THE SHED.
IF YOU MAKE A SOUND, I'LL KILL YOU RIGHT NOW.
THE POLICE...? NO, I ONLY HEAR ONE PERSON. A PARK MAINTENANCE WORKER...?
ZURU (SLUMP)
I THOUGHT THIS SHED HAD BEEN ABANDONED FOR YEARS... MAYBE MY DESIRE WAS CLOUDING MY JUDGMENT?
SU (SHFF)

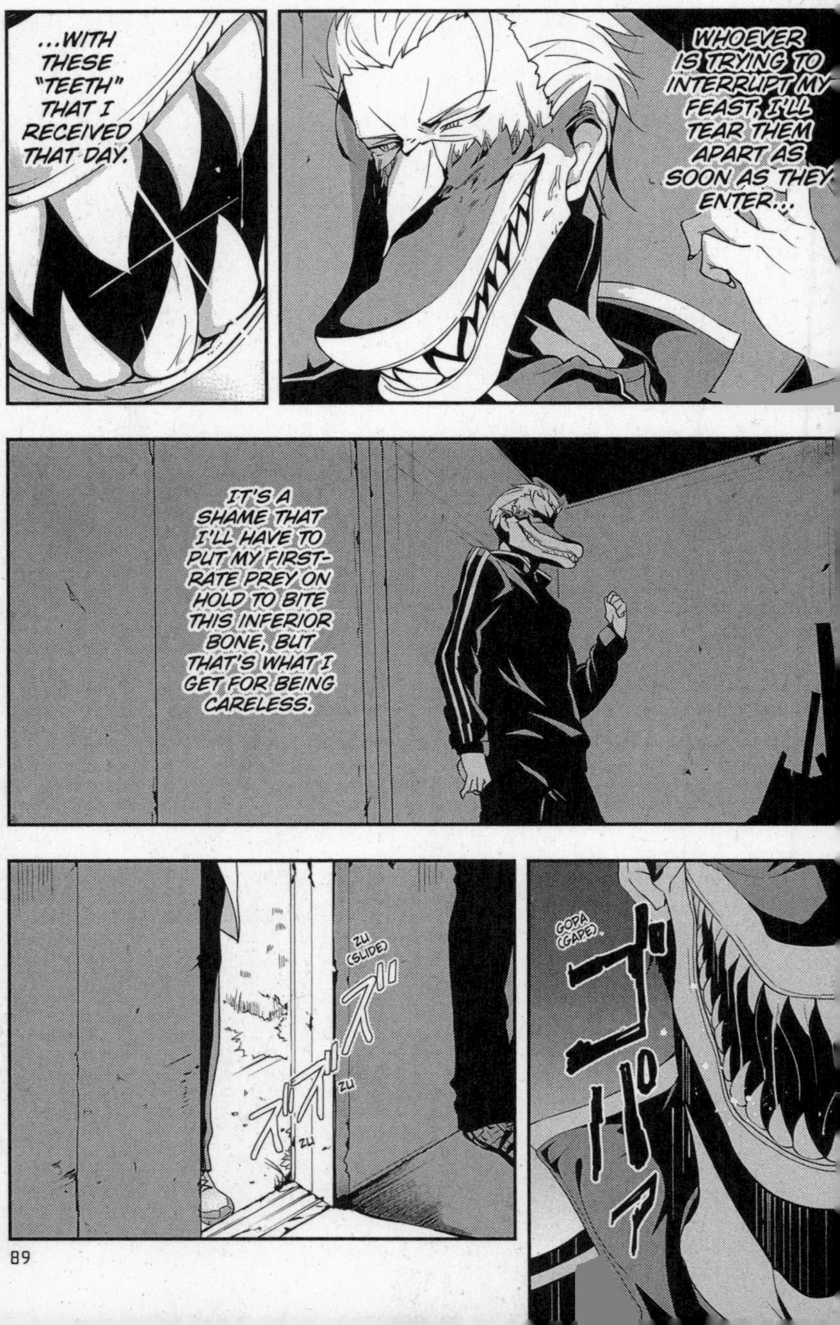
WHOEVER IS TRYING TO INTERRUPT MY FEAST, I'LL TEAR THEM APART AS SOON AS THEY ENTER...
...WITH THESE "TEETH" THAT I RECEIVED THAT DAY.
IT'S A SHAME THAT I'LL HAVE TO PUT MY FIRST-RATE PREY ON HOLD TO BITE THIS INFERIOR BONE, BUT THAT'S WHAT I GET FOR BEING CARELESS.
GOPA (GAPE)
ゴパァ
ZU (SLIDE)
ズ
ZU
ズ
ZU
ズ

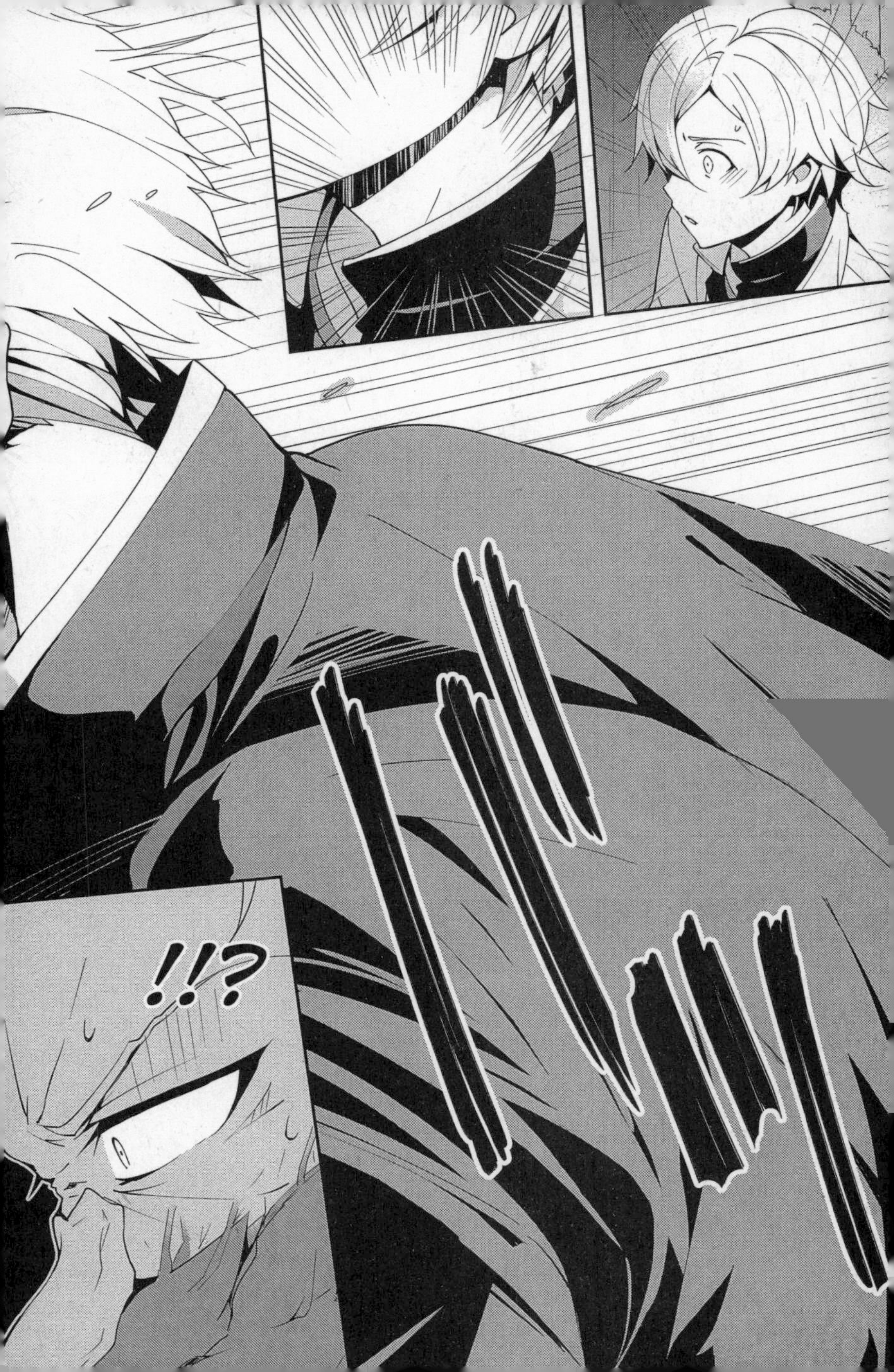
!!?

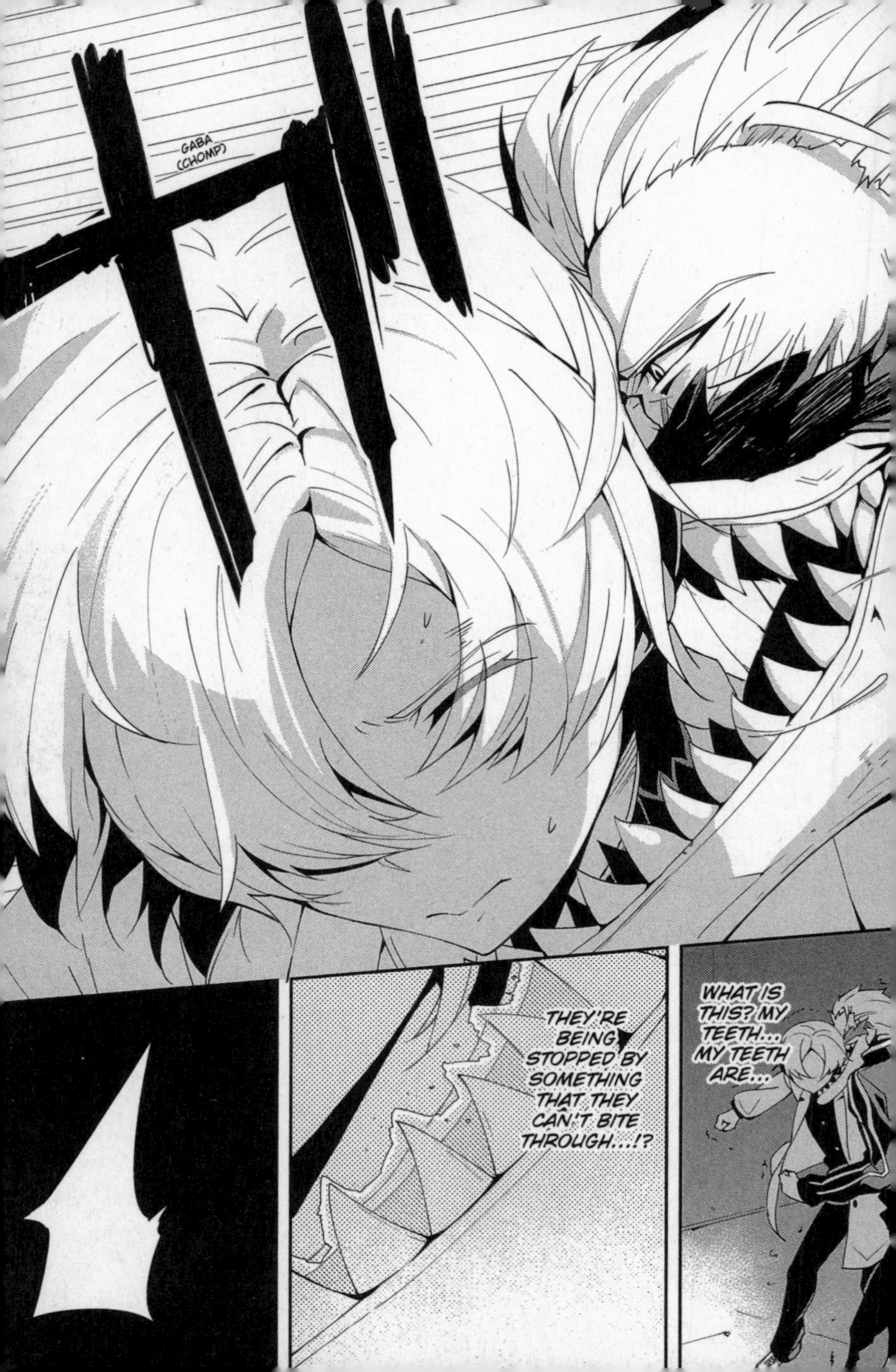
GABA (CHOMP)
WHAT IS THIS? MY TEETH... MY TEETH ARE...
THEY'RE BEING STOPPED BY SOMETHING THAT THEY CAN'T BITE THROUGH...!?

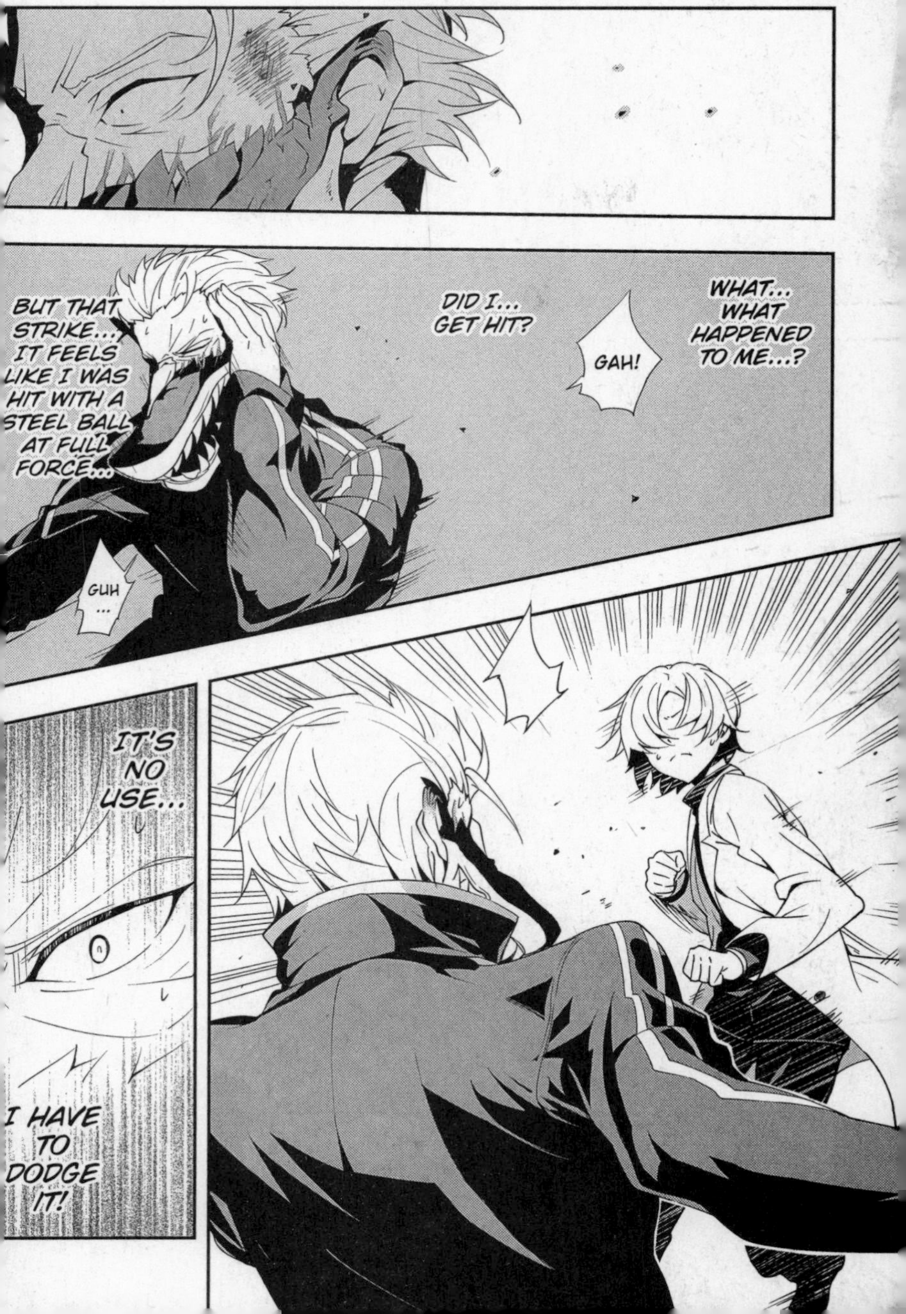
WHAT... WHAT HAPPENED TO ME...?
GAH!
DID I... GET HIT?
BUT THAT STRIKE... IT FEELS LIKE I WAS HIT WITH A STEEL BALL AT FULL FORCE...
GUH ...
IT'S NO USE...
I HAVE TO DODGE IT!

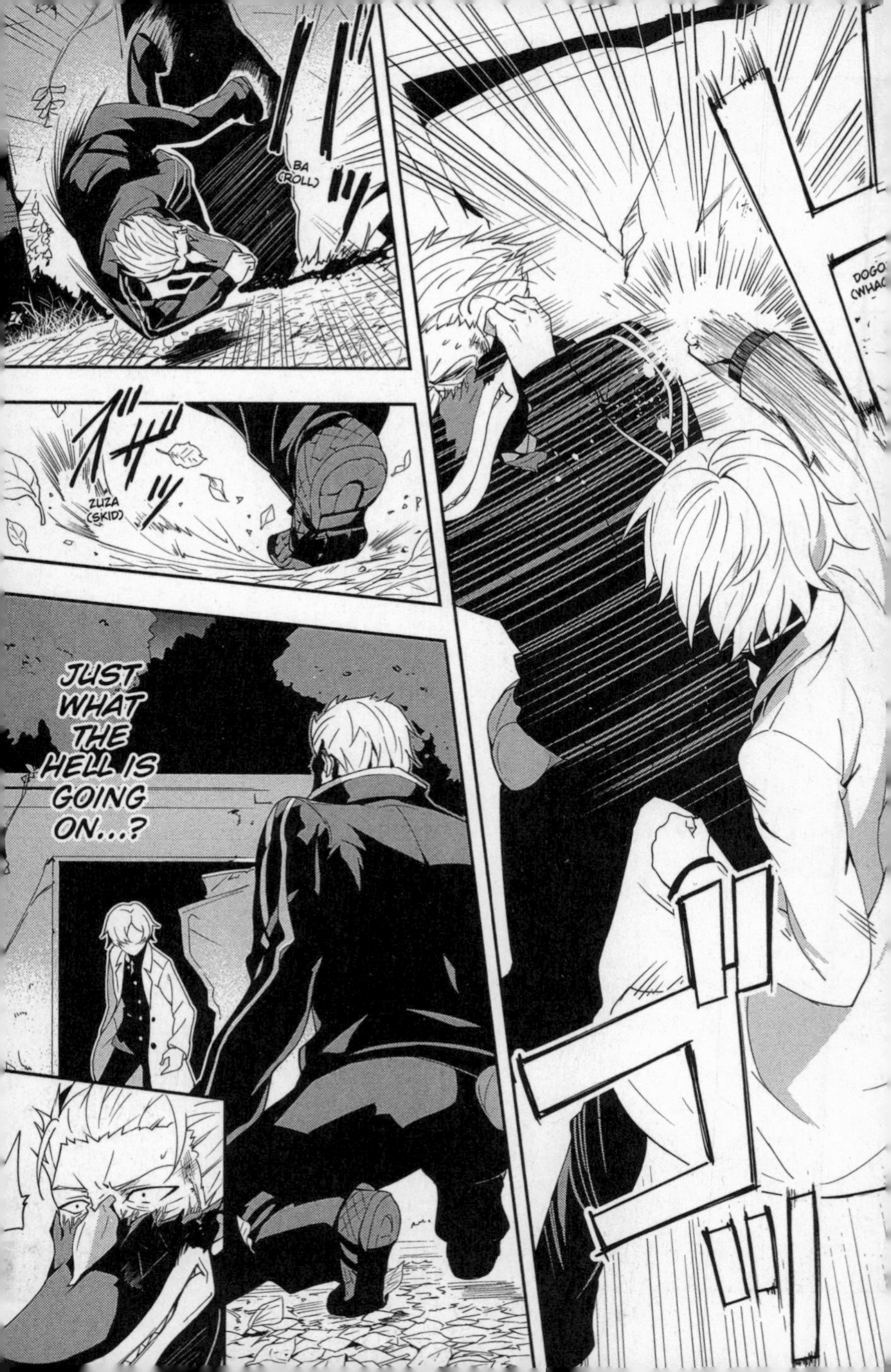
DOGO (WHAC
BA (ROLL)
ZUZA (SKID)
JUST WHAT THE HELL IS GOING ON...?

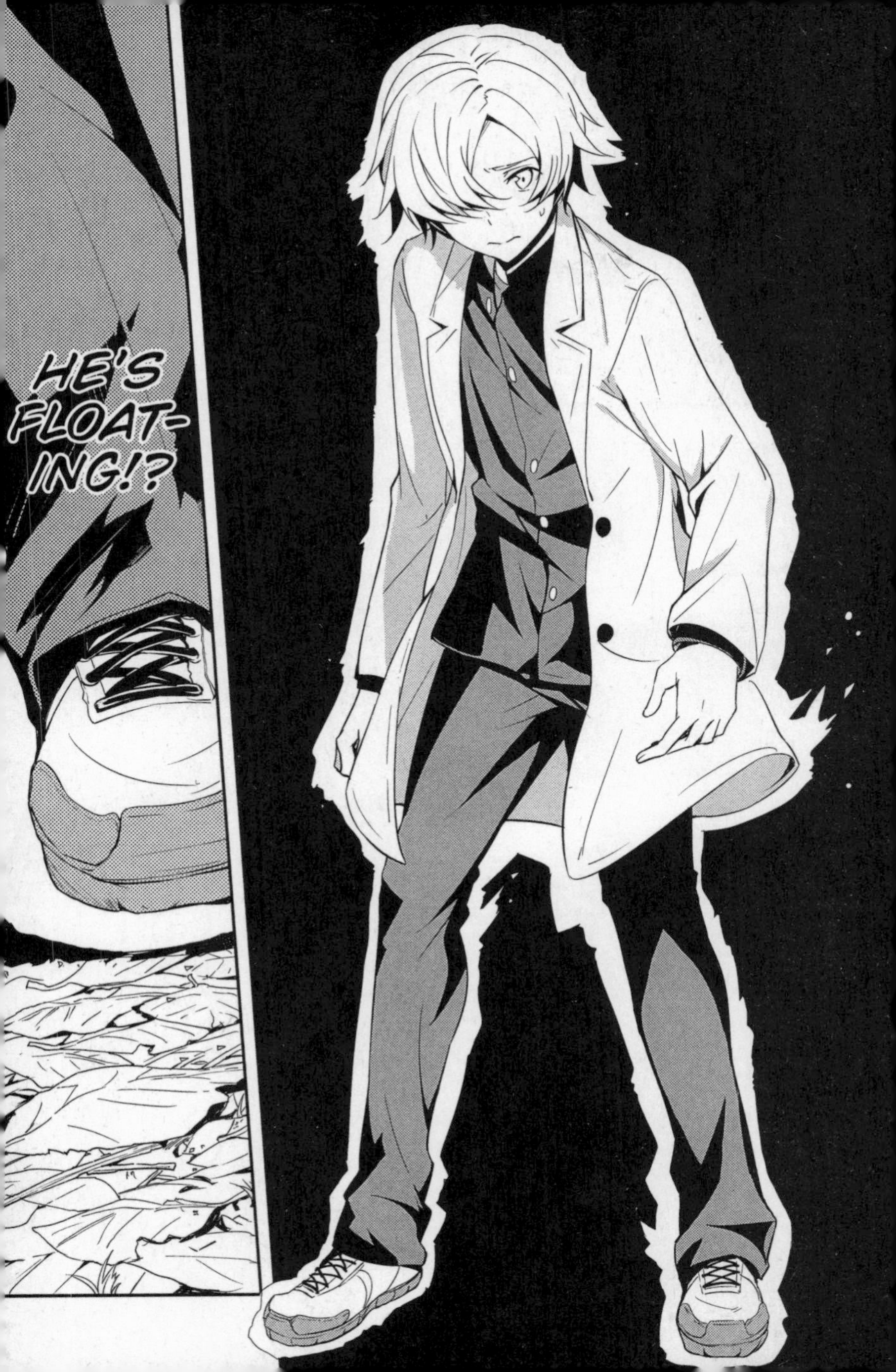
HE'S FLOAT-ING!?

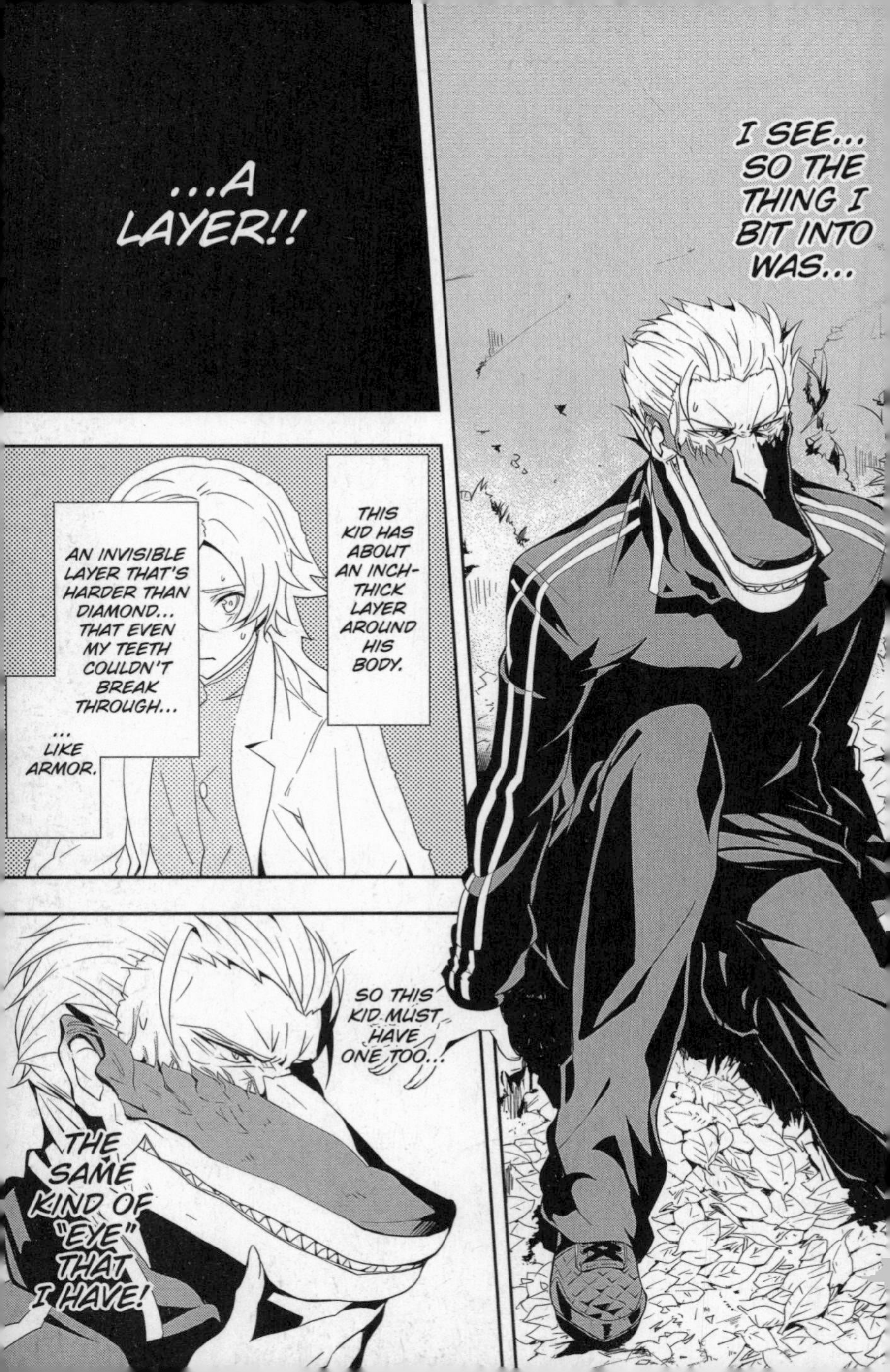
I SEE... SO THE THING I BIT INTO WAS...
...A LAYER!!
THIS KID HAS ABOUT AN INCH-THICK LAYER AROUND HIS BODY.
AN INVISIBLE LAYER THAT'S HARDER THAN DIAMOND... THAT EVEN MY TEETH COULDN'T BREAK THROUGH...
...LIKE ARMOR.
SO THIS KID MUST HAVE ONE TOO...
THE SAME KIND OF "EYE" THAT I HAVE!

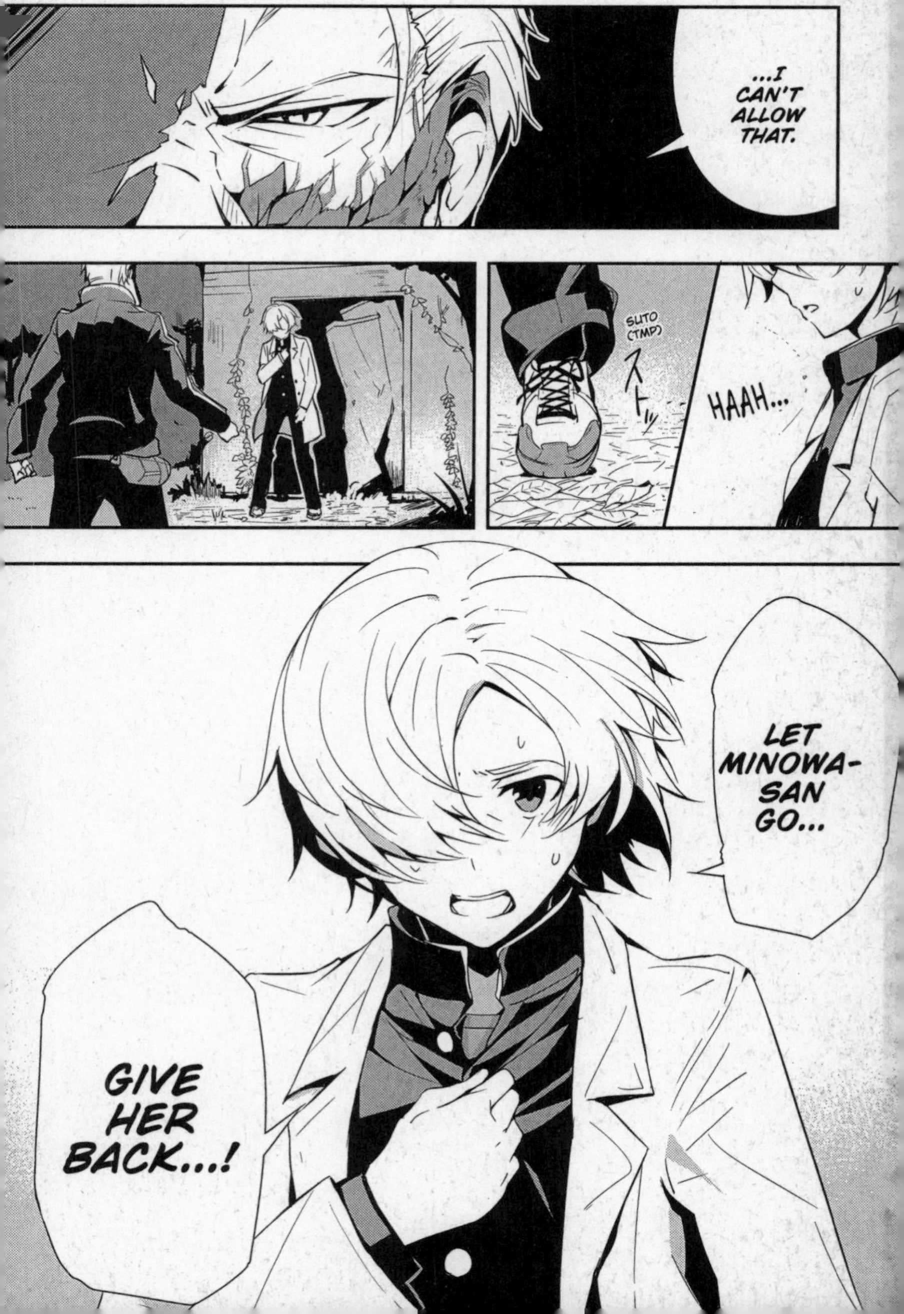
...I CAN'T ALLOW THAT.
HAAH...
SUTO (TMP)
スト
LET MINOWA-SAN GO...
GIVE HER BACK...!

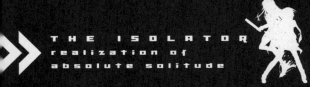

THE ISOLATOR
realization of
absolute solitude

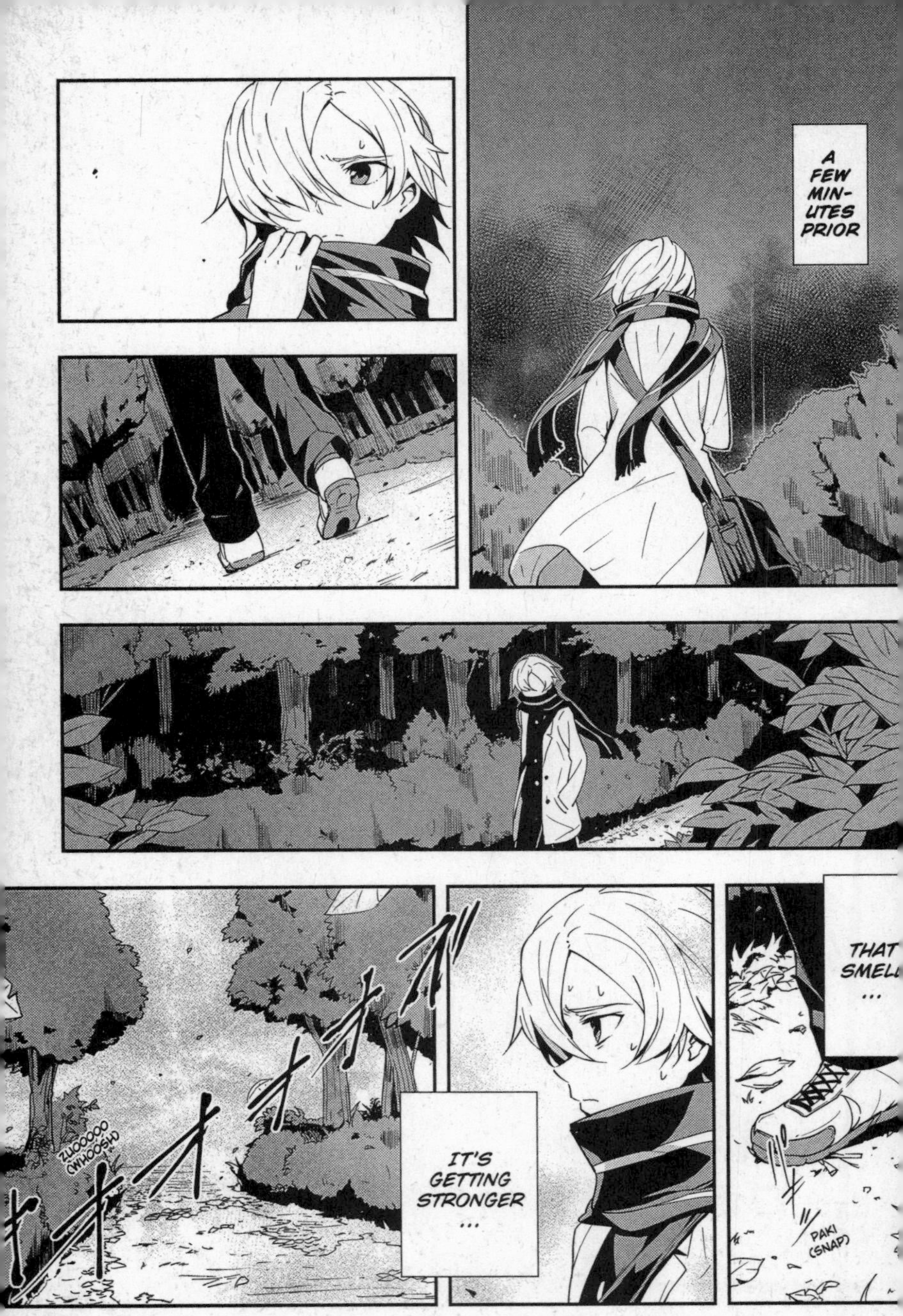
A FEW MIN-UTES PRIOR
THAT SMELL ...
PAKI (SNAP)
IT'S GETTING STRONGER ...
ZUOOOOO (WHOOSH)

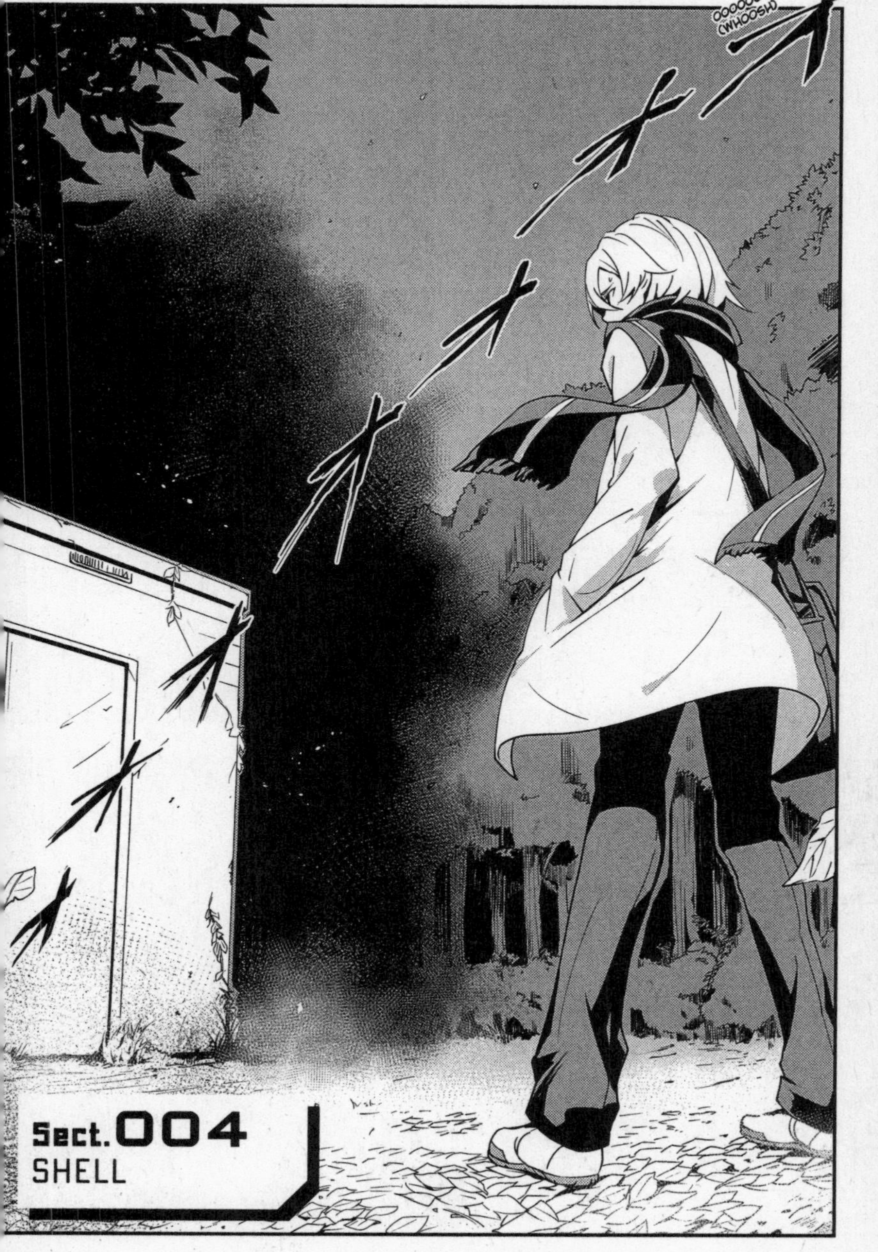
OOOOOOO
(WHOOSH)
Sect.004
SHELL

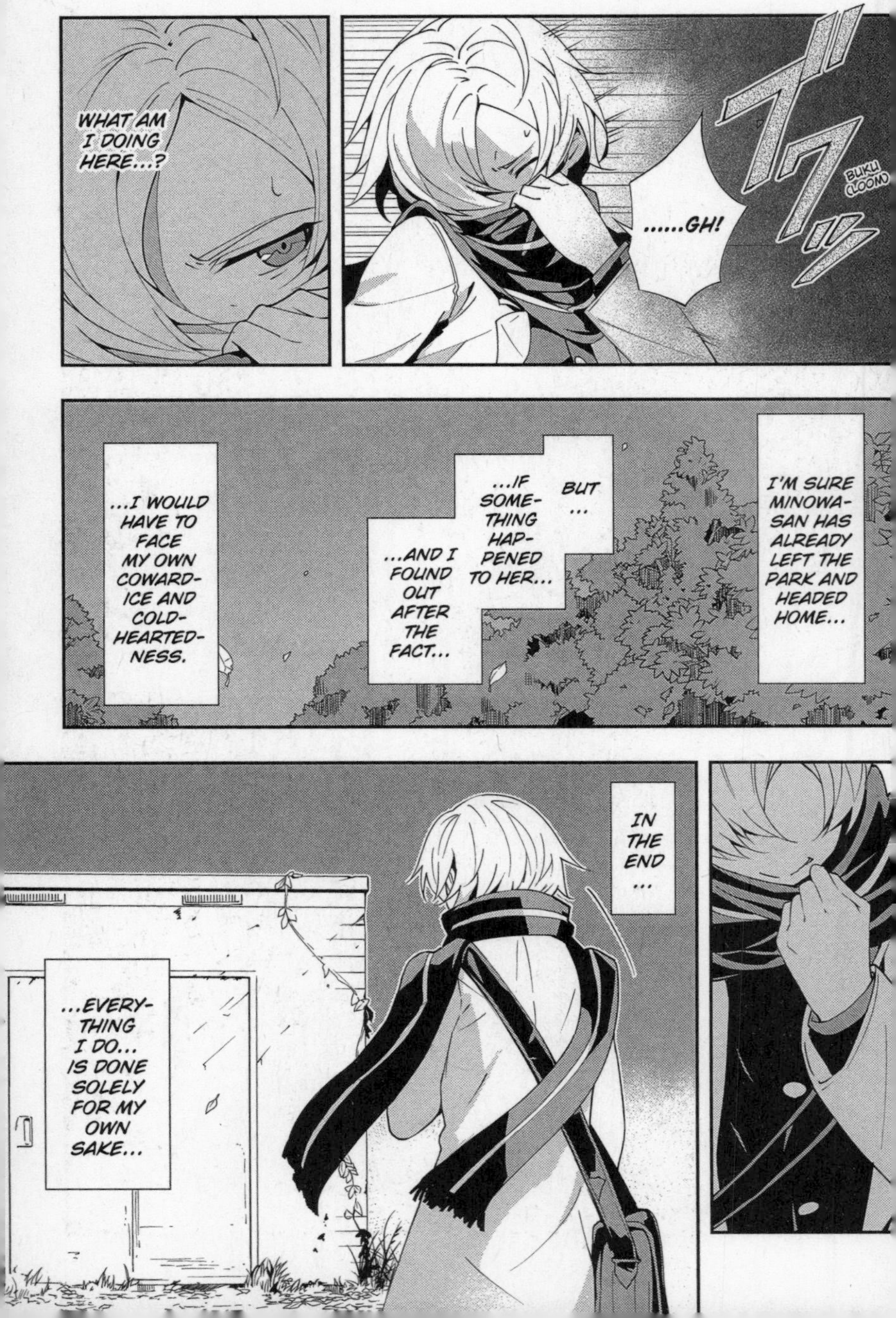
......GH!
BUKU (LOOM)
WHAT AM I DOING HERE...?
I'M SURE MINOWA-SAN HAS ALREADY LEFT THE PARK AND HEADED HOME...
BUT...
...IF SOMETHING HAPPENED TO HER...
...AND I FOUND OUT AFTER THE FACT...
...I WOULD HAVE TO FACE MY OWN COWARDICE AND COLD-HEARTEDNESS.
IN THE END...
...EVERYTHING I DO... IS DONE SOLELY FOR MY OWN SAKE...

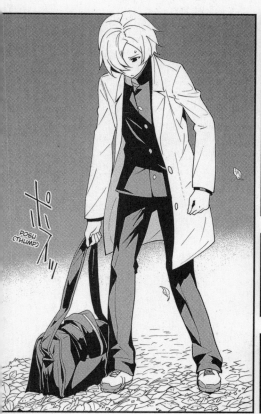

POSU
(THUMP)

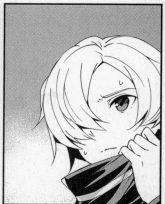

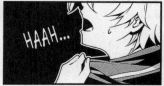

HAAH...

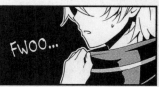

FWOO...

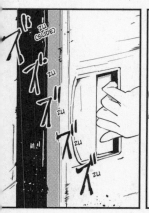

ZU
(SLIDE)

ZU

ZU

ZU

ZU

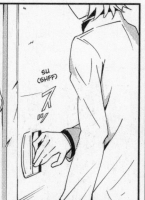

SU
(SHFF)

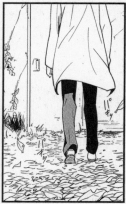

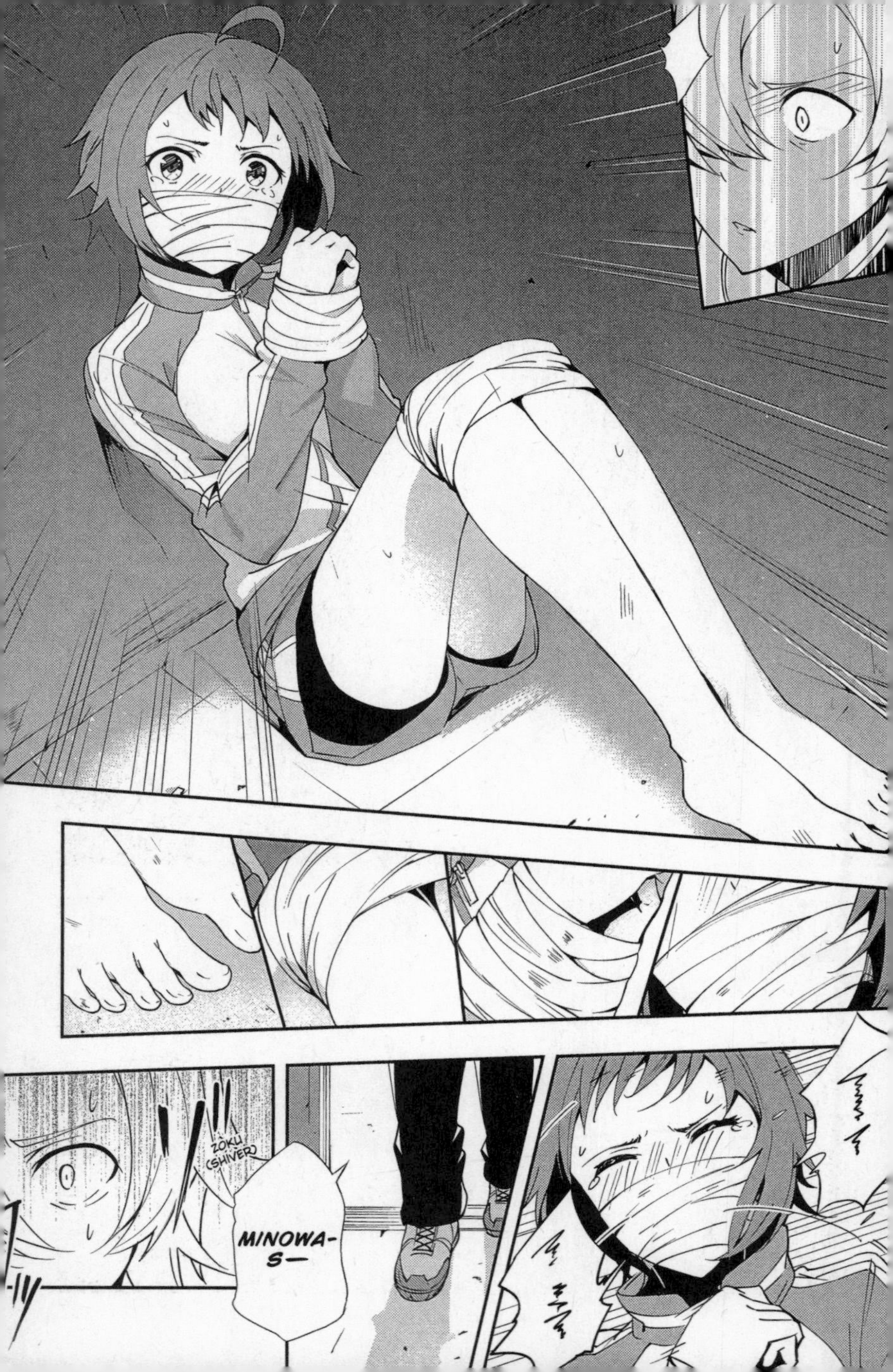
ZOKU (SHIVER)
MINOWA-S—

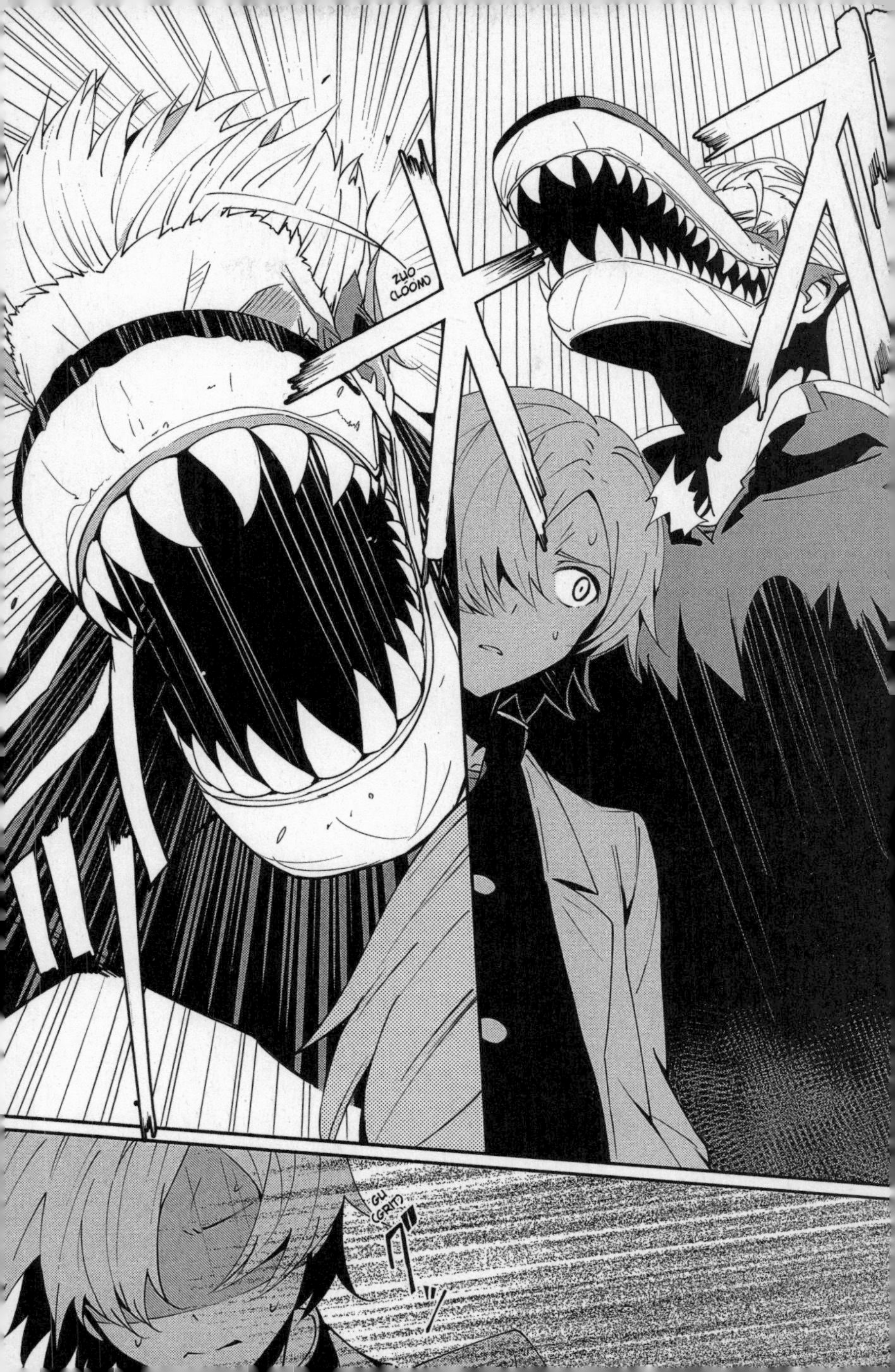
ZUO
(LOOM)
GU
(GRIT)

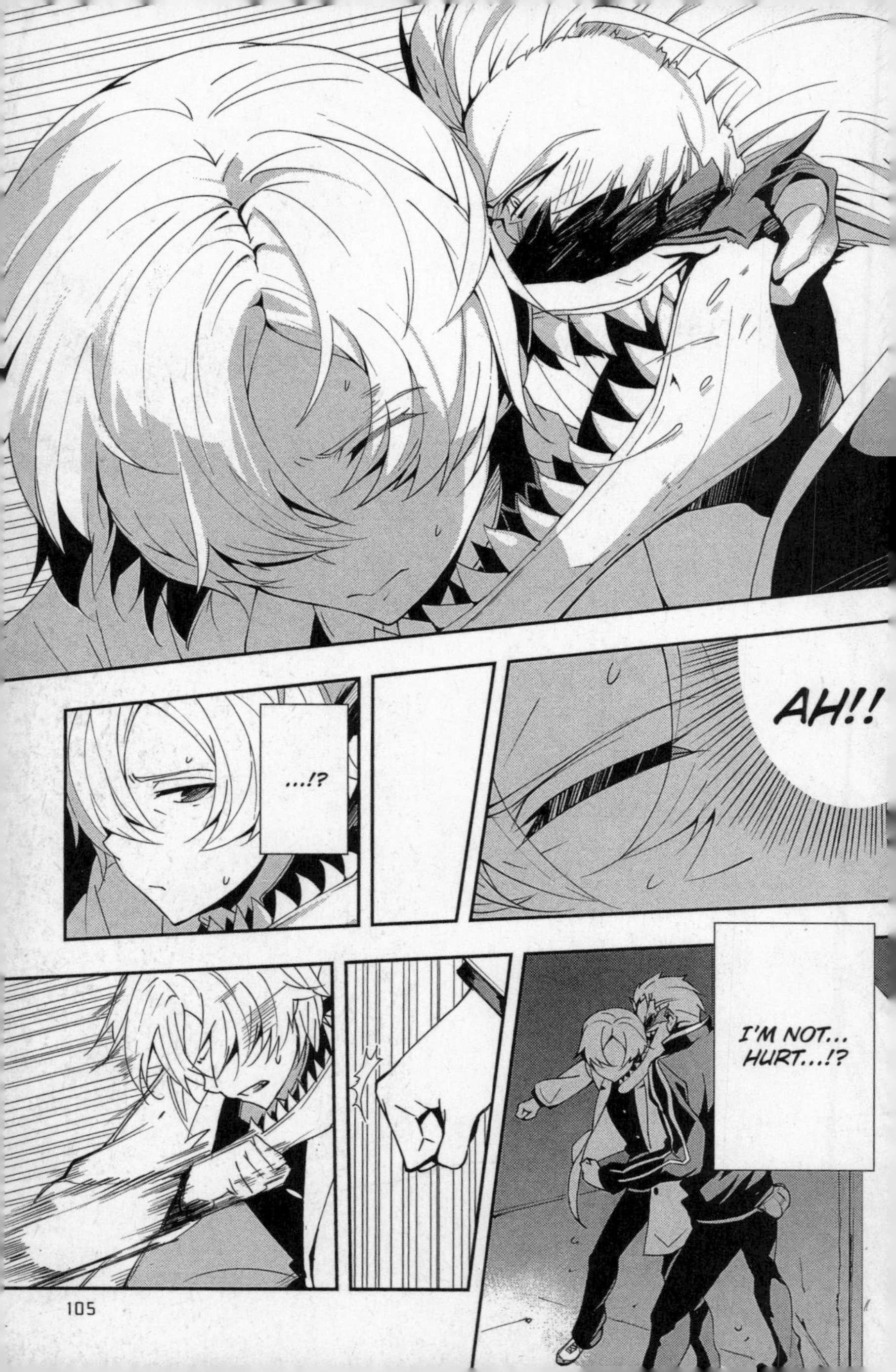
AH!!
...!?
I'M NOT... HURT...!?

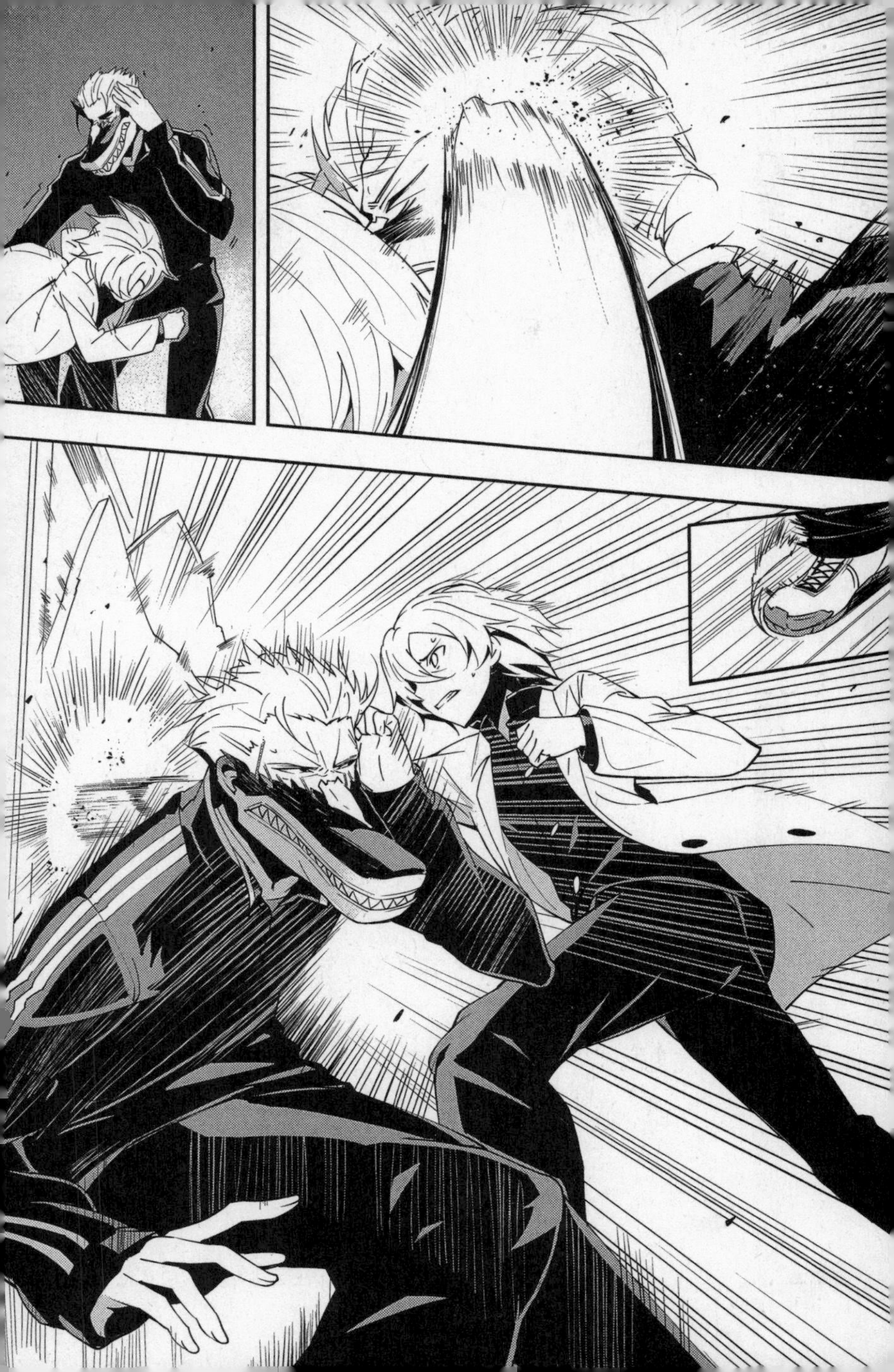

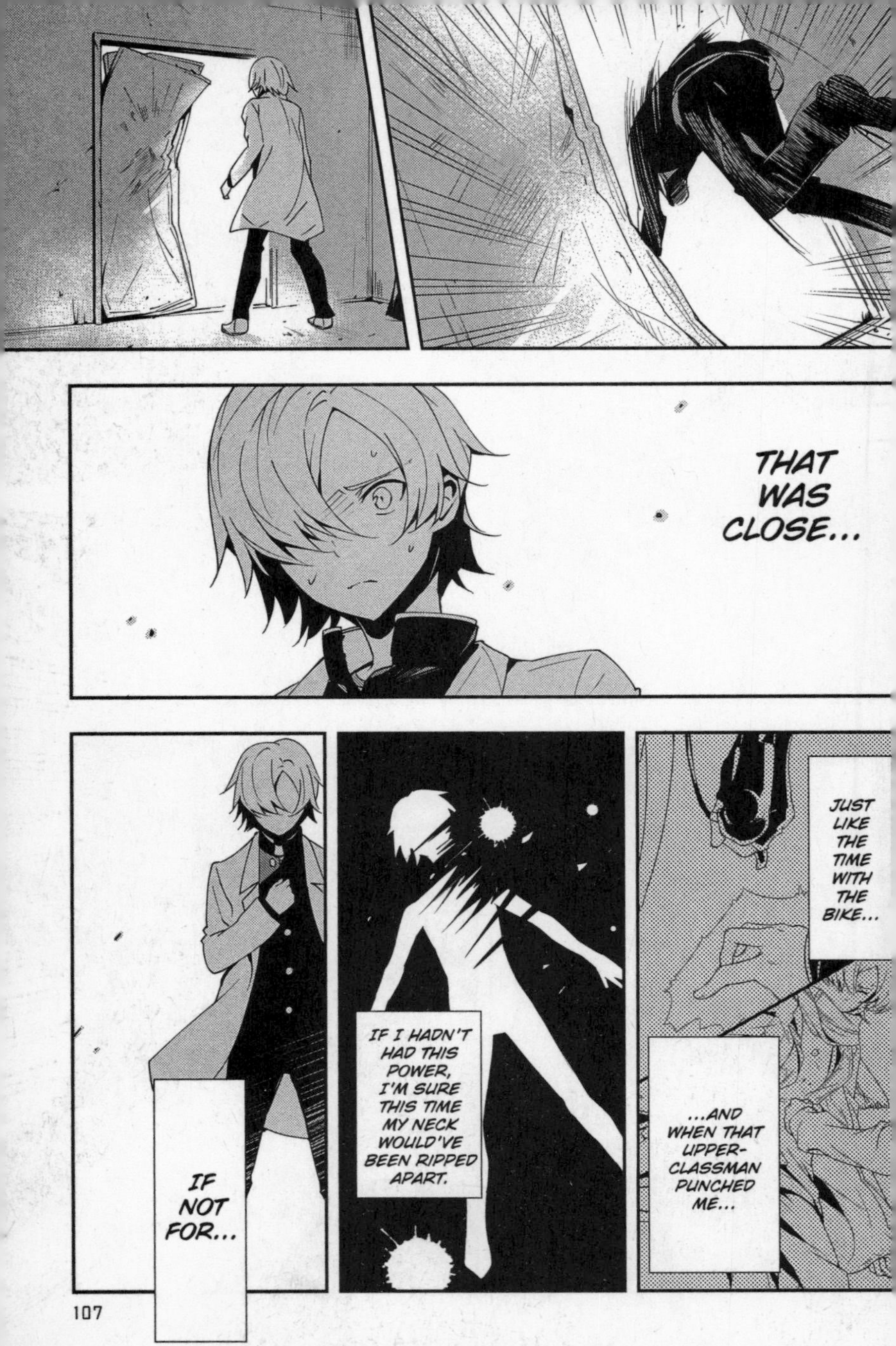
THAT WAS CLOSE...
JUST LIKE THE TIME WITH THE BIKE...
...AND WHEN THAT UPPER-CLASSMAN PUNCHED ME...
IF I HADN'T HAD THIS POWER, I'M SURE THIS TIME MY NECK WOULD'VE BEEN RIPPED APART.
IF NOT FOR...

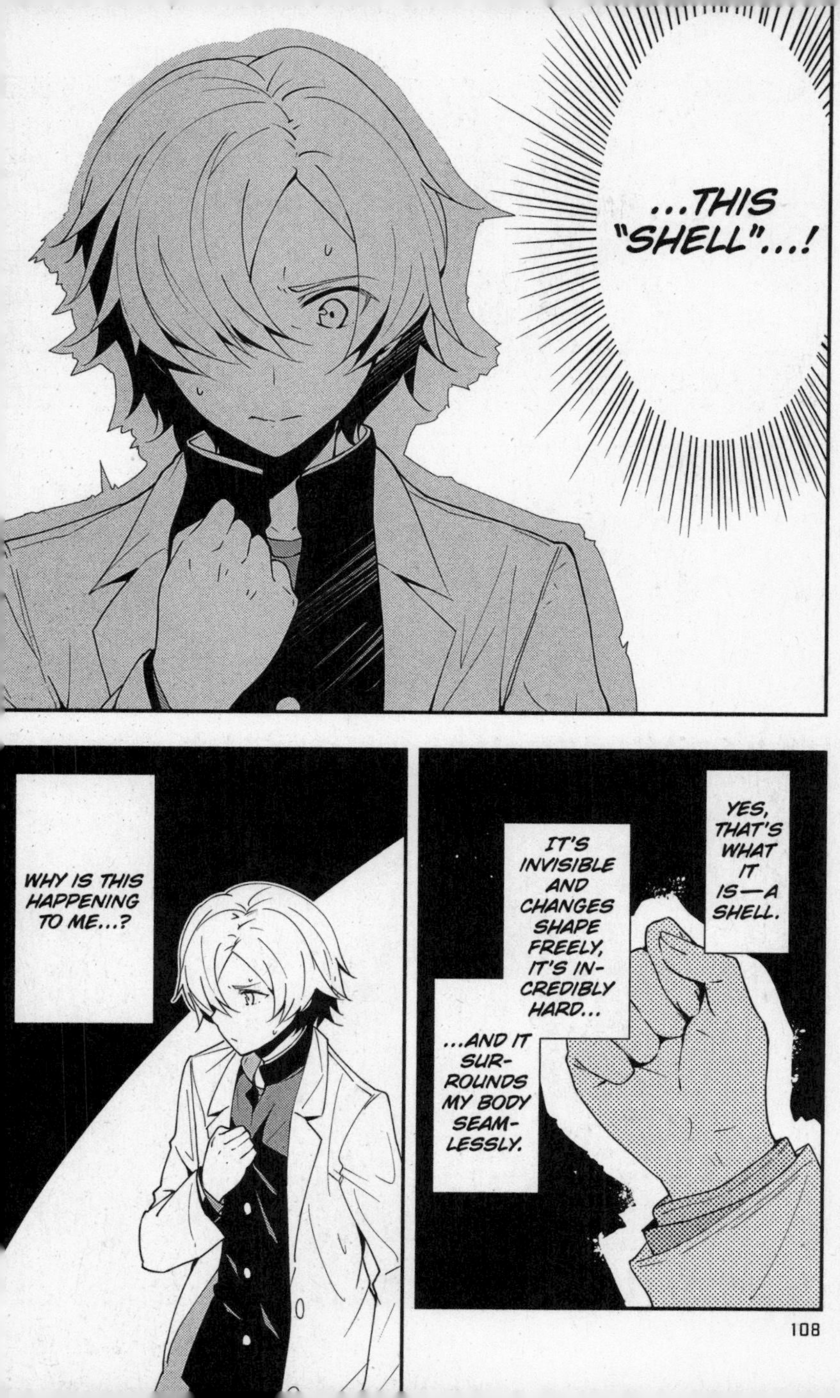
...THIS "SHELL"...!
YES, THAT'S WHAT IT IS—A SHELL.
IT'S INVISIBLE AND CHANGES SHAPE FREELY, IT'S INCREDIBLY HARD...
...AND IT SURROUNDS MY BODY SEAMLESSLY.
WHY IS THIS HAPPENING TO ME...?

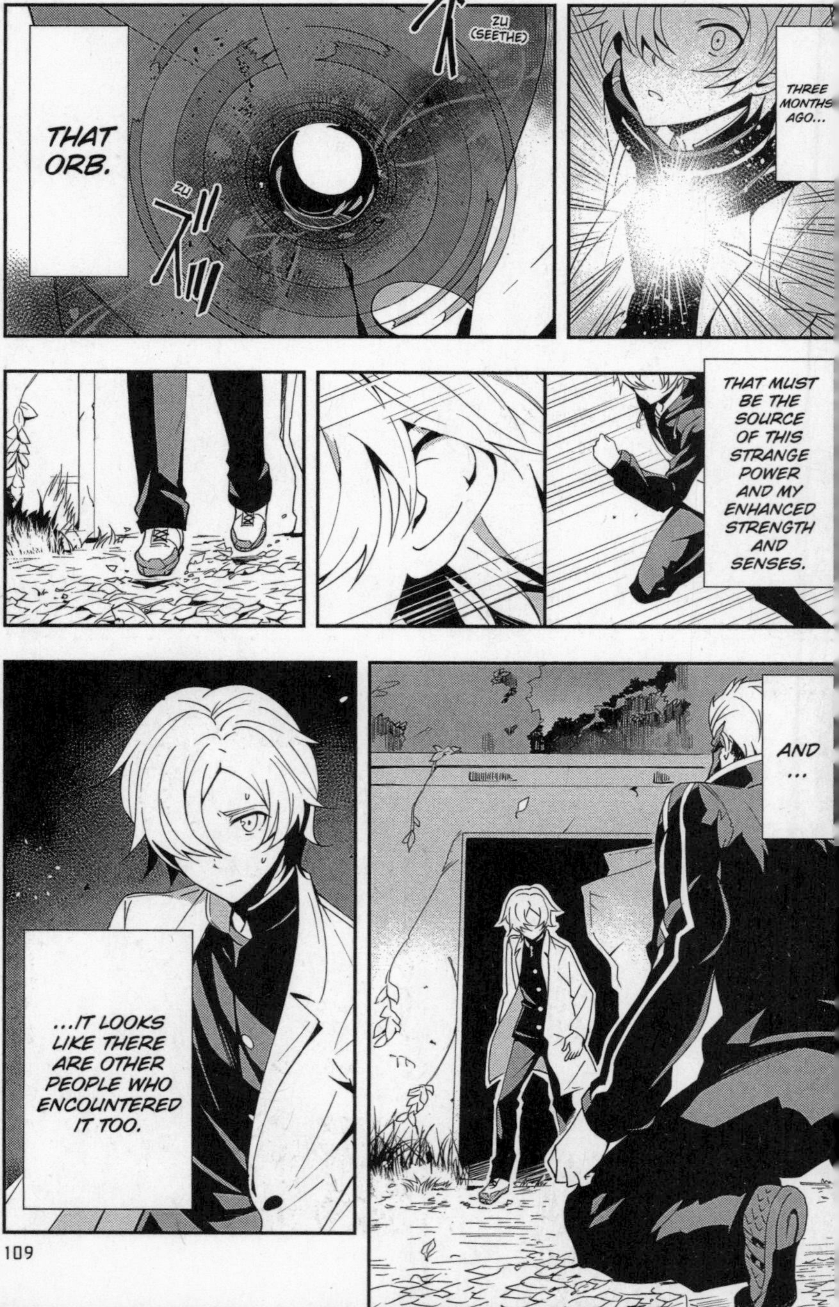
THREE MONTHS AGO...
ZU (SEETHE)
THAT ORB.
ZU
THAT MUST BE THE SOURCE OF THIS STRANGE POWER AND MY ENHANCED STRENGTH AND SENSES.
AND ...
...IT LOOKS LIKE THERE ARE OTHER PEOPLE WHO ENCOUNTERED IT TOO.

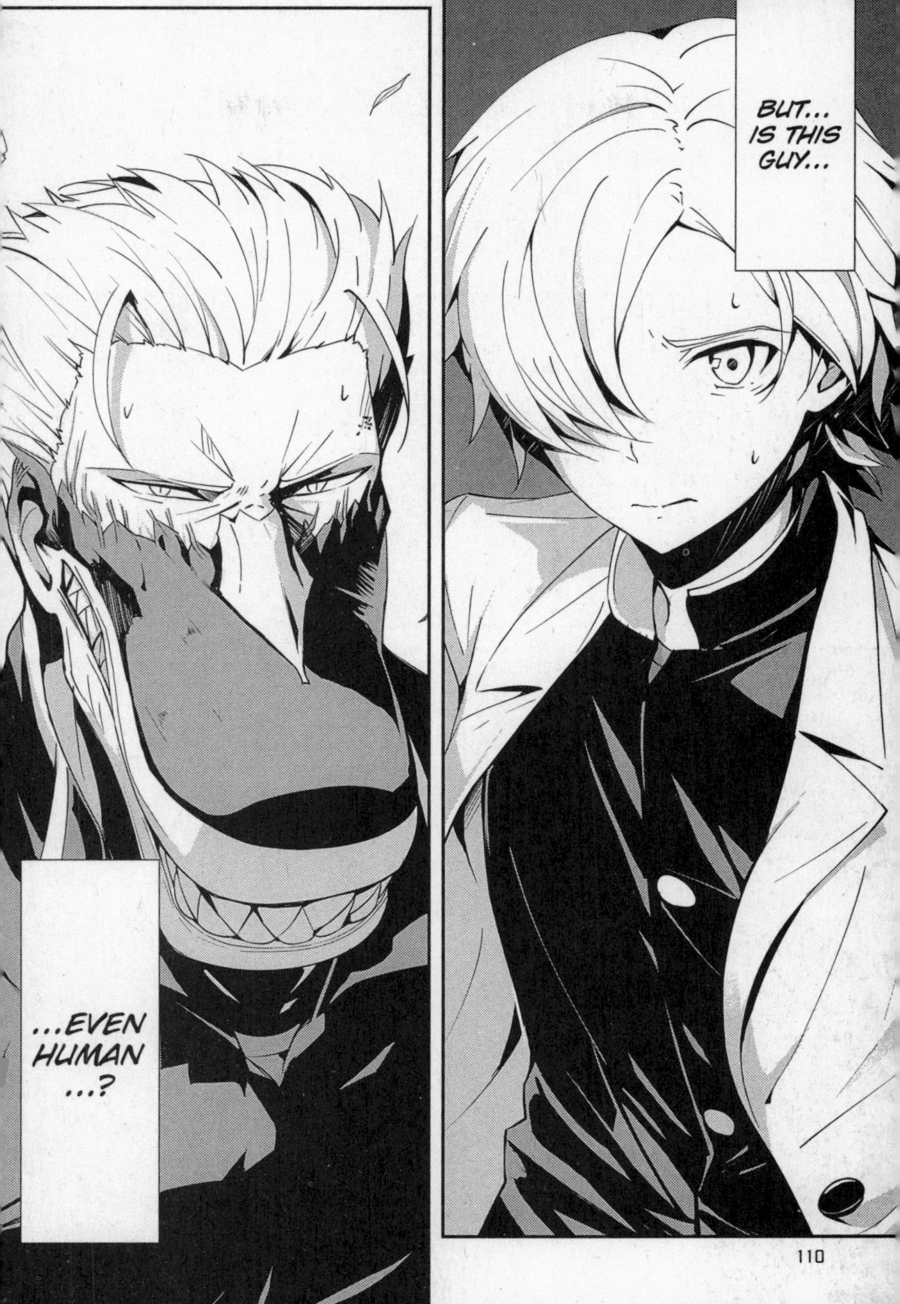
BUT... IS THIS GUY...
...EVEN HUMAN ...?

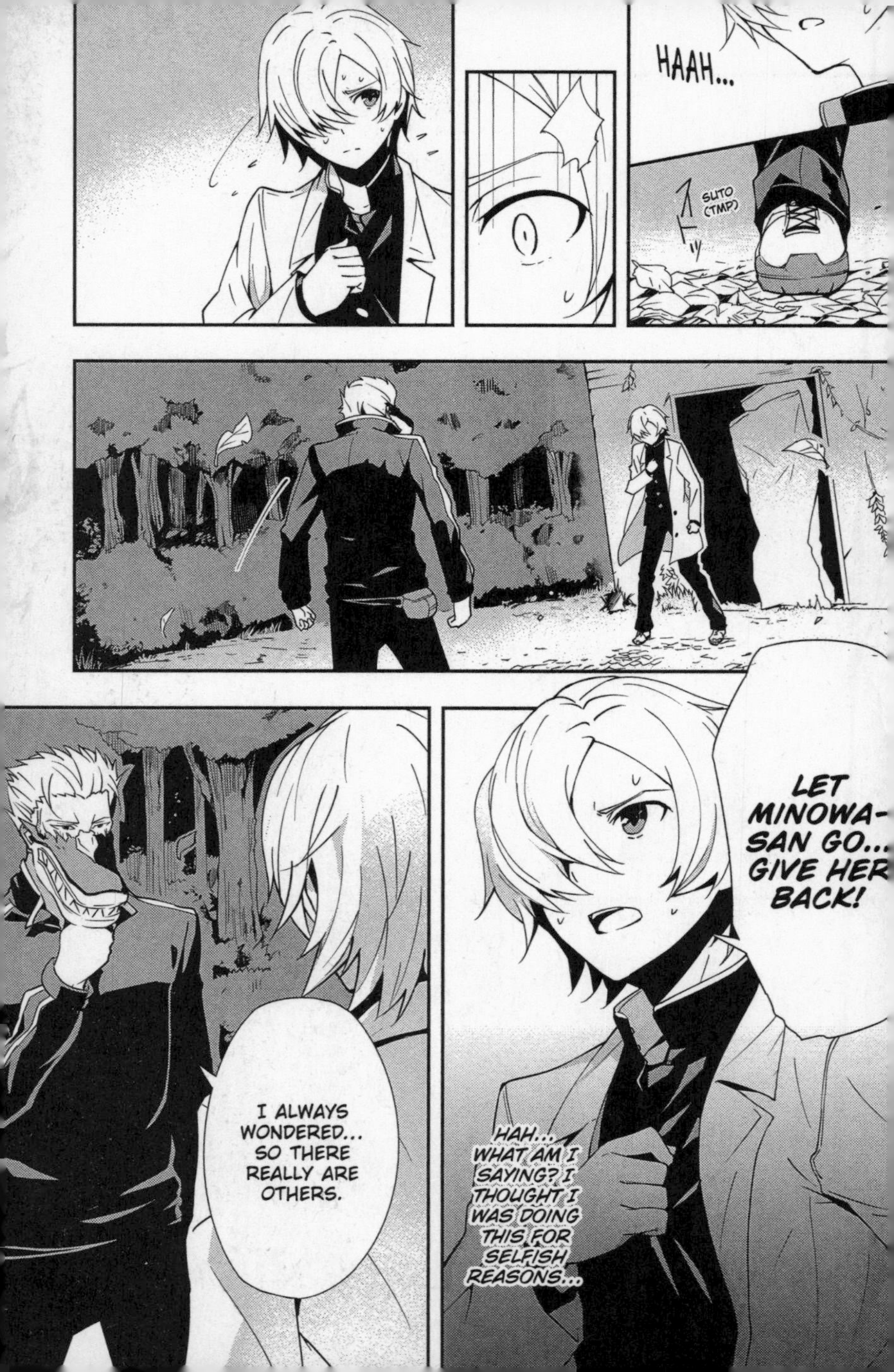
HAAH...
SUTO (TMP)
LET MINOWA-SAN GO... GIVE HER BACK!
HAH... WHAT AM I SAYING? I THOUGHT I WAS DOING THIS FOR SELFISH REASONS...
I ALWAYS WONDERED... SO THERE REALLY ARE OTHERS.

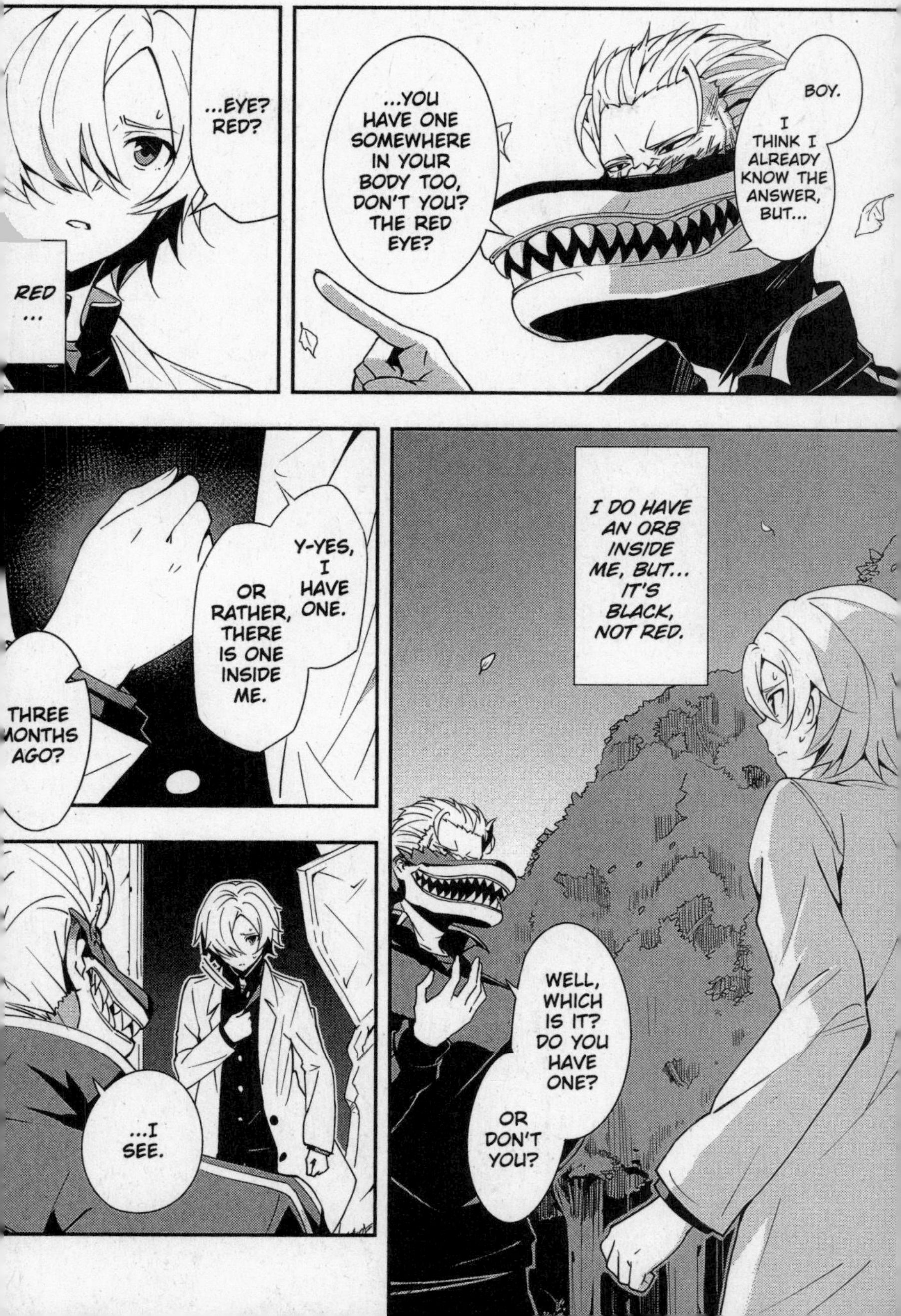
BOY.
I THINK I ALREADY KNOW THE ANSWER, BUT...
...YOU HAVE ONE SOMEWHERE IN YOUR BODY TOO, DON'T YOU? THE RED EYE?
...EYE? RED?
RED ...
I DO HAVE AN ORB INSIDE ME, BUT... IT'S BLACK, NOT RED.
WELL, WHICH IS IT? DO YOU HAVE ONE?
OR DON'T YOU?
Y-YES, I HAVE ONE.
OR RATHER, THERE IS ONE INSIDE ME.
THREE MONTHS AGO?
...I SEE.

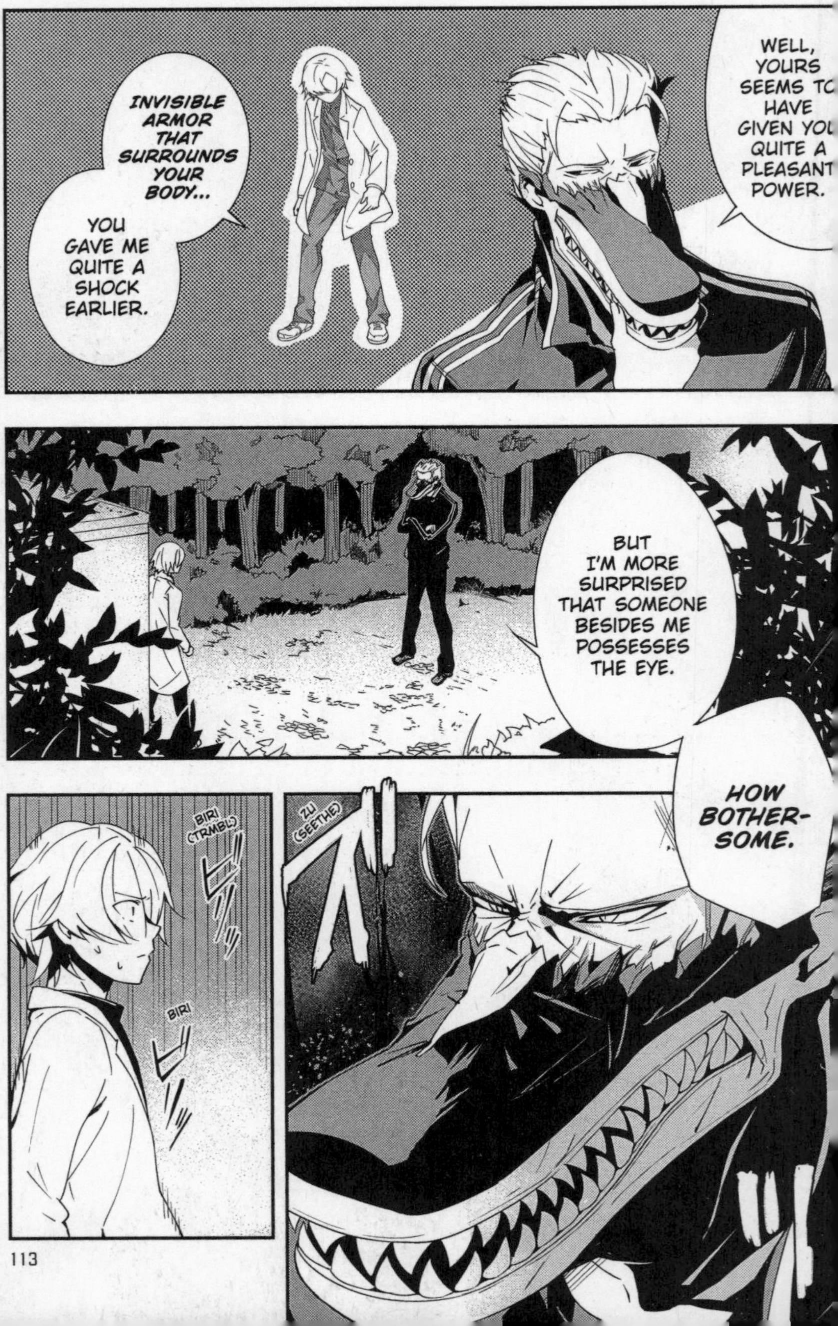
WELL, YOURS SEEMS TO HAVE GIVEN YOU QUITE A PLEASANT POWER.
INVISIBLE ARMOR THAT SURROUNDS YOUR BODY...
YOU GAVE ME QUITE A SHOCK EARLIER.
BUT I'M MORE SURPRISED THAT SOMEONE BESIDES ME POSSESSES THE EYE.
HOW BOTHER-SOME.
ZU (SEETHE)
BIRI (TRMBL)
BIRI

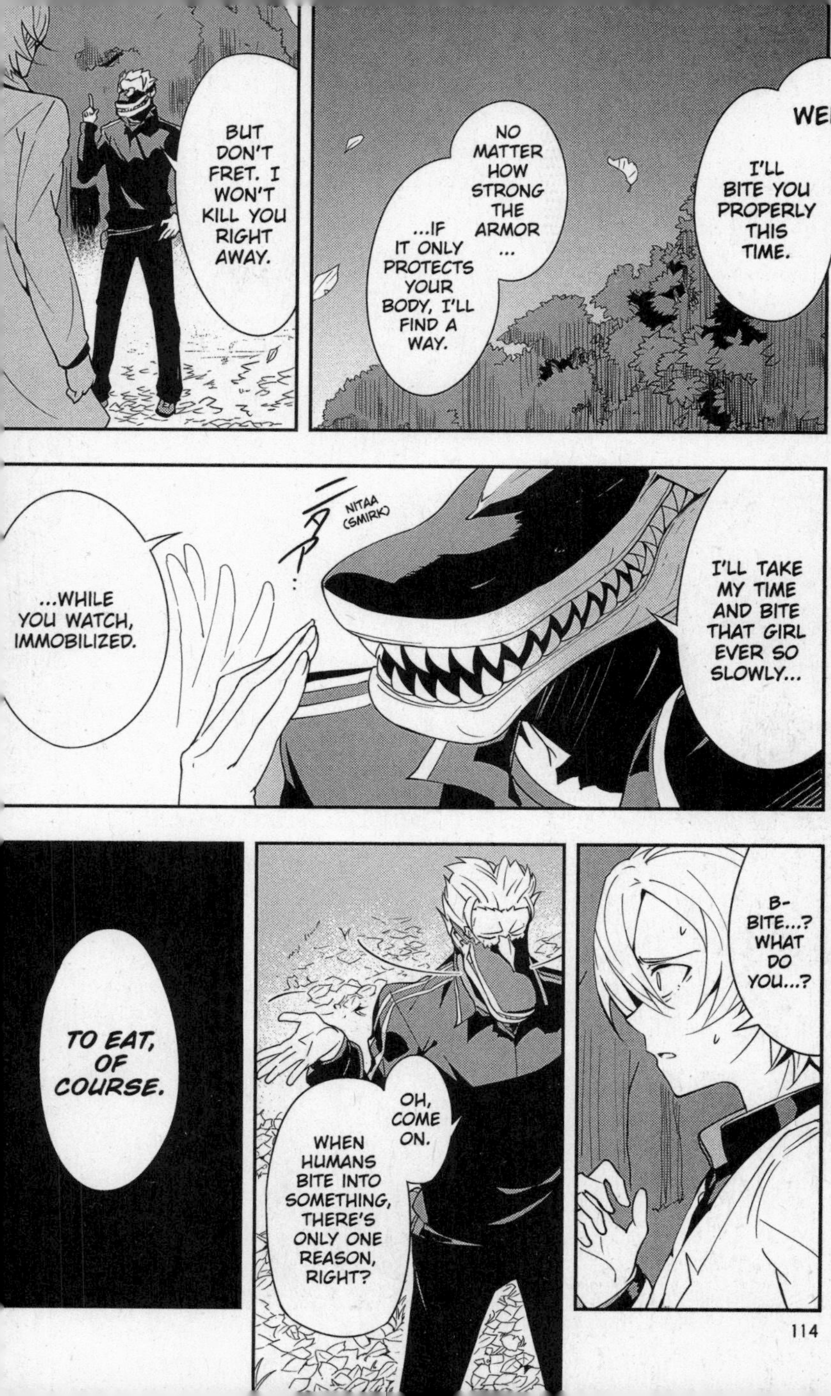
WELL.
I'LL BITE YOU PROPERLY THIS TIME.
NO MATTER HOW STRONG THE ARMOR...
...IF IT ONLY PROTECTS YOUR BODY, I'LL FIND A WAY.
BUT DON'T FRET. I WON'T KILL YOU RIGHT AWAY.
I'LL TAKE MY TIME AND BITE THAT GIRL EVER SO SLOWLY...
NITAA (SMIRK)
...WHILE YOU WATCH, IMMOBILIZED.
B-BITE...? WHAT DO YOU...?
OH, COME ON.
WHEN HUMANS BITE INTO SOMETHING, THERE'S ONLY ONE REASON, RIGHT?
TO EAT, OF COURSE.

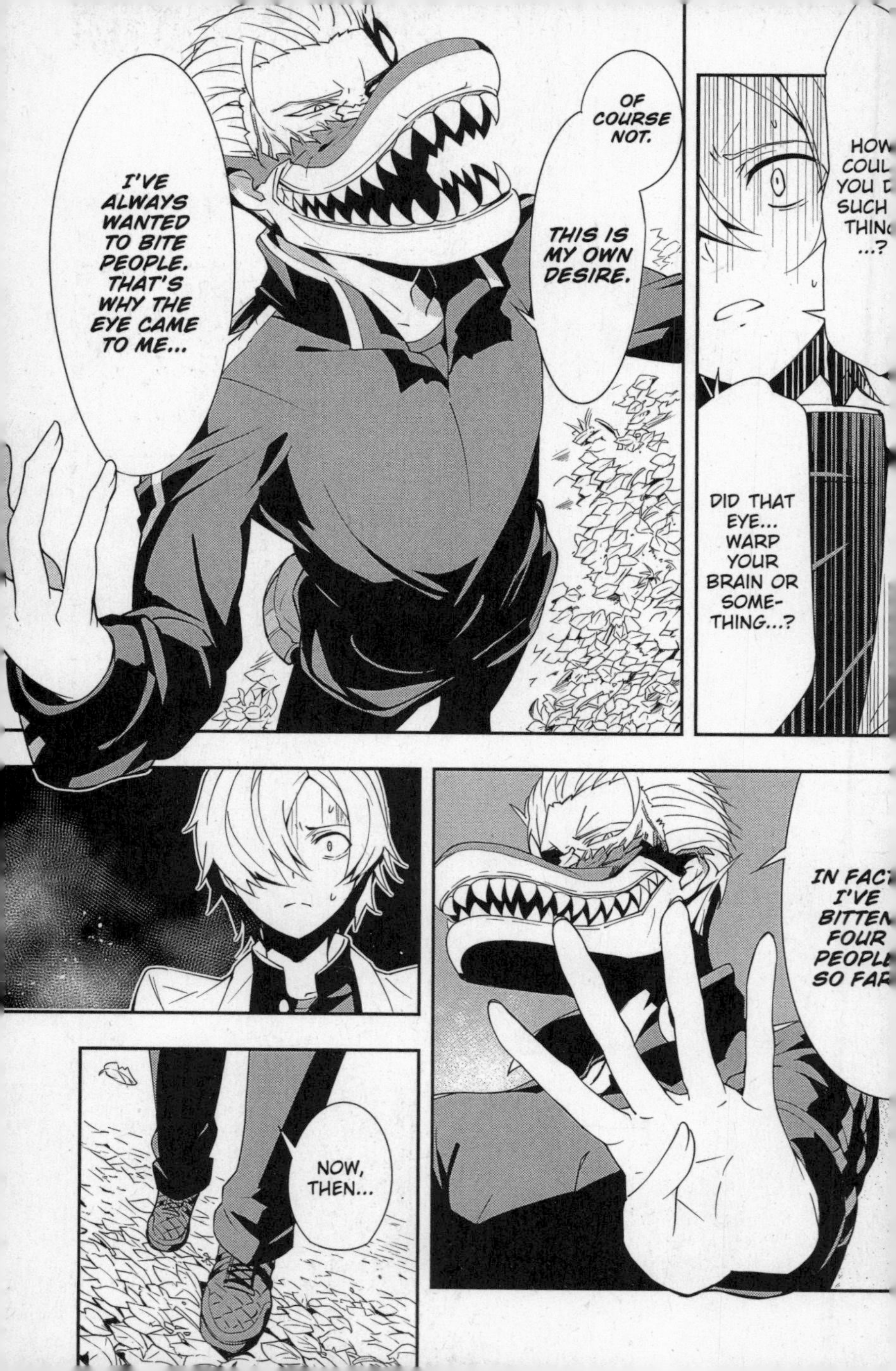
HOW COUL YOU D SUCH THIN ...?
DID THAT EYE... WARP YOUR BRAIN OR SOME-THING...?
OF COURSE NOT.
THIS IS MY OWN DESIRE.
I'VE ALWAYS WANTED TO BITE PEOPLE. THAT'S WHY THE EYE CAME TO ME...
IN FAC I'VE BITTEN FOUR PEOPL SO FAR
NOW, THEN...

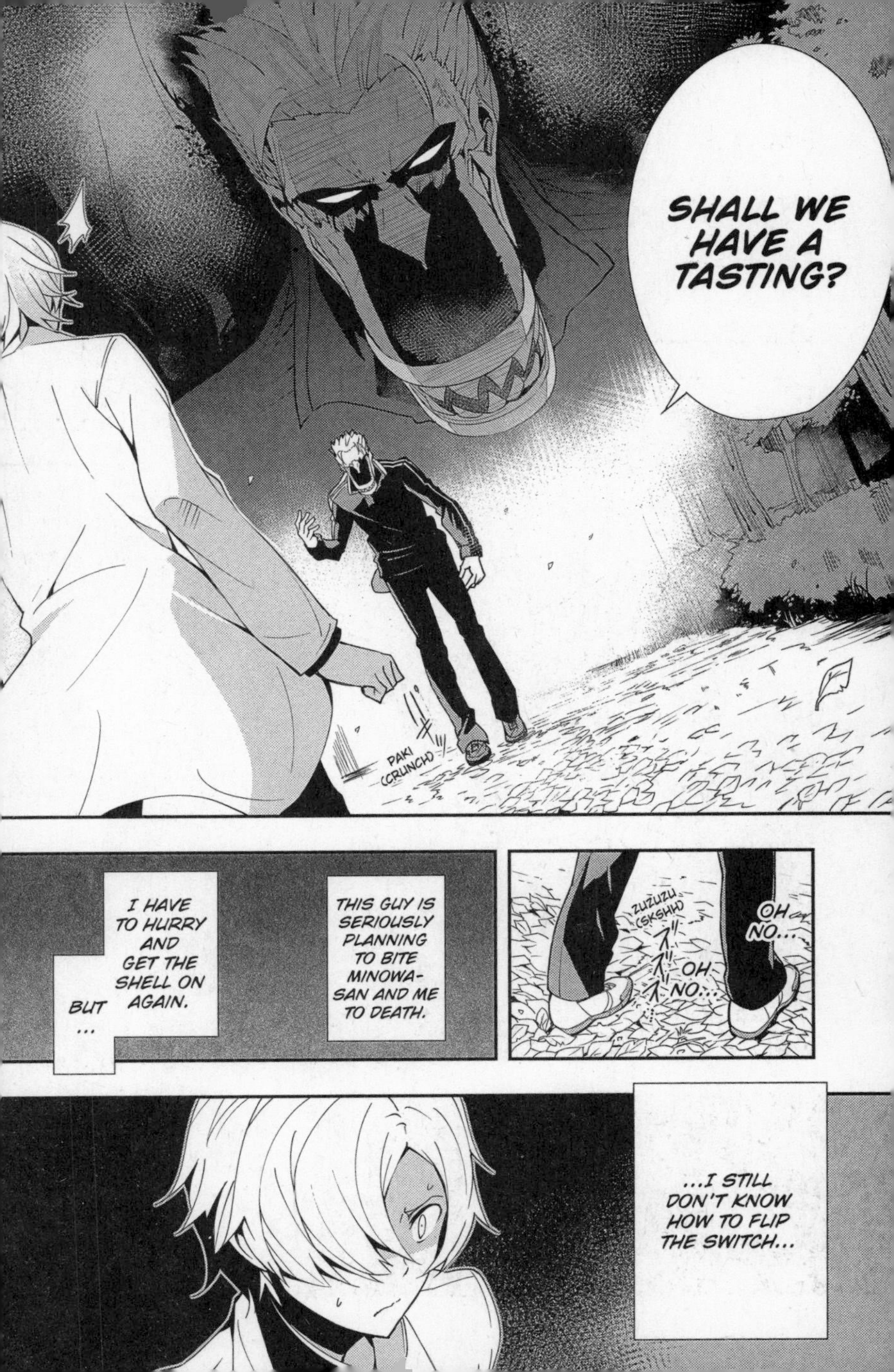
SHALL WE HAVE A TASTING?
PAKI (CRUNCH)
ZUZUZU (SKSHH)
OH NO...
OH NO...
THIS GUY IS SERIOUSLY PLANNING TO BITE MINOWA-SAN AND ME TO DEATH.
I HAVE TO HURRY AND GET THE SHELL ON AGAIN.
BUT...
...I STILL DON'T KNOW HOW TO FLIP THE SWITCH...

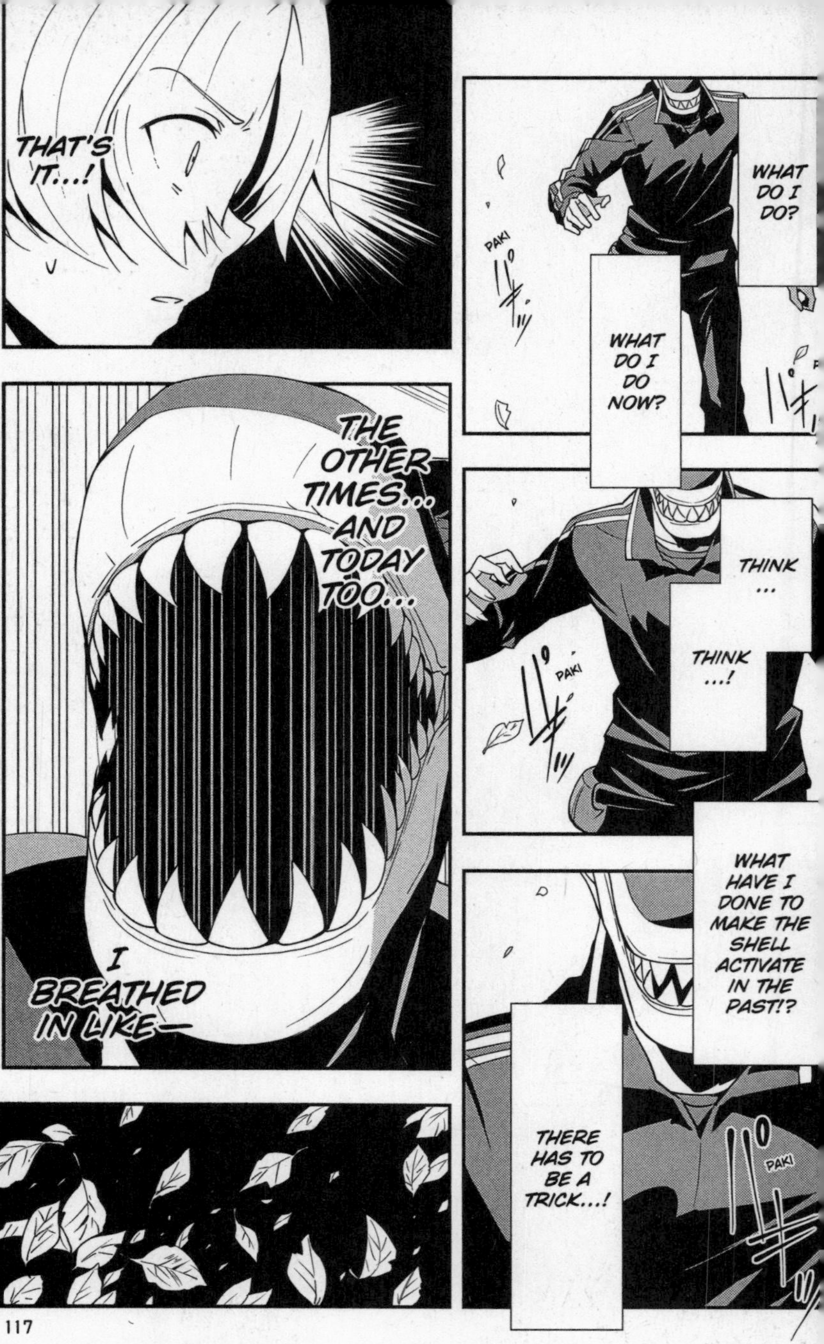
WHAT DO I DO?
PAKI
WHAT DO I DO NOW?
PAKI
THINK ...
THINK ...!
PAKI
WHAT HAVE I DONE TO MAKE THE SHELL ACTIVATE IN THE PAST!?
THERE HAS TO BE A TRICK...!
PAKI
THAT'S IT...!
THE OTHER TIMES... AND TODAY TOO...
I BREATHED IN LIKE—

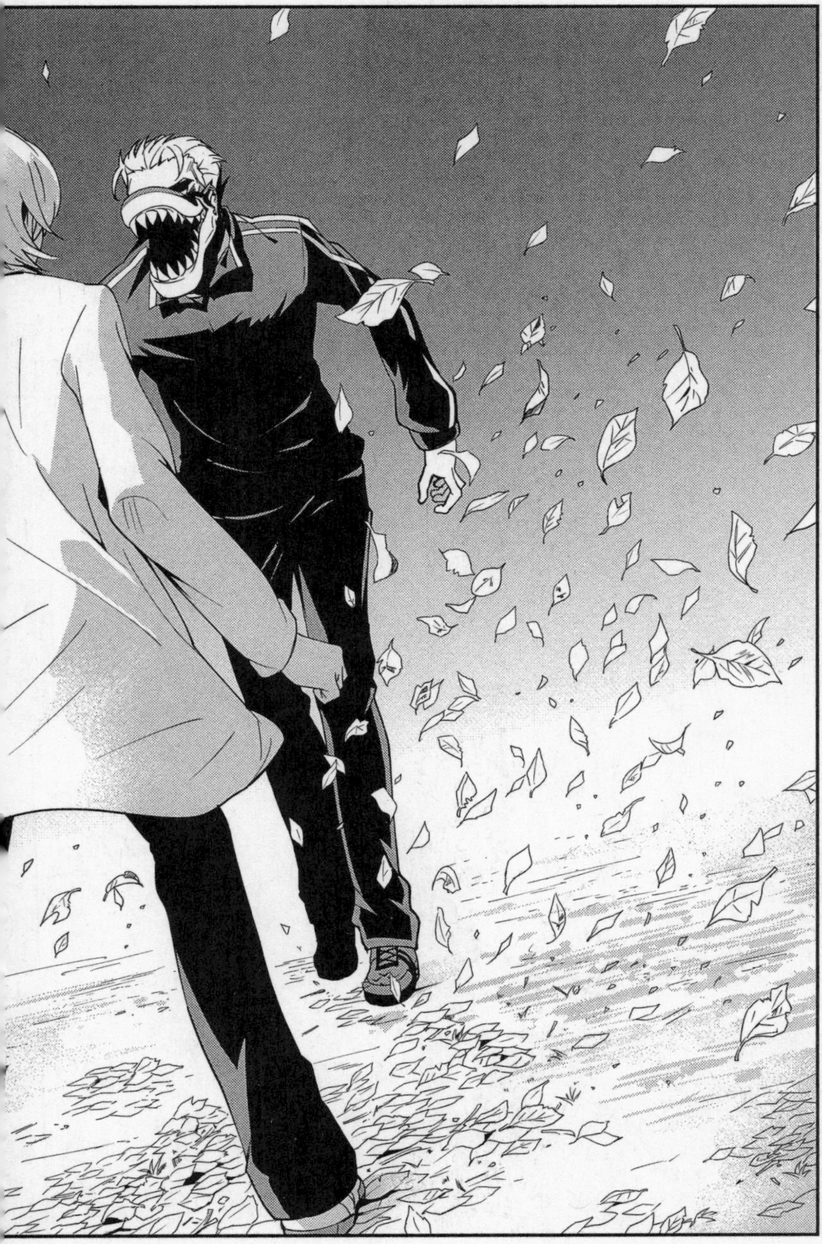

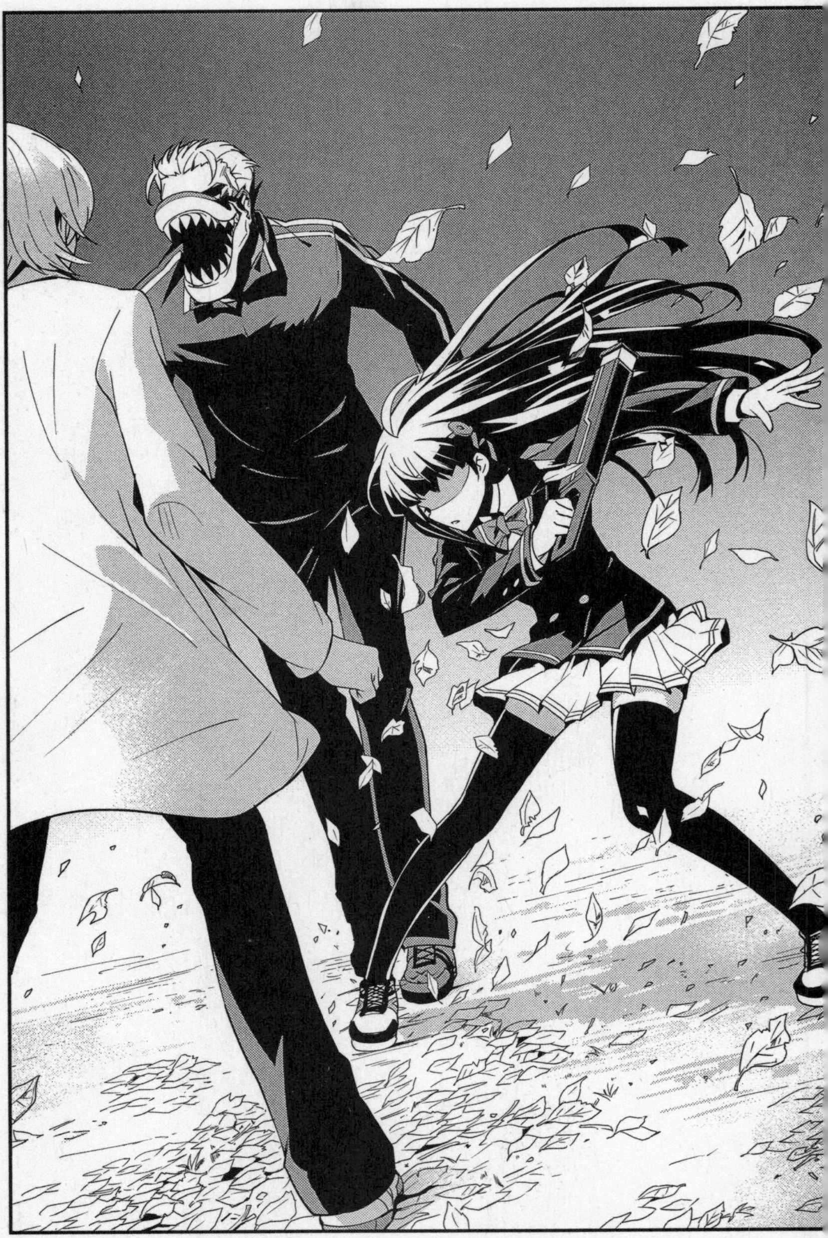

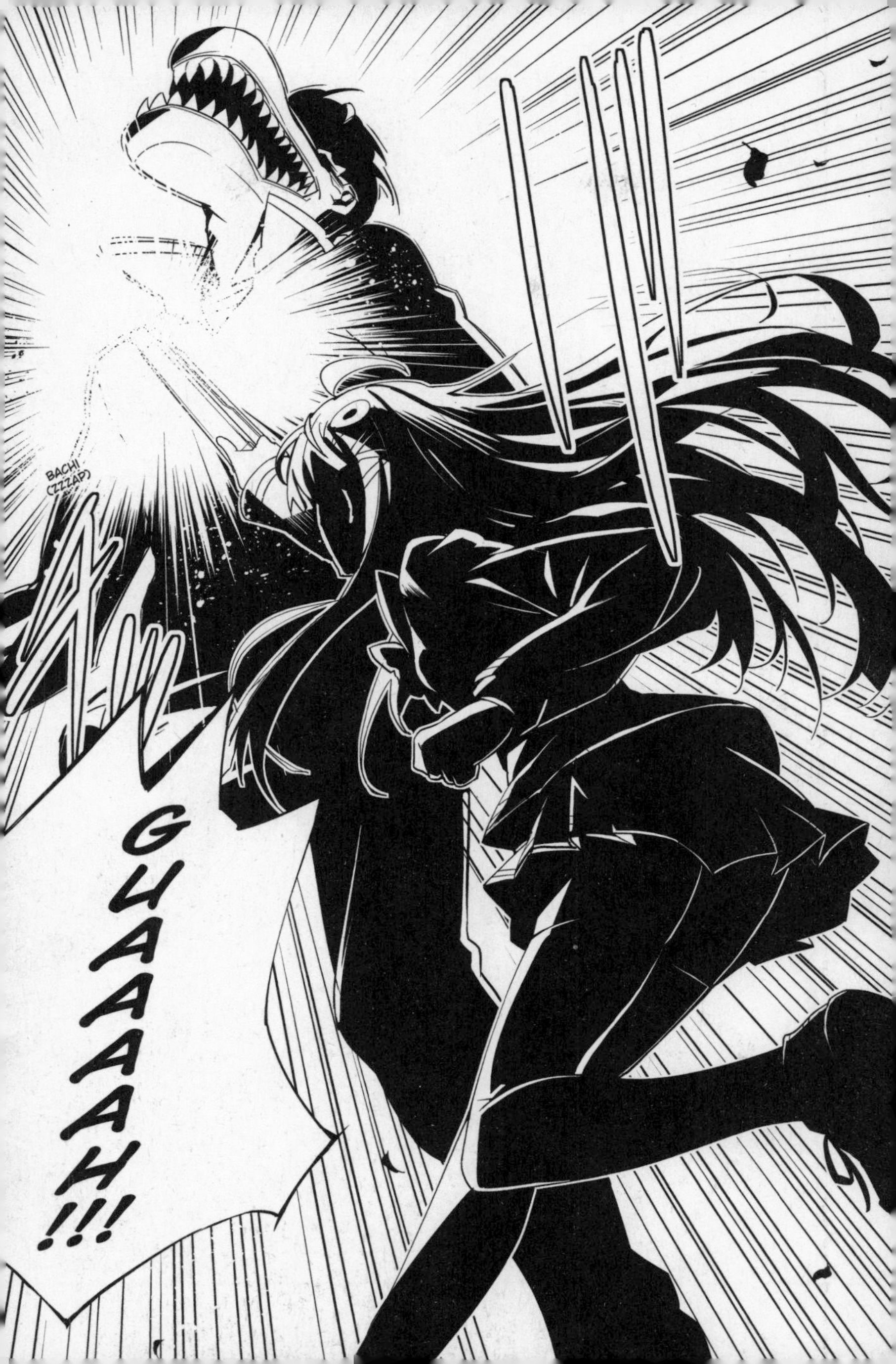
BACHI
(ZZZAP)
GUAAAAH!!!

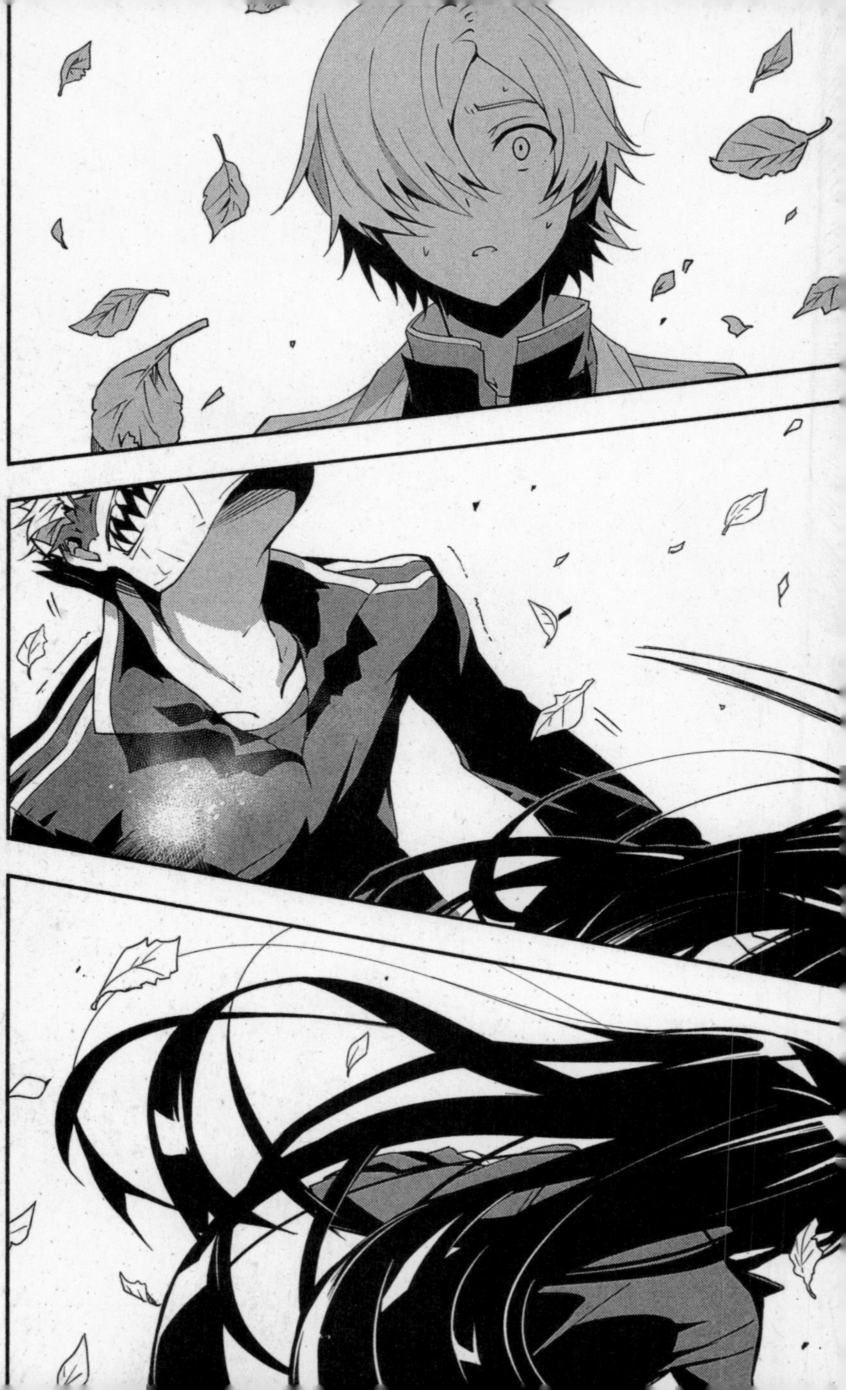

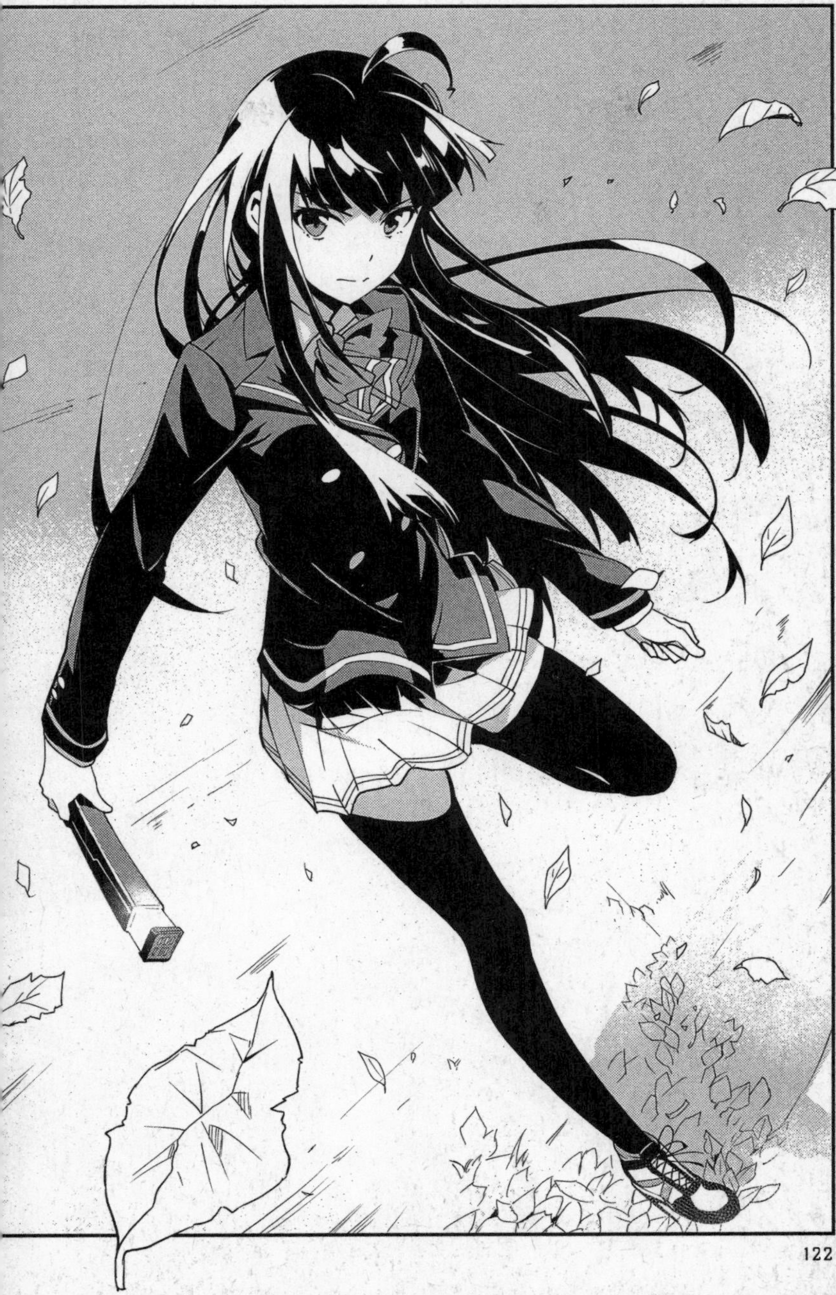

THE ISOLATOR
realization of
absolute solitude

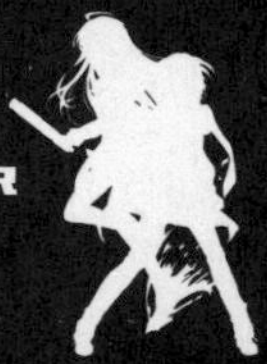

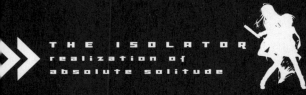

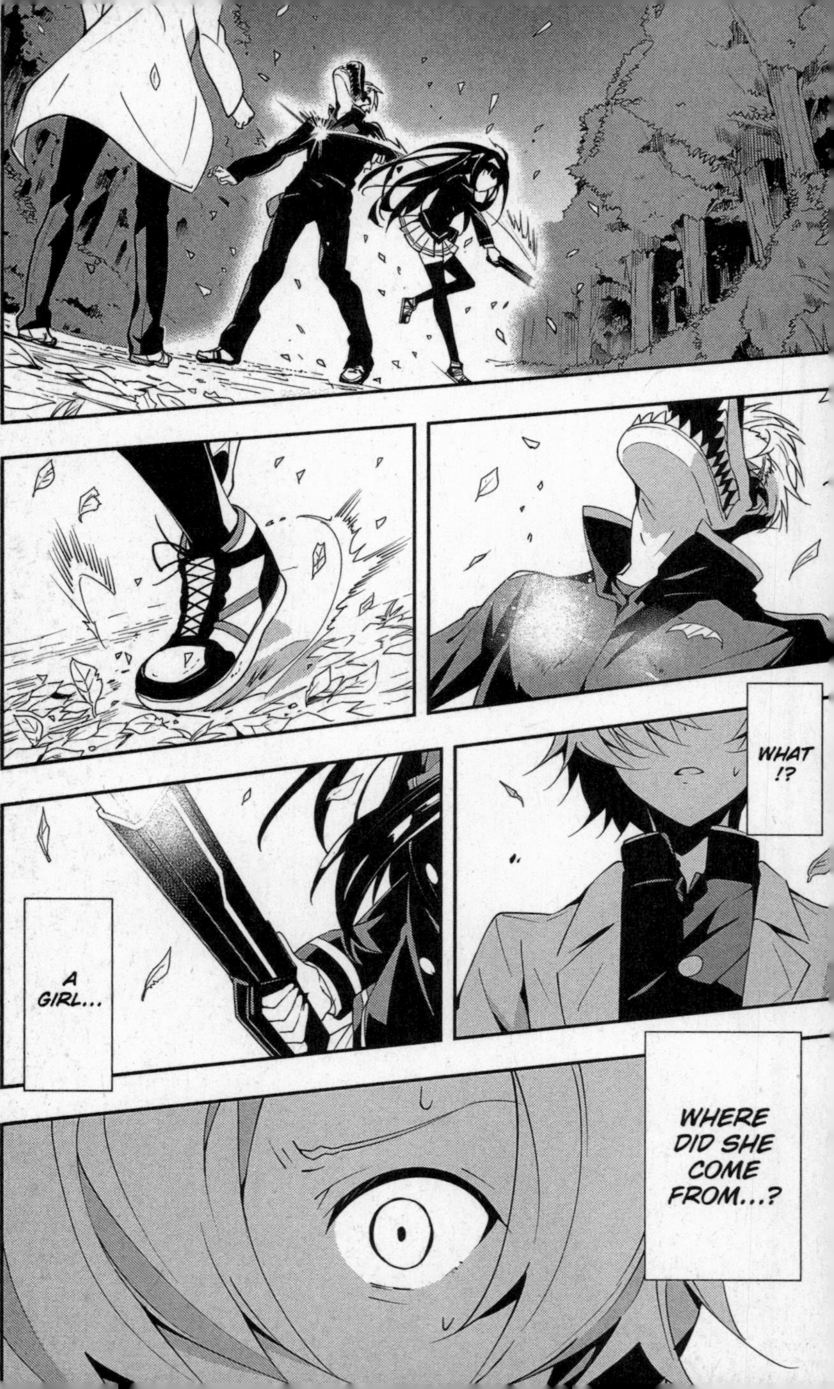
WHAT !?
A GIRL...
WHERE DID SHE COME FROM...?

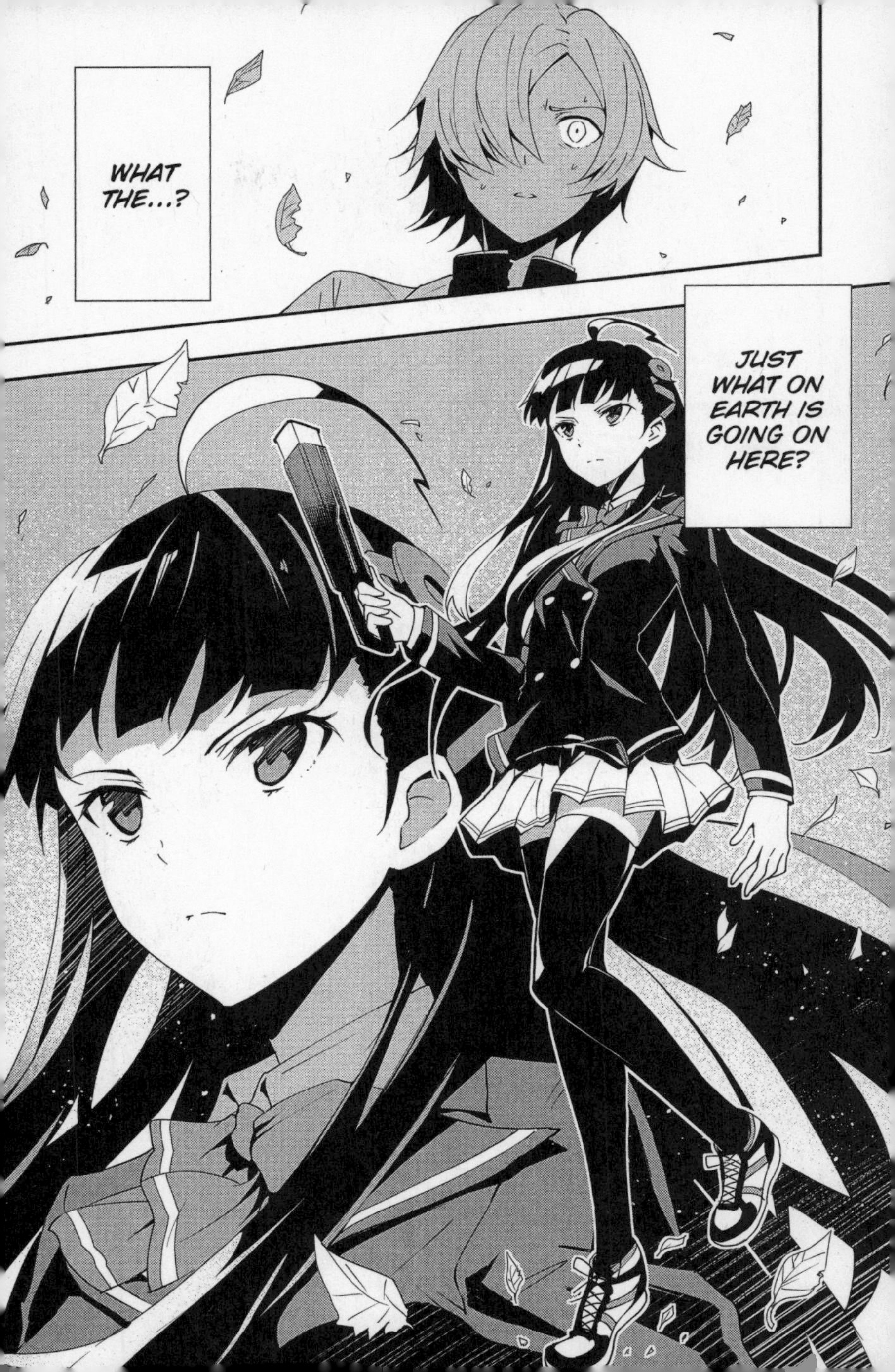
WHAT THE...?
JUST WHAT ON EARTH IS GOING ON HERE?

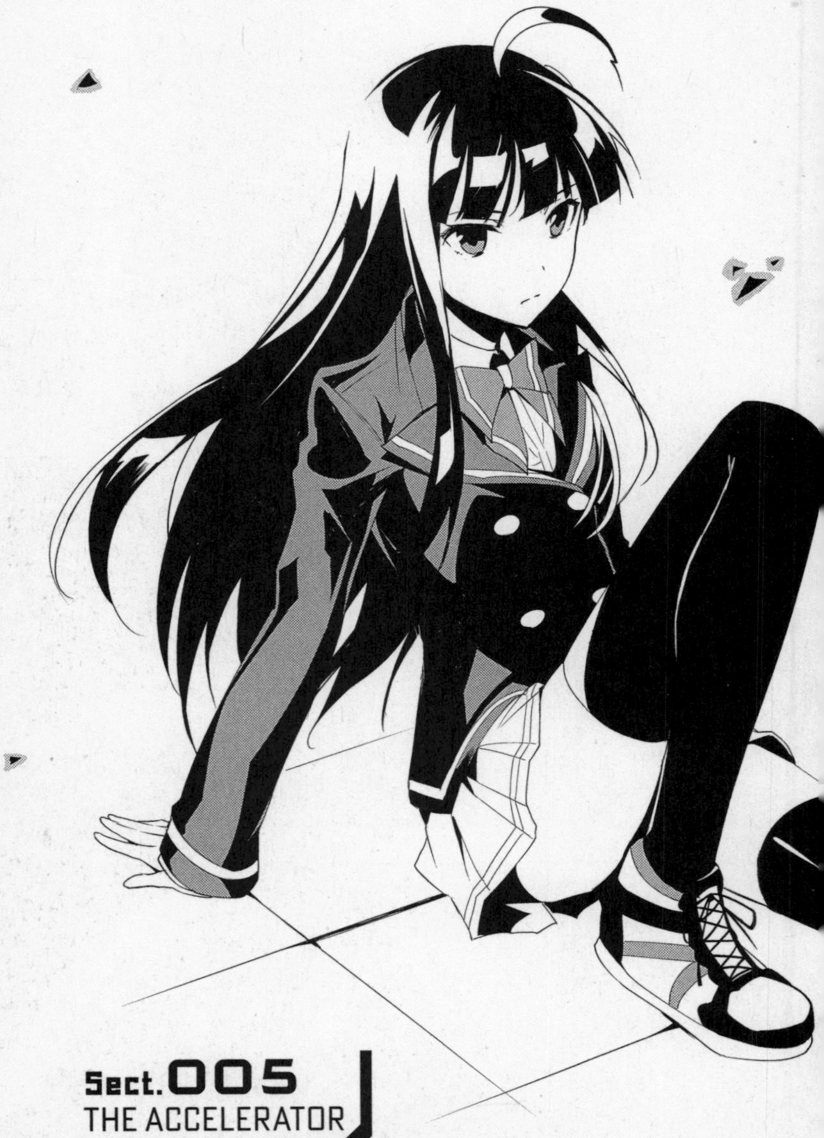

Sect.005
THE ACCELERATOR

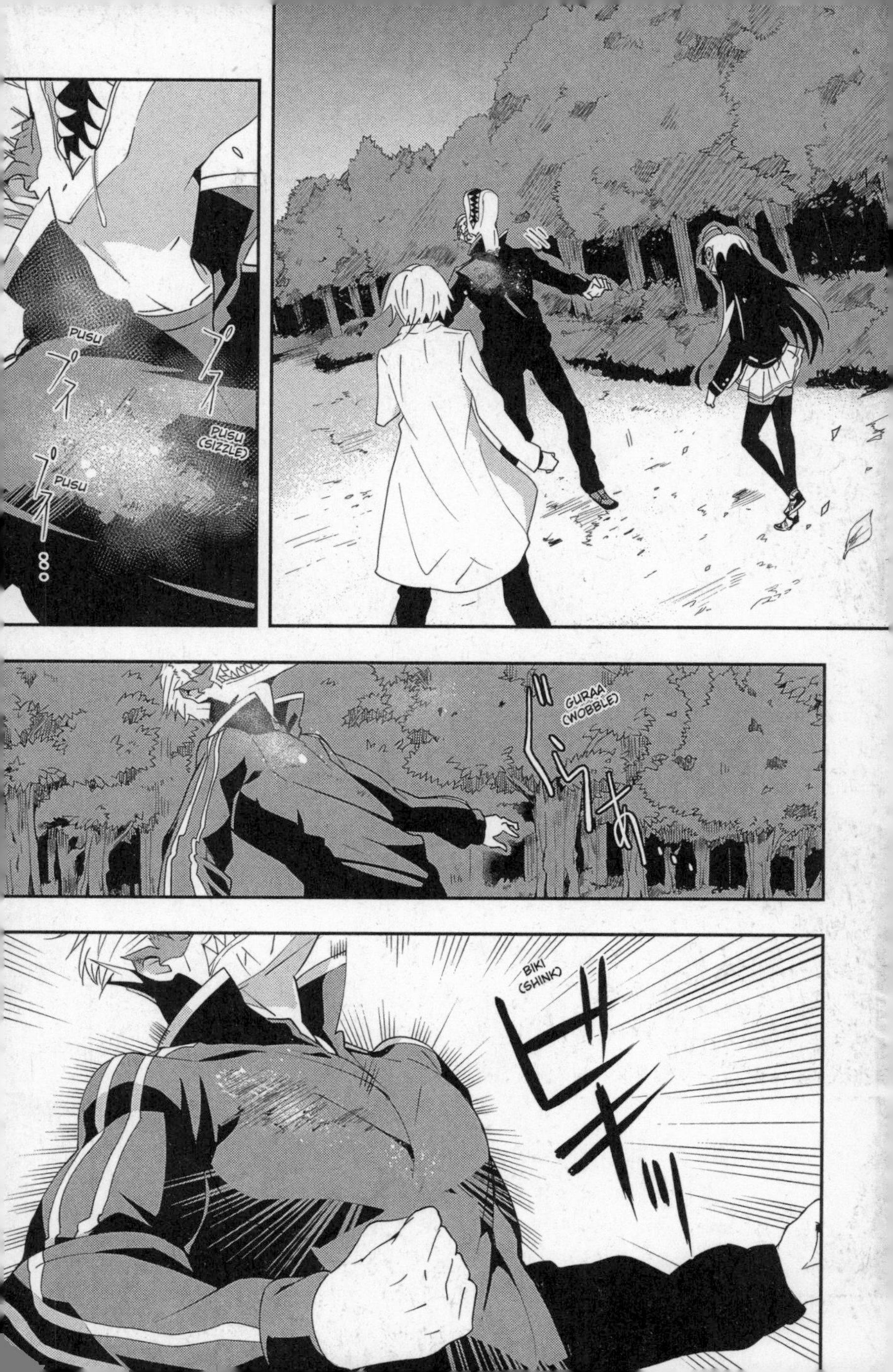
PUSU
PUSU (SIZZLE)
PUSU
GURAA (WOBBLE)
BIKI (SHINK)

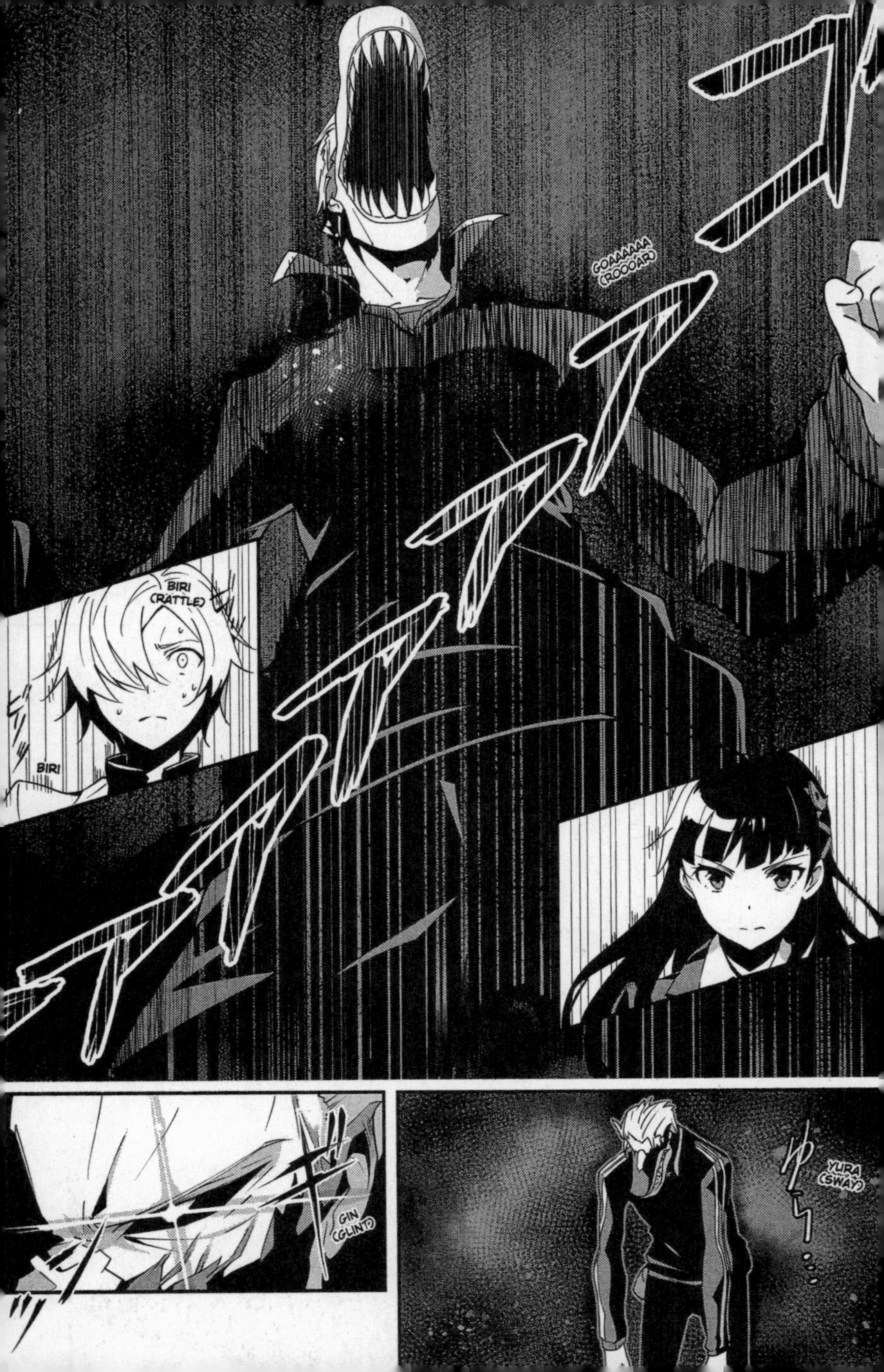
GOAAAAAA (ROOOAR)
BIRI (RATTLE)
BIRI
YURA (SWAY)
GIN (GLINT)

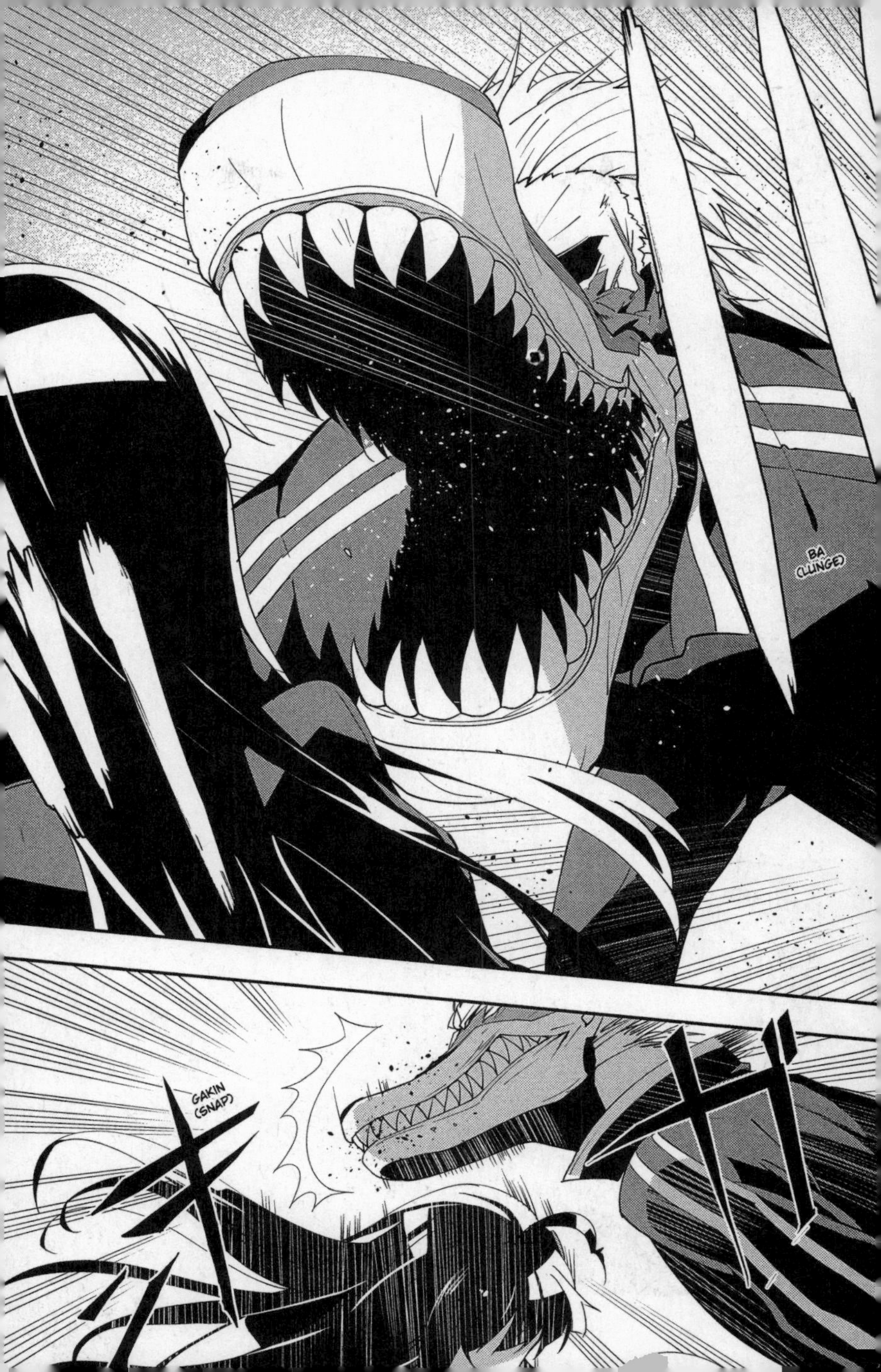
BA
(LUNGE)
GAKIN
(SNAP)

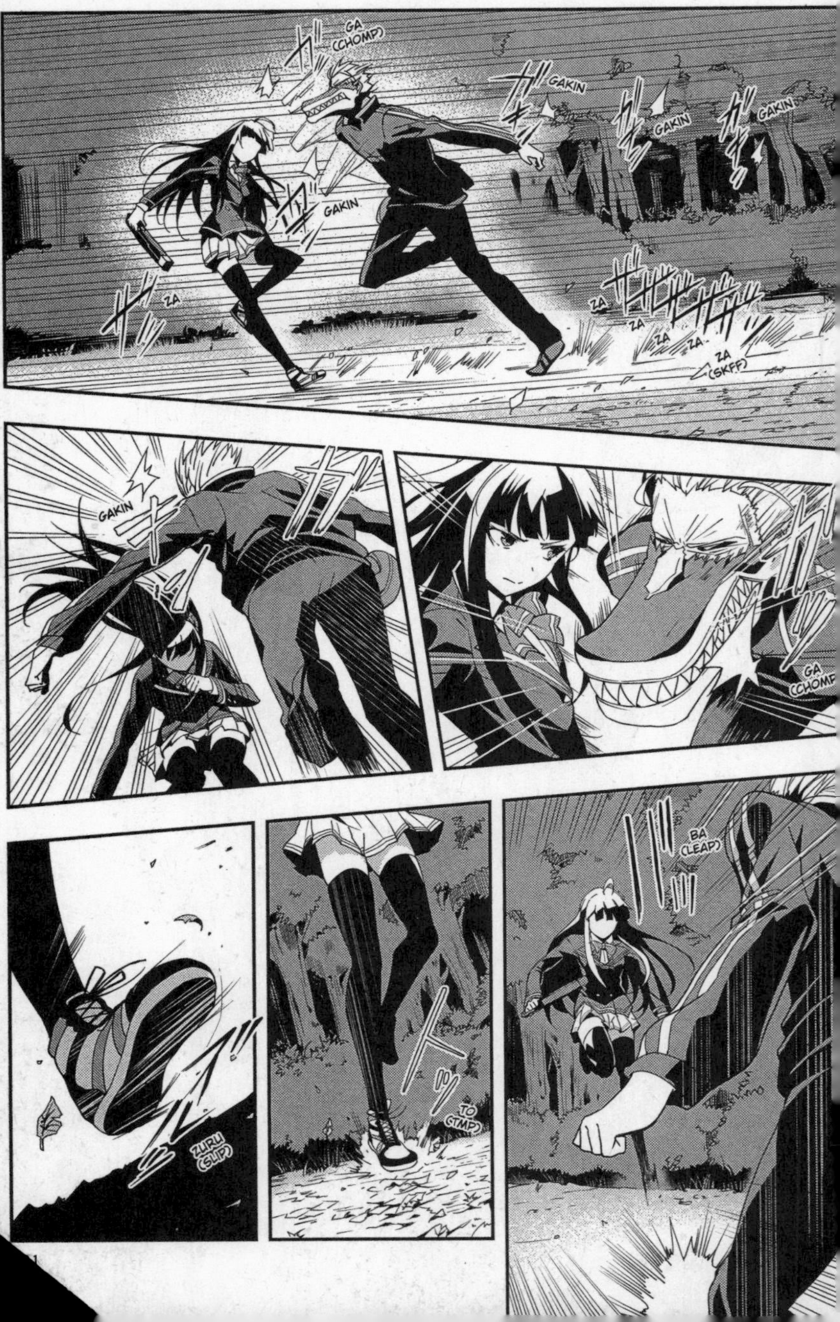
GAKIN
GAKIN
GAKIN
GA (CHOMP)
GAKIN
ZA
ZA
ZA
ZA
ZA (SKFF)
ZA
GA (CHOMP)
GAKIN
BA (LEAP)
TO (TMP)
ZURU (SLIP)

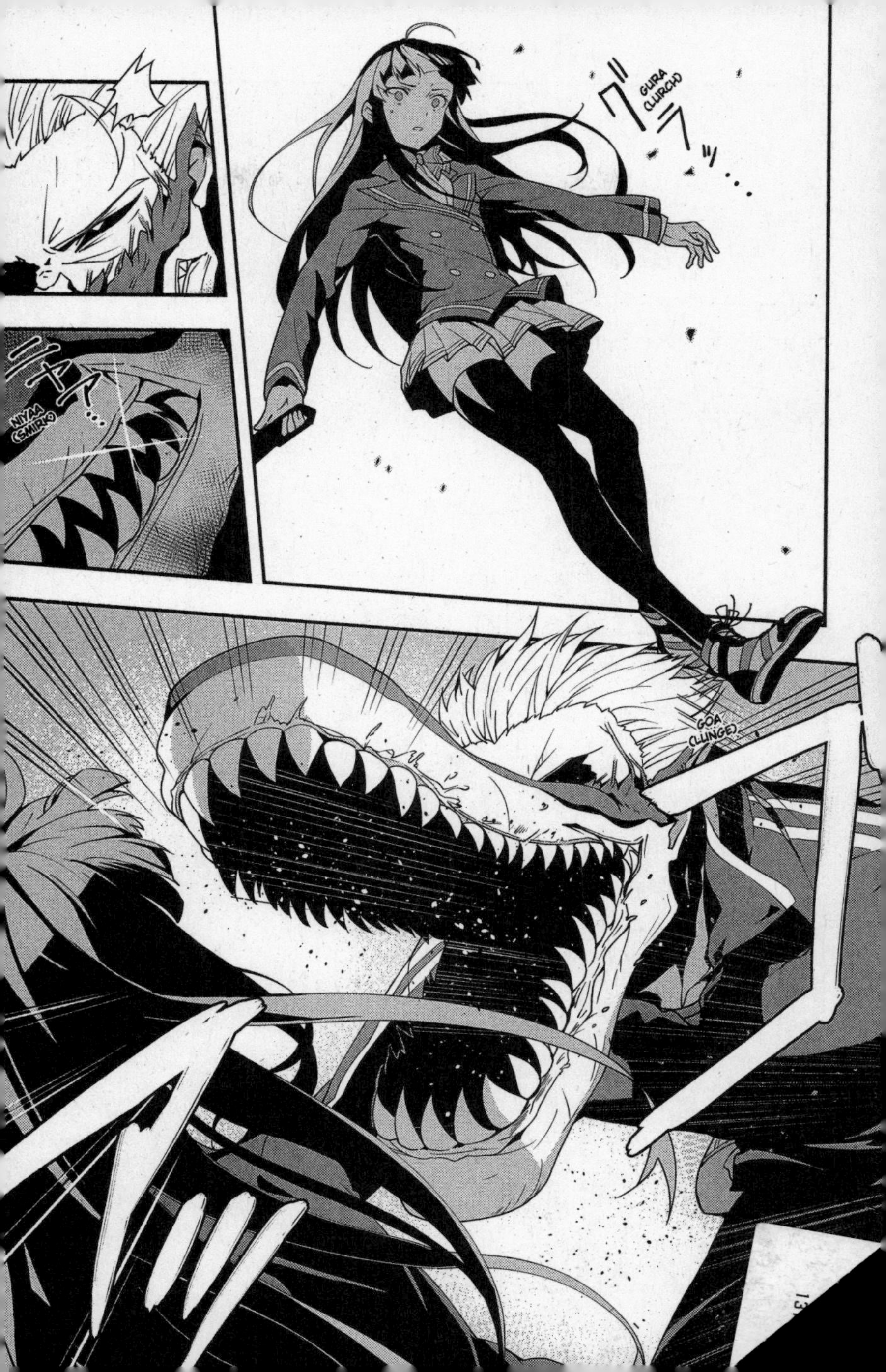
グラッ…
GURA (LURCH)
ニヤァ…
NIYAA (SMIRK)
GOA (LUNGE)

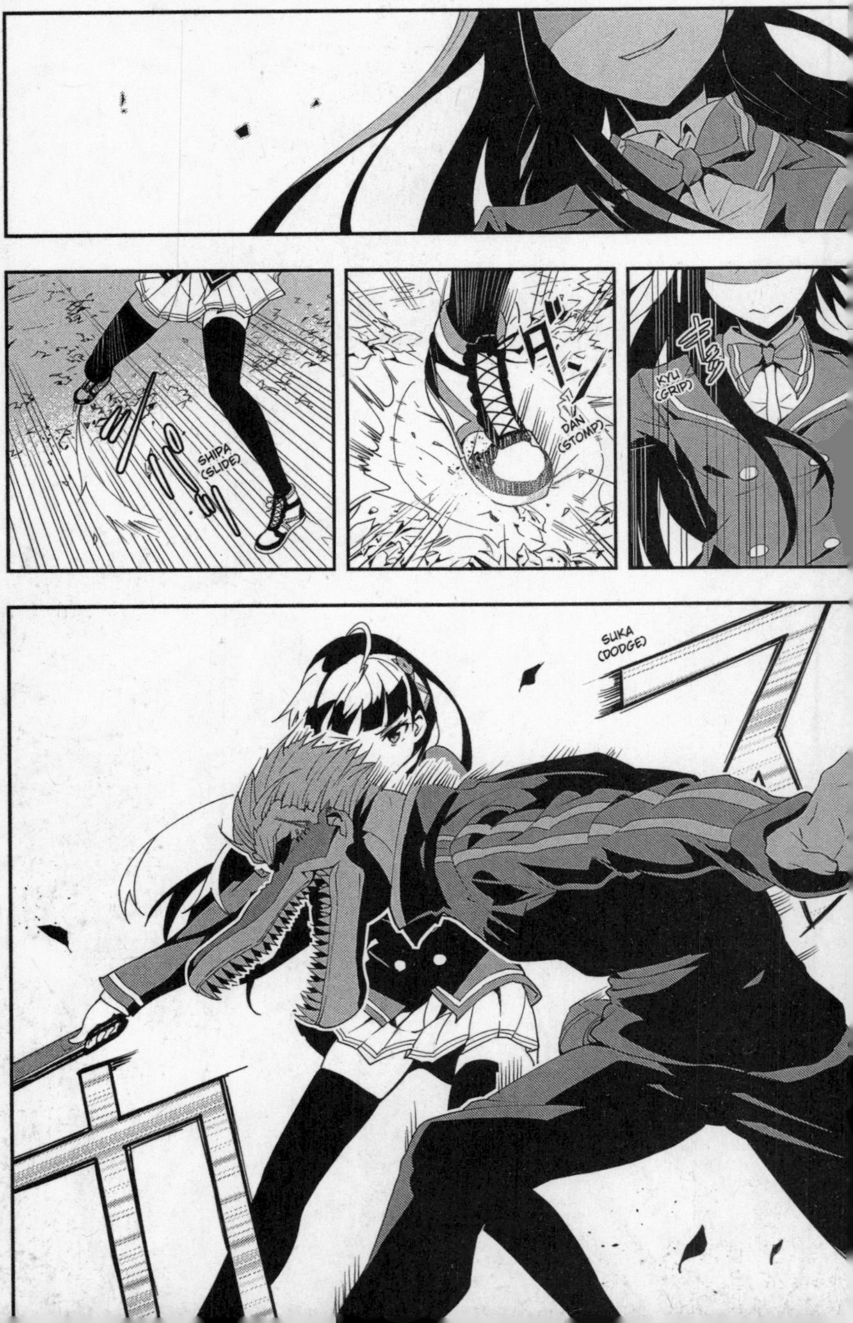
KYU (GRIP)
DAN (STOMP)
SHIPA (SLIDE)
SUKA (DODGE)

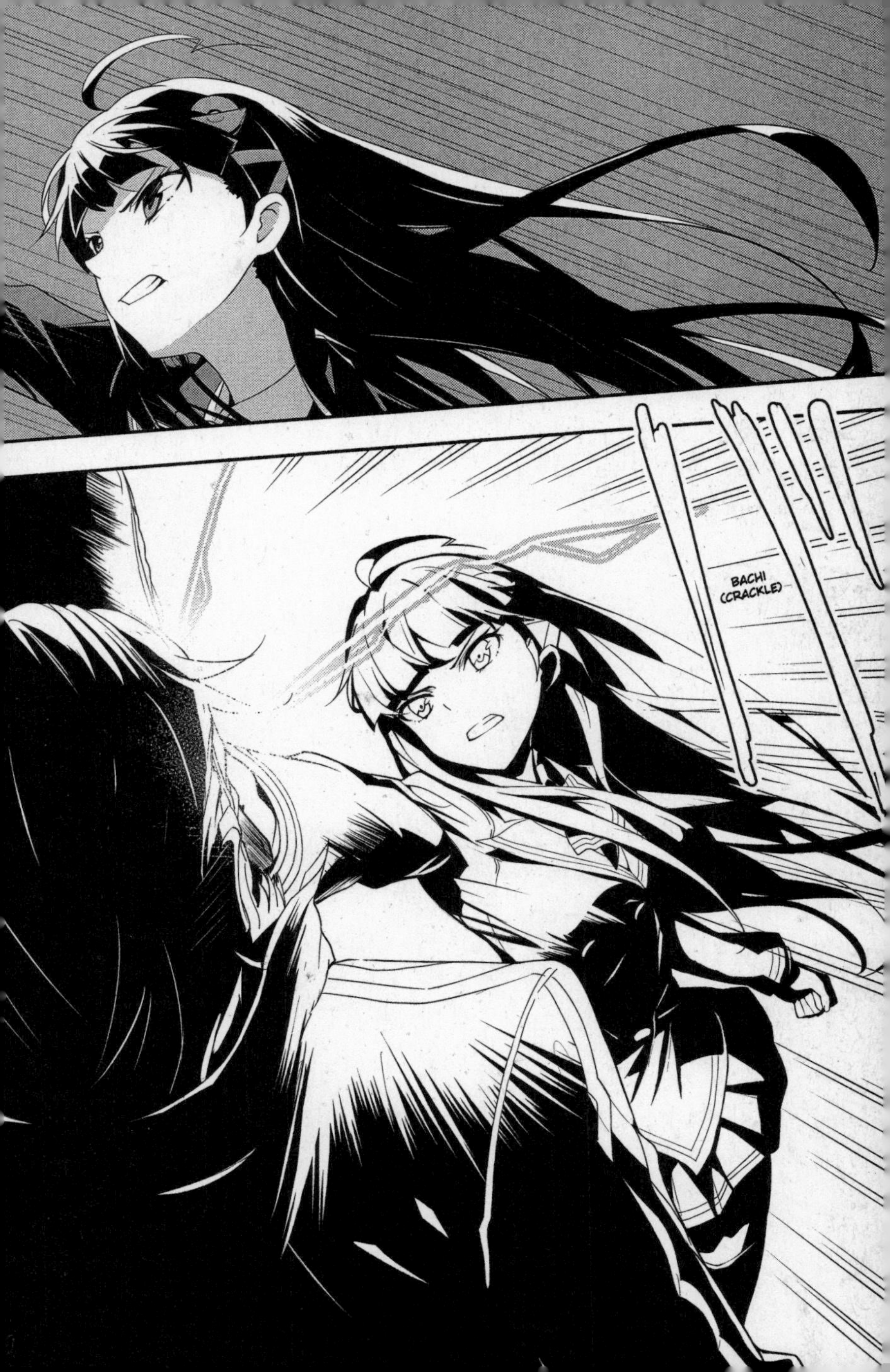
BACHI
(CRACKLE)

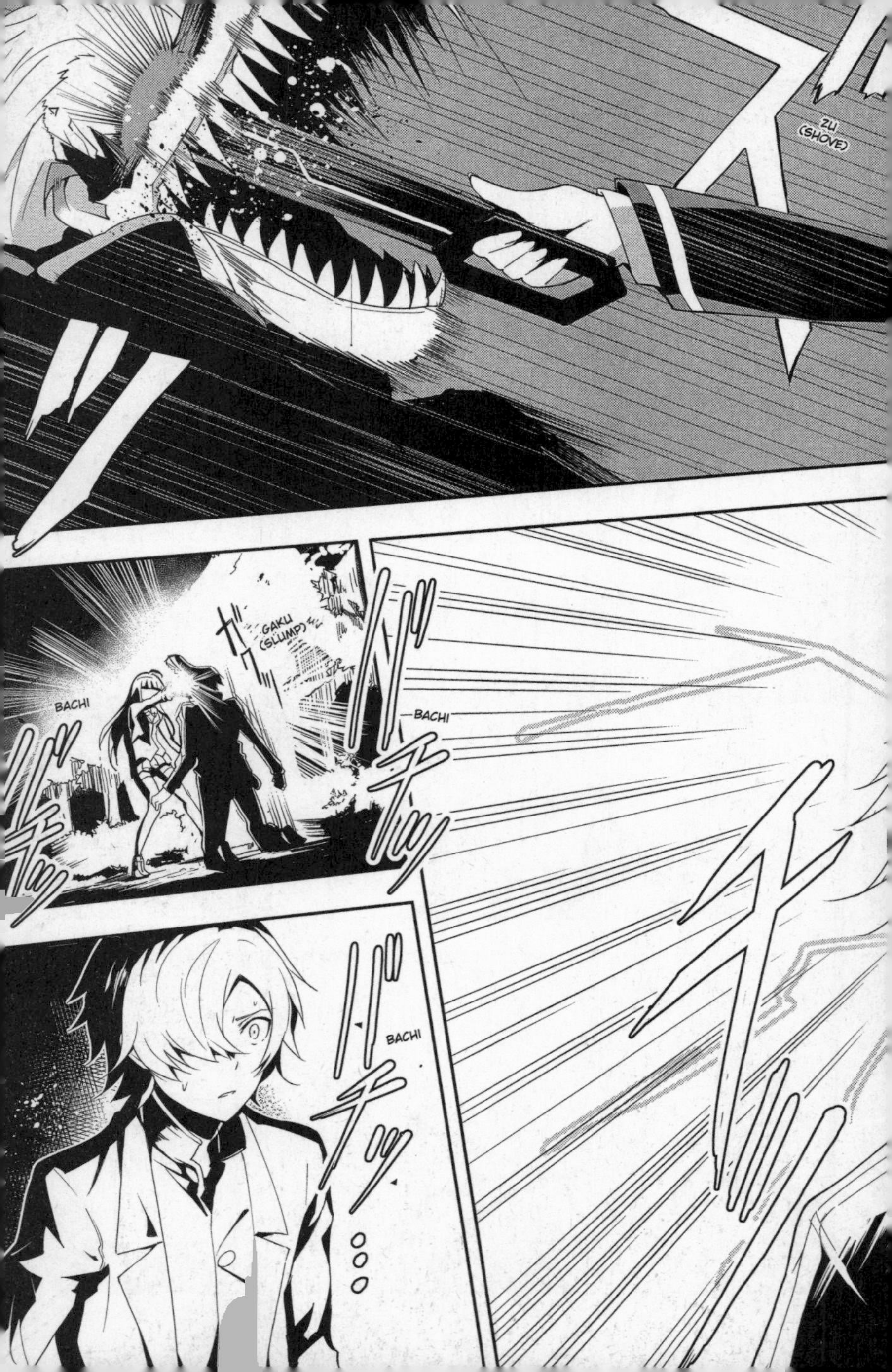

ZU
(SHOVE)
BACHI
GAKU
(SLUMP)
BACHI
BACHI
...

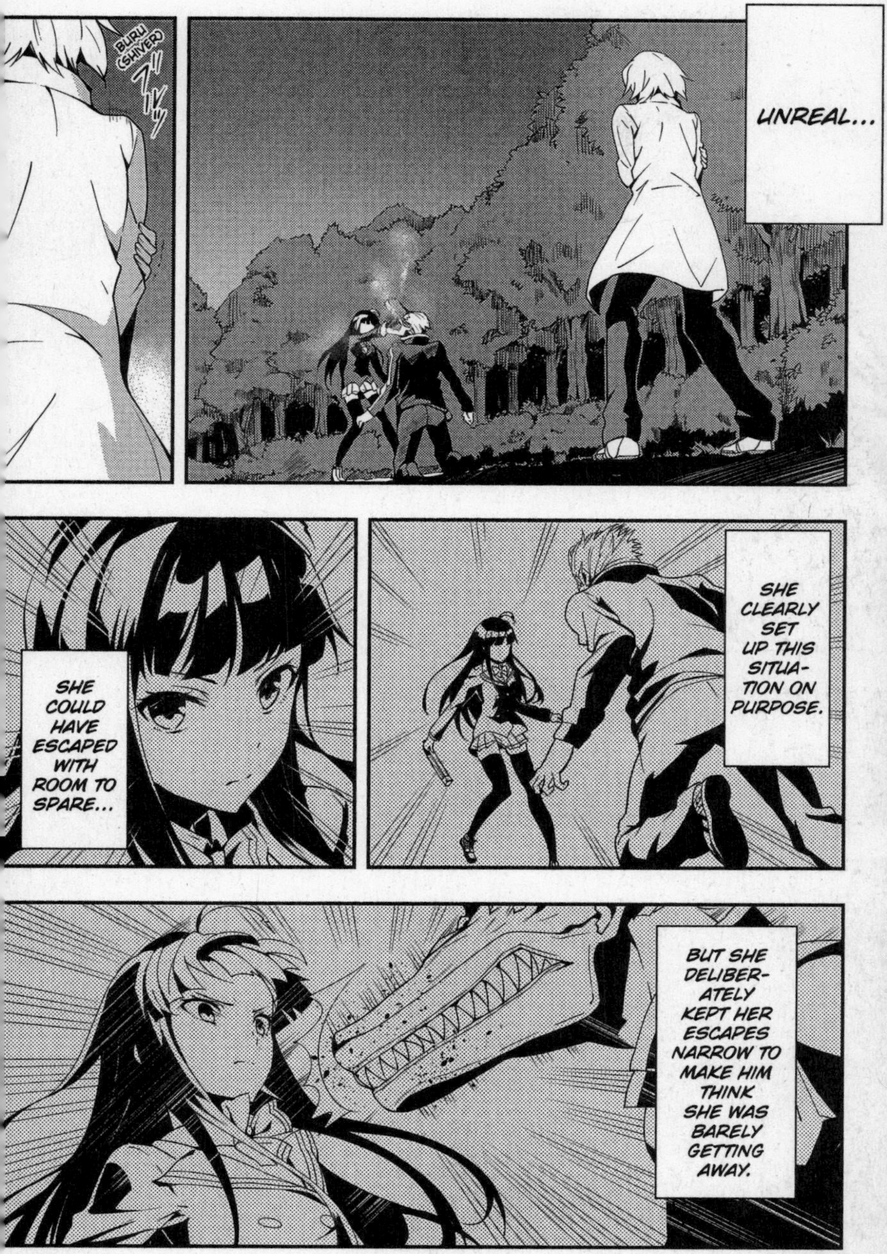
UNREAL...
BURU (SHIVER)
SHE CLEARLY SET UP THIS SITUATION ON PURPOSE.
SHE COULD HAVE ESCAPED WITH ROOM TO SPARE...
BUT SHE DELIBERATELY KEPT HER ESCAPES NARROW TO MAKE HIM THINK SHE WAS BARELY GETTING AWAY.

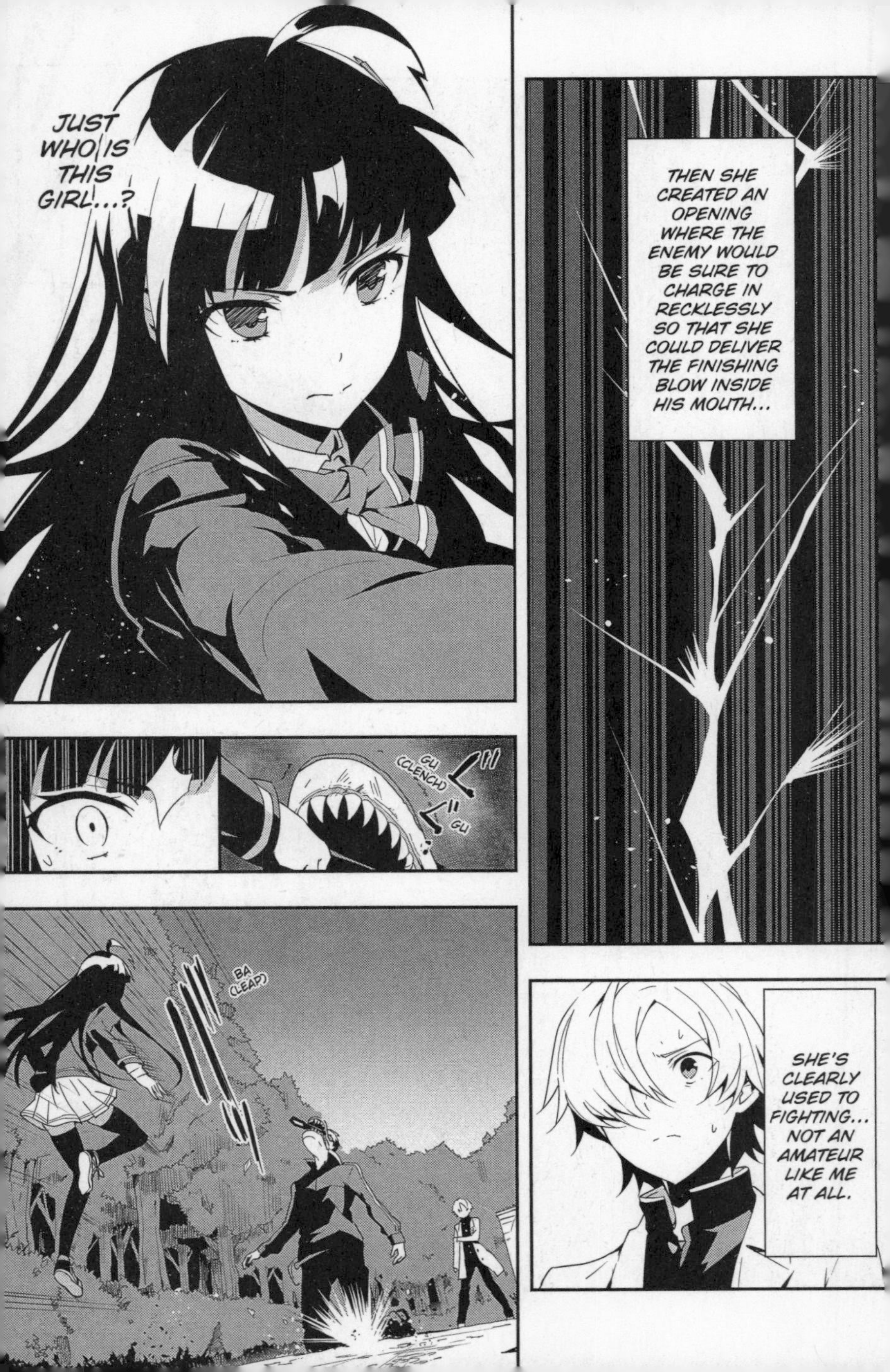

THEN SHE CREATED AN OPENING WHERE THE ENEMY WOULD BE SURE TO CHARGE IN RECKLESSLY SO THAT SHE COULD DELIVER THE FINISHING BLOW INSIDE HIS MOUTH...
JUST WHO IS THIS GIRL...?
GU (CLENCH)
GU
SHE'S CLEARLY USED TO FIGHTING... NOT AN AMATEUR LIKE ME AT ALL.
BA (LEAP)

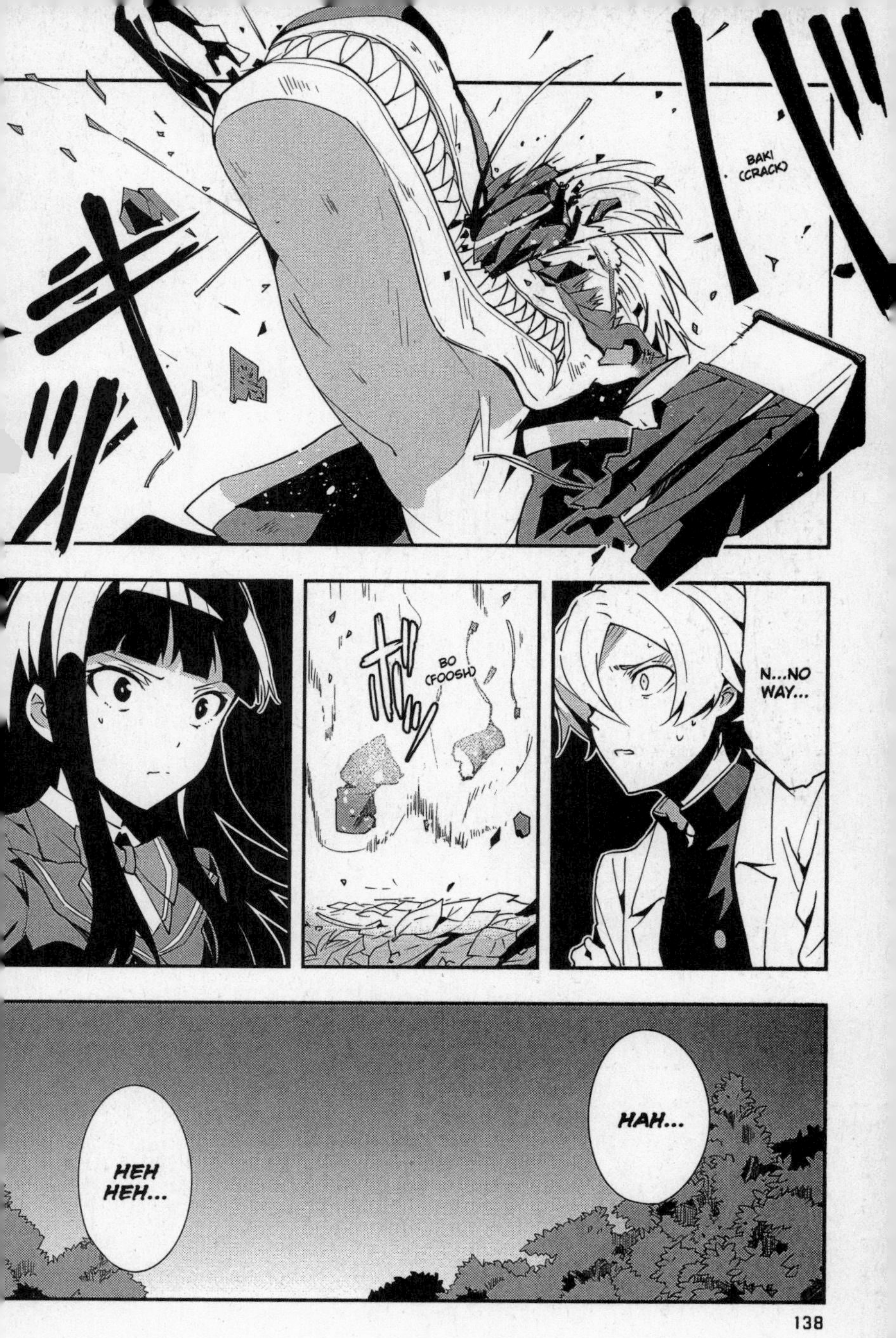
BAKI (CRACK)
N...NO WAY...
BO (FOOSH)
HAH...
HEH HEH...

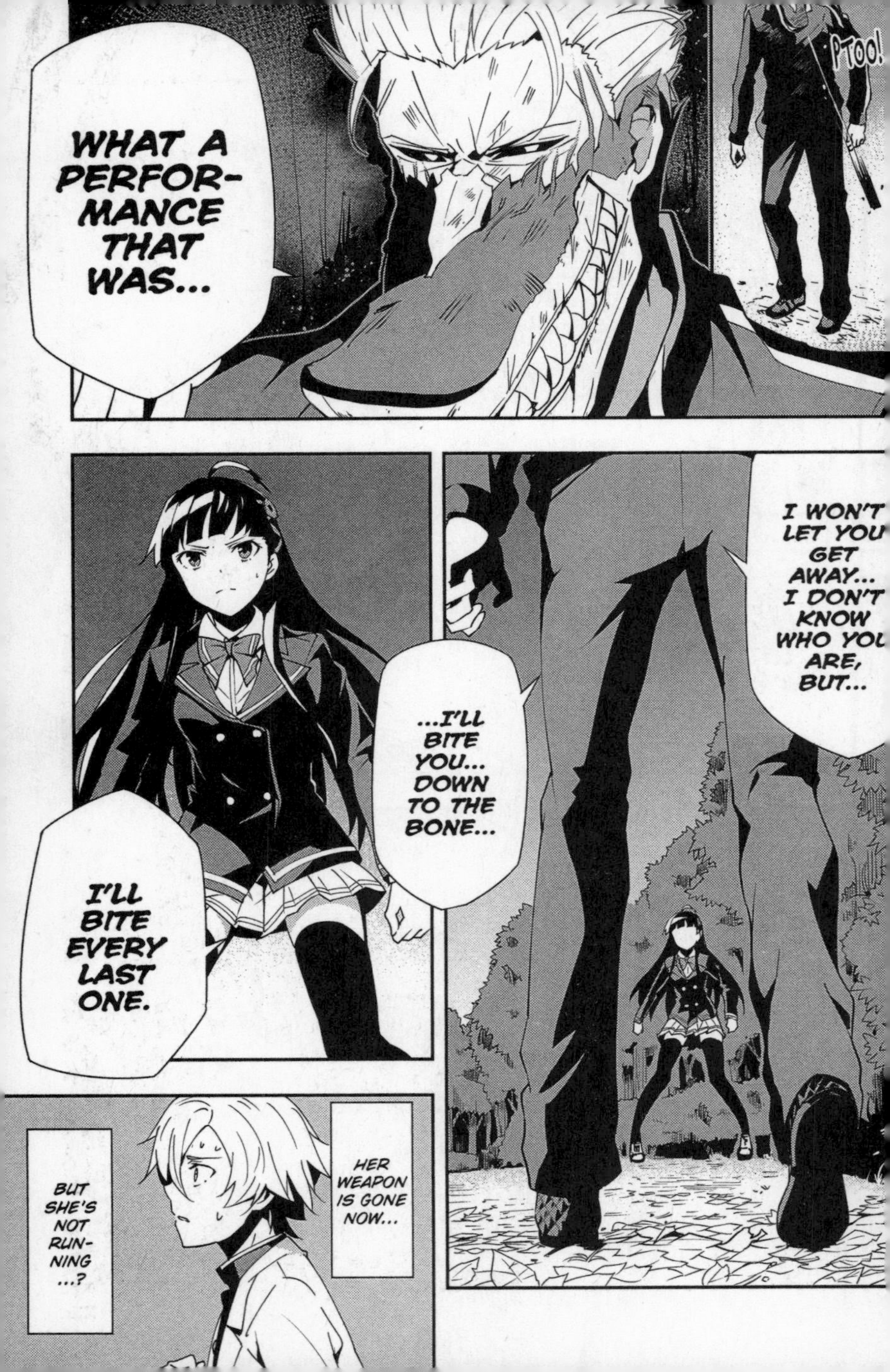
PTOO!
WHAT A PERFORMANCE THAT WAS...
I WON'T LET YOU GET AWAY... I DON'T KNOW WHO YOU ARE, BUT...
...I'LL BITE YOU... DOWN TO THE BONE...
I'LL BITE EVERY LAST ONE.
HER WEAPON IS GONE NOW...
BUT SHE'S NOT RUNNING...?

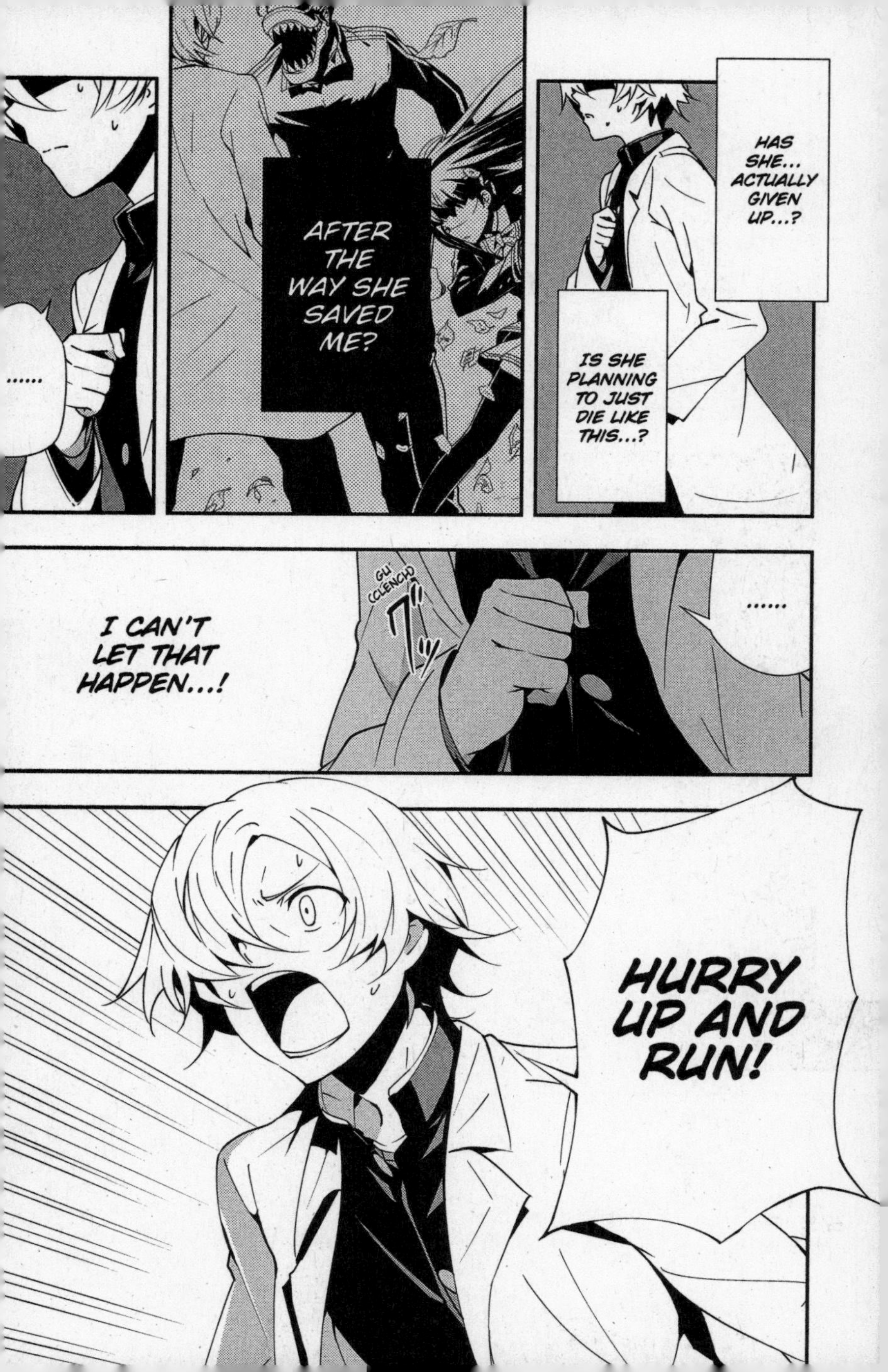
HAS SHE... ACTUALLY GIVEN UP...?
IS SHE PLANNING TO JUST DIE LIKE THIS...?
AFTER THE WAY SHE SAVED ME?
......
......
GU (CLENCH)
I CAN'T LET THAT HAPPEN...!
HURRY UP AND RUN!

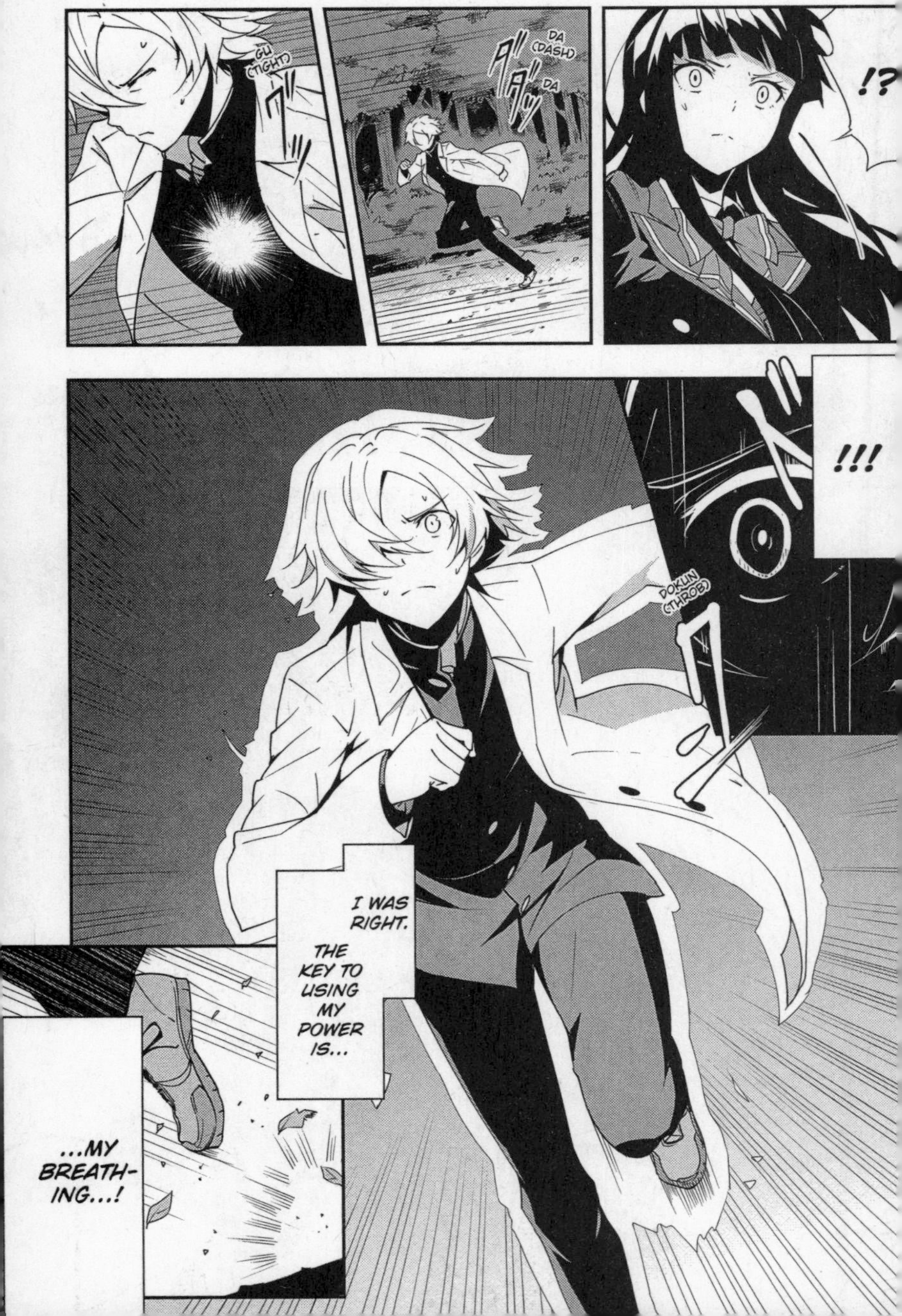
!?
DA (DASH)
DA
GU (TIGHT)
!!!
DOKUN (THROB)
I WAS RIGHT.
THE KEY TO USING MY POWER IS...
...MY BREATHING...!

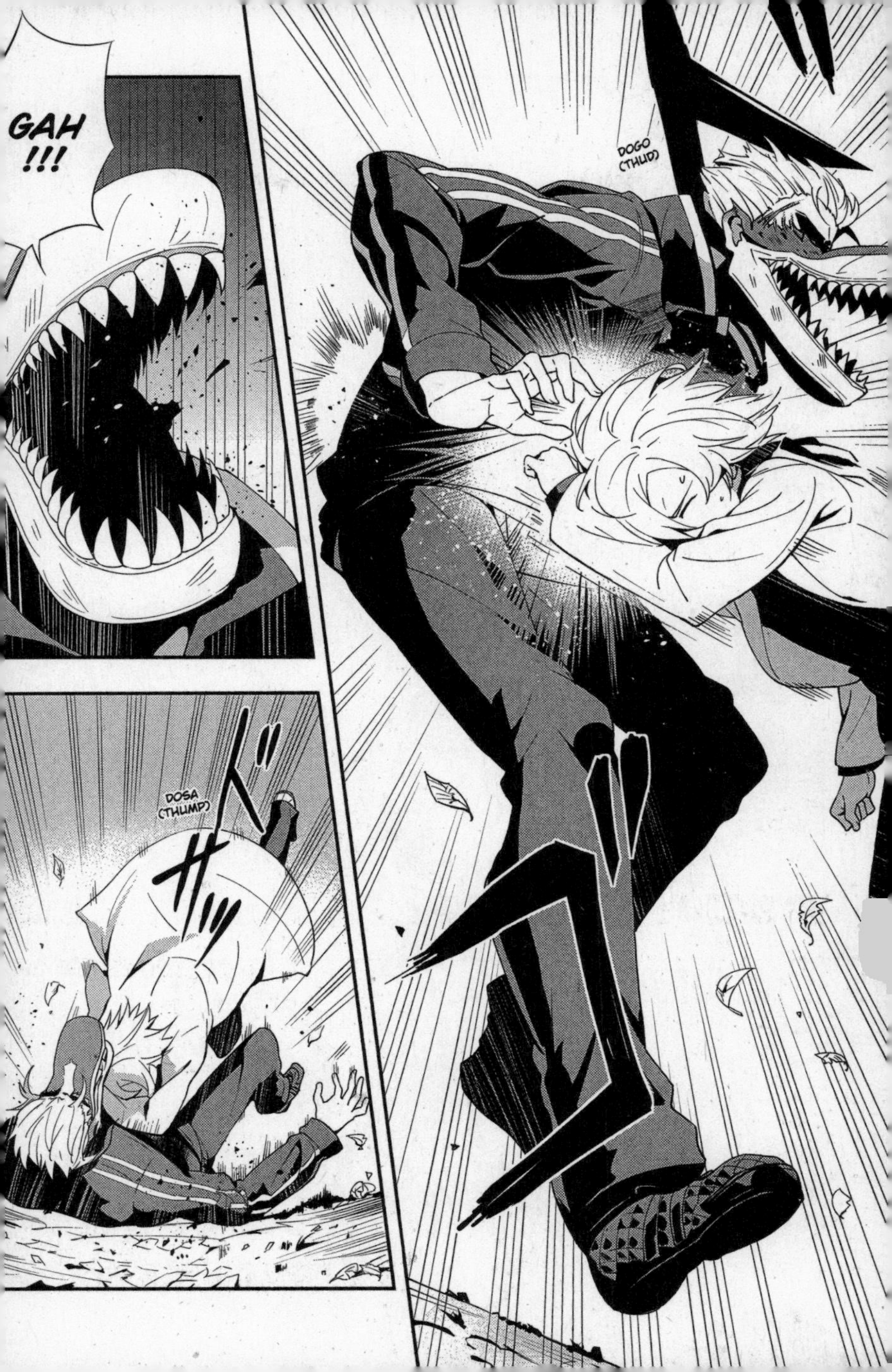
DOGO
(THUD)
GAH
!!!
DOSA
(THUMP)

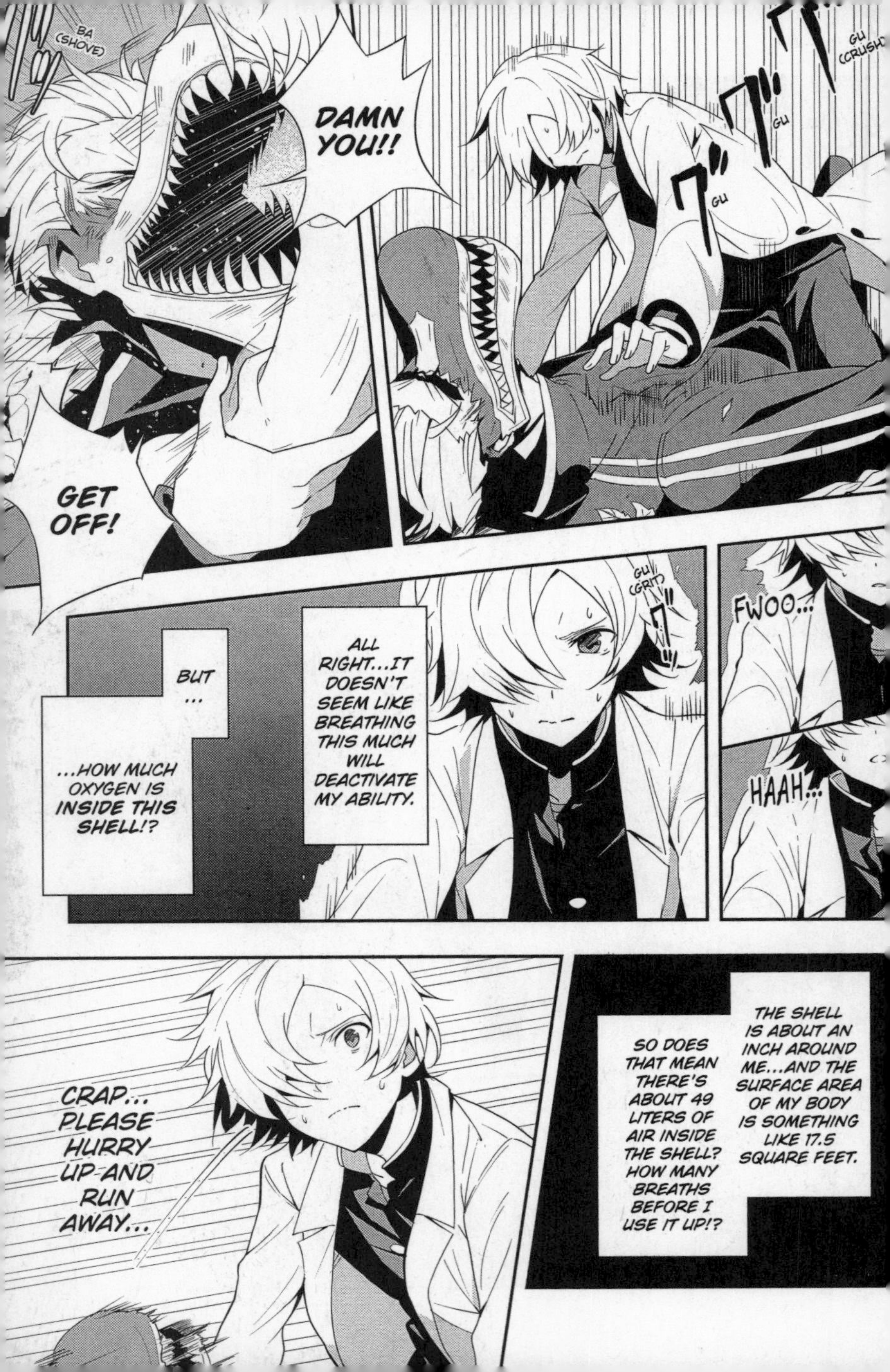
GU (CRUSH)
GU
GU
BA (SHOVE)
DAMN YOU!!
GET OFF!
FWOO...
HAAH...
GU (GRIT)
ALL RIGHT...IT DOESN'T SEEM LIKE BREATHING THIS MUCH WILL DEACTIVATE MY ABILITY.
BUT...
...HOW MUCH OXYGEN IS INSIDE THIS SHELL!?
THE SHELL IS ABOUT AN INCH AROUND ME...AND THE SURFACE AREA OF MY BODY IS SOMETHING LIKE 17.5 SQUARE FEET.
SO DOES THAT MEAN THERE'S ABOUT 49 LITERS OF AIR INSIDE THE SHELL? HOW MANY BREATHS BEFORE I USE IT UP!?
CRAP... PLEASE HURRY UP AND RUN AWAY...

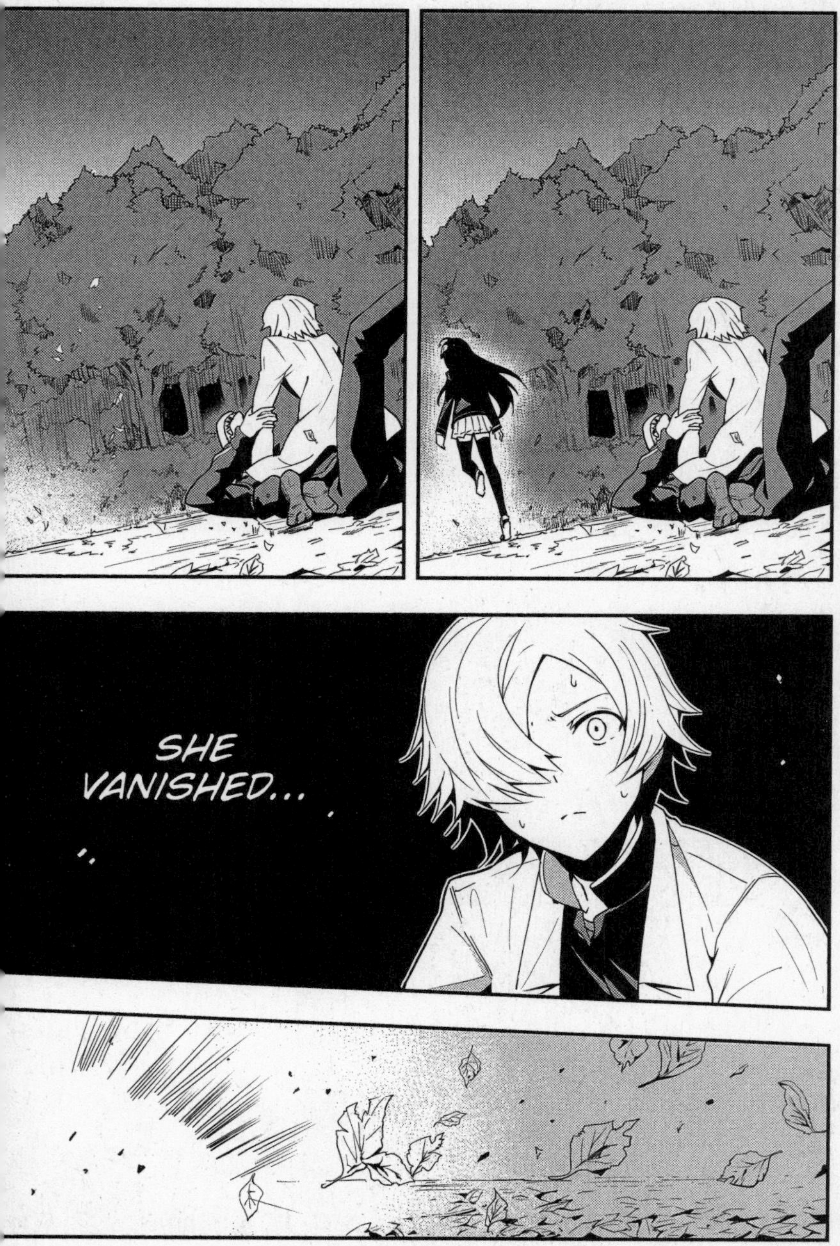
SHE VANISHED...

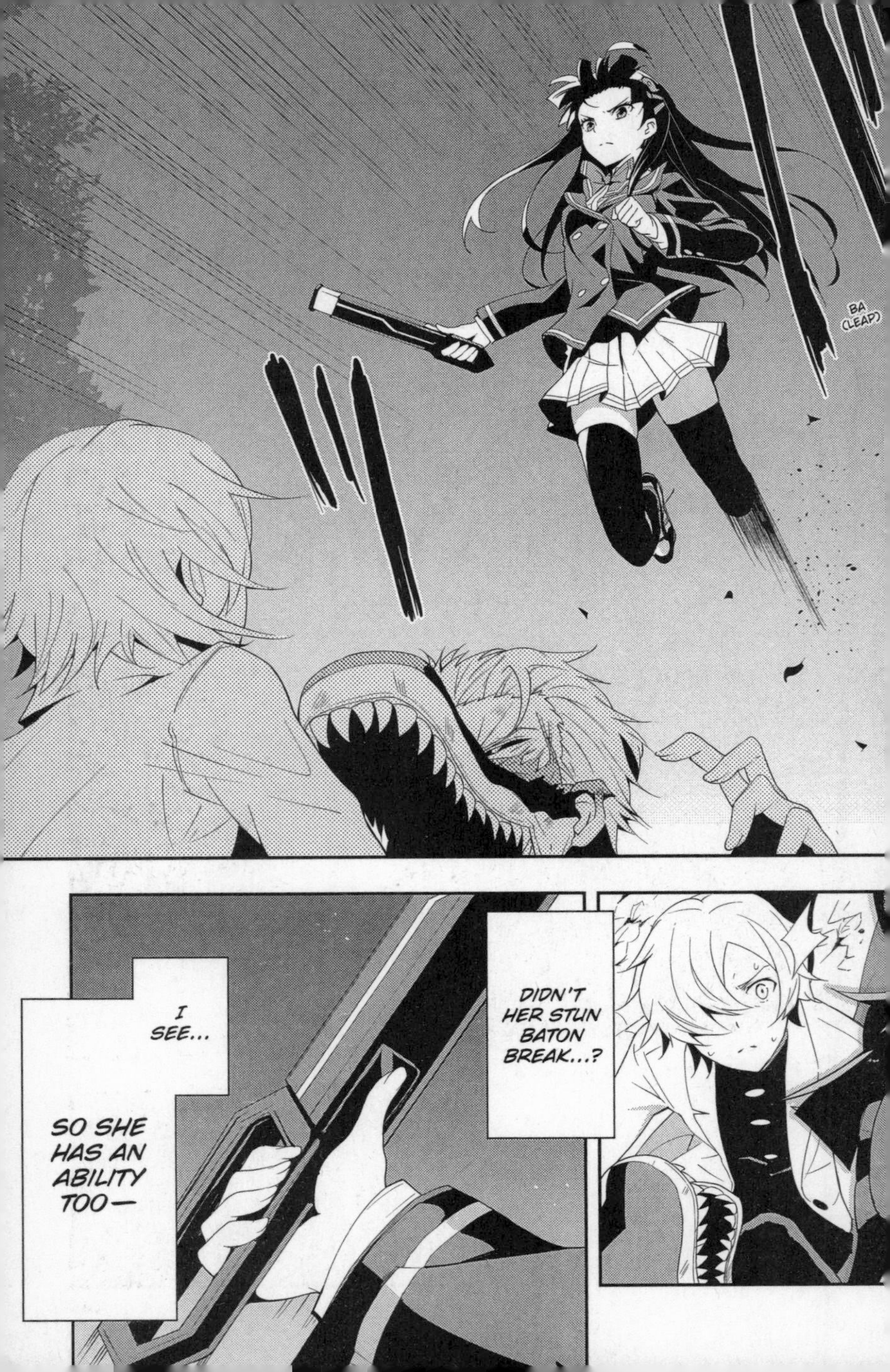
BA
(LEAP)
DIDN'T HER STUN BATON BREAK...?
I SEE...
SO SHE HAS AN ABILITY TOO—

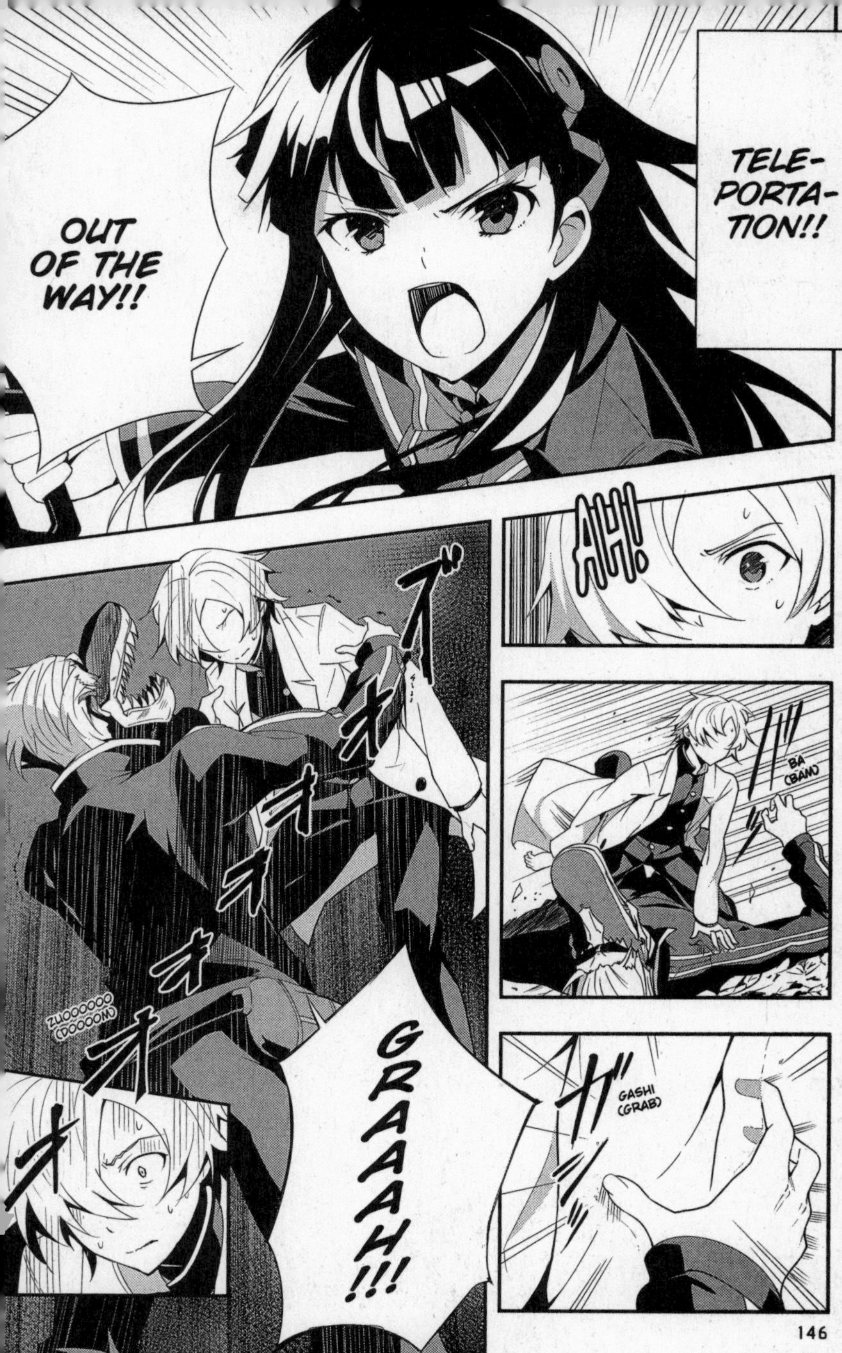
TELE-PORTATION!!
OUT OF THE WAY!!
AH!
BA (BAM)
GASHI (GRAB)
ZUOOOOOO (DOOOOM)
GRAAAAH!!!

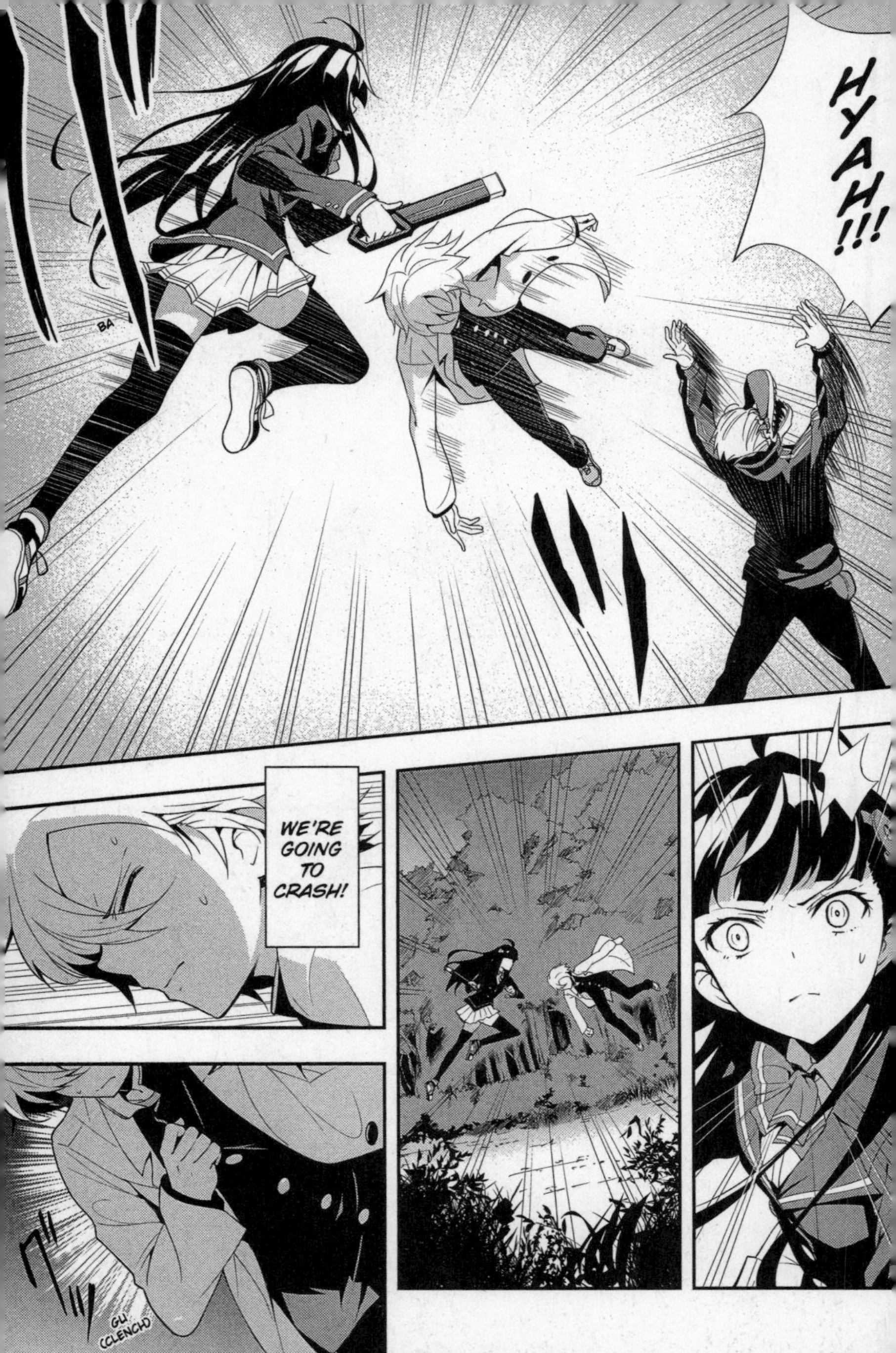
HYAH!!!
BA
WE'RE GOING TO CRASH!
GLI (CLENCH)

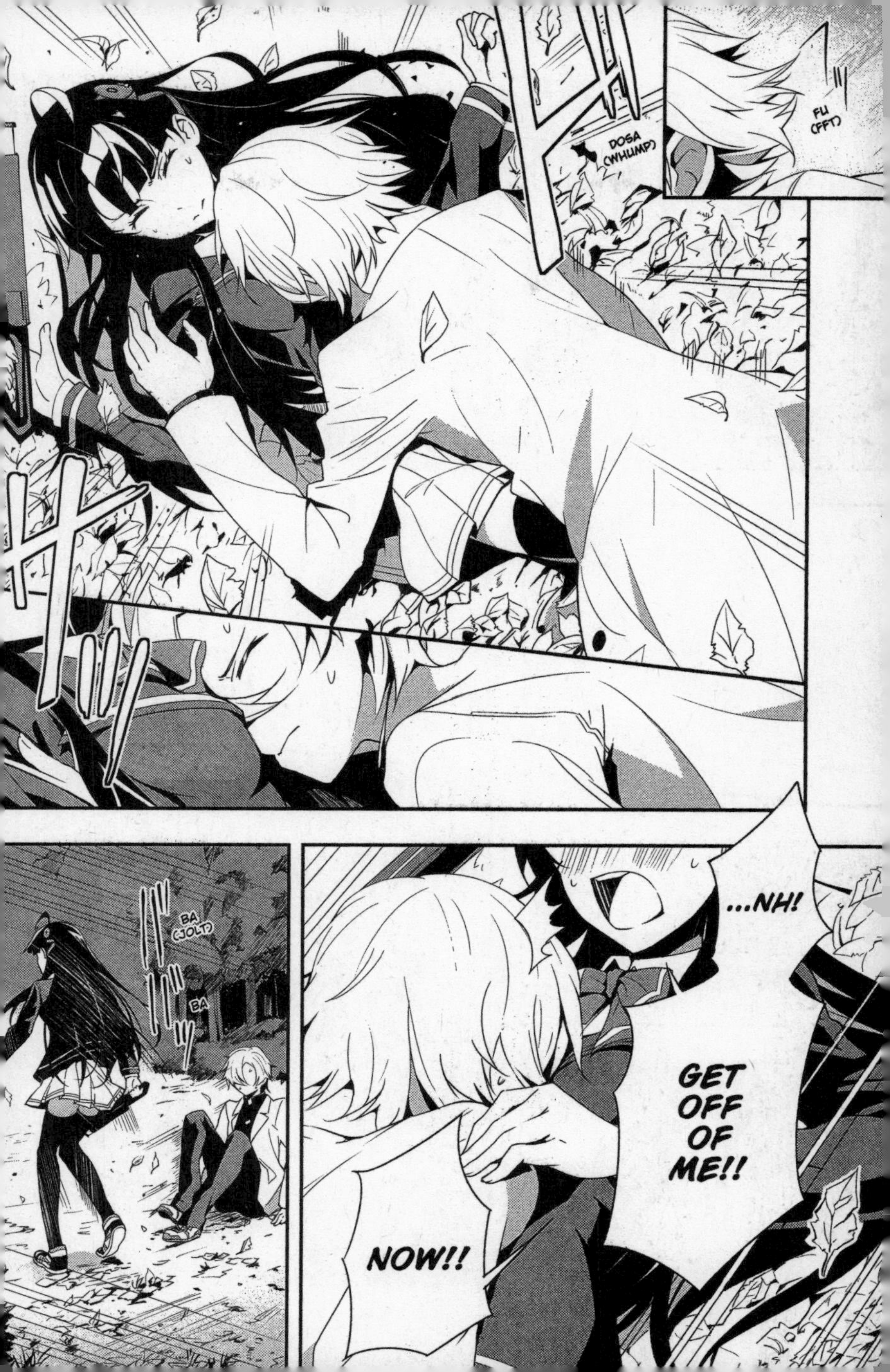
FU (FFT)
DOSA (WHUMP)
...NH!
GET OFF OF ME!!
NOW!!
BA (JOLT)
BA

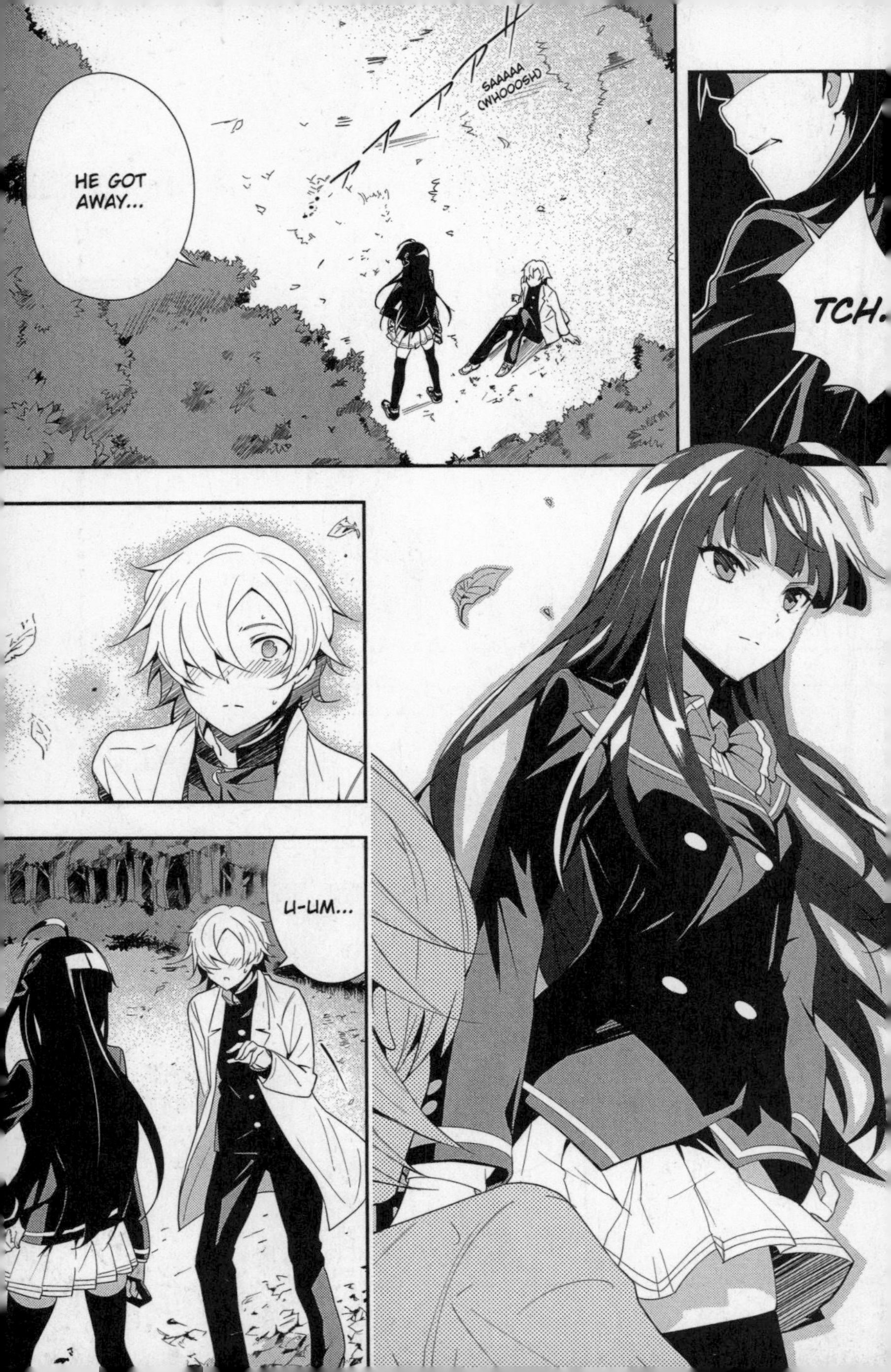
TCH.
SAAAAA (WHOOOSH)
HE GOT AWAY...
U-UM...

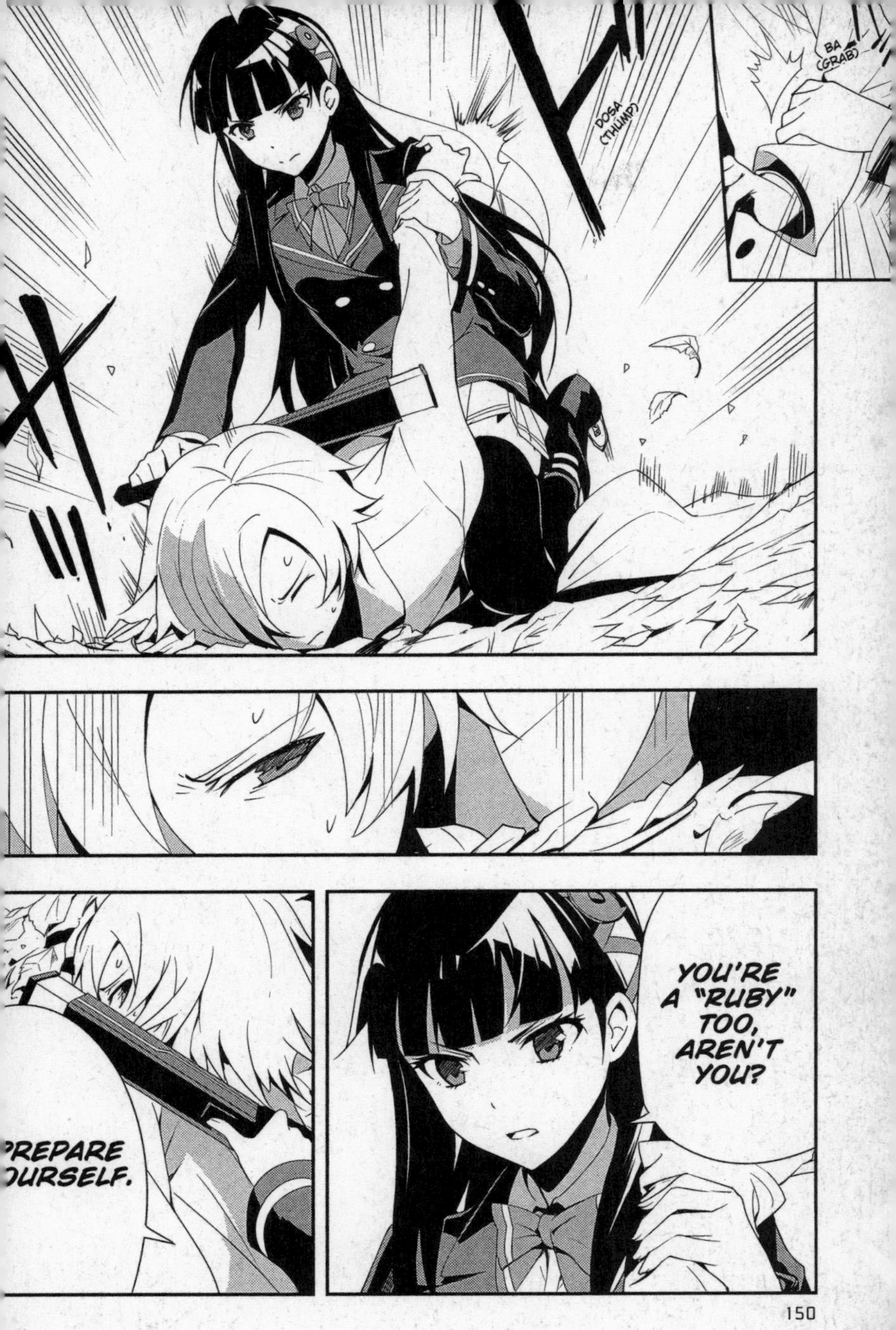
BA (GRAB)
DOSA (THUMP)
YOU'RE A "RUBY" TOO, AREN'T YOU?
PREPARE OURSELF.

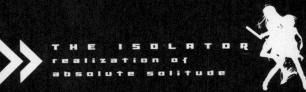

THE ISOLATOR
realization of
absolute solitude

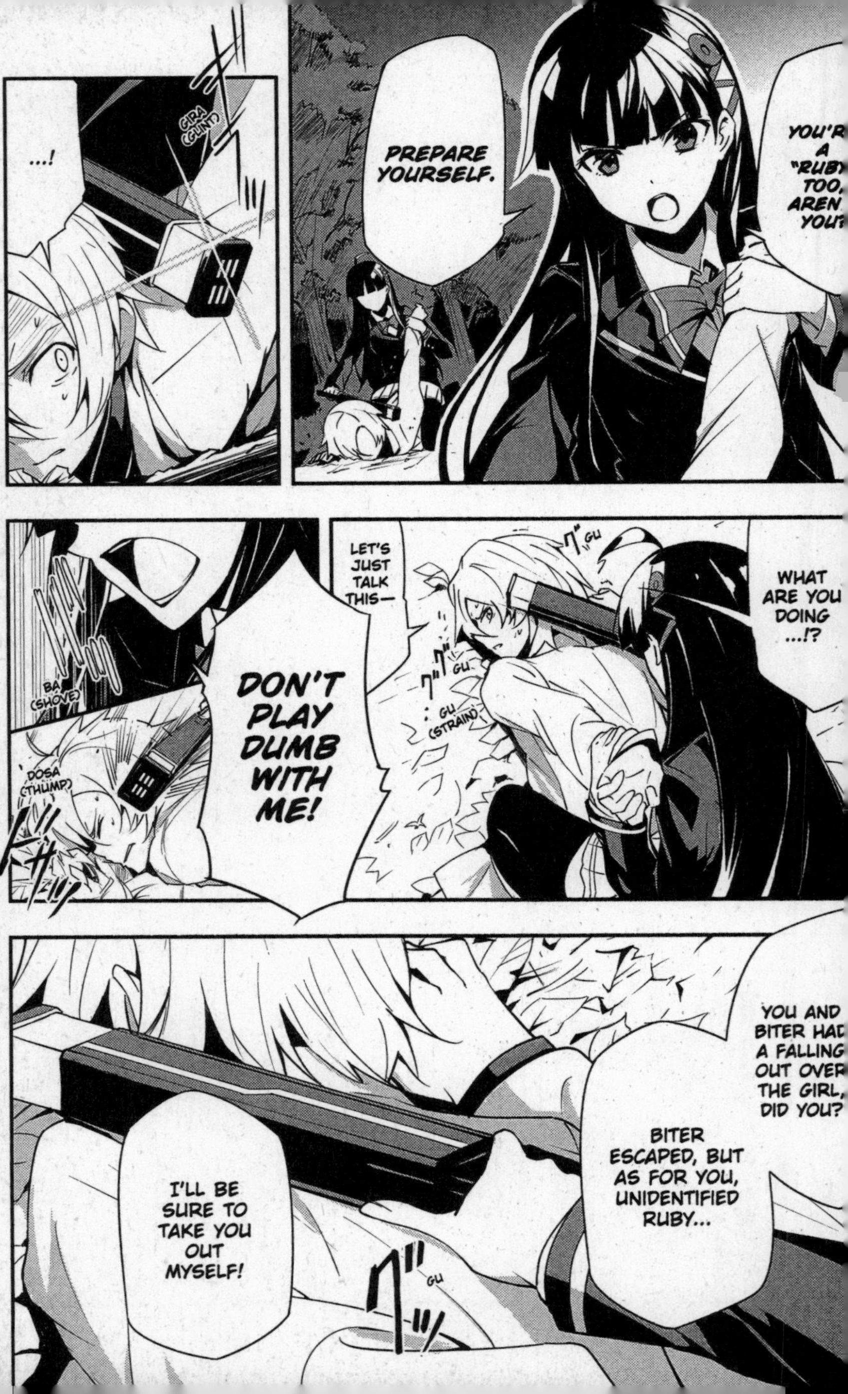
YOU'R A "RUBY TOO, AREN YOU?
PREPARE YOURSELF.
GIRA (GLINT)
...!
WHAT ARE YOU DOING ...!?
GU
GU
GU (STRAIN)
LET'S JUST TALK THIS—
DON'T PLAY DUMB WITH ME!
BA (SHOVE)
DOSA (THUMP)
YOU AND BITER HAD A FALLING OUT OVER THE GIRL, DID YOU?
BITER ESCAPED, BUT AS FOR YOU, UNIDENTIFIED RUBY...
GU
I'LL BE SURE TO TAKE YOU OUT MYSELF!

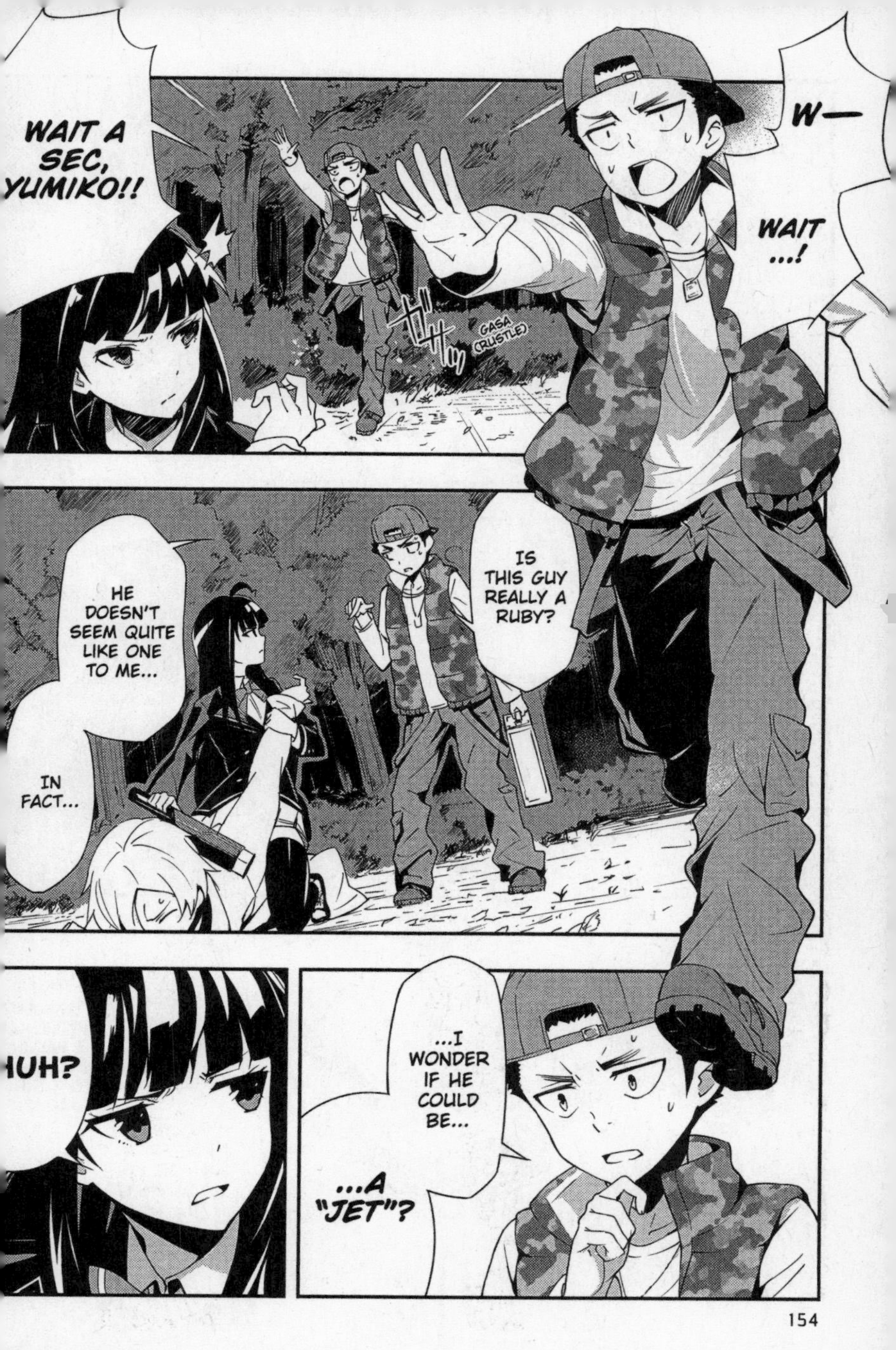
W—
WAIT ...!
WAIT A SEC, YUMIKO!!
GASA (RUSTLE)
IS THIS GUY REALLY A RUBY?
HE DOESN'T SEEM QUITE LIKE ONE TO ME...
IN FACT...
...I WONDER IF HE COULD BE...
...A "JET"?
HUH?

Sect. 006
JET EYE

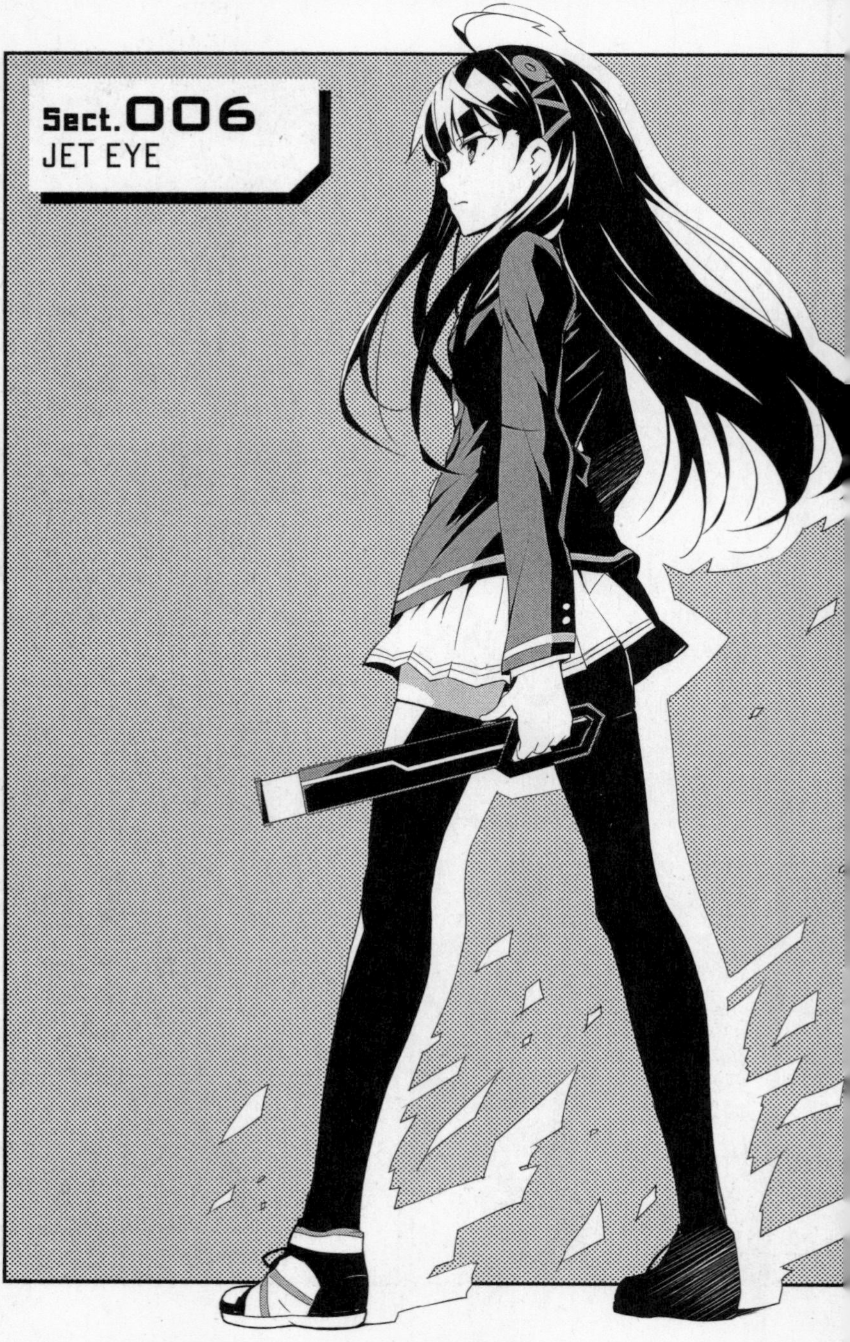

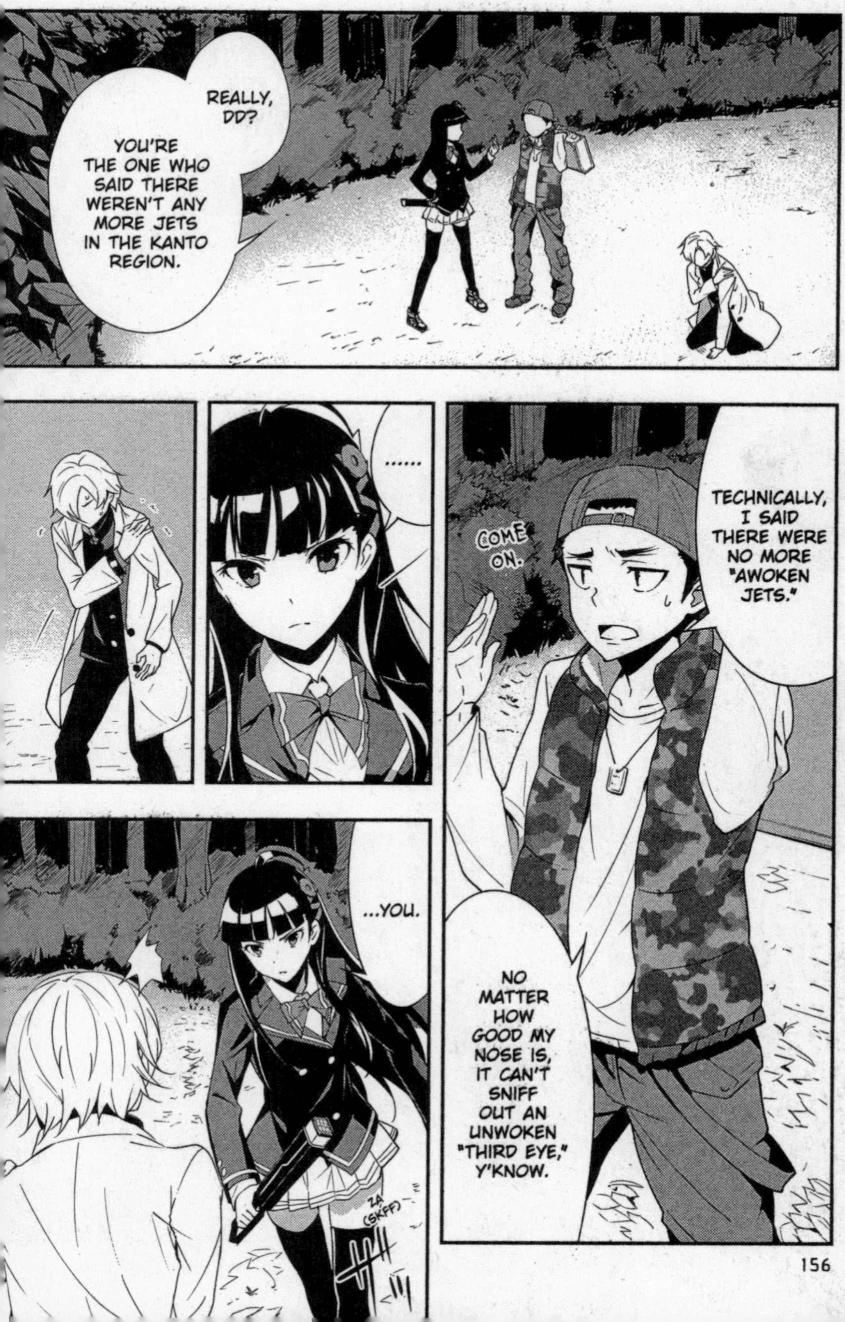
REALLY, DD?
YOU'RE THE ONE WHO SAID THERE WEREN'T ANY MORE JETS IN THE KANTO REGION.
TECHNICALLY, I SAID THERE WERE NO MORE "AWOKEN JETS."
COME ON.
NO MATTER HOW GOOD MY NOSE IS, IT CAN'T SNIFF OUT AN UNWOKEN "THIRD EYE," Y'KNOW.
......
...YOU.
ZA (SKFF)

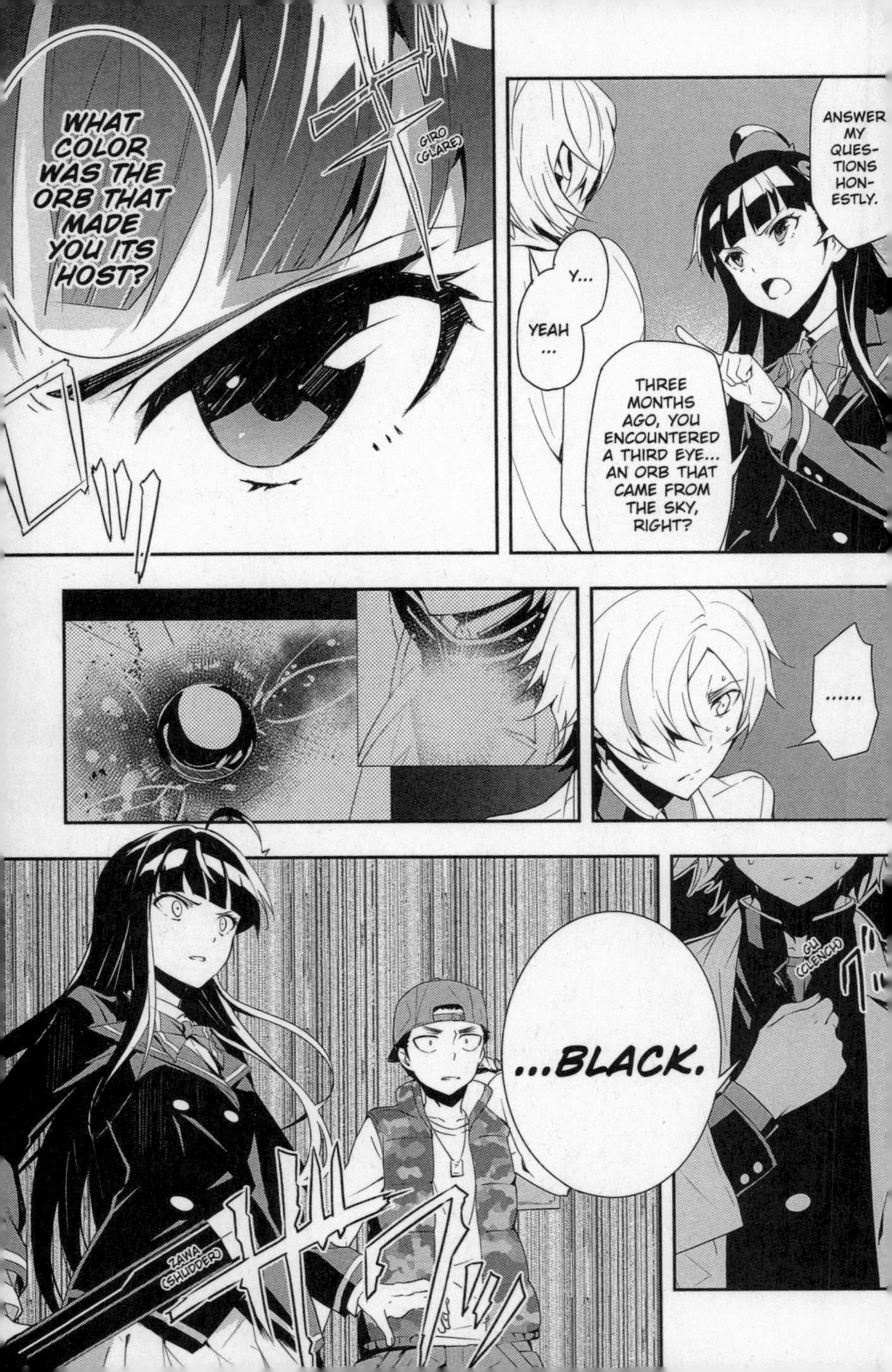
ANSWER MY QUES-TIONS HON-ESTLY.
THREE MONTHS AGO, YOU ENCOUNTERED A THIRD EYE... AN ORB THAT CAME FROM THE SKY, RIGHT?
Y...
YEAH ...
WHAT COLOR WAS THE ORB THAT MADE YOU ITS HOST?
GIRO (GLARE)
......
GU (CLENCH)
...BLACK.
ZAWA (SHUDDER)

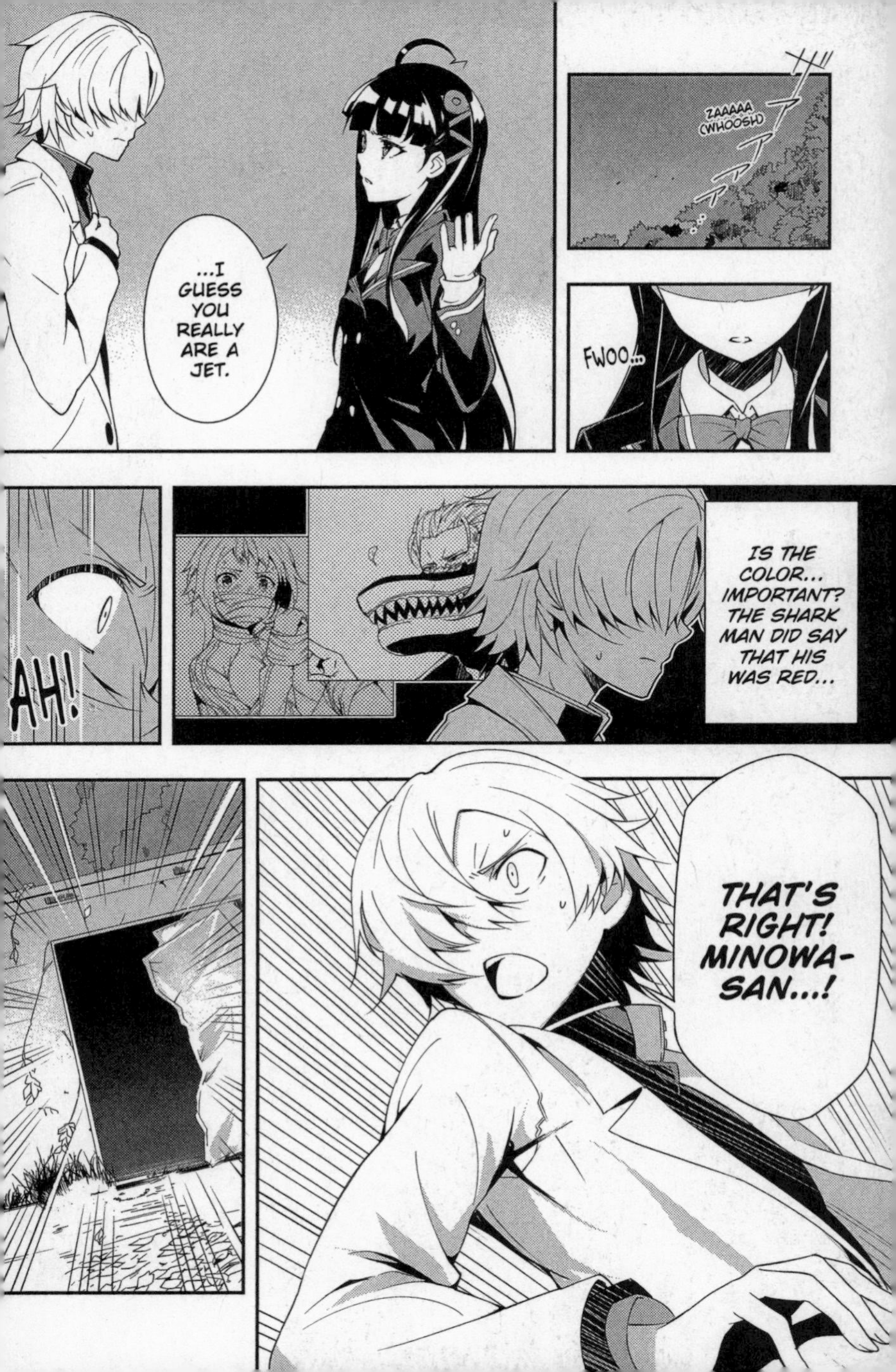
ZAAAAA (WHOOSH)
FWOO...
...I GUESS YOU REALLY ARE A JET.
IS THE COLOR... IMPORTANT? THE SHARK MAN DID SAY THAT HIS WAS RED...
AH!
THAT'S RIGHT! MINOWA-SAN...!

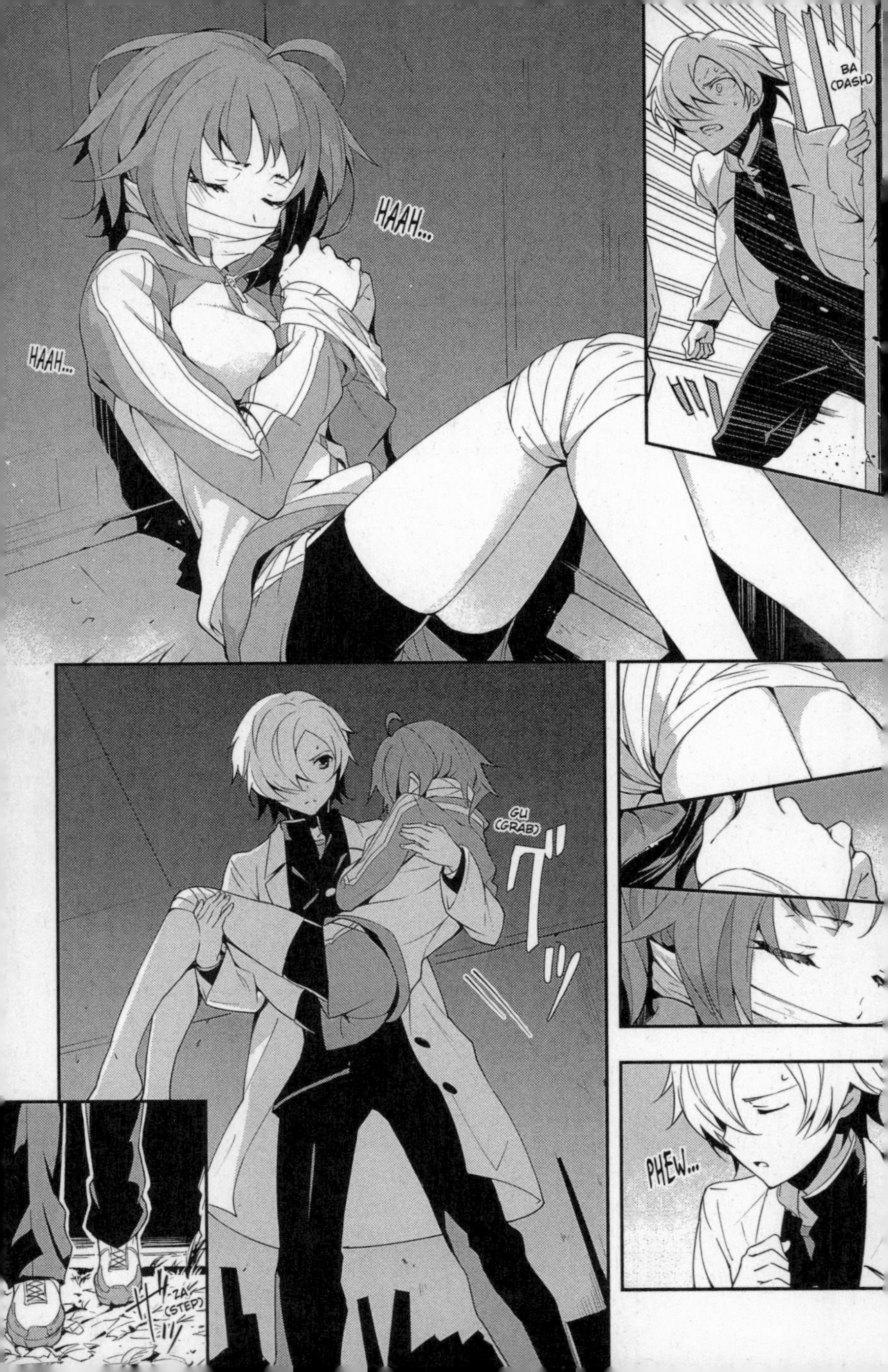
BA
(DASH)
HAAH...
HAAH...
PHEW...
GU
(GRAB)
ZA
(STEP)

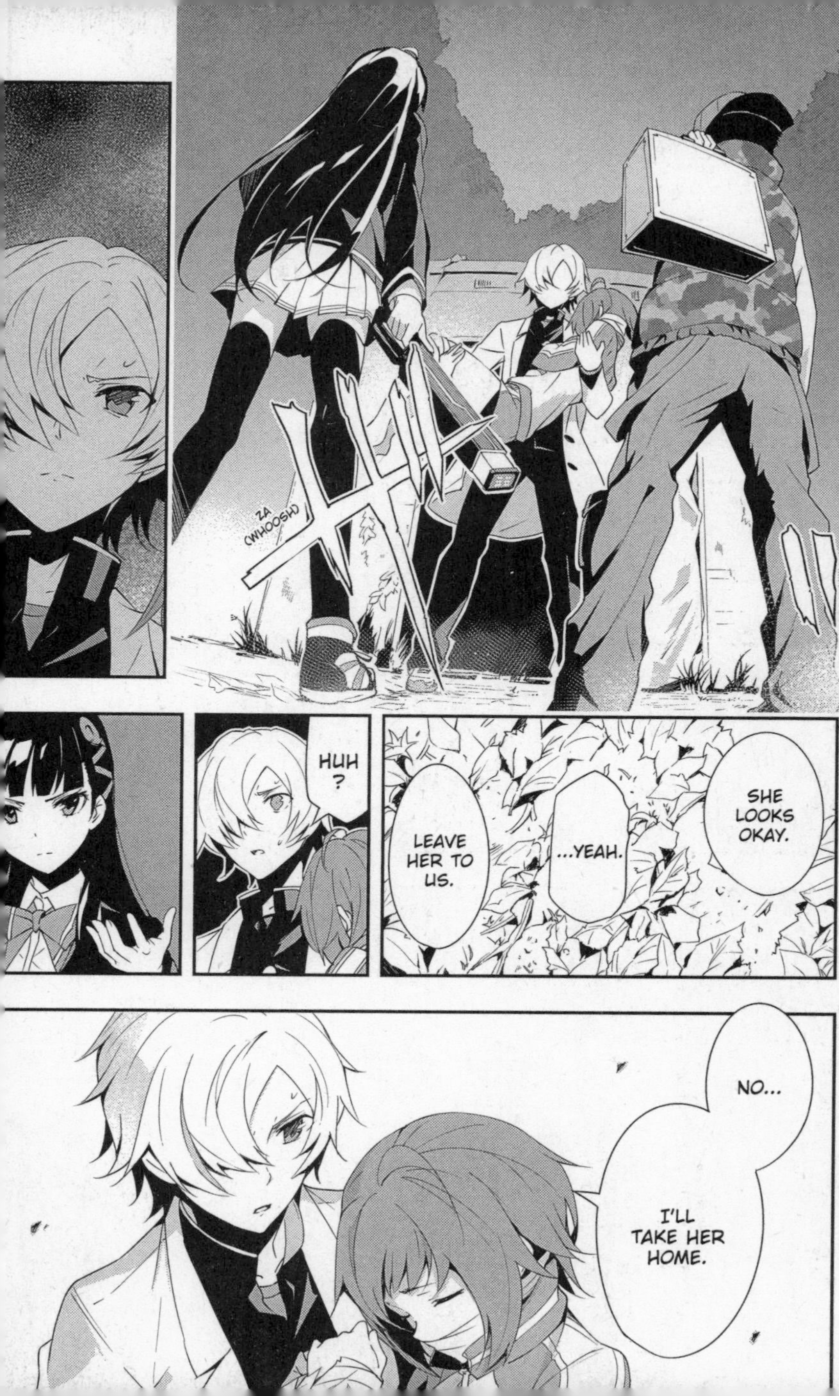
ZA (WHOOSH)
SHE LOOKS OKAY.
...YEAH.
LEAVE HER TO US.
HUH?
NO...
I'LL TAKE HER HOME.

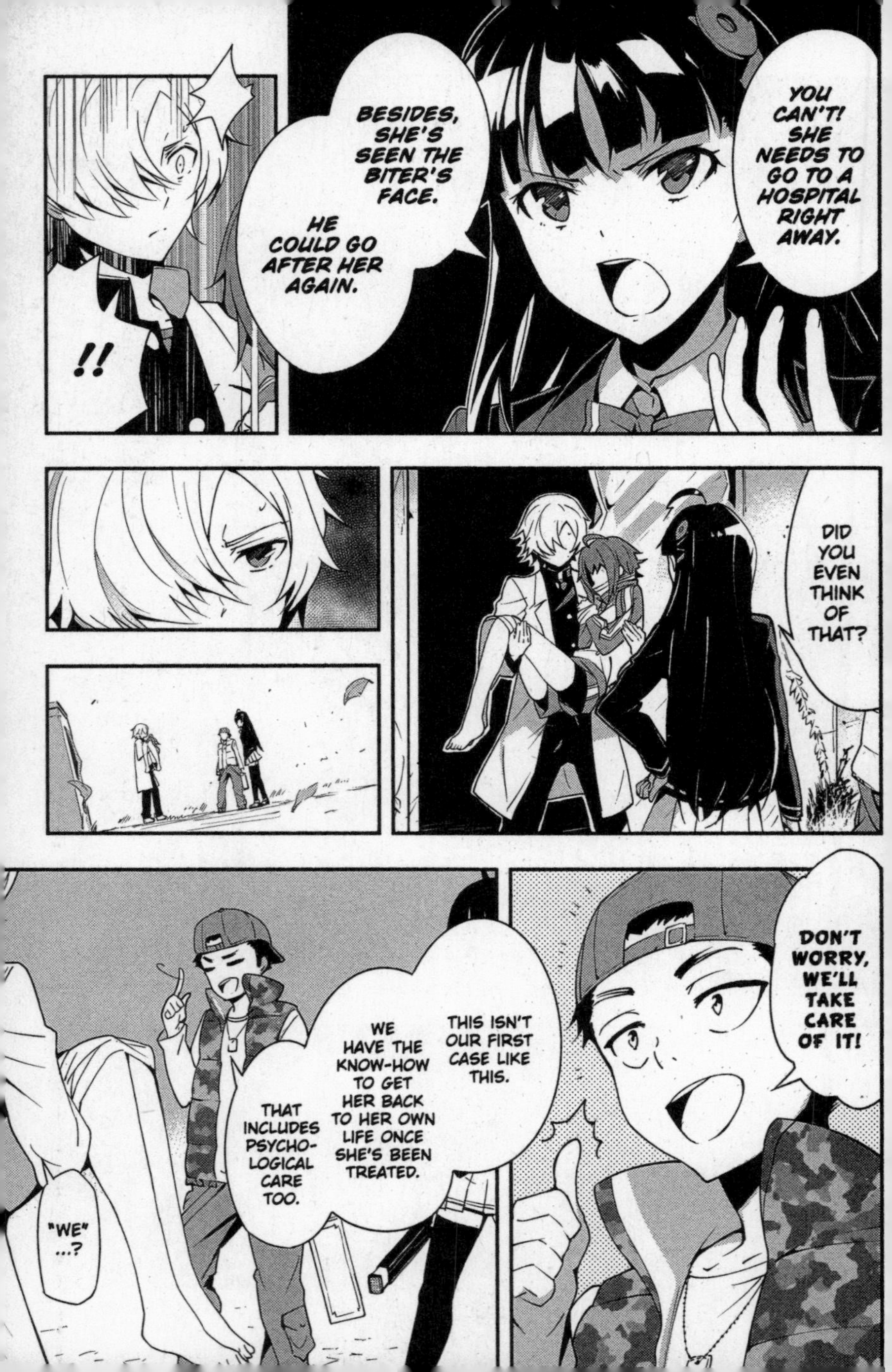
YOU CAN'T! SHE NEEDS TO GO TO A HOSPITAL RIGHT AWAY.
BESIDES, SHE'S SEEN THE BITER'S FACE.
HE COULD GO AFTER HER AGAIN.
!!
DID YOU EVEN THINK OF THAT?
DON'T WORRY, WE'LL TAKE CARE OF IT!
THIS ISN'T OUR FIRST CASE LIKE THIS.
WE HAVE THE KNOW-HOW TO GET HER BACK TO HER OWN LIFE ONCE SHE'S BEEN TREATED.
THAT INCLUDES PSYCHO-LOGICAL CARE TOO.
"WE" ...?

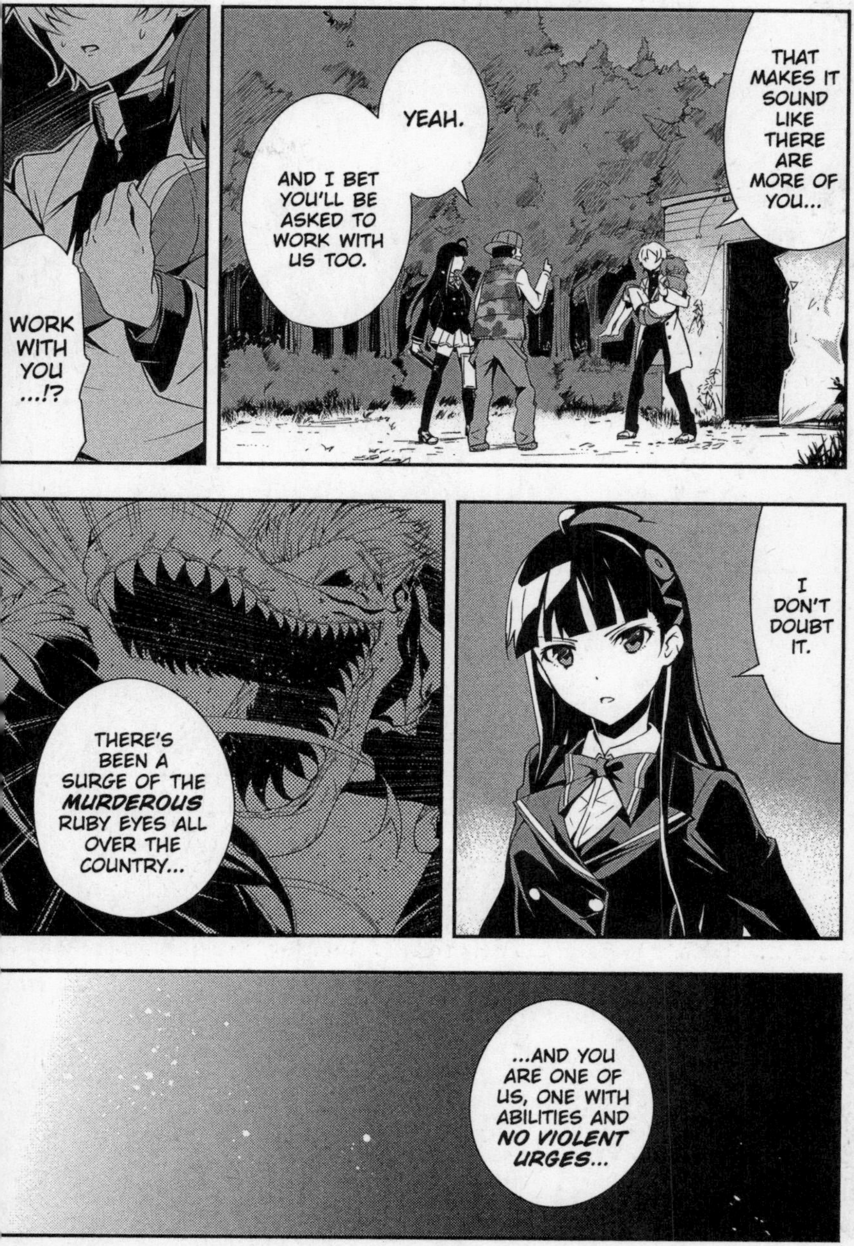
THAT MAKES IT SOUND LIKE THERE ARE MORE OF YOU...
YEAH. AND I BET YOU'LL BE ASKED TO WORK WITH US TOO.
WORK WITH YOU ...!?
I DON'T DOUBT IT.
THERE'S BEEN A SURGE OF THE MURDEROUS RUBY EYES ALL OVER THE COUNTRY...
...AND YOU ARE ONE OF US, ONE WITH ABILITIES AND NO VIOLENT URGES...

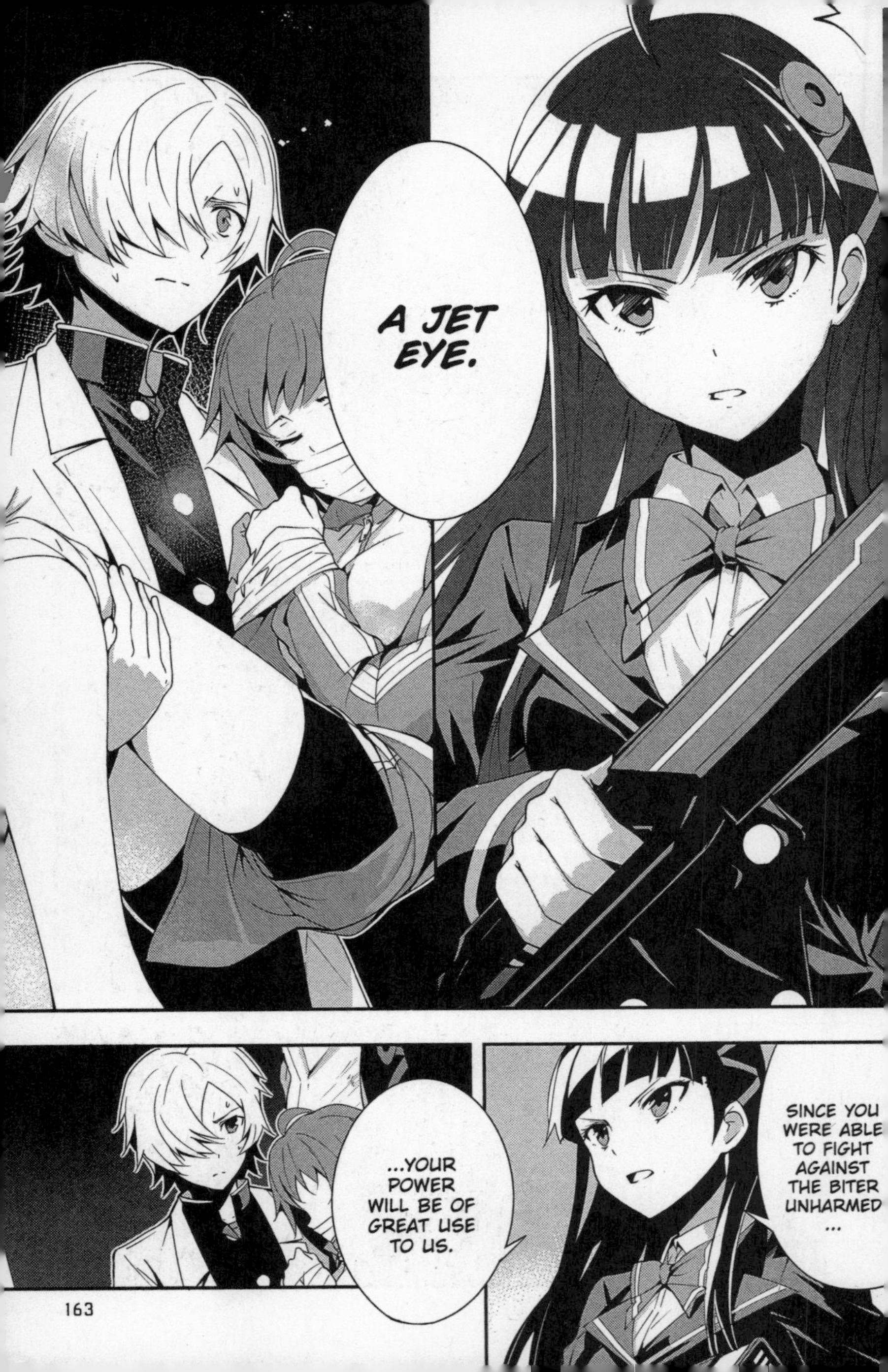
A JET EYE.
SINCE YOU WERE ABLE TO FIGHT AGAINST THE BITER UNHARMED...
...YOUR POWER WILL BE OF GREAT USE TO US.

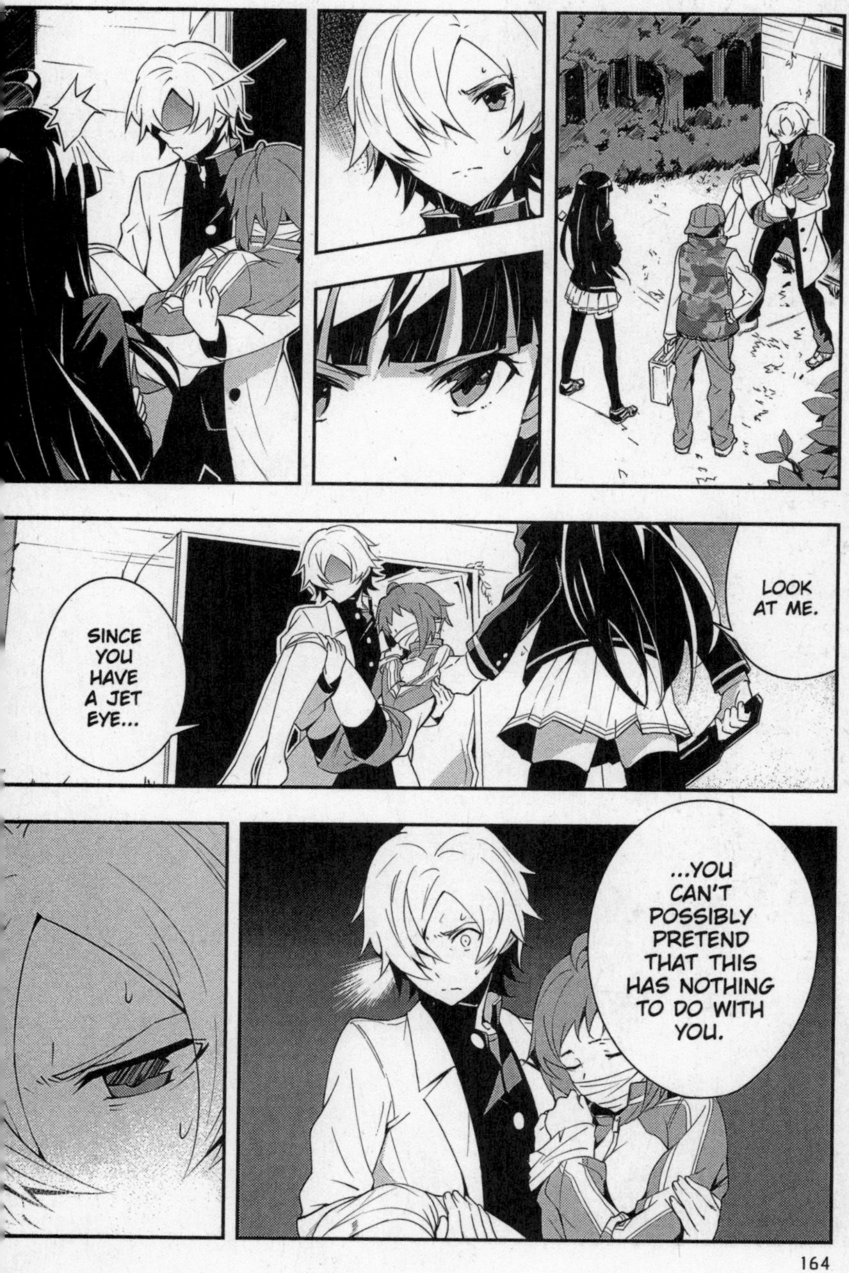
LOOK AT ME.
SINCE YOU HAVE A JET EYE...
...YOU CAN'T POSSIBLY PRETEND THAT THIS HAS NOTHING TO DO WITH YOU.

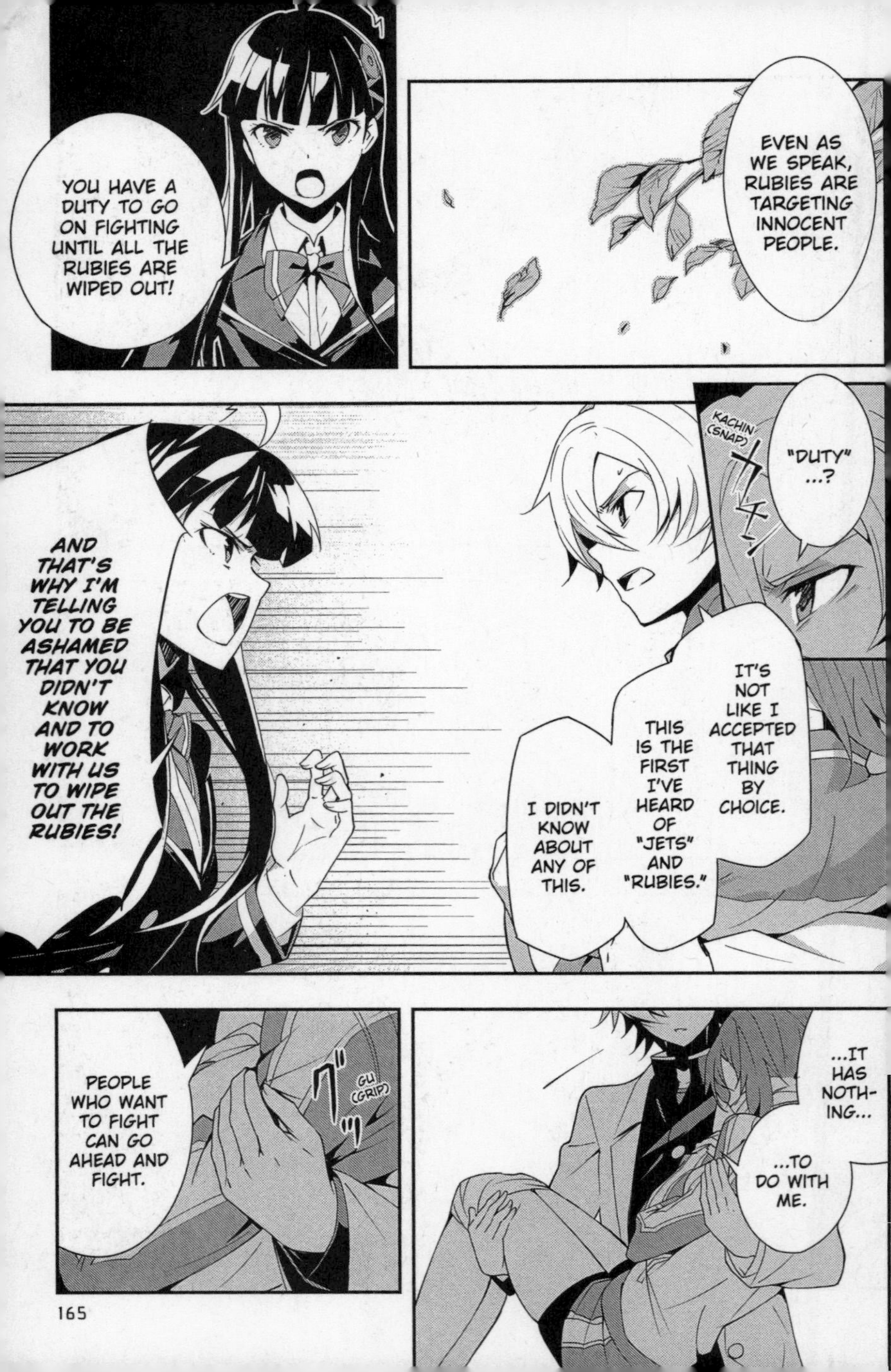
EVEN AS WE SPEAK, RUBIES ARE TARGETING INNOCENT PEOPLE.
YOU HAVE A DUTY TO GO ON FIGHTING UNTIL ALL THE RUBIES ARE WIPED OUT!
KACHIN (SNAP)
"DUTY" ...?
IT'S NOT LIKE I ACCEPTED THAT THING BY CHOICE.
THIS IS THE FIRST I'VE HEARD OF "JETS" AND "RUBIES."
I DIDN'T KNOW ABOUT ANY OF THIS.
AND THAT'S WHY I'M TELLING YOU TO BE ASHAMED THAT YOU DIDN'T KNOW AND TO WORK WITH US TO WIPE OUT THE RUBIES!
...IT HAS NOTHING...
...TO DO WITH ME.
GU (GRIP)
PEOPLE WHO WANT TO FIGHT CAN GO AHEAD AND FIGHT.

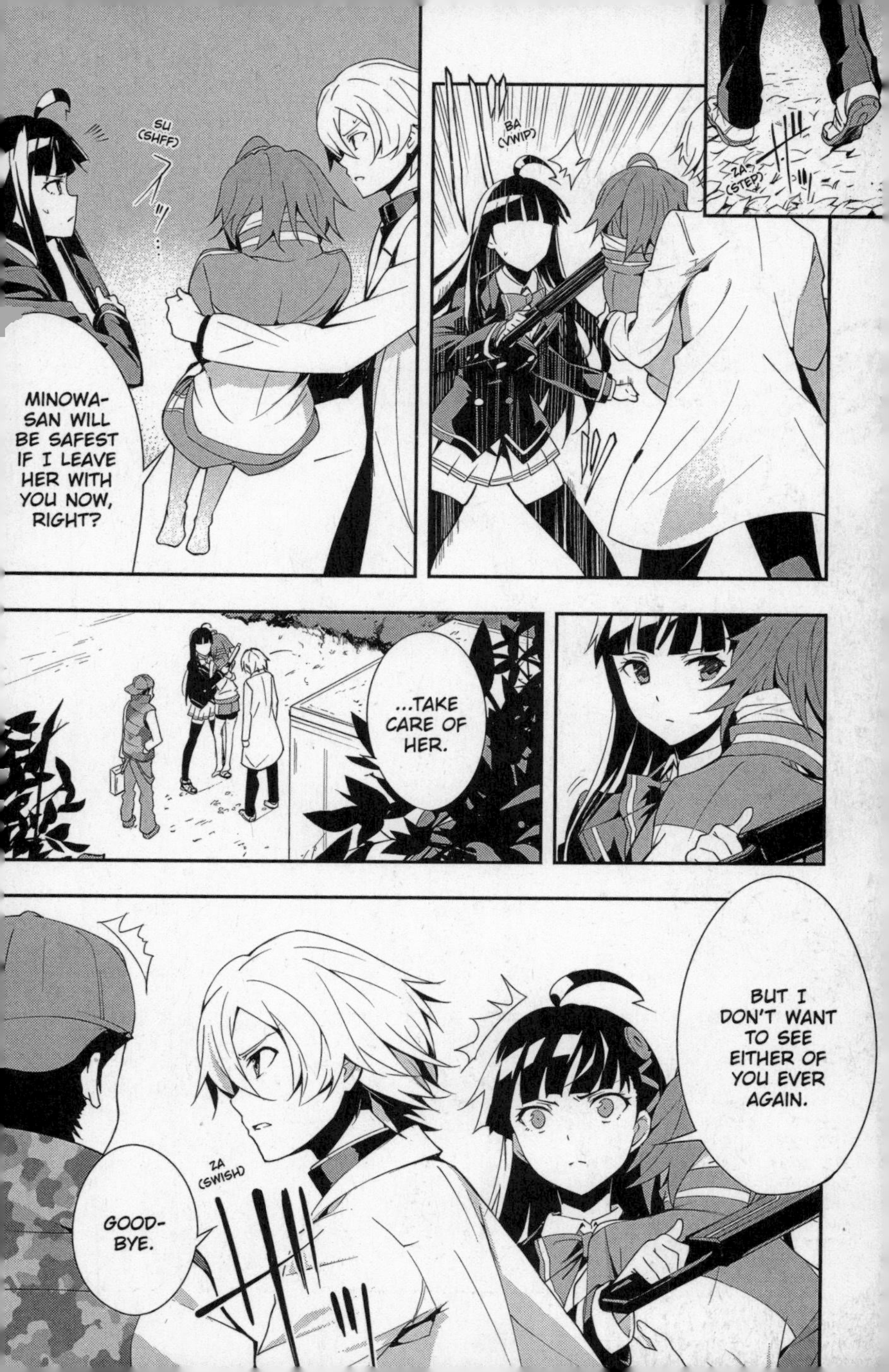
ZA (STEP)
BA (VWIP)
SU (SHFF)
MINOWA-SAN WILL BE SAFEST IF I LEAVE HER WITH YOU NOW, RIGHT?
...TAKE CARE OF HER.
BUT I DON'T WANT TO SEE EITHER OF YOU EVER AGAIN.
ZA (SWISH)
GOOD-BYE.

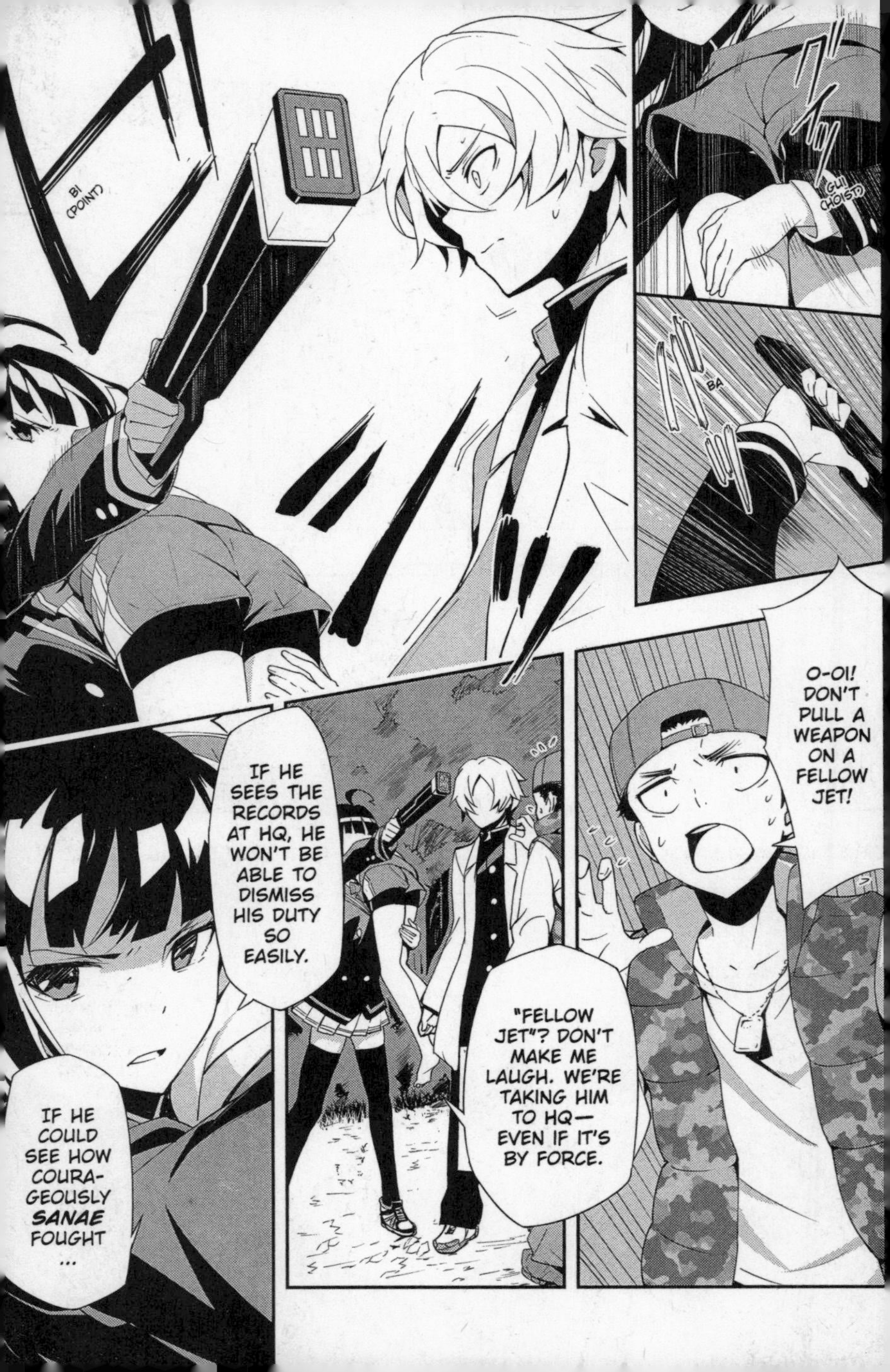
GUI (HOIST)
BA
BI (POINT)
O-OI! DON'T PULL A WEAPON ON A FELLOW JET!
"FELLOW JET"? DON'T MAKE ME LAUGH. WE'RE TAKING HIM TO HQ— EVEN IF IT'S BY FORCE.
IF HE SEES THE RECORDS AT HQ, HE WON'T BE ABLE TO DISMISS HIS DUTY SO EASILY.
IF HE COULD SEE HOW COURAGEOUSLY ***SANAE*** FOUGHT ...

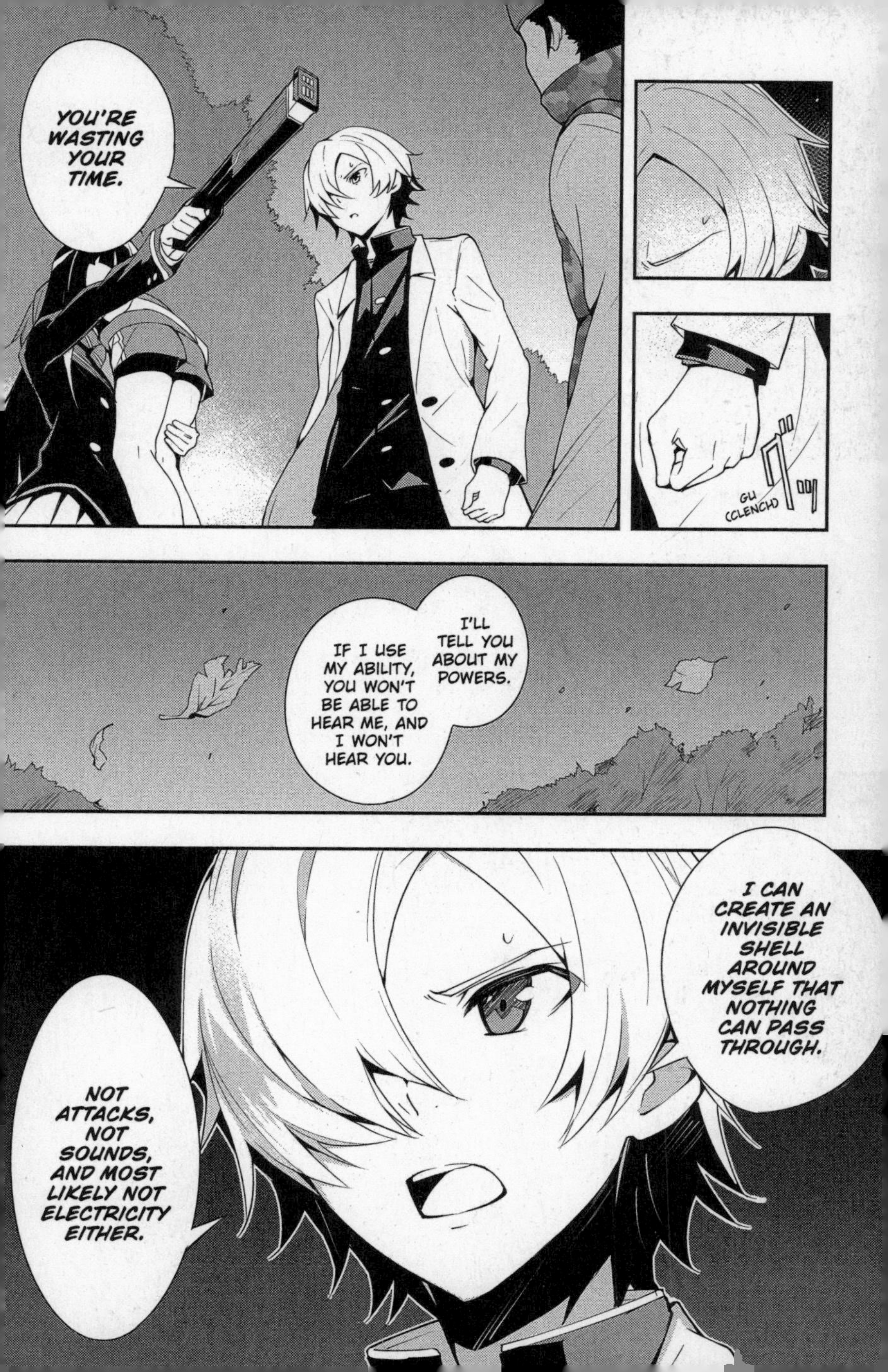
GU
(CLENCH)
YOU'RE WASTING YOUR TIME.
I'LL TELL YOU ABOUT MY POWERS.
IF I USE MY ABILITY, YOU WON'T BE ABLE TO HEAR ME, AND I WON'T HEAR YOU.
I CAN CREATE AN INVISIBLE SHELL AROUND MYSELF THAT NOTHING CAN PASS THROUGH.
NOT ATTACKS, NOT SOUNDS, AND MOST LIKELY NOT ELECTRICITY EITHER.

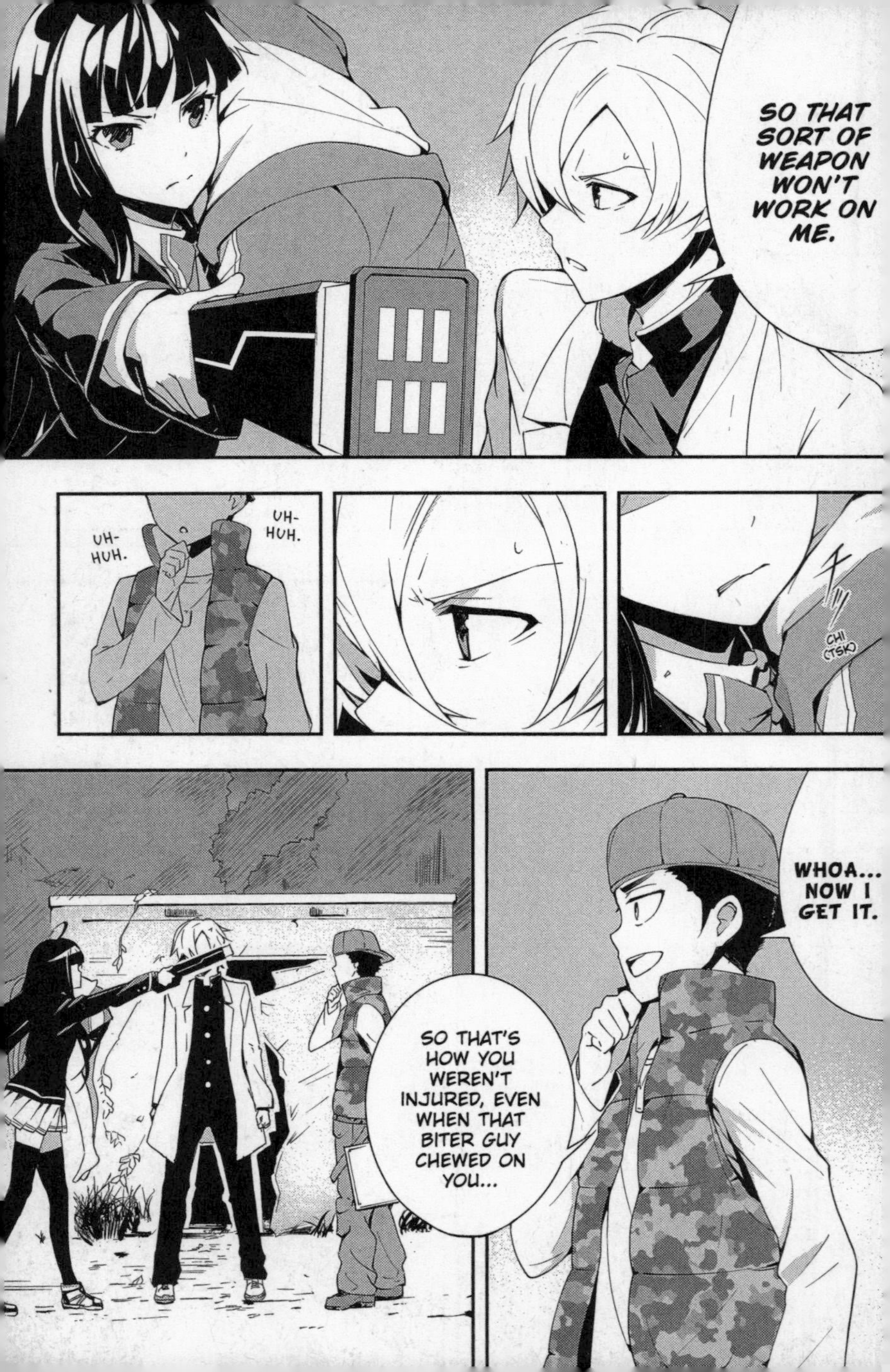
SO THAT SORT OF WEAPON WON'T WORK ON ME.
CHI (TSK)
UH-HUH.
UH-HUH.
WHOA... NOW I GET IT.
SO THAT'S HOW YOU WEREN'T INJURED, EVEN WHEN THAT BITER GUY CHEWED ON YOU...

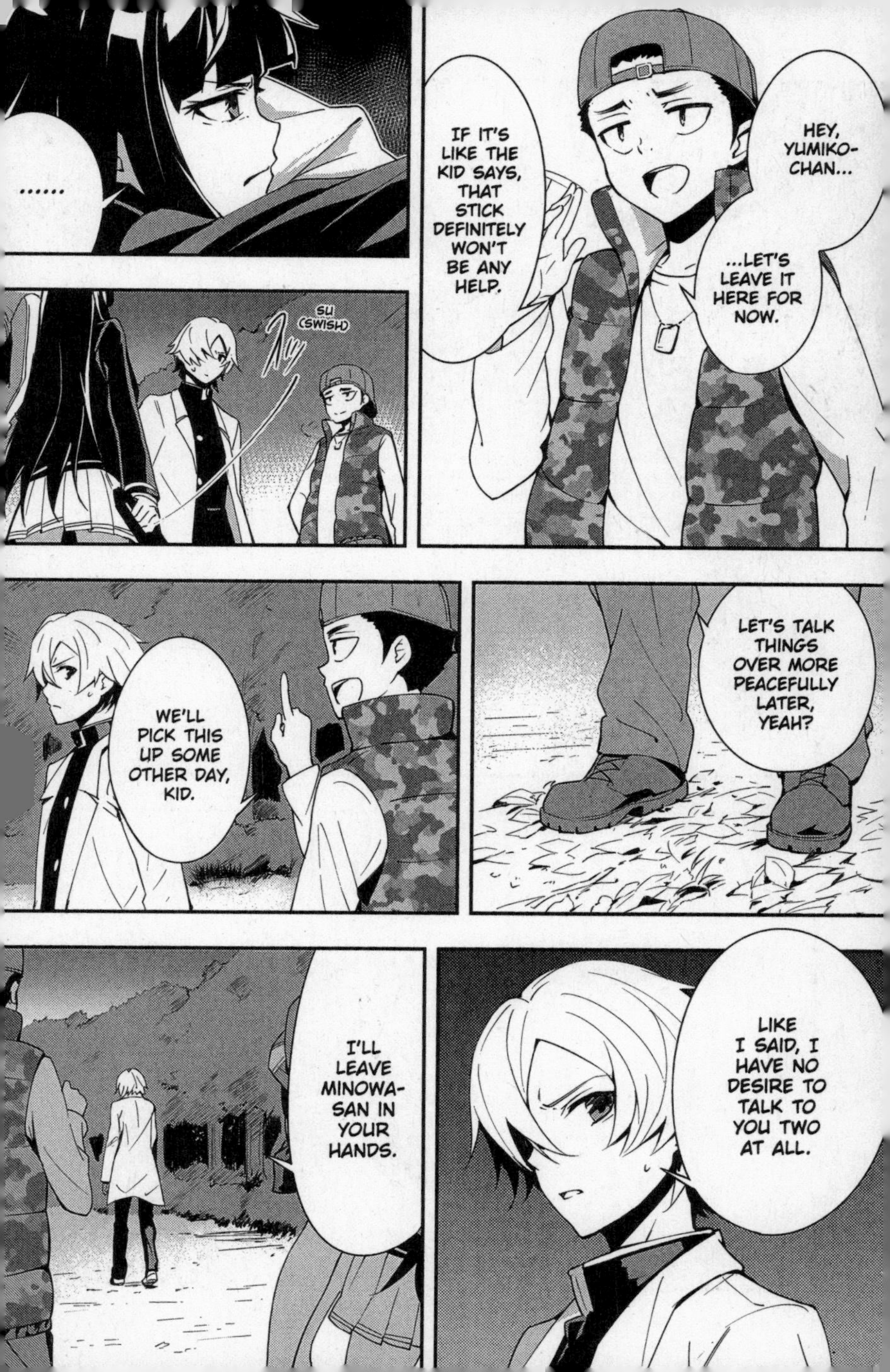
HEY, YUMIKO-CHAN...
...LET'S LEAVE IT HERE FOR NOW.
IF IT'S LIKE THE KID SAYS, THAT STICK DEFINITELY WON'T BE ANY HELP.
......
SU (SWISH)
LET'S TALK THINGS OVER MORE PEACEFULLY LATER, YEAH?
WE'LL PICK THIS UP SOME OTHER DAY, KID.
LIKE I SAID, I HAVE NO DESIRE TO TALK TO YOU TWO AT ALL.
I'LL LEAVE MINOWA-SAN IN YOUR HANDS.

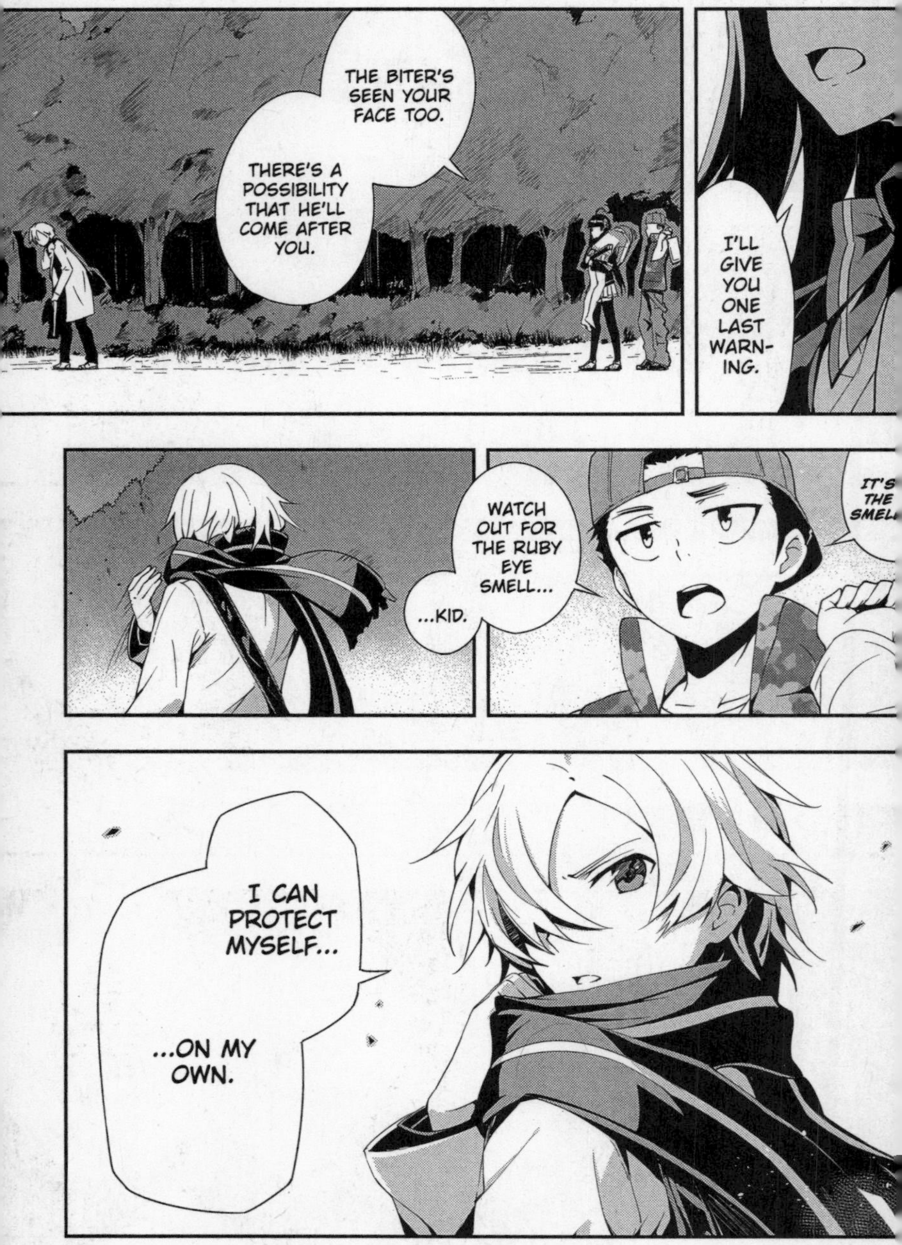
I'LL GIVE YOU ONE LAST WARN-ING.
THE BITER'S SEEN YOUR FACE TOO.
THERE'S A POSSIBILITY THAT HE'LL COME AFTER YOU.
IT'S THE SMEL
WATCH OUT FOR THE RUBY EYE SMELL...
...KID.
I CAN PROTECT MYSELF...
...ON MY OWN.

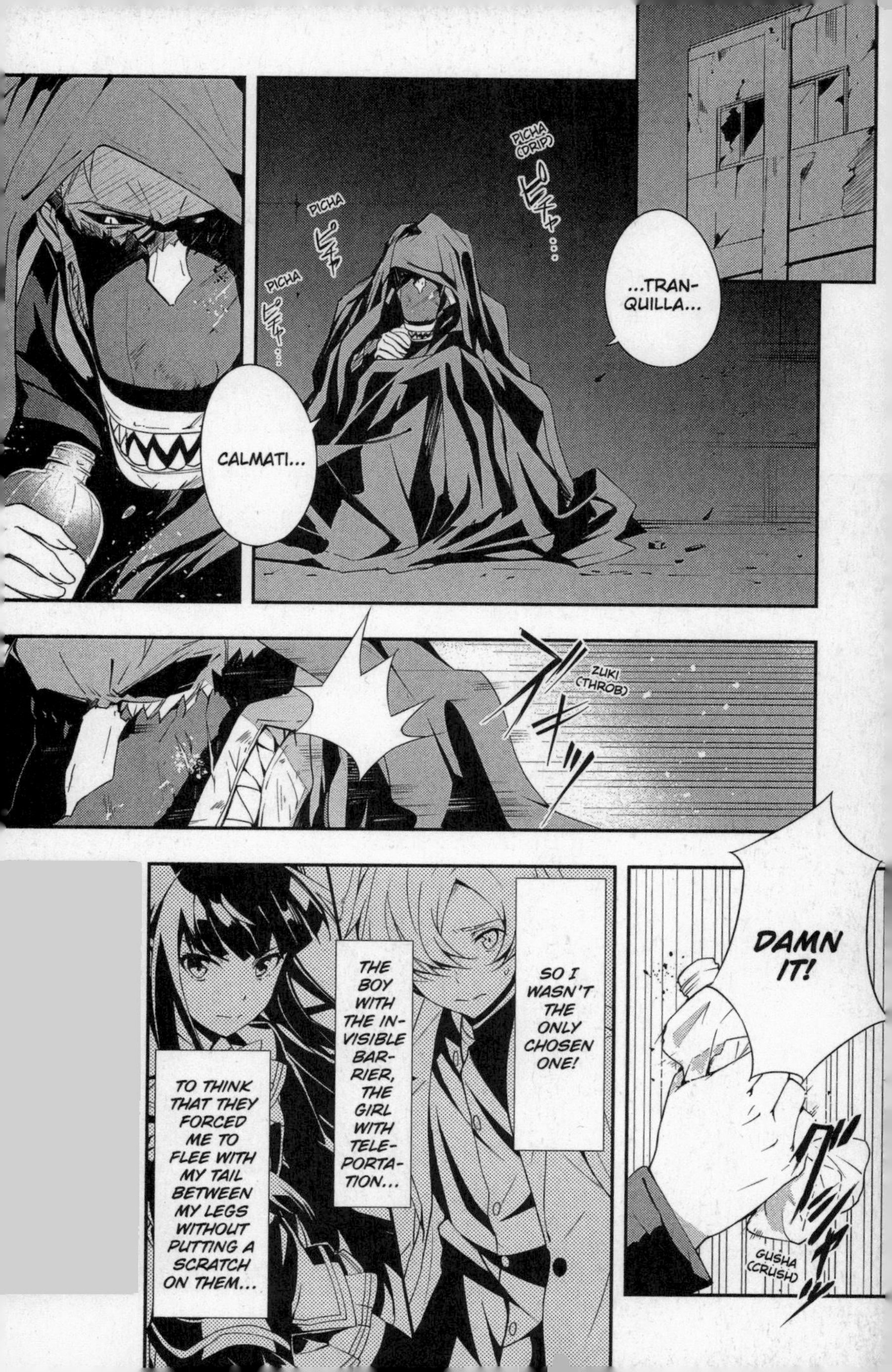
PICHA (DRIP)
...TRAN-QUILLA...
PICHA
PICHA
CALMATI...
ZUKI (THROB)
DAMN IT!
GUSHA (CRUSH)
SO I WASN'T THE ONLY CHOSEN ONE!
THE BOY WITH THE IN-VISIBLE BAR-RIER, THE GIRL WITH TELE-PORTA-TION...
TO THINK THAT THEY FORCED ME TO FLEE WITH MY TAIL BETWEEN MY LEGS WITHOUT PUTTING A SCRATCH ON THEM...

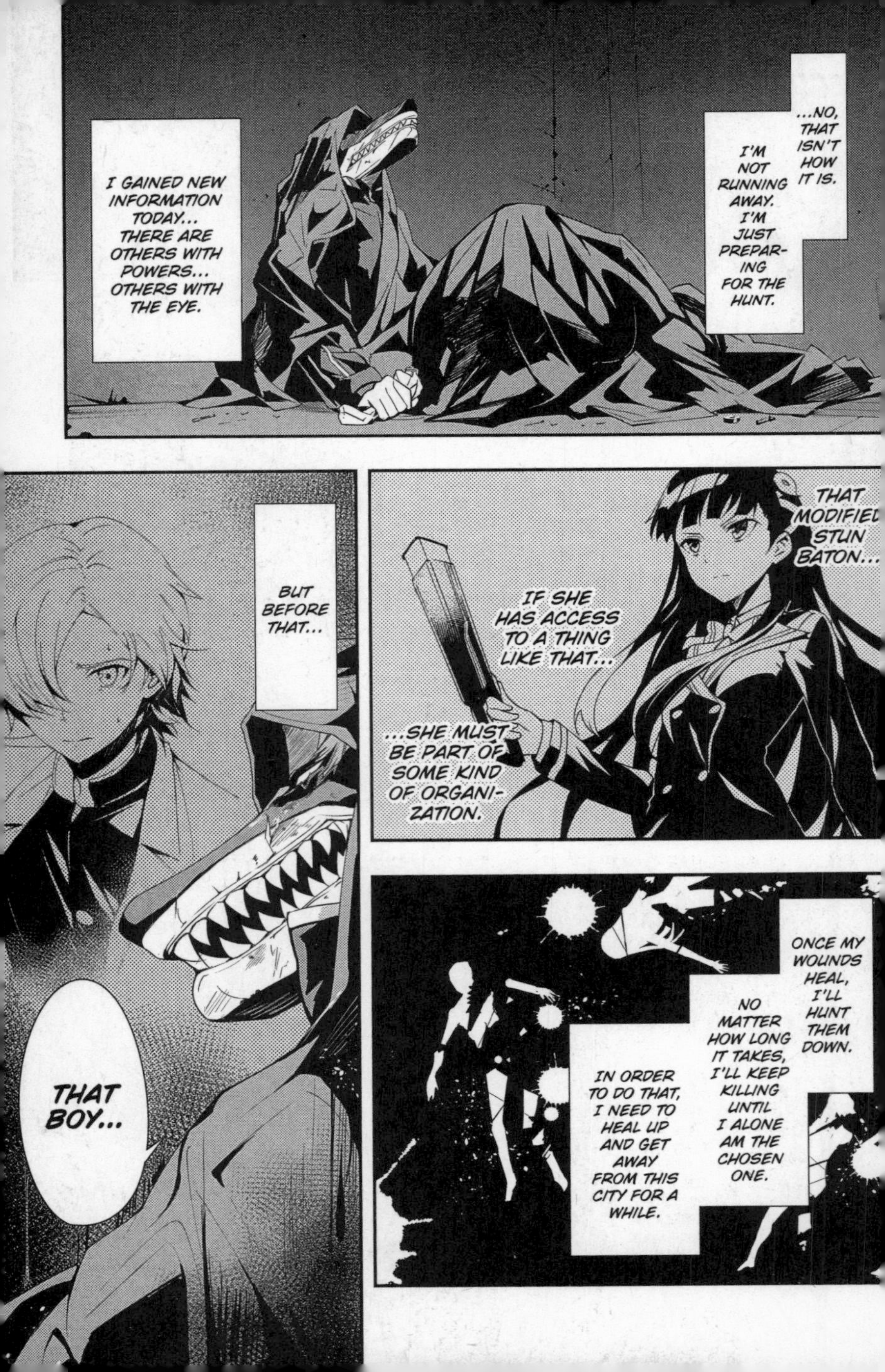
...NO, THAT ISN'T HOW IT IS.
I'M NOT RUNNING AWAY. I'M JUST PREPARING FOR THE HUNT.
I GAINED NEW INFORMATION TODAY... THERE ARE OTHERS WITH POWERS... OTHERS WITH THE EYE.
THAT MODIFIED STUN BATON...
IF SHE HAS ACCESS TO A THING LIKE THAT...
...SHE MUST BE PART OF SOME KIND OF ORGANIZATION.
ONCE MY WOUNDS HEAL, I'LL HUNT THEM DOWN.
NO MATTER HOW LONG IT TAKES, I'LL KEEP KILLING UNTIL I ALONE AM THE CHOSEN ONE.
IN ORDER TO DO THAT, I NEED TO HEAL UP AND GET AWAY FROM THIS CITY FOR A WHILE.
BUT BEFORE THAT...
THAT BOY...

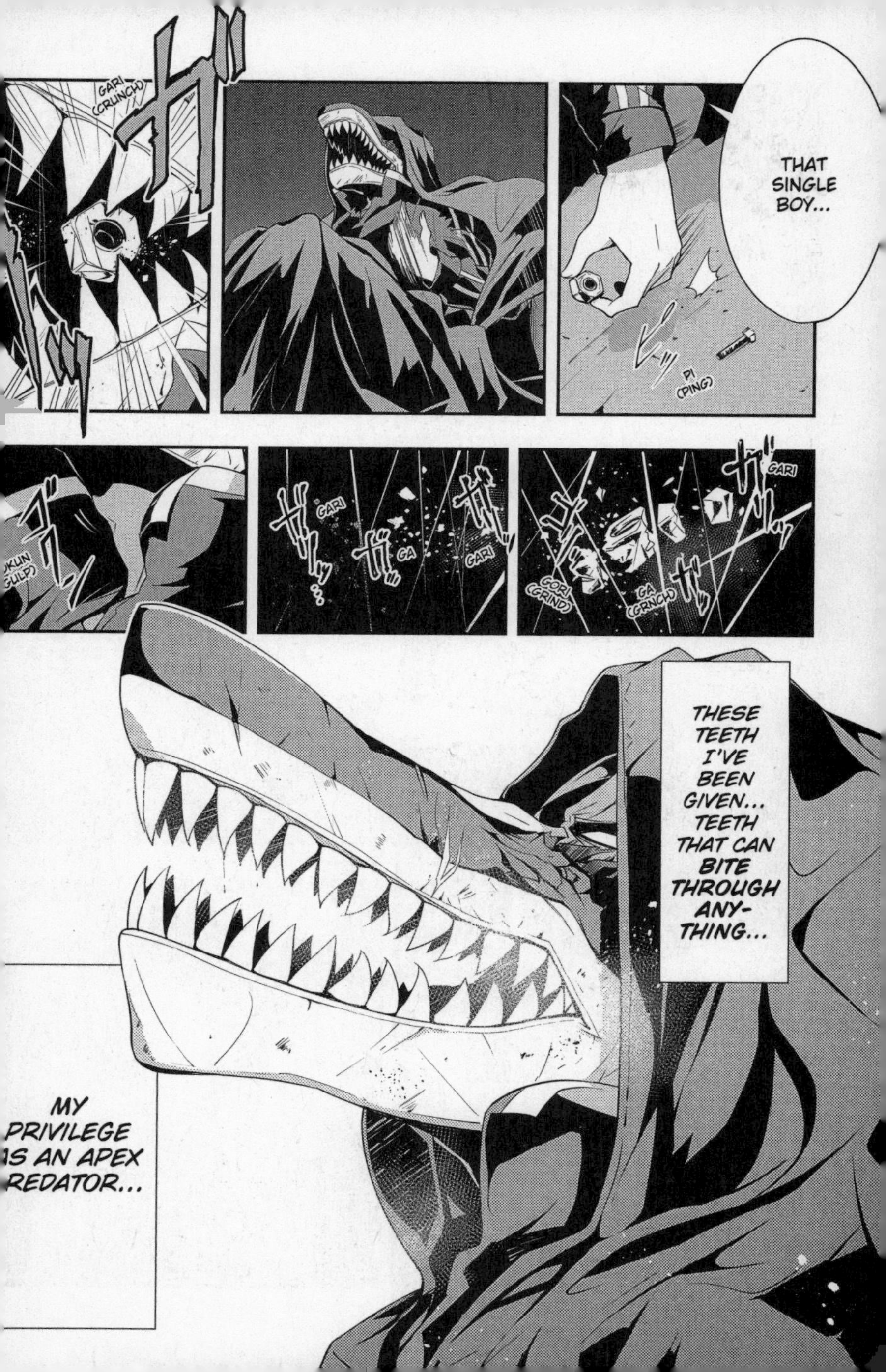
THAT SINGLE BOY...
PI (PING)
GARI (CRUNCH)
GARI
GORI (GRIND)
GA (GRNCH)
GARI
GA
GARI
THESE TEETH I'VE BEEN GIVEN... TEETH THAT CAN BITE THROUGH ANY-THING...
MY PRIVILEGE IS AN APEX REDATOR...

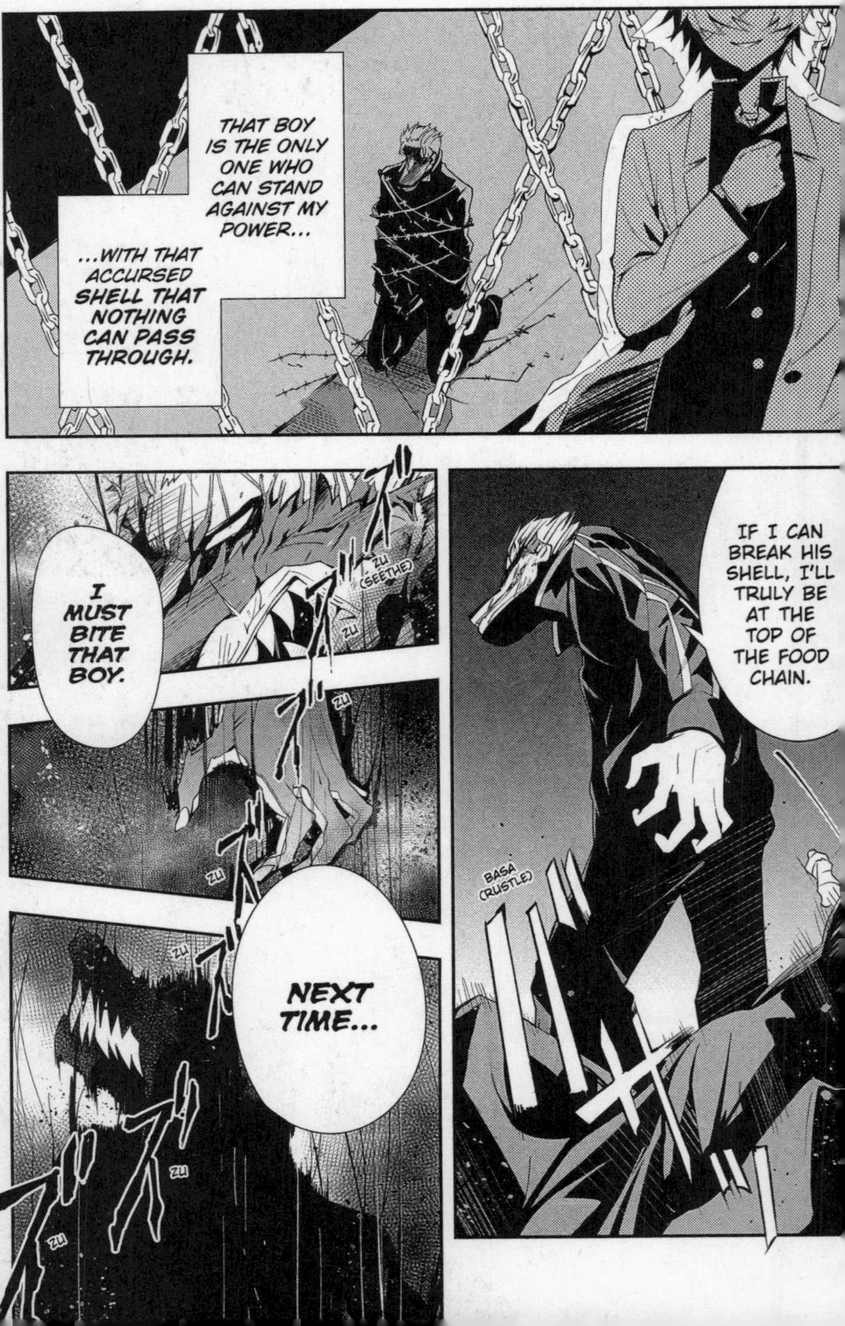
THAT BOY IS THE ONLY ONE WHO CAN STAND AGAINST MY POWER...
...WITH THAT ACCURSED SHELL THAT NOTHING CAN PASS THROUGH.
IF I CAN BREAK HIS SHELL, I'LL TRULY BE AT THE TOP OF THE FOOD CHAIN.
BASA (RUSTLE)
ZU (SEETHE)
ZU
I MUST BITE THAT BOY.
ZU
ZU
ZU
NEXT TIME...
ZU
ZU

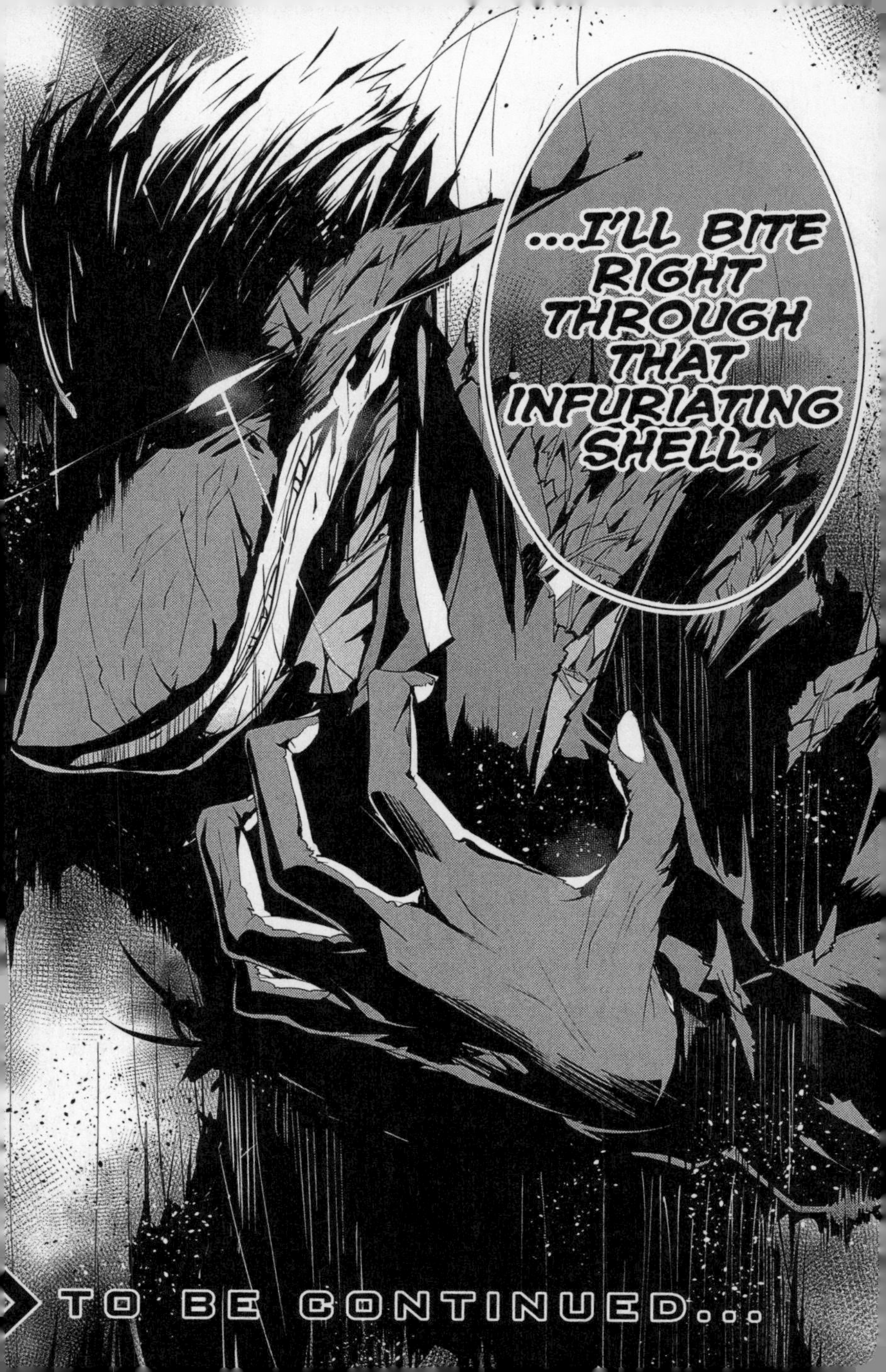
...I'LL BITE RIGHT THROUGH THAT INFURIATING SHELL.
TO BE CONTINUED...

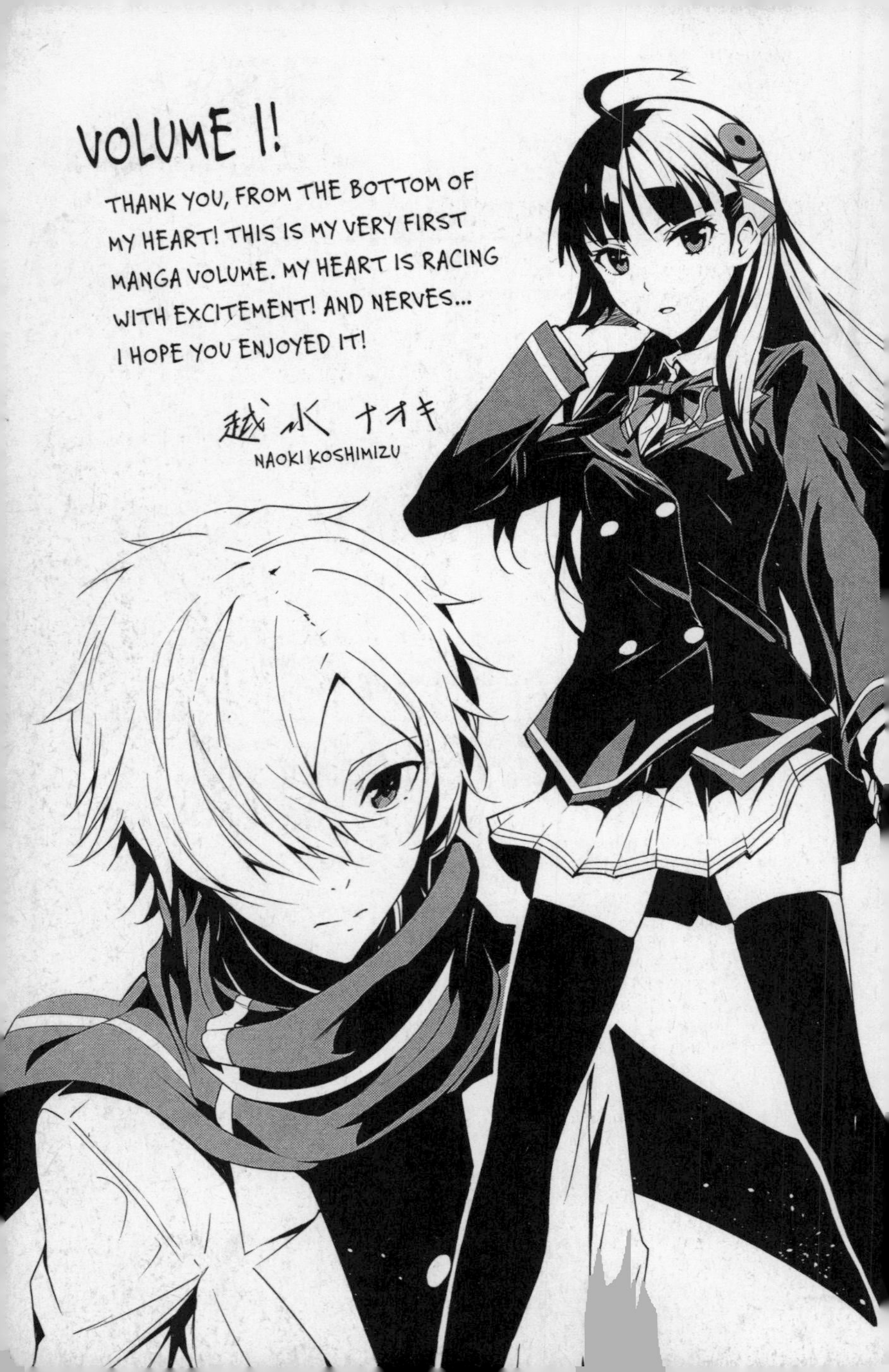
VOLUME 1!
THANK YOU, FROM THE BOTTOM OF MY HEART! THIS IS MY VERY FIRST MANGA VOLUME. MY HEART IS RACING WITH EXCITEMENT! AND NERVES... I HOPE YOU ENJOYED IT!
越水 ナオキ
NAOKI KOSHIMIZU

THE ISOL

Art: NAOKI KOSHIMIZU

Original Story: REKI KAWAHARA

D Xian Michele Lee

...acters, places, and incidents
... or are used fictitiously. Any
... persons, living or dead, is

THE ISOLATOR Volume 1
© REKI KAWAHARA/NAOKI KOSHIMIZU 2016
All rights reserved.
Edited by ASCII MEDIA WORKS
First published in Japan in 2016 by KADOKAWA CORPORATION,Tokyo.
English translation rights arranged with KADOKAWA CORPORATION,Tokyo,
through Tuttle-Mori Agency, Inc., Tokyo.

English translation © 2017 by Yen Press, LLC.

Yen Press
1290 Avenue of the Americas
New York, NY 10104

Visit us at yenpress.com • facebook.com/yenpress • twitter.com/yenpress •
yenpress.tumblr.com • instagram.com/yenpress

First Yen Press Edition: January 2017

Yen Press is an imprint of Yen Press, LLC.
The Yen Press name and logo are trademarks of Yen Press, LLC.

The publisher is not responsible for websites
(or their content) that are not owned by the publisher.

Library of Congress Control Number: 2016958581

ISBNs: 978-0-316-50464-5 (paperback)
          978-0-316-55847-1 (ebook)

10 9 8 7 6 5 4 3 2 1

BVG

Printed in the United States of America